Reconstructing Twentieth-Century China

Studies on Contemporary China

The Contemporary China Institute at the School of Oriental and African Studies (University of London) has, since its establishment in 1968, been an international centre for research and publications on twentieth-century China. *Studies on Contemporary China*, which is edited at the Institute, seeks to maintain and extend that tradition by making available the best work of scholars and China specialists throughout the world. It embraces a wide variety of subjects relating to Nationalist and Communist China, including social, political, and economic change, intellectual and cultural developments, foreign relations, and national security.

Series Editor
Dr Frank Dikötter, Director of the Contemporary China Institute

Editorial Advisory Board

Dr Robert F. Ash	Professor Bonnie S. McDougall
Professor Hugh D. R. Baker	Professor David Shambaugh
Professor Elisabeth J. Croll	Dr Julia C. Strauss
Dr Richard Louis Edmonds	Professor Lynn T. White III
Mr Brian G. Hook	Dr Jonathan Unger
Professor Christopher B. Howe	

Reconstructing Twentieth-Century China

State Control, Civil Society, and National Identity

Edited by

KJELD ERIK BRØDSGAARD
and
DAVID STRAND

CLARENDON PRESS · OXFORD
1998

Oxford University Press, Great Clarendon Street, Oxford OX2 6DP

Oxford New York

Athens Auckland Bangkok Bogotá Buenos Aires Calcutta
Cape Town Chennai Dar es Salaam Delhi Florence Hong Kong Istanbul
Karachi Kuala Lumpur Madras Madrid Melbourne Mexico City Mumbai
Nairobi Paris São Paolo Singapore Taipei Tokyo Toronto Warsaw

and associated companies in
Berlin Ibadan

Oxford is a registered trade mark of Oxford University Press

Published in the United States
by Oxford University Press Inc., New York

British Library Cataloguing in Publication Data
Data available

Library of Congress Cataloging in Publication Data
Data available
ISBN 0–19–829311–9

1 3 5 7 9 10 8 6 4 2

Typeset by Hope Services (Abingdon) Ltd.
Printed in Great Britain
on acid-free paper by
Biddles Ltd,
Guildford and King's Lynn

Preface

The chapters in this volume were originally presented as papers at a series of conferences held at the Department of Asian Studies, University of Copenhagen, under the auspices of the State and Society in East Asia Network. The Network brings together scholars from universities and research institutes in Europe, the United States, and Asia to explore the evolving nature of state–society relations in East Asia. Support for the Network, for conferences, and for the preparation of this volume came from the Danish Research Council for the Humanities. Additional support was provided by the Chiang Ching-kuo Foundation, Dickinson College, and the National Humanities Center, North Carolina.

K.E.B.
D.S.

Contents

List of Contributors   ix

1   Introduction   1
    Kjeld Erik Brødsgaard and David Strand

I. STATE CONTROL

2   Calling the Chinese People to Order: Sun Yat-sen's Rhetoric
    of Development   33
    David Strand

3   The Essence of Contemporary Chinese Bureaucracy:
    Socialism, Modernization and Political Culture   69
    Ryosei Kokubun

4   Control as Care: Interaction between Urban Women and
    Birth Planning Workers   92
    Cecilia Milwertz

5   Ownership and Community Interest in China's Rural Enterprises   113
    Susan Young

II. CIVIL SOCIETY

6   Reconstructing Society: Liang Shuming and the Rural
    Reconstruction Movement in Shandong   139
    Stig Thøgersen

7   Bases for Civil Society in Reform China   163
    Thomas Gold

8   State and Society in Hainan: Liao Xun's Ideas on 'Small
    Government, Big Society'   189
    Kjeld Erik Brødsgaard

9   Is a Participant Culture Emerging in China?   216
    Torstein Hjellum

III. NATIONAL IDENTITY

10 Party Policy and 'National Culture': Towards a State-
    Directed Cultural Nationalism in China?   253
    Søren Clausen

11 Fostering 'Love of Learning': Naxi Responses to Ethnic
   Images in Chinese State Education   280
   Mette Halskov Hansen

12 China Deconstructs? The Future of the Chinese Empire-
   State in a Historical Perspective   310
   Harald Bøckman

Index   347

List of Contributors

HARALD BØCKMAN is the coordinator of the Network for Pacific Asia Studies at the University of Oslo and the General Secretary of the European Association for Chinese Studies. His publications include works on Chinese nationalism and cultural history and he has translated Chinese poetry into Norwegian.

KJELD ERIK BRØDSGAARD is Associate Professor of Modern East Asian History and Society with particular reference to China at the University of Copenhagen. Recent works include *China after Deng* (1997) and articles on private business and private entrepreneurs in Hainan and on state capacity and the informal economy in rural China.

SØREN CLAUSEN is Associate Professor of Chinese Studies at the Department of East Asian Studies, University of Aarhus, Denmark. Among his recent publications are *The Making of a Chinese City: History and Historiography in Harbin* (with Stig Thøgersen, 1995) and *Cultural Encounters: China, Japan and the West* (with Roy Starrs and Anne Wedell-Wedellsborg, 1995).

THOMAS GOLD is Associate Professor of Sociology at the University of California, Berkeley. He has published extensively on issues of youth, personal relations, and private business in China, as well as on the political economy and democratic change in Taiwan.

METTE HALSKOV HANSEN is a post-doctorate Research Fellow at the Department for East European and Oriental Studies and the Centre for Development and Environment at the University of Oslo. She is the author of a forthcoming monograph, *Lessons in being Chinese: State Education and Ethnic Identity in Southwest China*.

TORSTEIN HJELLUM is Associate Professor at the Institute of Comparative Politics, University of Bergen. He is the author of *From the Opium War to Deng Xiaoping* (1995) and coeditor of *The Chinese Challenge* (1997).

RYOSEI KOKUBUN is Professor at the Faculty of Law and Politics and Vice-Director of Centre for Area Studies, Keio University. His main publications include *Examination of the Asian Era from China's View* (1996), *Documentary History of Contemporary China: Politics* (1994), and *The Political Process and Democratization in China: an Analysis of Reforms and Open-Door Policies* (1992).

CECILIA MILWERTZ is a European Science Foundation post-doctoral Research Fellow at the Institute of Chinese Studies, Oxford University. She is author of *Accepting Population Control: Urban Chinese Women and the One Child Family Policy* (1997).

DAVID STRAND is Professor of Political Science, Dickinson College. He is the author of *Rickshaw Beijing: City People and Politics in the 1920s* (1989) and articles on civil society and the public sphere in China, Sun Yatsen's thought and leadership, and modern Chinese urban history.

STIG THØGERSEN is Associate Professor of Chinese Studies at the University of Aarhus. He is author of *Secondary Education in China after Mao* (1990) and has co-authored *The Making of a Chinese City: History and Historiography in Harbin* (with Søren Clausen, 1995).

SUSAN YOUNG is a lecturer at the Department of Asian Studies, University of Copenhagen. She is author of *Private Business and Economic Reform in China* (1995) and of articles on the private sector and rural property rights in China.

1

Introduction

Kjeld Erik Brødsgaard and David Strand

In this century, China has experienced reform and revolution by government fiat, by broader cultural and social movements, and by the accretion
(and loss) of technologies and public and private goods and services. The
impulse to reform and rebuild has erupted on a national scale every
several years since the turn of the century: the 'New Policies' (*xinzheng*) of
the Qing dynasty's last decade, early Republican constitutionalism, the
May Fourth Movement, the Nationalist Party 'Reorganization' of the
early 1920s, the Nanjing decade of 1927–37, the Yan'an reconsolidation
and expansion of Communism, Nanjing's post-war attempt at reconstruction, building socialism in the 1950s, the Great Leap, the Cultural
Revolution, the 1980 reforms, the Democracy Movement, and, most
recently, China's exploding economy.

These programmes and movements have led to or been followed by a
series of profound shocks of varying kinds and degrees: the Boxer
Uprising and the sack of Beijing in 1900, the 1911 Revolution, the North
China famine of 1920–1, the 1930s depression, the Second World War, the
Korean War, the famine of 1960–1, near-anarchy and civil war in 1967–8,
the 1971 Lin Biao affair, élite power struggles and the Tangshan earth-
quake in 1976, the Tiananmen massacre of 1989.[1] In some cases, for example the Nanjing decade and the Japanese invasion, an externally delivered
shock brought to a premature end a building programme; in others, such
as the Great Leap and the subsequent famine, a drive for development
self-destructed. In most cases the motivating agent pressing for development was the state. But in at least three (the May Fourth Movement, 1989,
and the current private economic boom) the driving force for change was
outside direct state control. The special nature of the present economic
surge may be its dual identities as developmental programme and shock,
indigenous product and global movement, and social initiative and state
policy.

Our theme of 'reconstruction' (*jianshe*) acknowledges that current
reform efforts are proceeding from a future-oriented past of comparable
leaps, revolutions, and reorganizations.[2] As David Strand points out in his
study of Sun Yat-sen's political rhetoric (Chapter 2), *jianshe* took hold

early in the century as a keyword that expressed an ardent desire to rebuild or reshape China. The word has survived to the present day in dilute form as 'building socialism with Chinese characteristics' (*jianshe Zhongguo tese de shehui zhuyi*). With 'wealth and power' (*fuqiang*) for China the goal, *jianshe* has been the oft-prescribed course of action. The enormity of the tasks at hand made state control and direction of this enterprise appealing to most, but not all, reformers and revolutionaries. As Stig Thøgersen notes in his essay on Liang Shuming (Chapter 6), village education was part of a larger, early twentieth-century effort aimed at 'rural reconstruction' (*xiangcun jianshe*). Liang was a cultural conservative, but he shared a commitment to *jianshe* with radical critics of traditional culture. The diagnosis of the problem, selection of materials for use, and design for renewal might differ, but a common interest in constructing or reconstructing a culture, political system, literary theory, or economy from the ground up made everyone a 'builder'. In this atmosphere, model villages, schools, newspapers, literary genres, factories, and armies proliferated across China. In the absence of a strong state, the accent was often on local initiative. Reform in areas like education proceeded unevenly in the absence of a national policy and a central state capable of enforcing a comprehensive agenda. Meanwhile social chaos and military disorder made protecting or expanding these local projects extremely difficult. As Thøgersen points out, even Liang Shuming, who hoped to carry out educational reforms free of state control and supervision, was finally obliged to seek protection and support from state authorities.

Diverse commitments to building a new China continued beyond mid-century and across ideological divisions. In the process, local projects were drawn together in forms that were decidedly statist and centralizing in their basic thrust. Big plans seemed to require big government. Even anti-Communist Nationalists in the 1940s found the Soviet super-state an inspiration in the realm of 'nation-building' (*jianguo*).[3] After the war, state-directed reconstruction received broad reinforcement in a world preoccupied by the problems of rebuilding war-damaged economies and societies and decolonizing imperial possessions.[4] On mainland China, the project of 'building socialism in our country'—*woguo shehuizhuyi jianshe*—was placed by Mao and his colleagues within the Stalinist framework of the Fel'dman–Preobrazhensky paradigm for economic growth: high accumulation rates, focus on heavy industry growth, and low investment in agriculture.[5] Funds were appropriated by the state from agriculture and were used to build mammoth public works like Shougang and Anshan—industrial complexes each with over a hundred thousand workers and a budget comparable to that of a small city. Such interventions stimulated and justified the growth of the state as an amalgam of party, government, and military systems. The monumental structures that resulted made development easy to see, even as the accompanying rhetoric about building socialism concealed the cost of this strategy to rural dwellers and consumers. Maoist departures into the realm of mass eco-nomic and political mobilization during the Great Leap and the Cultural Revolution, however notable as gestures towards a unique, Chinese road to socialism, left the fundamental strategy of centrally planned industrial growth intact. One can discern in the chaos of these movements the continued appeal of local initiatives and alternatives to centralized state control. But the high ground held by state socialism left the rest of the social and economic terrain defined more by mechanisms of extraction than by development. An 'aborescent', hierarchical system of state enter-prises and institutions absorbed the lion's share of economic resources.[6] These enterprises were in turn milked by the state to fund the costs of big government and new development projects.[7]

The implementation of the Deng reform policies from 1979 onwards can be seen as an attempt finally to break with the Fel'dman–Preobrazhensky strategy. This move, justified on the basis of economic productivity, has affected all other realms of policy and areas of state and social activity, from the fiscal basis of the regime to the willingness of citizens to comply with intrusive policies such as population control. Reduced profits from state enterprises (or the need to subsidize them) and greater incomes to be had from outside the 'unit' (*danwei*) system of guar-anteed employment have left the state with fewer carrots to proffer inde-pendent-minded local governments, firms, and individuals. A series of measures have been introduced involving decentralization and new forms of management and ownership. The importance of gigantic heavy-industrial state enterprises has been downgraded, and market principles have gained a competitive edge over strict central planning.[8] The resulting landscape now includes both huge projects like the Three Gorges high dam originally envisioned by Sun Yat-sen and the small, localized enter-prises discussed by Susan Young in Chapter 5. The fact that the latter represents an increasingly large share of total economic activity underlines the growing economic power of small, local, non-state or quasi-governmental enterprises. In this context, reconstruction as process has become, again, a multi-levelled affair of wildly differing scales and modes of operation. Aborescent state structures that concentrate resources and authority on a mammoth scale compete with 'rhizomatic' networks of economic, social, and cultural entrepreneurs growing and spreading in less predictable, often covert, fashion.[9]

The papers presented here examine how a range of actors—political leaders, village reformers, government bureaucrats, entrepreneurs, women of childbearing age, intellectuals, members of ethnic minorities, and local cadres—have reacted to these unstable yet structured transitions. Chapters are grouped around the study of three problems central to any larger explanation of how the parts of a developing China compose the whole and how the bigger picture is inscribed in the details: (1) the extent and limits of state control over economic, social, and cultural life; (2) prospects for the development of a civil society separate from state control; and (3) the renegotiation of a Chinese national identity caught between powerful nationalist traditions and manifest cultural diversity.

Our time frame includes early twentieth-century struggles to build a modern China with a mix of indigenous and foreign materials and techniques. As papers keyed to the start of the century (Strand and Thøgersen) suggest, China was neither a blank page awaiting the signature impressions of Western institutions and ideologies nor a stage on which modern players performed solely under the direction of ancient scripts. Other essays (Kokubun, Clausen, and Bøckman) span the century with analyses grounded in the great mid-century transition to communism. They focus on the contemporary fate of institutions and ideas associated with Mao's China. The remainder of the papers (Milwertz, Young, Gold, Brødsgaard, Hjellum, and Hansen) are concerned with the specific nature and broad consequences of Deng Xiaoping era reforms. After more than a decade and a half of state-initiated change, a growing tide of unintended consequences and the release of more independent economic, cultural, and social forces have complicated the original reform vision. As a result, early twentieth-century problems of preservation and innovation have returned with a communist rather than a Confucian base-line.

State Control

The imperial state-system,[10] represented at the end of empire by the Qing court and bureaucracy, was small by modern standards relative to China's large and growing population. A single Qing county magistrate had as many as several hundred thousand people within his jurisdiction, in contrast to a much thicker carpet of administrators in pre-revolutionary France, where the ratio of officials to population was about 1 : 3,000.[11] But the state-idea, represented by the emperor's charge to rule 'all under Heaven', was very ambitious. Any modern overhaul or replacement of this system and this idea might reasonably seek both a dramatic expansion of government personnel and the preservation of at least some elements of a ruling idea which, shorn of its sacred and religious character, invoked modern-sounding themes of protecting and nurturing the people.[12]

China's republican revolution overthrew rather than preserved the monarchy, and the early republic turned out to be weak, ineffectual, and corrupt. The republic required a new foundation of direct popular support. And yet, why would citizens support a government that repeatedly failed to defend the country's basic security interests and, at the national level, was little more than a tax burden and a political embarrassment?

Some interpretations of the twentieth-century Chinese state have stressed continuities in personnel, structure, and style of operation with the late imperial system. At a minimum, regime changes from empire to republic, from republic to party–state, and even from Chinese republic to puppet-state under the Japanese, have often included significant carry-overs in personnel. At most, as Ryosei Kokubun emphasizes in Chapter 3, deeper structures of political culture may have encouraged twentieth-century officials to behave in imperious if not imperial fashion and citizens to adopt a subject mentality.[13] Others have argued that the radical abolition of the imperial institution in 1911 left little room for such continuities and made the task of building a modern state incalculably more difficult.[14] As Sun Yat-sen put the problem in the early 1910s, it was rather like tearing down one's old house before building a new one. No wonder politicians like Yuan Shikai tried to re-enter the Forbidden City as emperor on the grounds that, as Yuan's supporters put it, a monarchical national polity (*guoti*) was more in tune with Chinese culture than a republican one.[15] Later leaders such as Mao Zedong and Deng Xiaoping seemed to assume an imperial persona at those moments when the new structures of the modern state proved inadequate to the task of mobilization or simple governance.

When the Chinese have contemplated the state from inside or outside its structures, their feelings about the state's capacity to save or build China have varied considerably. Sun Yat-sen was a great optimist in this regard, while Liang Shuming and turn-of-the-century anarchists were decidedly pessimistic. Mao had mixed feelings. He shared Sun's enthusiasm for an overarching and concentrated source of power but was suspicious of the state as a bureaucratic entity. Localism or regionalism encouraged advocacy of 'liberal' projects such as self-government and federalism while usually conceding to a centralized state the lion's share of authority.[16] Few liberals, anarchists, or federalists stayed the course they embarked on. Most finally perceived the contradiction between the strong China they wanted and the decentralized programmes they advocated, or became disenchanted with movements that fell prey to cynicism and opportunism.[17] In general, the juggernaut of statism and nationalism overwhelmed the alternatives.

Difficulties in defining or comprehending the role of the state in twentieth-century China are reflected in the ambiguous modern meanings attached to the Chinese word typically used for state: *guojia*, a term that can also be translated as 'nation'. Prior to the modern period, *guojia*—formed from the characters for 'kingdom' or 'country' and 'family'—variously connoted the fiefs that made up a kingdom, the public, the court, or the emperor himself.[18] In the late nineteenth century, officials like reformer Zhang Zhidong argued that in order for China to be saved the state had to be strengthened. In due course, *guojia* acquired the kind of concentrated, organized, and centralized meaning typical of Western usages of the term 'state'. 'According to Zhang, the state, for which he used the term *guojia*, was not only the dynasty itself but also its laws . . . which, "by creating binding ties . . . amongst different groups of the populace, allowed people to attend to their affairs in peace".'[19] For Zhang, the state was not only the central governmental institutions of the Qing but also a pattern of connections to the populace.

Other reformers, e.g. Liang Qichao, and revolutionaries like Sun Yat-sen also emphasized the importance of central state power and broad social organization.[20] When Sun called in 1906 for a 'racial *guojia*, a citizens' *guojia* and a social [concerned with social issues like land tenure] *guojia*', he was referring both to a state broadly understood to include Zhang Zhidong's 'binding ties' and to a nation with a strong, centralized organizational bent.[21] There were differences of opinion over whether or not an organized populace already existed as a power to be tapped, or needed to be created through a new mobilization. As Strand points out in Chapter 2, Sun Yat-sen was frustrated by what he saw as the unwillingness of many Chinese to use their abundant organizational capacities to serve the interests of state and nation. It was also apparent that, in a time of troubles and disorder, and in the absence of strong central control, many groups and localities were prepared to go their own way. These independent-minded localities, associations, and groups sometimes made explicit demands for autonomy and self-government.[22] But they also represented a residue of traditional parochialism and served to illustrate the plain fact that the state-system in existence through most of the first half of the century was barely a system at all, being too weak to do more than acknowledge, register, and occasionally tax or extort resources from individuals and groups in society. A 'civil society' was emerging, as much by default as by constitutional or cultural design. *Guojia* as state-and-nation promised to bridge the gap between government and people but also left open the question of where the initiative in closing the gap would come from.

Meanwhile, a new kind of centralized power was taking shape in the minds of leaders and followers and in political practice. While Leninism eventually gave structure to both the Nationalist and Community Party versions of this new entity, nationalism provided a pointed impetus and broad justification for such a move. The suppression of anarchist, federalist, and liberal alternatives to the party–state means that this ambiguity was resolved into an essential identity between state and nation. Support for a state capable of overcoming the weaknesses of the late Qing dynasty and early republic seemed to be the obligation of all true nationalists. State control of the 'national' economy and culture was a natural, perhaps inevitable, consequence of this fusion of state as centralized authority and nation as mobilized citizenry. Once the Communists had defeated all political rivals, a state-system was built in which the boundary between centralized power and other realms of political and social activity was effaced. The emergent state-idea or rationale for such an intrusion included the Marxist–Leninist mandate of history, the compelling interests of the *guojia* and, perhaps, a less conscious commitment to a more ancient dream of unity under the auspices of a benevolent, now militant, state. Every community now had 'state cadres' (*guojia ganbu*), whose job it was to enforce the centre's agenda. Therefore, the idea of extensive state control predated its implementation by decades, if not centuries. The rise of nationalism as a powerful force in the twentieth century gave great support to the construction of a socialist state-system and undermined alternative conceptions of a more limited government role or a balance between state on the one hand and society or localities on the other.

The power of statism as an idea and system in China makes the current 'retreat' or 'withdrawal' of the state from economy, society, and culture that much more remarkable. And suspect. Could this really be happening? Is not the alternative to strong state control in a Chinese context chaos and breakup rather than incipient federalism or democracy? It is difficult to discuss 'state and society' as a feature of early twentieth-century Chinese history because the strength of the state as an idea was rarely matched then by a systematic presence. Later, during the Maoist years, society was consumed at the state banquet table of socialization and collectivization. (In that sense, in contradistinction to Mao's morbid joke about the bloody nature of revolution, the Chinese revolution was a kind of dinner party for centralized state power.) Today, as a result of the disorders of late Maoism and the reforms of Deng, a shift in power, resources, and (perhaps) authority has taken place that has affected both the state and an emergent constellation of groups and individuals that displays some of the characteristics of an independent society.

Essays in this volume suggest elements of both design and default in the reconfiguration of state and society. At a minimum, 'state and society' now exist as distinguishable spheres of public and private, state-owned and privately-owned, government and non-governmental activity. The fact that much of this happened because the state 'let go' in the late 1970s through decollectivization and privatization does not diminish the scale and weight of what was relinquished. However, the state's hand in releasing rural families to farm, entrepreneurs to try to make money, and ordinary people everywhere to construct new lives from previously banned materials including bibles, TOEFEL examinations, and clan lineage records does raise questions about the permanence of this move and the state's capacity to continue to regulate and control.

As Kokubun shows in Chapter 3, the state may be undergoing a variety of stresses and strains, but it is still following societal developments both in a surveillance sense and in terms of its determination to regulate and control. As Cecilia Milwertz's research demonstrates in Chapter 4, for women in state-owned enterprises, 'Maoist' methods that mix coercion, propaganda, and intimate contact between cadre and citizen are still in force in the regulation of reproduction. That portion of the female body politic has not yet experienced release from the grip of the state except in so far as marketization and privatization have placed many families outside the unit-based system of control.

The growing size of the bureaucracy, despite the neat logic of a 'bigger' society leading to a 'smaller' state, suggests that the regime is not about to surrender either its authority or its power without a struggle. That this struggle not only involves simply a decision to lock up dissidents, but also attempts to regulate stock markets and other social and economic transactions and relationships, indicates that the state continues to hold a broad vision of its own mission. The 'hypertrophy' of the state mentioned by Kokubun seems tied to both the rational pursuit of regulatory leverage and patrimonial privilege. The result may be comparable to the combination of frenetic activity and political decay characterized by Prasenjit Duara for the republican period as 'involution':

What I call 'involution' is an alternative to state making as a means of conceptualizing the expanding and modernizing role of the state in 20th-century China. In state involution, the formal structures of the state grow simultaneously with informal structures, such as the entrepreneurial state brokers discussed previously. Although the formal state depends on the informal structures to carry out many of its functions, it is unable to extend control over them. As the state grows in the involutionary mode, the informal groups become an uncontrollable power in local society, replacing a host of traditional arrangements of local governance.[23]

The difference seems to be that the involution taking place today is within the bureaucracy itself, as informal networks 'take over' the real work of agencies and develop beyond the control of formal, legal–rational ordering. While this is normal in all complex organizations, the extent of this involution, or the proliferation of 'involuted' practices, seems striking. As a result, the party–state has increasing difficulty governing itself, a fact of which the public has not failed to take note. At the same time, the network dimension of government activity provides intimate access to activity outside the state in the form of informal relationships with groups such as businessmen and the Triads. This imbricated aspect of state–society relations prevents the regime from being wholly alienated from society at the same time that the typical mode of contact—corruption—provokes a crisis of legitimacy.

In a phenomenon that further complicates this picture of a state developing in regulatory capacity, staffing, and 'involuted' social practices as it loses legitimacy and overall control of the economy and society, many local, state-run enterprises are doing quite well in shifting management functions to tasks set by the market economy. As Vivienne Shue has noted in her study of a small city in northern China, retreat by the state in some spheres of urban life has been accompanied by a 'local state sprawl' in areas such as land management and city planning.[24] What is decaying at the top of the state structure by way of collectivist ideology and bureaucratic practice is being continued and revitalized at the lower levels. The result includes hybrid forms of enterprise in which local governments play decisive roles either as shareholders, direct owners, or close regulators. As Young observes in Chapter 5, in the 'poorly regulated, highly personalized environment of the reforms ownership is less important than control and rights less important than obligations'. The lineage or lineage-like basis of some of these enterprises suggests continuity with the family or clan-style of organization typical of Chinese firms in the past and in contemporary Taiwan and Hong Kong.[25] In this case, the reconstruction of the rural enterprises depends on a complex assortment of ideological (socialist), organizational (bureaucratic), and cultural (lineage) materials.[26]

Civil Society

The rise of the communist state from its imperial and republican antecedents seemed to consign non-state forces and institutions to history's dustbin. Defined negatively, 'society' could be understood only in terms of what was left over after the state took what it wanted of resources, power, and loyalty. This constituted a great deal of social and spatial territory in the first half of the twentieth century when the state was undeveloped and weak, and very little in the succeeding decades when the state seemed all-powerful. Now that state control, by design and happenstance, has been reconfigured to permit more independence by non-state actors, this left-over part of social reality invites re-evaluation. One way of accomplishing this task is to apply the notion of 'civil society' to the presence, emergence, and re-emergence of independent social activity in the twentieth century.

However, just as the use of 'state' generates problems of translation and interpretation, 'civil society' also requires care in its application to China. While the state as *guojia* has ancient antecedents, no such term for society existed in China before the modern period. Along with numerous other neologisms invented by the Japanese to cover Western terms, *shehui*, meaning literally 'ritual community-association', was imported in order to translate Western texts that treated the problem of 'society'.[27] Whereas in the past the conjuncture of the social and the spatial formed a nested, vertical structure of (in descending order) the world or 'all under Heaven' (*tianxia*), 'country' (*guo*), 'family' (*jia*), and person (*shen*), the foreign loan-word of 'society' described social life in more horizontal and implicitly national terms.[28] Instead of being *under* the authority of heaven, emperor and family, individuals were now *in* society as members of a larger community of fate. One could blame society for social ills or mobilize society in the search for remedies to problems such as poverty or backwardness. 'Civil society' entered the Chinese language only much later as *shimin shehui* (literally: city people's society) in translations of Marx's *Eighteen Brumaire of Louis Napoleon*.[29] More recently, in the context of greater intellectual openness and under the influence of revolutions in Eastern Europe, civil society has become a keyword in Chinese discussions of economic reform, democracy, and law.[30] Civil society has been translated as *shimin shehui* but also as *gongmin shehui* (citizen's society) and *minjian shehui* (civic, folk, popular, or non-state society), and even *wenming shehui* (civilized society).[31] The common ground in these various renderings is a longstanding concern with an organized social life imbued with a larger purpose. That purpose might be construed as class support for a regime, political participation in national affairs, solidarity with fellow citizens, or a sense of a higher, moral community.

In its European and North American context, civil society also carries diverse connotations. In Chapter 8 Brødsgaard notes that civil society can be positioned in as many as six different Western discourses: (1) the traditional, (2) the classical–liberal, (3) the Hegelian, (4) the Marxian, (5) the Gramscian, and (6) a newer Havelian, which takes its inspiration from East European experiences. The traditional discourse calls attention to the classic Greek concerns with how people organize themselves in a collective life in the polis. The classical–liberal discourse centres on the inalienable rights of the individual and non-interference in the market. The Hegelian views civil society as a realm of intermediate institutions and associations between the individual and the state. The Marxian identifies civil society with bourgeois society and the capitalist state, and thus implies that the concept is relative to a particular historical period. The Gramscian discourse operates with at least five different understandings of civil society and the state: the state in a balanced relationship with civil society, the state as an outer surface of civil society, the state as a massive structure *vis-à-vis* an autonomous civil society, the state as encompassing civil society, and the state as identical with civil society. In the East European or Havelian discourse, the concept refers to the organization of a plurality of interests outside the state and the party in an increasingly autonomous social sphere. Vaclav Havel's understanding appears to be related to Gramsci's third version and thus assumes a dichotomy in state–society relations. Finally, the Habermasian discourse imagines a public sphere of independent, critical opinion built on the foundations supplied by civil society.

To invoke civil society is to raise the general issue of how particular forms of social organization influence, shape, enable or obstruct that society's central political processes. Depending on which tradition (or which Gramsci!) one begins with, the questions one asks about linkages between social organization and political processes are bound to be quite diverse. Depending on how one reads late imperial and early republican social development, a Chinese civil society is either an entirely novel response to the decay and reform of the Maoist system or the revival of a much older pattern of autonomy and initiative among groups like guilds, poetry societies, self-government groups, chambers of commerce, and labour unions.[32] In Chapter 2 Strand argues that, while a civil society and an accompanying public sphere were emerging in Chinese cities early in the century, the full implications of these social and cultural changes were resisted even by democratic leaders like Sun Yat-sen on the grounds that autonomy translated into a level of social disorder that China as a nation could ill afford. In other words, there is little dispute that Chinese social organization is capable of considerable autonomy and independence; but the notion of civil society carries with it the idea of a whole social presence in political and public life greater than the sum of its local, corporate, or individual parts. At what point does evidence of autonomy in a guild, union, or locality prove the existence of a higher, more developed social formation? Can the kind of national regimes produced by a century of war and revolution in China accept or support such autonomy?

Focusing on the non-state sector of the economy and on society today, Thomas Gold and Kjeld Erik Brødsgaard see a clear line emerging between the state and an emergent civil society, and both take a Havelian perspective on the natural tendency of societal forces to contest the power of the state in large and small ways. Accordingly, in Chapter 7 Gold defines civil society as 'the realm between society and the state, or associations of autonomous individuals participating voluntarily, which enjoy autonomy to establish themselves, determine their boundaries and membership, and engage in relationships with other similar associations'. Social movements (such as the 1989 pro-democracy movement, religious bodies, women's groups, and intellectual currents) also could be included in the definition.

The emergence of a vibrant private economy and the associated rise of new social groups of private entrepreneurs can form important steps in the formation of a civil society in communist systems. Clearly, private-sector expansion creates space for a sphere of economic activity which is not easily controlled by the state. First, a strong private sector reduces the role of the plan and the planning bureaucracy of the state. Second, the Communist party will be absent in most of the new small private and individual enterprises, creating autonomy and space for new social forces. Third, 'growing out of the plan' eventually will mean growing out of the old state–society matrix and creating the foundation of a more pluralistic and open configuration.[33] In sum, market reform and private-sector expansion seem to stimulate the emergence of a civil society. Forces unleashed by Deng Xiaoping's economic policies have taken on an independent momentum rooted in economic interests, transnational and 'greater China' connections, and strategies for social organization that do indeed show strong points of continuity with imperial and early twentieth-century experiences.

Drawing a clear line between state and society has analytical value in sorting through the various transactions currently taking place between officialdom and extra-bureaucratic forces over issues such as taxation, group autonomy, cultural independence, and private property. The insurgency of society against the state during moments like the pro-democracy movement of 1989 has also suggested the possibility of a much broader, constitutional focus to such tensions and relationships. However, as Brødsgaard observes, in a number of areas, e.g. the status of private property, the regime has moved to redefine the state–society relationship in ways that have fostered considerable ambiguity. Ceding property rights to individuals is a radical idea, and a logical extension of the release of private activity from state control. This is one of the hallmarks of the Deng reforms and a decidedly liberal one. The state's desire to legitimate private business originally flowed from purely economic considerations. But the unintended consequences helped consolidate the independence of entrepreneurs in ways that are socially and politically challenging to a 'socialist' China. Whether this autonomy, rooted in an emergent notion of private property, will come to rest juridically and culturally speaking in a civil society is less clear. The nature of property rights has been entangled from the beginning with state power in ways that restrict and undercut any prospect for legal autonomy. Brødsgaard points out the broad consequences of activity by individual entrepreneurs (*getihu*) while at the same time cautioning against making too much of the right to engage in private business in a China where, historically or culturally, such rights were always contingent on state approval or indifference.

State policy has led to the enlargement of a society freer of state control in many areas—for example the realms of family life, hobbies, and private money-making. These spheres can be described as 'civil' in the sense of being predominantly urban and market-oriented (*shimin*) as well as popular, consumerist, and non-state in orientation (*minjian*). Whether or not the groups Gold describes as having autonomy can make the complete journey to *gongmin shehui* (a 'citizen's society') remains to be seen. *Gongmin shehui* assumes that civil society either equals or naturally leads to political society. In such a civil society political relationships between state and society are based on principles of citizenship, rights, representation, and the rule of law.[34] Here the experiences of the states and societies of the former Soviet Union offer a cautionary note. The victory of civil society, understood as the private and corporate world of contacts and loyalties outside state control, over the state has done as much to empower criminals and ex-Communists as ordinary people. In China, the return of secret societies, the prevalence of corruption, and the victimization of vulnerable individuals and groups in various labour-contracting, prostitution, and consumer fraud practices promise a level of 'criminalization' that flies in the face of hopes for both rule of law and more civil (*wenming*) relations within society itself.

The pressures and turbulence of recent years, including regime efforts to guide and tax the private economy, sporadic demands for democracy, government crackdowns on dissident activity, and entrepreneurial efforts to carve out room for money-making and culture-making outside the state, have encouraged Chinese attempts to rethink and renegotiate the relationship between state and society. As Ann Anagnost has observed, some of these efforts have included top-down programmes to consolidate party control through new community-based systems that stress control at the expense of both disorder (*luan*) and freedom.[35] In comparable fashion, as Thøgersen shows in Chapter 6, Liang Shuming praised spontaneity and freedom from state control while building strong state-like elements into his *social* initiative. The local officials described by Young in this volume are similarly concerned with maintaining order within their realms. Other reformers, like the ones Brødsgaard discusses in Hainan, have re-envisioned the state as 'small' in contrast to an economically insurgent and socially developing 'big' society. In the first instance, this is a matter of scale rather than values. But the new importance being applied to social groups (*shetuan*) by social investigators and the prevalence of 'popular' (*minban*) organizations suggests a broader and deeper set of changes in process.

One distinguishing feature of the promotion of civil society as social goal and analytical tool in China is the weight attached to economics as a driving factor. Theorists and activists in the initial phases of resistance to communist regimes (e.g. Vaclav Havel) imagined civil society as a cultural realm of freedom linked to 'living in the truth' rather than freedom of the marketplace.[36] In contrast, Chinese intellectuals writing on the problem of civil society in the 1980s sought to ground a new, more independent sense of citizenship in the economic realities of a reformed Chinese economy. The Deng reforms granted individuals and firms the right to buy and sell in the marketplace without risking the past, punishing effects of labels like 'bourgeoisie' and 'capitalist'. By their account, the resulting *shimin shehui* (city people's society) began to make possible the emergence of a new citizen (*gongmin*) who could be legally protected. As Ju Mingzhou argued in 1989, ' . . . without [civil] society, there is no citizen. Society creates citizens and [the formation of] a citizenry represents the perfection of individuals.'[37] As Shu-Yun Ma points out, advocacy on behalf of a new citizenship based on an economically freer society did not lead to a direct attack on state authority.[38] This appears to have been less a matter of simple prudence than a continued belief that state and society should be in harmony rather than conflict.[39]

Since 1993, under the impact of the 1989 defeat of the pro-democracy movement and the continuing momentum of economic reform, the ground of the debate over civil society has shifted in mainland China. Discussions have returned more narrowly to the theme of economic reform as the basis of a *shimin shehui*, citing both Deng's recommitment in 1992 to marketization and the 'small government, big society' formulation of Hainan reformers.[40] For example, instead of promoting a new, more active citizenship, legal researcher Xu Guodong emphasizes the importance of civil law (*minfa* or *shiminfa*) in protecting the rights of the individual as a 'private person' and 'legal entity' (*faren*).[41] The civil law of contracts and the marketplace of economic exchange define and undergird civil society as a realm separate from that of the state and its concern with criminal law and citizenship.[42] Another writer, Qi Heng, using a Marxian framework of base and superstructure, summed up the differences between state and society as a basic, non-antagonistic division of social and political function:

The state [*zhengzhi guojia*] takes political life as its nucleus. Civil society [*shimin shehui*] takes economic life as its main component. The state takes class and social strata as its basic structure. Civil society takes the bond of human relationships [*renji guanxi*]. The state depends on political power and other related coercive forces, while civil society relies on contracts, trust, and a naturalized authority. The state belongs to the realm of the superstructure, while civil society is located in the economic base. The state takes political power as its goal, while civil society makes gaining material interest its guide.[43]

While the dynamic element of the two spheres is plainly civil society, the importance of the state is acknowledged: 'The appearance of the state truly [represents] progress in human history. With the aid of coercive power, the state mediates conflicts in society between opposing classes and guarantees the continuation of society. Consequently the state is not a monster but rather an object worthy of veneration, humankind's loftiest "myth".'[44] While the problem of potential conflicts between state and society over boundaries and rights is not addressed in any detail, authors seem to accept a diminished role for state power in future. 'The tendency to reform markets in China is promoting deep changes in the relationship between society and political power. The power of politics and the state is gradually withdrawing and shrinking while the power of society and the individual is quickly developing, leading, finally to the formation of a Chinese civil society.'[45] While at present the main changes are taking place in the economic realm, eventually, as the centre cedes more power to localities and as organizations relinquish power to individuals, the state will 'give social power back to society'.[46] These perspectives suggest a residue of respect, if not veneration, for state power as an overarching authority, but also a deeper interest in forces current in China today: privatization, consumerism, and anxieties about security of persons and property. The assumption seems to be that a strengthening of these elements of social life, legitimized through the medium of law, will finally 'check' (*kongzhi*) the power of the state without the necessity of open opposition or a revolution.

Adjustments in the concept of civil society required for use in interpreting social change and its political ramifications in China appear to be in two areas: the authority of the state as system and idea over social life, and the network-oriented nature of Chinese society. Before the twentieth century, the idea of totalistic imperial authority, in the context of the 'great systemic whole' (*da yitong*) discussed in Harald Bøckman's paper (Chapter 12), was offset by the limited nature of the imperial state system. Concessions to central authority were matched by the reality of local and group independence in practice. As Chinese writers frequently note, in the absence of both citizenship and absolutism in the Chinese historical experience, the western liberal turn towards building a concept of society on the foundations of property and private life never happened, even though private property and corporate life in China represented a considerable zone of independent endeavour. Independent initiative in commerce, religion, and social life was normally consistent with formal or ritual subservience to the emperor. At the same time, high politics was hostile to the representation of interests except through the rhetoric of paternal concern or the reality of networks and patronage. The emergence of a robust realm of associational life in the early twentieth century was built on this tradition of corporate and individual initiative and retained a definite vertical or hierarchical orientation. Although one might now be a member of society and a citizen of China, those statuses still hinged for most people on the recognition granted one and one's group or community by higher powers.

The radical expansion of the state under communism brought official power and the means of repression and protection close to virtually everyone in China. The 'retreat' of the state has left officialdom still in close proximity to entrepreneurs, artists, worshippers, and students, who can take advantage of this shift without experiencing anything like complete freedom. This is not simply a matter of continued surveillance and police state controls. Proximity fosters collaboration as well as disengagement or conflict. In some cases official and social spheres overlap in ways that make a definite line between state and society difficult to draw. As Benjamin Lee notes in his comments on the social and cultural activism in the months leading up to the crisis of 1989:

Coffee clubs, alternative bookstores and magazines, think tanks, and intellectual salons all blossomed in what looked like the counterpart to the English literary public sphere of the eighteenth century. The major difference was that most of these organizations were either 'underground' or developed in niches in state organizations; they were therefore extremely susceptible to government pressure and had not yet formed a self-producing and semi-autonomous network of organizations.[47]

Partly because of this tendency to burrow into the state for protection, the withdrawal of the state from some areas of life and the softening of some controls has not led to a clear break between state and society.

Even with the private economy leading the way and social and cultural change proceeding by its own logic, the state, in its 'realm of the superstructure', is expected to sanction events 'below'. Hainan provides a case of considerable independent social initiative. However, from the moment the new province was established, authorities were laying blueprints for the social, economic, and political development of the island. Liao Xun's 'small government and big society' ideas represent such a guide. In this sense, a Chinese civil society absolutely depends on state initiatives and protection. The state in some instances protects civil society against encroachments by local governments and cadres. Or local government may protect local society against hostile actions by the centre. As society becomes localized and fragmented, so the state too, as a system, is no longer a monolith. Stability and predictability under these conditions, and in the context of Chinese political culture's reliance on hierarchy, depends on social actors seeking the protection of officials, either openly through official registration or covertly through connections (*guanxi*). For their part, officials need the support of society to gain some measure of compliance and to supplement through taxes or bribes their shrinking revenues.

The fact that it is necessary to say that the state is not a 'monster' but rather a useful 'myth' is an indication of the erosion of the state-idea in recent decades in China. As Milwertz shows in her study of women living under the one-child regime, citizens are still willing to subject themselves to state surveillance and regulation for both practical and cultural reasons, but the state can no longer count on unquestioned obedience. Conditions may be ripe either for growing strife and friction or for a gradual read-justment of functions and roles of the kind suggested by some civil society theorists in China and by comparativists who have surveyed a range of such settings.[48] Here Gold is led to soften earlier assertions of the opposition of civil society in China to the state, and Brødsgaard sketches a Hainan experiment which presupposes state support.

Secondly, conflicts of interest and pressures that do arise from realms of social life outside state control are often articulated informally, through networks. Just as the Chinese state from a certain angle is more a creature of networks than formal organization, Chinese society seems naturally inclined towards *guanxi*. The continued prevalence of such networks based on family, school, workplace, and hometown connections has persuaded Mayfair Yang that one should focus first on the phenomenon of *guanxi* when discussing civil society in the Chinese context. She argues that Chinese society is rooted in dyadic relations of family and kin radiating outward to all types of interpersonal relationships. Through the art of connections (discussed on the mainland as literally that—*guanxi xue*) one can gain a degree of autonomy from state regulations and the bureaucracy. Like rhizomatic tubers, *guanxi* networks can be broken at any spot by state intervention. But they can never be uprooted as an aborescent structure can be. Chinese networks will grow again, taking up where they were interrupted, to form new connections.[49] For example, in the 1980s old business families in Xiamen, long persecuted and seemingly 'uprooted' by the

Communist regime, were able quickly to reconstitute local and regional connections broken off decades before once conditions abruptly changed.[50] According to Yang, we can expect civil, or *minjian*, society in China to appear first in private relations and networks, not in public groups or in a public sphere. In short, whereas the history of civil society in the West was propelled by a discourse of rights, specifically individual rights, and the formation of a social realm outside the state, in China the relevant discourse is one of relatedness and obligations.

Yang's theoretical perspective links the centrality of what Qi Heng calls the 'bond of human relationships' in Chinese social life to changes in the balance of power between state and society. Whereas Havel finds social resistance to tyranny 'hidden' in the human heart and friendships among those who choose to 'live in truth', Yang finds comparable resources more openly available as part of a Chinese culture stimulated in the direction of networking by the decay of a still potent state socialism. However, since this patterning of relationships holds not only for friends, colleagues, and co-believers but also for entrepreneurs and other economic actors, one wonders whether *guanxi* makes possible a unique Chinese *minjian* society or simply facilitates in novel fashion the emergence of the kind of economic organizations and interest groups normally associated with civil society in a Western sense. While many organizations and associations that have developed in China in recent years are either openly or informally *guanban* (run by the state), the Hainan case provides examples of far more autonomous groups. In many cases these *minban* (run by the people) organizations have spontaneously formed, elected their own leadership, and drafted their own rules and regulations. In any case, the particular weave of a Chinese civil society will likely depend on the warp and weft of statism and *guanxi*.

In Chapter 9, Torstein Hjellum raises questions about what this new economic and social environment means for popular political attitudes and suggests ways in which continuity and change in political culture might lead to political action. In doing so, he demonstrates the importance of keeping in mind the network dimension of Chinese social life. Using the results of Chinese survey data, one can identify elements of the classic 'civic culture' typology of parochial, subject, and participant profiles. But it also seems clear from Hjellum's use of these categories that relative degrees of isolation or awareness, indifference or engagement mean different things in Chinese culture. In a classic work of Chinese sociology cited by Hjellum, Fei Xiaotong has identified 'differential' (*chaxugeju*) links that permit an individual continuously to redefine social reality to include and exclude family, neighbours, fellow workers and compatriots in order to achieve goals such as self-protection and economic advancement. Within this context and its rich possibilities for redefining social reality and connections, no Chinese in the late imperial (or twenti-eth-century, if continuity is the rule) period would be as isolated as a European counterpart. A circle of village acquaintances was (and is) read-ily extendable via hometown or kinship ties. So it is quite possible, for example, both to be 'parochial' in outlook and to participate in the modern world of commerce. When a Ningbo man did business in Shanghai, he did it with fellows from Ningbo. When Sun Yat-sen founded the 'Reconstruction' (*Jianshe*) journal in Shanghai, he did so with sup-porters from his home province of Guangdong. As Lu Fangshang points out, this does not mean that *Jianshe* was a 'Guangdong magazine'.[51] But it did mean that the pathway to broad discussions about China was the far narrower one of *tongxiang* identity. By the same token, participant behav-iour (joining a political party or engaging in protest) may be much nar-rower in meaning than it appears on the surface. That is, the reason for joining a group of demonstrators headed for Tiananmen Square in 1989 might have had more to do with workplace identity than with a commit-ment to democracy. Or a participant sentiment ('if something is unfair I can do something about it') is likely to be manifest through the use of *guanxi* rather than the more rational-legal techniques of 'civil society'. A lack of formal options in the public realm of politics is offset by a range of informal strategies that mirrors the network and imbricated tactics of bureaucrats within the regime.

National Identity

'Nation' and nationalism are slippery terms ideologically and analytically. They take forms that are both state-centred and de-centred, explicitly ideological and more diffusely cultural, and clearly invented and more subtly evolved. Ernest Gellner points out that nationalism tends to be focused on the core political processes of the nation-state.[52] As noted above, the Chinese notion of nation has been strongly identified for more than a hundred years with centralized state authority. The development of Chinese nationalism from the late Qing embodies massive and fateful changes including the turns from empire to a scaled-down Han heartland and back to the appropriation of as much of the Qing imperium as possi-ble. Struggles leading to the 1911 Revolution effected a shift from racial conceptions of nationalism to openly statist formulations.[53] In the process, 'racial revolution' gave way to a belief in 'assimilating the Manchus, Mongolians, Muslims and Tibetans into the Han race to become a great nationalist country [*daminzu zhuyi de guo*]' and to gestures of accommodation such as 'the five races united in the Chinese nation [*Zhonghua minzu*]'.[54]

The state manufactures 'official' nationalism in the form of flags, anthems, school curricula, and the 'restricted code' of 'formalized language'.[55] But citizens may also create an 'unofficial nationalism' in the context of community and society.[56] Nationalism can draw on broad cultural traditions for anchorage or move through the vehicle of distinctively modern ideas such as race. The state is an important, perhaps indispensable, focus of national energies and ideas. But nationalism as an act of imagination will involve other economic and cultural institutions like print capitalism and popular culture.[57] In a 1929 book on nationalism, He Luzhi bemoaned the fact that parts of China could be 'sliced off'; and still 'many officials and people are undisturbed':[58]

The Japanese revile us for not being a nation. Although we are angry, we must calm down and think a bit. Have we made ready the organized conditions for a modern nation or not? In a modern, organized nation, there are elections so that people can participate in politics, a free press to disseminate accurate news, and various kinds of associations that combine the feelings of a part of the people [into the whole]. There exist means of communications so that the life of the whole nation can be more and more intimately connected.

China needed a 'nervous system' to permit the whole country to feel the pain it was enduring and a 'nerve centre'—a strong state—to guide its reactions.

Despite the ideological power of statism, the weakness of republican successor states often left open the precise expression of what the nation actually meant to the broad inventiveness of the population. This was partly due to the fact that ordinary people shared with élites a real sense of threat of national extinction or loss of national patrimony. The texts written in blood mentioned by Strand contained language written or spoken by élites, but the acts themselves were taken and dramatized by all kinds of groups and individuals. David Apter has pointed out that the broad appeal of Mao's inversionary rhetoric hinged in part on an alignment between Mao's Yan'an stories and a concrete sense of threat to local communities.[60] This connection between national and local-level narratives of community had been imagined by Sun Yat-sen and other early nationalists. But it took the Japanese invasion to bring this national discourse down to earth over most of the country. Today the changing nature of state control in China and the presence of more independent spheres of social and cultural life create the prospect of the parts (individuals, regions, or groups) no longer feeling the dramatic sense of wholeness evoked by He Luzhi, or responding in accord with state directions.

Finally, one may stress the ethnic foundations of nationalism and the importance of religion, myths, and sacred languages and scripts.[61] As Bøckman points out, Chinese history offers a deep, almost bottomless, tradition to drop an anchor into. Nationalist revolutionary Zou Lu gave classic rejoinder to the didactic pressure of the outside world when he observed: 'If we are to reply to Russians who ask us about the principles [*daoli*] of the Chinese Revolution, we can say it begins with Yao and Shun, Xia and Tang, Wen and Wu, the Duke of Zhou and Confucius.'[62] The recent ceremonies to honour the Yellow Emperor discussed by Bøckman continue that effort to secure the cultural footings of today's China. Søren Clausen (Chapter 10) and Bøckman both question the 'culturalism to nationalism' paradigm which sharply distinguishes between traditional Chinese culture and the modern Chinese nation. The pre-modern Chinese achievement of cultural integration keyed to empire is now seen as prefiguring (or in Bøckman's approach dominating) rather than denying the principles of modern nationalism.[63] On the one hand, as Bøckman suggests, it is possible to misjudge the reserves of unity in China by discounting the feelings and ideas associated with the 'empire-state' that stands behind modern Chinese nationalism. On the other, ethnic minorities and regional cultures like the Tibetans and the Cantonese have found the means to resist or alter nationalist formulations that seemed irresistible and inalterable only a few decades ago.

In his essay on the failure of the current regime to re-engineer national culture, Clausen shows how, when the state and its propagandists falter, other 'layers' of society are available to continue the work of reinterpreting or even 'reinventing' the nation. This is partly because, as Clausen points out, quoting Robin Fox, culture is always 'under active construction'. The process of sustaining the discourse of national culture involves a complex set of negotiations from the regime through establishment intellectuals and iconoclasts down to (and back from) the realm of popular culture. As Frank Dikötter has suggested for the nineteenth century, these exchanges can be imagined as a 'phenomenon of circularity, or constant interaction, rather than one of strict autarky' based on class or official status.[64] This multi-levelled social arrangement for the construction of national identity is further complicated by spatial tensions—from centre to periphery—and includes pressure from regionalism and localism.

Clausen presents a state that has lost its grasp of what Sun, Mao, and Liang seemed to have had so firmly in view if not under complete control. But if China's national culture changes in ways not sanctioned by the state, there may yet be a role for state power, either as an obstacle to the unfolding of alternatives or as a facilitator of such developments. The most obvious example of this continuing statist dimension would be in the repression of secessionist or regional autonomy movements in places like Tibet or Guangdong. But there are other, more subtle, roles that the state may choose to play or not to play. In a recent essay, Torbjørn Lodén has predicted a kind of 'downsizing' of Chinese nationalism in a fashion consistent with greater individualism.[65] This might also include a more catholic attitude towards the other Chinas like Taiwan, Hong Kong, and the Chinese diaspora. But will these more narrow ambitions, in terms of mobilization, finally require active intervention by the nation-state? As Thøgersen's portrait of educational reformers indicates, attempts to escape the state through an emphasis on the local community led reformers back to the state as part of their search for security, legitimacy, and financial resources. Individualism, or liberalism, also requires a strong regime to guarantee rights like freedom of speech and the protection of private ownership. Is it possible to rethink the problem of being Chinese without 'bringing the state back in'? Is it likely that any Chinese state will reconfigure itself to be more amenable to the 'liberalism' of individual, regional, and national rights?

Envisioning China during the revolution meant, as Apter points out, constructing a 'simulacrum' capable of compressing and condensing the narrative of the nation into a story that could be told convincingly anywhere within the borders originally drawn in broad stroke by Manchu conquerors in the seventeenth and eighteenth centuries.[66] This was no easy task. The story of 'lost patrimony' was never completely convincing to peoples outside Han culture but still within the borders. As Mette Halskov Hansen points out, the PRC's accommodation of 'national minorities' was partial from the very beginning of the regime's history. Only 56 out of 400 applicants for minority status were approved. Those that were granted official status have had to cope with the complex challenge of improving the relative position of their group within the parameters set by Han racial dominance and an evolutionary discourse that labelled various cultural practices primitive or advanced. For the Naxi, this has meant accepting the game of ethnicity as designed by the state. The rules of this game, for example, privilege a written script (which the Naxi luckily possess) over oral traditions and enshrine a pseudo-science called 'minority psychology'. But at the same time, as Naxi urban intellectuals have found, it is possible, by working within the Chinese discourse of nation, to push past other minorities towards higher status. Unlike the Tibetans, the Naxi's rising ethnic consciousness poses no threat to official Chinese nationalism, although it promises to alter the precise content of China's national identity.

Where this identity in the largest sense is moving is a matter of debate. On the one hand, if Lodén is correct about the shift 'away from' the *fuqiang* (wealth and power) and *wangguo* (threat of national extinction) mentality, then the state's ritual evocation of the original and successful quest for patrimony's return will mean less and less.[67] On the other hand, the *Heshang* (River Elegy) television critique of Chinese xenophobia assumes the Chinese are still susceptible to fits of national hysteria. Events in 1995 and 1996, such as the publication of *The China that Can Say 'No'*, popular reaction over President Lee Teng-hui's visit to the United States and the PLA's missile firings near Taiwan, and student protests on the anniversary of the Japanese invasion of Manchuria all suggest that powerful national feelings still exist and can surface in ways that the regime may seek to exploit or stifle.

What is the most convincing narrative of nation told today? And who is telling it? What is the most decisive force in shaping national culture and consciousness? The death of Mao as embodiment of the ethic of sacrifice (and victimization) has not eliminated him as an artefact of popular culture. In fact, he has become both a commodified souvenir of China and the Maoist past and a religious protector of ordinary people ('Big Daddy Mao', in at least one temple dedicated to him in his native Hunan).[68] This reorientation of desire and demand has been achieved through marketplace reforms, including the market for Mao memorabilia as amulets and fashion statements and calendars to serve as 'gate gods' (*menshen*), and the creation of new spaces (*kongjian*) for cultural production, including the positive assertion of 'subjectivity' by philosophers, the celebration of Cantonese or Shanghai culture, the articulation of a new Chinese feminism, and a reassertion of family and clan values. Perhaps, in an atmosphere of political uncertainty and economic explosion, notions of nationhood will have to be inscribed within new economic, political, and social identities. Whether or not the nation in its racial, cultural, or political meanings has the power to encircle (or 'superscribe' in Prasenjit Duara's conception of this kind of process)[69] rival identities as it once did remains to be seen. This may depend on what Bøckman sees as the largest potential force of all: Chinese culture in its broadest and deepest sense.

In addition, global forces and discourses have conspired to create a context in which ideas that speak to the relationship between state and society, such as democracy or civil society, can be both indigenous and foreign, in a manner analogous to the inside/outside histories of other keywords such as nation and communism. Nationalism can be thought of as proceeding through stages of development in a contest between 'derivative' and indigenous forces towards some point of balance or resolution.[70] In his notion of 'grabism' (*nalai zhuyi*), Lu Xun sought such a resolution through the active appropriation of foreign things for Chinese use in what he hoped would be a non-derivative spirit.[71] To paraphrase Lu Xun, today there is lots more to 'grab' and bring inside, and the state is no longer the customs agent of ideas it once was. The nation, long in the grip of communism as arbiter of what it meant to be Chinese in both political and cultural terms, has been freed from 'national communism'. But, unlike the newly free nations of Eastern Europe or the radically deconstructed republics of the former Soviet Union, China offers no immediate answers to questions designed to gauge either the power or nature of a new Chinese nationalism. At one level the question is whether or not China will 'fall apart'; at another, as Bøckman, Clausen and Hansen, suggest, it is about what it means for China to stay together, within the boundaries of either the Manchu conquests or the older and smaller Han heartland. The state seems to have lost its ability to 'engineer' consciousness, and there seems no definite candidate for a settled, much less 'hegemonic' reconstruction. That has not prevented intellectuals, artists, film-makers, and ordinary people from trying to work out what it means to be Chinese today and in a historical context. These concerns about identity help explain how a programme like *Heshang* could capture the national imagination so completely even if it could not hold it for very long.

Conclusion

Since the turn of this century, the visions of Chinese leaders and the sentiments of the broader citizenry have helped chart a course notable for its abrupt changes of direction. The projects and practices that resulted left a wave-like pattern of rising and falling motions in political, economic, social, and cultural life. Governments, prices, and literary fashions rose and fell. Populations were pulled to cities by economic opportunity and pushed around by war and revolution. State policy (sometimes the policies of competing states) shifted in ways that turned over and rerouted the lives of individuals and communities. These twists and turns and reversals raise questions about the nature of the forces driving processes of change in China.

Is this the natural shape of development in a continent-sized country? Forces spend themselves to exhaustion before plans or trends can be completed. Course corrections in turn call forth counterforces of great magnitude leading to 'over-corrections', in the form of recessions that become depressions and reforms that escalate into revolutions. Or are radical changes in political regimes or cultural orientations due to an élite or collective determination to try every alternative available until one that completes the modern Chinese quest for wealth and power is found? As

China's twentieth century nears its close, the latest developments and undulations can be placed in the context of this long historical progression in ways that focus both on the nature of change and the effects of change on consciousness and culture.

NOTES

1. For the notion of 'shocks' and a more detailed list of such events as they relate to the prewar Chinese economy, see Thomas G. Rawski, *Economic Growth in Prewar China* (Berkeley: University of California Press, 1989), xxix.
2. See Jiwei Ci's discussion of how utopianism made thoughts of the future a powerful force in 20th-cent. Chinese history: Ci, *Dialectic of the Chinese Revolution: From Utopianism to Hedonism* (Stanford: Stanford University Press, 1994).
3. Wang Jueyuan, *Zhongguo jianshe gailun* (An Outline of Chinese Reconstruction) (Chongqing: Duli chubanshe, 1943), 1.
4. As e.g. in the case of the World Bank, inaugurated in 1946 as the 'International Bank for Reconstruction and Development': see World Bank, *The International Bank for Reconstruction and Development, 1946–1953* (Baltimore: Johns Hopkins Press, 1954).
5. For the Fel'dman–Preobrazhensky paradigm for economic growth, see Kjeld Erik Brødsgaard, 'Paradigmatic Change: Reform and Readjustment in the Chinese Economy, 1953–1981, Part I', *Modern China*, 9:1 (January 1983), 37–83.
6. The state as an 'aborescent' structure that suppresses 'rhizomatic' alternatives is described in Mayfair Yang, *Gifts, Favors, and Banquets: The Art of Social Relationships in China* (Ithaca, NY: Cornell University Press, 1994), ch. 8.
7. For 'cities as cash cows' for the regime during this period, see Barry Naughton, 'Cities in the Chinese Economic System: Changing Roles and Conditions for Autonomy', in Deborah S. Davis, Richard Kraus, Barry Naughton and Elizabeth J. Perry (eds.), *Urban Spaces in Contemporary China: The Potential for Autonomy and Community in Post-Mao China* (New York: Cambridge University Press, 1995), 67–70.
8. Kjeld Erik Brødsgaard, 'China's Political Economy in the Nineties', *China Report*, 27:3 (1991), 177–96.
9. Yang, *Gifts, Favors, and Banquets*.
10. Philip Abrams makes a useful distinction, followed here, between the state as an idea or 'ideological power' and the 'state-system' of agencies and institutions: Abrams, 'Notes on the Difficulty of Studying the State', *Journal of Historical Sociology* 1:1 (March 1988), 79–80.
11. Joseph W. Esherick and Mary Backus Rankin, 'Introduction', in Esherick and Rankin (eds.), *Chinese Local Elites and Patterns of Dominance* (Berkeley: University of California Press, 1990), 3.
12. See Marianne Bastid's study of the rhetoric and politics of late Qing reforming officials like Zhang Zhidong who helped create a 'new vision of the Chinese state' 'by detaching the principle of unity represented by the monarchy from the religious and ritualistic ties of kingship, and by linking strongly this principle of unity with the very substance of state power'. Marianne Bastid, 'Official Conceptions of Imperial Authority at the End of the Qing Dynasty', in Stuart R. Schram (ed.), *Foundations and Limits of State Power in China* (Hong Kong: Chinese University Press, 1987), 185.

13. In an essay more even-handed than the title might suggest, Yan Jiaqi explores continuities and discontinuities in the transition from imperial to Communist rule: Yan Jiaqi, 'Zhongguo zhengzhi tizhi de san dabiduan' (Three Great Abuses in the Chinese Political System), in Yan Jiaqi, *Lianbang Zhongguo gouxiang* (Thoughts on the Bases of a Federal China) (Hong Kong: Mingbao chubanshe, 1992), ch. 2. For example, Yan notes that under communism China has had 'imperial succession struggles' without 'imperial succession rules' (p. 26).

14. For the later interpretation, see Karl Bunger, 'The Chinese State between Yesterday and Today', in Stuart Schram (ed.), *The Scope of State Power in China* (New York: St Martin's Press, 1985), xxiii.

15. Liang Qichao responded to this justification for Yuan's dictatorial brand of monarchy by making a distinction between *guoti*, referring to the nature of the state, and *zhengti*, or form of government. From Liang's perspective, while *guoti* did define differences between the nature of republics and monarchies, Yuan's actions and intentions were simply unconstitutional, an aspect related to governmental form rather than state type. Yan Jiaqi, *Guojia zhengti* (Politics of the State) (Beijing: Renmin chubanshe, 1982), 2–3.

16. On the broad twentieth-century significance of federalism see Arthur Waldron, 'Warlordism Versus Federalism: The Revival of a Debate?' *China Quarterly* 121 (March 1990).

17. Yan Jiaqi, *Lianbang Zhongguo gouxiang*, 6–19. Before the 1911 Revolution, many reformers and revolutionaries like Liang Qichao and Sun Yat-sen saw federalism as a means of building a strong state from the ground up. Later on Sun changed his mind, on the grounds that the idea promoted division and had become the tool of militarists. Ironically, but understandably, the Communist Party remained a supporter of federalism through the 1940s, based, according to Yan, on a realistic appreciation of the threat posed by centralizers like Chiang Kai-shek.

18. See the entry under *guojia* in the *Hanyu dacidian* (Comprehensive Chinese Dictionary), ed. Luo Zhufeng (Shanghai: Hanyu dacidian cubanshe, 1989), 3, 640.

19. Bastid, 'Official Conceptions', 175. Zhang's essay is dated 1898.

20. Liang in 1901 provided an appreciative commentary on the Swiss political theorist Johann Bluntschli's 'Theory of the Modern State' (*Lehre vom modernen Staat*), which Liang rendered as *Guojia xue*. Liang noted the differences that existed between the ideology of the now realizable 'perfect state' (*wanquan guojia*), in which 'state and people are united', and China's 'old ideology', in which they are 'completely separated'. 'Guojia sixiang bianda yitong lun' (On Similarities and Differences in the Transformation of State Ideology), in Liang Qichao, *Liang Qichao xuanji* (Selected Works) (Shanghai: Shanghai renmin chubanshe, 1984), 184–93.

21. Sun Yat-sen, 'Sanmin zhuyi yu Zhongguo minzu zhi qiantu' (The Three Principles of the People and the Future of the Chinese Race), in Sun Wen [Sun Yat-sen], *Zongli quanji* (Complete Works of the Zongli), ed. Hu Hanmin (Shanghai: Minzhi shuju, 1930), 2, 81.

22. For a discussion of this 'society of associations' see Strand, 'Changing Dimensions of Social and Public Life in Early Twentieth Century Chinese Cities', in Leon Vandermeersch, *La société civile face à l'État: dans les traditions chinoise, japonaise, coréenne et vietnamienne* (Paris: École-Française Extrême-Orient, 1994).

23. Prasenjit Duara, *Culture, Power, and the State: Rural North China, 1900–1942* (Stanford: Stanford University Press, 1988), 74.

24. Vivienne Shue, 'State Sprawl: The Regulatory State and Social Life in a Small Chinese City', in Davis *et al.*, *Urban Spaces*, 92–3, 97–106.

25. Madeline Zelin, 'The Rise and Fall of the Fu-Rong Salt-Yard Elite: Merchant Dominance in Late Qing China', in Esherick and Rankin, *Chinese Local Elites*. Zelin explains that in these enterprises lineage trusts (*tang*) served as 'an analogue of the business corporation' (p. 91). For the family basis of Taiwan enterprises see Laurids Lauridsen, 'The Role of Workers and Labour Institutions in Flexible Capitalism and Political Transformation in Taiwan', paper presented at the conference on 'Regionalism and Globalism in East Asia', Gentofte, Denmark, 12–15 May 1994.

26. For a discussion of the complex rendering of local 'public enterprises' in rural areas, see Andrew Walder, 'The Industrial Organization of Zouping County: Agency and Ownership in Local Public Enterprise', paper presented to the conference on 'Regionalism and Globalism in East Asia', Gentofte, Denmark, 12–15 May 1994.

27. Wang Hui and Leo Ou-fan Lee, with Michael M. J. Fischer, 'Is the Public Sphere Unspeakable in Chinese? Can Public Spaces (*gonggong kongjian*) Lead to Public Spheres?' *Public Culture*, 6 (1994), 599. See also Alexander Woodside, *Community and Revolution in Modern Vietnam* (Boston: Houghton-Mifflin, 1976), 54, for a discussion of *shehui*'s meaning in a larger, East Asian, revolutionary context.

28. According to Mencius, 'The world is rooted in the country, the country in the family, and the family in the person.' See *Hanyu dacidian*, 3, 640.

29. Wang *et al.*, 'Is the Public Sphere Unspeakable . . . ?' 101.

30. For an analysis and overview of the emergence of civil society as a keyword on mainland China, see Shu-Yun Ma, 'The Chinese Discourse on Civil Society', *China Quarterly*, 137 (March 1994), 180–93. Ma cites a 1986 article on the 'rights of city people' (*shimin quanli*) as the first in a series of essays on the subject running through 1990.

31. *Minjian* society has been used for some time in Taiwan to refer to protest movements: Wang *et al.*, 'Public Sphere', p. 101. For an assessment of the difficulty in achieving a 'citizen's society', see Liu Zhiguang and Wang Xuli, 'Cong "Qunzhong shehui" zouxiang "gongmin shehui"' (From 'Mass Society' to 'Civil Society'), *Xinhua wenzhai* (New China Digest), 11 (1988), 119.

32. For a review of the controversies surrounding the debate over this question, see 'Symposium: "Public Sphere"/"Civil Society" in China?' *Modern China*, 19:2 (April 1993).

33. Barry Naughton, *Growing Out of the Plan: Chinese Economic Reform, 1978–1993* (Cambridge: Cambridge University Press, 1996).

34. See Gordon White, 'Prospects for Civil Society in China: A Case Study of Xiaoshan City', *Australian Journal of Chinese Affairs*, 29 (January 1993), 63–88.

35. Ann Anagnost, 'Socialist Ethics and the Legal System', in J. N. Wasserstrom and E. J. Perry (eds.), *Popular Protest and Political Culture in Modern China* (Boulder, Colo.: Westview Press, 1992).

36. In his key essay on the problem of social resistance to government oppression, Havel expresses scepticism about the supposed advantages of a consumer society and focuses instead on cultural freedom embodied in individual freedom of thought, underground presses, and 'flying universities': Havel, 'The Power of the Powerless', in Jan Vladislav (ed.), *Vaclav Havel, or Living in Truth* (London: Faber and Faber, 1986).

37. In Ma, 'Chinese Discourse', 185.

38. ibid.

39. For a discussion of this premiss of harmony rather than conflict in the relationship between state and individual as a longstanding feature of Chinese democratic thought, see Andrew J. Nathan, *Chinese Democracy* (New York: Knopf, 1985).

40. See a series of articles by legal researcher Xu Guodong: 'Shimin shehui yu shimin fa: minfa de diaozheng yanjiu' (Civil Society and Civil Law: Research on the Revision of Civil Law), *Faxue yanjiu* (Studies in Law), 4 (1994), 3–9; 'Lun shiminfazhong de shimin' (On the Citizen in the Citizen Code), *Tianjin shehui kexue* (Tianjin Social Science Review), 6:6 (1994), 94–100; and 'Minfadian yu guanli kongzhi' (The Civil Code and Checks on Power), 1 (1995), 64–9.

41. Xu, 'Shimin shehui . . . '.

42. Xu, 'Minfadian . . . ', 69.

43. Qi Heng, 'Guanyu "shimin shehui" ruoyou wenti de sikao' (Reflections on Some Issues related to 'Civil Society'), *Tianjin shehui kexue*, 5 (1993), 60.

44. ibid. 59.

45. Guo Dingping, 'Woguo shimin shehui de fazhan yu zhengzhi zhuanxing' (The Development of a Chinese Civil Society and Models of Political Transition), *Shehui kexue* (Social Science) (Shanghai), 12 (1994), 52.

46. ibid. 55.

47. Benjamin Lee, 'Going Public', *Public Culture*, 5 (1993), 174.

48. For the notion that the state and the activities of civil society may be mutually empowering, see Joel Migdal, 'Introduction: Developing a State-in-Society Perspective', in Joel S. Migdal, Atul Kohli, and Vivienne Shue (eds.), *State Power and Social Forces: Domination and Transformation in the Third World* (Cambridge: Cambridge University Press, 1994), 7–34.

49. Yang, *Gifts, Favors, and Banquets*, 308.

50. David Wank, 'Merchant Entrepreneurs and the Development of Civil Society: Some Social and Political Consequences of Private Sector Expansion in a Southeast Coastal City', presented to a panel on 'Civil Society in People's China', Association of Asian Studies, New Orleans, 13 April 1991.

51. Lu Fangshang, *Zhu Zhixin yu Zhongguo geming* (Zhu Zhixin and the Chinese Revolution) (Taibei: Sili dongwu daxue, 1978), 237.

52. Ernest Gellner, *Nations and Nationalism* (Oxford: Blackwell, 1983).

53. Zhu Hongyuan, 'Zong zuguo dao guozu: Qingmo minchu geming pai de minzu zhuyi' (From Fatherland to Nation: Nationalism among Revolutionaries at the End of the Qing and the Beginning of the Republic), *Si yu yan* (Thought and Word), 30:2 (June 1992): 7–38.

54. The formulations are those of Sun Yat-sen quoted and analysed in Li Zehou, 'Lun Sun Zhongshan di sixiang' (On Sun Yat-sen's Thought), in Li Zehou, *Zhongguo jindai sixiang shilun* (A History of Contemporary Chinese Thought) (Taibei: Fengyun shidai chubanshe, 1990), 376, and Zou Lu, *Zhongguo guomindang shigao* (A Draft History of the Chinese Nationalist Party) (Shanghai: Minzhi shudian, 1929), 612, 617.

55. Michael Schoenhals, *Doing Things with Words in Chinese Politics* (Berkeley: Chinese Research Monographs, 1992), 1–29.

56. Thomas H. Eriksen, 'Formal and Informal Nationalism', *Ethnic and Racial Studies*, 16:1 (January 1993).

57. See Benedict Anderson, *Imagined Communities: Reflections on the Origin and Spread of Nationalism* (London: Verso, 1982, 2nd edn 1992).

58. He Luzhi, *Guojia zhuyi gaiyao* (An Outline of Nationalism) (Shanghai: Zhongguo renwen yanjiusuo, 1948, first published 1929), 12.

59. ibid. 13–14.

60. See David E. Apter, 'Foucault's Paradox: From Inversionary Discourse to Hegemonic Power in Mao's "Republic"', *Copenhagen Journal of Asian Studies*, 10 (1995), 6–39..

61. See Anthony D. Smith, *Ethnic Origins of Nations* (Oxford: Basil Blackwell, 1986).

62. Zou Lu, *Zhongguo guomindang shigao*, 605.

63. See Prasenjit Duara, *Rescuing History from the Nation: Questioning Narratives of Modern China* (Chicago: University of Chicago Press, 1995).

64. Frank Dikötter, *The Discourse of Race in Modern China* (Stanford: Stanford University Press, 1992), 35. Dikötter borrows the notion of 'circularity' from the work of Mikhail Bakhtin.

65. See Torbjorn Lodén, 'In Search of Whose Wealth and Power? Nationalism Reconsidered in Post-Mao China', paper presented at the First Annual Conference of the 'State and Society in East Asia' Network, Copenhagen, 29 April–2 May 2 1993.

66. Apter, 'Foucault's Paradox'.

67. See Lodén, 'In Search of Whose Wealth and Power?'.

68. Wei Shui, 'A Temple Poses a Dilemma', *China Focus* (1 October 1995), 3. The 'Temple of the Three Protectors' was built and paid for by local peasants and dedicated to Mao, Zhou Enlai, and Zhu De. See also Geremie R. Barme, *Shades of Mao: The Posthumous Cult of the Great Leader* (Armonk, NY: M. E. Sharpe, 1996).

69. Prasenjit Duara, 'Superscribing Symbols: The Myth of Guandi, Chinese God of War', *Journal of Asian Studies*, 47:4 (November 1988): 778–95.

70. See Partha Chatterjee, *Nationalist Thought and the Colonial World: A Derivative Discourse* (Minneapolis: University of Minnesota Press, 1993).

71. Discussed in Zhang Longxi, 'Western Theory and Chinese Reality', *Critical Inquiry*, 19 (Autumn 1992), 107.

I
STATE CONTROL

2

Calling the Chinese People to Order: Sun Yat-sen's Rhetoric of Development
David Strand

Modern leaders benefit both from the power of the state as a likely instrument of their will and from crises that cast doubt on the ability of government or other political agencies to respond to social demands and interests. A strong leader can expose the weakness of a state and the latent power of a particular social reform or political constituency, or employ state power to recast society through reform or revolution from above. Alternatively, a political leader may contribute to both state power and social upheaval and so drive state and society towards higher levels of influence and mobilization. In this latter process, at certain moments of political and social conjuncture leaders may seem to take possession not only of a regime or a movement, but also of an entire country and era.

China never belonged to Sun Yat-sen in the same way the country later became 'Mao's China' or 'Deng's China', though his failure to take hold of the Chinese nation was not for lack of trying.[1] During his career Sun helped expose the weaknesses of the Qing state and tap the power of nationalism as a social force. But he struggled without success for decades to win paramount power, only holding the post of provisional president for a few weeks in 1912 before surrendering the position to Yuan Shikai. Although Sun was later given titles of 'Extraordinary President', 'Generalissimo', and 'Party Leader' by the southern regimes he led, he died in 1925 before he could reclaim the national presidency for himself and power for his Nationalist movement.

If we accept the proposition that leadership is as much a matter of a willingness to follow as it is the expression of an individual leader's qualities and capacities,[2] Sun's repeated failures testify to the resistance China offered would-be national leaders in the early part of the century. Leading China was not a simple matter of grafting modern statesmanship on to the role of emperor or imperial institution. The trunk of that structure had been cut down in the 1911 Revolution. However, the roots of an imperial China were still in place, and the monarchical turns taken later by leaders such as Mao Zedong and Deng Xiaoping testify to the continuing power of an emperor-like political persona.[3] Lacking a firm power base, Sun was never permitted the luxury of such governing poses. Instead, by conviction and circumstance, he faced the continuous and daunting problem of how to construct a new style of leadership that directly engaged the 'people' as the foundation of the state. Sun did not leave the connection between state and citizen merely implied or latent. He spoke directly to the people and insisted on their support. He called them to a new political order as if his voice and personal authority could reach beyond the confines of lecture rooms and scattered political bases and stir and shape China's millions. In doing so, he pioneered the role of leader as speaker and ideologue, preparing the ground for combining militant state power and a mass citizenry.

Sun's efforts at speech-making, manifesto-writing, and other forms of propaganda were accompanied by a search for ideological content suitable for winning popular support. His 'Three Principles of the People' (*Sanmin zhuyi*)—nation (*minzu*), democracy (*minquan*), and people's livelihood (*minsheng*)—provided the framework for these ideas. The multidimensional, eclectic character of his agenda represented a shift from the simple racial appeals of anti-Manchu revolution to a complex rhetoric of development or reconstruction (*jianshe*). He foresaw a China of railways, modern ports, dams, and schools developed by a powerful state and supported by a modern people. Sun's talk about a new China, sometimes taken to extravagant lengths, drew derisive comments but also admiring support.

Sun Yat-sen therefore acquired not proprietary control of the China of the 1910s and 1920s, but instead a vision of a future, developed China. He bequeathed this vision to contemporary and future political leaders along with a willingness to try almost anything to achieve such dreams. In doing so, he helped set the stage for later leaps and bounds towards Chinese wealth and power as well as for the stumbles and catastrophes that often attend breakneck development.

Writing Sun's Obituary

Sun Yat-sen died suddenly of cancer on 12 March 1925 in Beijing in the midst of a final political adventure. He had journeyed there from his Guangdong base in a vain attempt to make peace with northern warlords and unify the country. An outpouring of editorials, death notices, and commemorative statements mourned Sun as a philosopher, political founder, and martyr.[4] Supporters compared him to Confucius, Jesus, George Washington, and Dr Stockmann, the altruistic protagonist in playwright Henrik Ibsen's *Enemy of the People*. But others were just as quick to attack him as an opportunist, a shallow thinker, and a failure. An editorialist in a Shanghai newspaper, *Shishi xinbao* (Current Events), jeered that, politically speaking, Sun had been dead for years. 'Therefore, when I consider Sun's death today, I cannot avoid thinking it came too late.'[5] Sun was also blamed for a 'blind reliance on military force', 'agitating among young people', concluding a dangerous alliance with the Soviet Union, and being personally fickle and unreliable.[6] While alive Sun had been a target for exaggerated, vindictive attacks;[7] in death his failure to achieve significant political power and thereby to begin to make good on his promises and plans cast doubt on his status as political founder and framer.

Sun's life embodied the central paradox of the early Republic: radical commitment to revolutionary change had led instead to stalemate, fragmentation, and stagnation at the national level. Cultural ferment and labour unrest in the cities, the massing of revolutionary armies in the south, and the reorganization of the Nationalist Party along Leninist lines with the help of the fledgling Communists held the promise of a new breakthrough. But these forces looked to many at the time as further symptoms of chaos and disorder. Sun himself was dismissed as someone afflicted by 'revolution-itis' (*geming pi*), forever attacking and opposing without a sense of where he and the country were going. It was joked while he was alive that if his son, Sun Fo, became president, Sun would still call for revolution.[8]

In fact, Sun did have definite ideas about China's future. It was just that the connection he made between the then-existing state of warlordism, poverty, and civil strife and a hoped-for era of political stability and economic prosperity was not always clear or convincing. The very grandeur and completeness of Sun Yat-sen's vision variously inspired and dismayed compatriots who found his ambitious plans for building a new China either tremendously appealing or completely unrealistic. The most notorious example had been his 1912 plan for building 67,000 miles (200,000 *li*) of rail line in China in a project Sun estimated would take ten years, require the labour of 2 million workers and cost 6 billion Chinese silver dollars.[9] During the same year he broached the idea of raising a 10 million man army in the event that war broke out with Russia.[10] Sun later proposed building a new 'Great Northern Port' the size of New York harbour; colonizing Mongolia and Xinjiang through the state-supported transfer of 10 million Chinese from overpopulated areas; reconstructing the Grand Canal; building a 'Great Eastern Port' on Hangzhou Bay to replace Shanghai; relocating the centre of Shanghai across the Huangpu River in Pudong; improving navigation and rebuilding cities on the Yangzi River (including damming the Three Gorges above Yichang); restoring Canton as a world port and ending its dependence on Hong Kong; building state-run locomotive and automobile factories; constructing a nationwide system of grain elevators; exporting soy bean foodstuff technology to Europe and America to relieve meat shortages in Western countries; building a million cheap, modern houses a year (for fifty years) to replace outmoded Chinese-style architecture; replacing all Chinese furniture with modern items made in special 'bedroom', 'kitchen', 'bathroom', 'toilet', 'parlour', and 'library' room factories; making telephones available to every family in China; and opening one million miles of public roads.[11] Supporters felt obliged to defend Sun against the charges that his ideals were so elevated they 'exceeded reality', that his plans and proposals amounted to little more than 'empty talk', and that he had a poor sense of actual conditions in the country.[12]

The gap between Chinese realities and the China envisioned by Sun was a factor in his favour as long as utopian thinking and lofty standards could be construed as practical virtues. That for many Chinese utopianism made sense was as characteristic of the times as the disorders that drove people to imagine better, more orderly worlds. Educator and language reformer Qian Xuantong saw Sun in the stubborn, heroic mould of Ibsen's Dr Stockmann, a man who had the courage to convey an unpopular message:

The people wanted the Qing emperor or the true son of Heaven sitting on a golden throne. Dr Sun wanted to overthrow the Manchus and also eliminate the emperorship. The people wanted to crawl before county magistrates who could have them stripped and beaten on the buttocks. Dr Sun was determined that the people would manage their own governmental affairs. The people regarded the happiness of the wealthy and the persecution of the poor as a matter of course. Dr Sun called for equalizing the land and restricting capitalism . . . The people were fond of spitting and farting, letting finger and toenails grow long and not cleaning their teeth. Dr Sun encouraged everyone to take care of their bodies and to use their time well.[13]

Like Ibsen's Dr Stockmann, Sun's message carried a threat to established ways of life and an enormous price tag. Stockmann's Norwegian town needed its faulty water system 'ripped out' and replaced for 300,000 crowns.[14] China needed a whole new transportation infrastructure costing billions of silver dollars. Sun advocated 'destroying' (*pohuai*) or ripping out the old as the first step towards building a new China. Fortunately for Sun, many politically conscious Chinese, unlike the townspeople in *Enemy of the People*, were willing to contemplate destructive and expensive forms of change.

Sun Yat-sen's idealism earned support from those who shared his belief that a broad vision and a long view offered leverage against the weight of

China's current afflictions. Hu Shi insisted that 'the greatest false charge against [Sun] is that everyone says he is a "dreamer", not a realist'.

Actually, anyone without an idealistic plan cannot be a genuine realist. I therefore say that Dr Sun has been a realist precisely because he has had the courage to settle on an idealistic *Outline of National Construction*. Most politicians simply loaf around. As soon as they hear of a ten-year or twenty-year plan, it flies out of their ears. And they say, 'We do not value empty talk'.[15]

For Hu, the opposition between idealism and realism was a false dichotomy, especially if dreams could be transcribed into plans. And Sun delighted in taking a bold idea like the construction of a national railway system and embellishing it with cost figures, maps, and projected dates of completion.

The common thread in Sun's ideas and actions lay in the general, though not unanimous, recognition that he was a visionary—a leader ahead of his time at a time when many hoped to put the current crises behind them. Nor was his reputation for failure necessarily fatal to his political prospects. Through his past and present setbacks and suffering, Sun personified China's plight. Whether one found his ideas convincing or overblown and his story ennobling or pathetic, Sun's words and deeds held centre stage in Chinese public life. They were framed in the stirring settings of kidnapping, 'ten great defeats' in attempting to overthrow the Qing before the 1911 Revolution, escapes, exile, sudden triumph, abrupt fall from power, *coup d'état*, celebrity marriage, betrayal, and a highly public illness and death. Sun's personal reversals coincided with China's national saga of defeat, disaster, and hoped-for redemption. For this reason, comparisons to Jesus had a certain logic. The need to 'save the nation' (*jiuguo*) implied a saviour.

Jesus brought about unlimited love. Zhongshan [Sun] brought about the Three principles and the Five Powers. The spirit of their creations is the same. Jesus sacrificed everything to save everyone in the world. During the Zhongshan revolution, [Sun] sacrificed himself, his family and his clan to save China . . . Their spirit of sacrifice was the same.[16]

This last was a bit of hyperbole. Unlike Mao, who lost several family members killed in revolution and war, Sun was spared that kind of blood sacrifice except among close associates and followers killed in abortive uprisings he led or sanctioned. The wounds were primarily, but significantly, to his pride, and were so extreme that there were those who believed the liver cancer that killed him could be traced to events like Chen Jiongming's 1922 coup against Sun and the 1924 Canton Merchant Corps uprising against his government.[17] Even harsh critics acknowledged that Sun's life had often been a 'living hell'.[18] Either Sun Yat-sen bore responsibility for this sorry personal and national history, or his life and the life of the republic had merged in some profound way to efface such distinctions between cause and effect. Sun certainly believed the latter to be the case. He had a Charles de Gaulle-like belief that his destiny was the same as his country's. If he could endure these trials, so could China. If China shared in the prospect of collective immortality characteristic of modern nationalism, Sun could live on as a token of that larger identity. Defeat for either was then a prelude to rebirth rather than simple failure.

Since Sun's thought was utopian and his leadership rhetorical, imagery and style were necessarily crucial elements of his political persona. This is not to say that Sun lacked a practical dimension to his politics, but rather that, beyond attending to the nuts and bolts of political intrigue and organizing, Sun found image-making and propaganda the central means by which he distinguished himself from his rivals and made his claim to national leadership. One explanation of Sun's influence, especially after death, is the way in which the Nationalist Party promoted a cult of Sun as part of its drive for legitimacy. But it was also the case that while he was alive Sun packaged himself, his image, and his ideas for wide distribution. In addition to the content of Sun's words and deeds, there was the form of what he said and did: his speech-making, public appearances, travel, distinctive clothing, and a particular style of political address. His trademark 'Sun Yat-sen suit' (*Zhongshan zhuang*) served this function,[19] as did the dramatic stories he told and retold about his life as a revolutionary.[20] His name alone became synonymous with the anti-Manchu revolution and the republic that followed. A commentator with decidedly mixed feelings about Sun as a leader admitted in 1912 that Sun's name was constantly being invoked:

Nowadays people regard revolution as being like [an affair between] mutual enemies. Because [people] do not understand what revolution is, that it is not some individual's revolution but rather a revolution to benefit the people, they simply call out the name [of Sun].[21]

Under the conditions of incomplete communications and marginal literacy prevailing in China, Sun could not hope to achieve wide influence unless he indexed his ideas and programmes through easily recognizable symbols and slogans. His voluminous writings and innumerable speeches had a limited circulation relative to the masses he wanted to reach.[22] Conveniently, Sun's public persona included both a basic cluster of images and ideas and a more extended ensemble of theories, stories, and personal impressions. All of these made him in death, according to the left-wing *Weekly Guide*, a 'symbol of the Chinese revolution'. Sun the man might be gone, but ' "Sun Zhongshan" will never die.'[23] Bracketed in quotation marks, the absent 'Sun' remained morally and ideologically present, absorbed into political imagery, sloganeering, and ritual. In the absence of a workable political system, Sun and his ideas and image held a place for a yet-to-be-completed modern polity.

Sun the Cannon: Force and Discourse

Sun helped sustain a republic of words through the manifold political crises of the 1910s and early 1920s. In turn, this flood of words buoyed him up. The commonplace observation that the republic was a mere 'sign-board' without a real structure to back it implied the need to construct national armies in place of militarist hordes, representative parliaments in place of clusters of 'piggish' political factions, and dynamic parties in place of passive bands of cronies. In the short term a paucity of constructive actions stimulated an outpouring of critical and rhetorical language: a prolonged 'What is to be done?' phase in China's long revolution.

Sun's heavy commitment to public speaking and visionary language about such questions was reflected in the nickname given him by fellow Cantonese: 'Sun the Cannon' (Sun Dapao).[24] This was a sarcastic reference to Sun's predilection for big talk on military and other issues.[25] While hardly a compliment, being a 'big gun', as the word has been applied to other twentieth-century Chinese political figures, can connote toughness as well as bluster and the ability to impose one's own will on others.[26] In the most negative sense, this image of Sun confirms his reputation for empty talk delivered in a heavy-handed manner. More positively, Sun's ability to 'lay down heavy artillery fire' (*kai dapao*) in his speeches and writings suggests some of the appeal that his blunt, bold message had in the context of national crisis.[27]

In the absence of the kind of military power his rivals were able to obtain, Sun was often obliged to use words instead of force to try to achieve his political goals. In 1912, after having stepped aside in favour of Yuan Shikai, Sun was still described, somewhat humorously, as a political figure 'without equal in his exalted position, having filled reams of newspaper pages and [acquired] 2,000 Mauser pistols'.[28] Sun managed to stay ahead in the realm of words but fell behind in the arms race that broke out among political contenders in China. During Sun's failed 'Second Revolution' in 1913, Yuan's weapons trumped Sun's ability to command public opinion and pen manifestos. The lesson of the pivotal importance of military power was absorbed by Sun as it was later by Mao Zedong and the Communists. Sun was not an unarmed prophet of the kind Machiavelli warned was doomed to fail, but he was often lightly or inadequately armed compared with his rivals. When circumstances turned against him, as they often did, there was little Sun could do save retreat and try to write and talk his way back into a more favourable position.

Guns and words, Mausers and newsprint, or 'force and discourse', in social theorist Bruce Lincoln's turn of phrase,[29] echo Rousseau's dictum that 'The strongest is never strong enough unless he succeeds in turning might into right and obedience into duty.' In the ideologically charged atmosphere of early twentieth-century China, force alone made you a bandit or warlord. Weaponless, words risked ridicule as the blank product of 'big guns'. Sun saw his efforts as including both the deployment of force and an equally pointed 'psychological offensive' to win the heart/mind of the Chinese populace. In 1924 Sun stated that the two major tasks for that year were building up the Whampoa Military Academy near Canton and giving a series of Three People's Principles lectures.[30] But he also insisted that 'doctrine [*zhuyi*] [always] prevails over force',[31] and that the 'quickest means of completing the revolution required 90 per cent propaganda and 10 per cent military force'.[32] Sun acknowledged the existence of force and discourse as separate kinds of power. Favouring norms over violence was consistent with Confucian cant as well as modern theories of legitimation. But Sun had a mind not just to convert might to right, but to use right doctrine to give birth to military academies, armies, and mass support. Given Sun's precarious hold on military power, attempting to convert 'right into might' or discourse into force was a matter of both wishful thinking and practical necessity. Sun sensed that discourse could become force as supporters and armies rallied to his words, or even that words by themselves could win the day. In 1924, on the eve of Sun's final journey north to negotiate with warlords in Beijing, he asked citizens to send him telegrams of support:

I can take these 10,000 telegrams to Beijing to struggle with the warlords and use 10,000 telegrams in a peaceful form of struggle to defeat 100,000 soldiers.[33]

In another context he claimed that the advantage of propaganda as a 'weapon' was that, once you have gained power over a person, that individual will stay on your side (which is 'not to be compared to a military unit seizing a walled city and later being expelled').[34]

The militarization of political rhetoric dovetailed with the realization that propaganda was essential to revolutionary war. We know that revolutionary armies emerged from the remnants and models of late Qing and early Republican military reform. But the story of how words came to be used like weapons is less clear. Sun's emergence as an expert in the use of revolutionary rhetoric, and especially the spoken word, is instructive in this regard.

The idea of using words to generate political order is a powerful one in the Chinese tradition. Through their essays and other 'literary compositions' (*wenzhang*), the literati (*wenren*) might imagine themselves writing their political and cultural world into existence.[35] Referring to this literary mission, the fourth-century AD scholar Lu Ji observed that a writer 'traps heaven and earth in the cage of form; he crushes the myriad things under the tip of his brush'.[36] In the past, writing (*wen*) had been 'a public matter',[37] analogous to public speaking in the West or in the modern period. But, as Joseph Esherick and Jeffrey Wasserstrom have pointed out, public speaking in the sense of an official or other figure addressing an indoor or outdoor crowd was exceedingly rare.[38] In addition, though forceful writing might have the power to 'crush', *wen* was conceived as the civilized, cultured opposite of 'martial' (*wu*), the supposed strategy of last resort for the Confucian statesman. Writing was superior to speaking, and words, though key to gaining and keeping power, ought to lead away from war and violence.

Beginning at the turn of the century, as a result of a number of different borrowings and adaptations, China acquired a new tradition of rhetoric that was at once more oral and more martial.[39] As one of Sun's biographers suggests, in China public speaking was 'an ultra-modern role and one in which [Sun] had few rivals'.[40] However, Sun's success in this realm had as much to do with the growing numbers of fellow speakers as it had with his rhetorical gifts. Reflecting the rise of this new style of speech-making, Sun could add the spoken to the written word in his attempt to 'trap' constituents and adversaries in the 'cage' of ideological form. That enemies might blast their way out, or that Sun himself might choose violence instead of discourse, did not diminish the seductive power of the word as close companion to the gun.

For Sun Yat-sen, discourse was a matter of both the written and spoken word. He followed the typical course of his contemporaries through the media of petition, essay, manifesto, newspaper articles, journals, and book-length theories and proposals. Sun also developed considerable prowess as a public speaker during his years in exile from China. He spoke to overseas Chinese audiences throughout the world in his quest for political support and funds. Meanwhile, speaking and lecturing was gaining ground in China. Political groups engaged in 'revolutionary harangues' (*gaotan geming*) within institutions like schools and in public places like parks.[41] These speeches were often immediately transcribed and published for propaganda purposes.[42] For example, the revolutionary newspaper *Subao* regularly and prominently published lectures given in Zhang Park, one of Shanghai's most famous recreation complexes.[43] In other cases, readers of revolutionary magazines and newspapers were moved to found societies dedicated to lecturing and publishing on topics related to social and political reform.[44] The written and spoken word became closely entangled in the revolutionary enterprise. For Sun, whose fondness for *gaotan geming* was well-known, the expansion of this public dimension of politics offered a suitable opening.[45]

Ideally, from the point of view of an inveterate public speaker like Sun Yat-sen, a speech carried the conventional authority of the written word plus an extra measure of emotional and psychological impact. Sun argued that 'public speaking (*yanshuo*) is like essay-writing (*zuowen*) except that the "air" (*qi*) one has about one is primary.'[46] Observers who witnessed the rise of public speaking were much intrigued by the difference between the classic art of *zuowen* and the new methods of lecturing (*yanshuo*):

The written word is projected into the iris of the eye and one can then know its meaning. Sound shakes the membrane of the ear and also stirs the emotions. Lecturers wail and shout with anger. Emotional excitement causes them to make sounds in choked voices.[47]

While acknowledging that content was important, the spectacle of public speaking seemed to prove that the way one stood, spoke, and gestured was a key determinant of success or failure. One commentator identified 'words, tone, and looks' as the components of a successful speech, making lecturing 'no different than singing Beijing opera on stage'.[48] The word 'looks' (*zirong*) referred to female beauty, an engendered term that underlined the perceived difference between the masculine realm of the reasoned essay under the 'tip of the brush' and a new arena where speakers appealed to emotions and subjected themselves to the scrutiny of an audience. A new political aesthetic emerged to accommodate the task of mass mobilization. Bridging the two realms through the control of emotion, in oneself and in one's audience, made it possible to prevail in the arena of the spoken word. In a 1912 newspaper article entitled 'Getting up and giving a speech isn't easy', Zhang Jianyuan argued that, if the audience is to be stirred (*dongxin*), a speaker's 'outward demeanour must exhibit vitality (*jingshen*)' even as one's inner self remains 'composed'.[49] The challenge might be great but the rewards were potentially high, given that 'Everyone knows that public speaking is a quicker way of inciting people than reading.'[50]

By all accounts, Sun knew how to 'get up and give a speech'. His personal secretary in the last years of his life noted that 'In public speaking, he was a ready and eloquent speaker. He could get up before an audience and speak for several hours on a stretch. His speeches were not flowery . . . [they] were inspirational and stirring in grass roots language.'[51] In public and in other group settings, Sun placed great store in being composed:

When you ascend the podium, your bearing and demeanour should put everyone in the whole place at ease. When you open your mouth to speak, the way you commence should further create an atmosphere [*qi*] that is peaceful and auspicious. A flippant attitude must be shunned. Everything should be natural. Be grave at times. Arouse their attention without startling them.[52]

Sun was not a wailer or a shouter, but he recognized the emotional as well logical nature of this new form of political rhetoric. He also succeeded in being persuasive through sheer volubility. He was one of the great, perhaps the greatest, talkers of the revolution. He sometimes spoke several times a day in his quest for support and recognition, another reason for his 'cannon' nickname.[53] As in battle, sometimes quantity will win out over quality. Those who knew Sun well noted that 'he talked a lot' and that 'Nothing about him strikes you till he talks—a low and uninflected tone with a rapid flow of words.'[54] Some of his speeches lasted three or four hours.[55] A Chinese pastor who served as an aide to Sun during a visit to New York in 1904 remembered that he was a 'fascinating and fluent speaker . . . [who] could hold his audiences spellbound for hours at a time, whether they numbered by the hundreds and thousands or only a handful'.[56]

Joining speaker to audience, both in the institutional settings of school, guild, or army camp and also during mass protest rallies, served the immediate goal of conveying a message and mobilizing support. The sight of a speaker on podium or stage and an audience in chairs, on stools, or standing in a city square also graphically represented the new polity that was emerging in twentieth-century China. Audiences, singly and as a sequence of constituencies, helped model and lend concreteness to the novel notion of a national 'people'. Sun's experience of speaking to Chinese students in Japan from many different provinces had been important in shaping his and their sense of a single Chinese citizenry. After Sun's return to China in 1911, he lectured both to composite audiences of that type and to specific 'circles' (*jie*) of, say, Shanghai journalists, Canton female students, or Guangdong residents in Beijing.

The newness of leaders facing followers in the expectation of applause (or of negative gestures like the hurling of stools or catcalls) was striking. Leaders invoked the needs or interests of the people just as emperors and officials had. But also, they sought out and actually faced the people. Admittedly, the percentage of citizens reached in this fashion was limited by the size of assembly halls and stadia as well as by the undeveloped state of modern communications. However, the act of public speaking itself implied interaction beyond ritual expectations. Citizens faced leaders rather than kow-towing to them; leaders sought to persuade and inform rather than simply to awe and notify their followers.

Perhaps the most famous example of Sun's speech-making was his marathon 1924 'Three Principles of the People' lectures given weekly over a period of months.[57] In transcribed form, these lectures alone amounted to 150,000 characters.[58] The lectures are lengthy, complex, and sometimes contradictory. They form a kind of bulletin board for the ruling ideas of Sun's day, and they reflect the pressures on Sun as a political figure. They also comprise an attempt by Sun to talk his personal followers, the Nationalist Party, the residents of Canton, and the larger population of China into some kind of political order. That Sun's audience was meant to be broader than a lecture hall full of officials, teachers, and students is suggested by his reference to the final product as a propaganda (*xuanchuan*) device.[59] As he mentioned to a supporter at the time, 'Although the theory of the Three People's Principles is quite profound, anyone who is literate must be able to read and understand it. Only then can it reach the masses.'[60] And so 'he made great use of popular expressions in order that everyone would easily accept them'. He said that the Three People's Principles was [really] patriotism and the Principle of People's Livelihood was the 'principle of getting rich [*facai zhuyi*]'.[61] He used visual aids like a blackboard to demonstrate concepts and once pulled a flower out of his pocket to illustrate a point.[62] He insisted that the first edition of the lectures be published in large print so that even old people with weak eyes could read them.[63] In May 1924 Sun recorded a four-record set of lectures on the Three Principles and other, related, topics.[64]

Sun's goal in this endeavour, and in other speeches, news conferences, and informal discussions he gave and granted, was to persuade his listeners to follow him and his doctrines. Persuasion presumed understanding, and Sun took little for granted even in speaking to an audience that was relatively well educated and informed about revolutionary politics and national affairs. He included long digressions on subjects like natural evolution, the American Civil War, international economics, and the history of democratic thought. Since he also needed to persuade his listeners to persuade others, he couched his remarks in the context of what worked and what did not work in appealing to a Chinese audience. That is, the content of his remarks included a running commentary on problems of rhetoric and propaganda.

Sun equated his principle of 'people's livelihood' (*minsheng*) with the salutation 'Get rich!' (*facai*), not because they were precisely the same thing (*minsheng* is more a collective notion of national development than a matter of gaining individual riches), but because he believed that the latter phrase stood a better change of grabbing the attention of those he sought to mobilize. He argued that using the word *facai* in China has an impact on Chinese comparable to the use of 'freedom' in Europe and

America.[65] Chinese politicians hoping to stir a mass audience with talk of 'freedom' alone will not achieve anything like the effect their counterparts in Europe or America register with that word.

Simply taking words like 'freedom' and 'equality' and going out and trying to elevate the spirit of people [*minqi*] is not realistic. There will be no sharing in the acute pain felt by the people ... [and] if such sensations are missing they certainly will not come to agree with you.[66]

According to Sun, Chinese did not know what freedom was because, like the air they breathed, they had as much of it as they wanted. The power of the emperor and even that of local magistrates rarely touched their lives.[67] By contrast, all Chinese understood *facai* because most of them, being poor, never had enough money.[68] All Chinese wanted to be rich and, now, those whose sense of national identity had been awakened wanted their nation to be rich and powerful as well. The problem was that most Chinese could not see beyond the interest of self, family, and clan. Talking to them of freedom sent a signal that they were free to pursue these individual or familial ends without regard to national needs.

Those who *did* like the sound of words like 'freedom' and 'equality' tended to be the 'new youth' and other 'cosmopolitan' Chinese. They had fallen under the spell of Western democratic ideology. For them, freedom meant defying authority. The result, according to Sun, was 'indifference and recklessness: schools without rules and armies without regulations'.[69] In both cases—those of the majority of traditional Chinese and of the minority of Westernized intellectuals—the result was disorder and a lack of common purpose. China remained, in one of Sun's favourite similes, a 'plate of sand' (*yipan sansha*).

From Sun's perspective as would-be leader, China tended to collapse into an amorphous mass of protesting students, striking workers, mutinous soldiers, and feuding clans. In imperial China, there had been no real 'relationship between government and people'.[70] European monarchies (Sun's examples suggest he means the absolutist kings of the early modern period) were 'direct' and 'severe' (*lihai*) in their stances towards the population, while the oppression experienced by most Chinese was 'indirect'.[71] In China, political relationships in an immediate sense existed only at the top, among the emperor and his officials and between reigning emperors and those rebels who wanted to be emperor. The imperial regime touted the importance of the people (*min*) through various homilies but, aside from taxation, had little real contact with the population. The state was strong, even 'dictatorial', by way of having all power concentrated in the hands of the emperor. But that power was hardly used, and the state remained fundamentally disengaged from society. For their part, the people, though possessed of an ancient racial and cultural identity, had largely lost that identity in favour of Confucian cosmopolitan thinking that paved the way for foreign (Mongol and Manchu) rule.

The remedy Dr Sun prescribed was a strong state and a mobilized people. China's modernist avant-garde must sacrifice their personal free-dom in order to free the nation. The average person must expand his or her notion of belonging beyond the confines of family and clan. An admirer of Otto von Bismarck, Alexander Hamilton, and the Swiss statist theorist Johann Bluntschli, Sun favoured a powerful, centralized government.[72] The relationship between state and society he imagined was solid and seamless rather than composite and contractual. Sun envisioned a well-organized society of citizens mobilized to sacrifice for the national good. Although he accepted the necessity of modern bodies like labour unions, he much preferred 'traditional groups' (*guyou tuanti*) such as clan and native-place organizations. Communal bodies like these would be the building blocks of a 'great national family'. On the grand scale of his 10 million man army, national granaries, and a million miles of public roads, Sun called for a nationwide system of family name groups (of Chens, Wangs, Zhangs, and the hundreds of other common surnames) organized at county, provincial, and national levels to enable the country to over-come the sand-like fragmentation of China's 'Four Hundred Million'. This gathering of the clans would, Sun claimed, turn the sand of disorder and dispersed loyalties into the 'rock' of national unity.

Sun was deeply critical of the tendency in Europe and America for the relationship between government and people to be marked by continuous conflict.[73] He attributed this poor relationship to an unjustified, democra-tic fear of an 'all-powerful government' (*wanneng zhengfu*).[74] He also insisted that certain technical innovations such as referenda and recall bal-lots would keep even powerful governments accountable to the people.[75] The people, imagined as a natural, familial body, had to be joined to the state as a super-efficient, machine-like instrument. In order for this bond-ing to take place, the people had to be persuaded to give over the govern-ing of the country to a technocratic élite as the child-emperor A Dou gave over power to the genius-statesman Zhuge Liang during the 'Three Kingdoms' period following the collapse of the Han dynasty.[76] For their part, the political élite had to abandon individual dreams of 'wanting to be emperor' in favour of an orderly regime that placed ultimate authority, but not regular control of government, in the hands of the people.[77]

The scene in Sun's Canton lecture hall of an erudite, paternal, and far-seeing leader speaking to a respectful, quiet audience epitomized the kind of political order Sun seems to have had in mind. Sun argued that there were three kinds of people: 'those who were first to understand and comprehend', 'those who later understood and comprehended', and 'those who did not understand or comprehend" (but could be made to act).[78] The first group, like Sun, were the 'inventors' or founders. The second were 'propagandists'. The third were 'doers'. Reaching the majority who were to do the actual work of fighting, building, and producing required a rhetorical strategy that accepted the 'mentality' of the Chinese as different from Europeans or Americans. And, according to Sun, like the majority everywhere, they were unlikely to realize their own or their country's interests unless enlightened 'men of good will' 'awakened' them with propaganda.[79] Not surprisingly, Sun believed in the importance of great men like Bismarck, Lincoln, Lenin, and Hong Xiuquan. Even after the events of 1919 suggested a broader base of political activism, Sun interpreted the May Fourth Movement of that year as the initial work of one or two individuals who had influenced public opinion and triggered the student movement.[80] However, as the May Fourth Movement seemed to demonstrate, once ties between leaders and led have been cemented, there were further dangers of this relationship coming apart as the masses became more aware of their situation. The result would then be 'waves of rejecting leaders', which Sun found deeply objectionable no matter what their democratic rationale might be.[81] Many Chinese had gone from a 'psychology' of 'worshipping the emperor' to one of 'rejecting government' altogether.[82] Both kinds of mentalities had to be 'smashed'. If everything went according to plan in Sun's model of mobilization, the masses, convinced or 'conquered' by propaganda, would carry out the plans and blueprints of the country's natural élite. But for any of this to happen, Sun and 'propagandists' had to use the right words and present them in the right way.

As China progressed through the years of the early Republic, Sun kept his reputation as an authoritative practitioner of the written word (*wen*), the lecture (*yanshuo*), and modern political thinking or ideology (*sixiang*). In January 1924, as Sun commenced his Three Principles lectures, an editorialist for the North China Post (*Huabei xinbao*) praised Sun as someone who 'told the truth, was straightforward, and acted with complete composure' in response to the challenges of the day. Unlike those who 'take serving the will of the people as their mantra and chant abstractly [as if they were] the emperor ten thousand miles away', Sun truly believed in the republic and in his words:

There really is republican thinking (*minguo sixiang*). It can be published in essays and receive an immediate popular response. With the coming of the republic, aside from [Sun] we have not had one president like that. Yuan [Shikai] was an emperor-like president, certainly without a shred of republican thinking. Li [Yuanhong] had *minguo sixiang* but could not *write* (*buneng wen*). Xu [Shichang] could write but lacked *sixiang*. Feng [Guozhang] had neither *sixiang* nor *wen*. Cao Kun's essays were done by other people.[83]

The writer's only complaint was that Sun had taken to calling himself 'Great President' (*Da Zongtong*) and 'Generalissimo' (*Da yuanshuai*) and organizing his own national government—signs, he mused, of 'egomania'. Still, 'the force of his thought can open and close the twentieth century'.

Ridicule and Respect: Appeals of Reason and Sentiment

The scenes in Chinese lecture halls and meeting rooms were not always as placid as the one Sun gave his 'Three Principles' talks in. During that same month in Tianjin, the year opened with a meeting of the Zhili Provincial Education Society in which factional conflict nearly exploded into the streets. An indignant delegate to the meeting described her experiences in an article for the Tianjin *Women's Daily*:

There was a great shouting and running back and forth . . . without the slightest order. The rules of the meeting hall did not permit smoking. But these gentlemen were inhaling great clouds and spitting as well as engaging in all kinds of other bizarre behaviour . . . [the head of the Education Office] asked the members to elect a temporary chairman. Some people put forward Wu Delu for nomination. But when he got up on the platform, he was immediately pushed off and was not allowed to speak. There was complete chaos. Some said Wu was not from educational circles. Some feared a fight. There was not the slightest respect for the rules of how to hold a meeting. There was only the stopping of people from speaking and not letting anyone say anything at all. There arose a pandemonium. Someone got up on the stage—I don't know what his qualifications were—and announced that many people at the meeting were not really Education Society members. Therefore, a certain Zhang would examine credentials. From below there were great cries of 'Get off!' and 'Idiot!' Readers, do you know why they made this kind of disturbance? Originally Zhili provincial educational circles were divided into three great Tianjin, Beijing, and Baoding factions. Each faction imagined electing its own man as chair. Wu is from Tianjin so the Beijing and Baoding people did not approve and fought all afternoon over the chairmanship. During the disturbance they almost came to blows . . . It was lucky there were no tea cups or ink pots in the hall or they would have been flying around. No wonder the 'Pig' Parliament in Beijing is that way.[84]

Conflicts such as this one reflected the lively, contested nature of the civil society emerging in Chinese cities during this period. But such affairs also underlined the kind of 'plate of sand' turmoil and 'reckless' disregard of rules that Sun and others were keen to remedy. The Tianjin meeting finally came to order when *Women's Daily* editor and Communist activist

Deng Yingchao, in actions Sun surely would have approved, got up and shamed and scolded those present for 'fighting and cursing' and 'causing turmoil'.

Sun Yat-sen spoke to small groups and large crowds in an effort to win them over to his cause. But the controversies surrounding Sun suggest a mixed record in persuading people to accept his leadership and agree with the words he used and feelings he tried to evoke. If he rarely was greeted with the kind of reception faced by the putative leaders of the Zhili Educational Society, he often faced sceptical as well as appreciative audiences. After the 1911 Revolution he had to come to grips with competition from new voices and the challenge of audiences by now familiar with, or even cynical about, politics. Small circles of revolutionary comrades had been replaced by larger publics of diverse backgrounds and interests. Calling this more complex 'people' to disciplined followership tested Sun's capacity for persuasion and propaganda.

As his 1924 lectures suggest, Sun saw the young intellectuals of the May Fourth generation as a particularly unruly source of dissidence and dissonance. Although most of those around him like Dai Jitao and Hu Hanmin, as well as young recruits to the Nationalist Party, were strongly influenced by the new culture movement and the politics attending it, Sun was resistant and even 'psychologically unattuned to it'.[85] During a conversation with Zou Lu in the course of editing the lectures in 1924, Sun even accused young Chinese of imperilling the survival of the race through their iconoclasm and individualism. One of Sun's obsessions was the belief that China was faced with a crisis of *under*-population, that soon China's Four Hundred Million and the yellow races as a whole would be outstripped by whites. While educated people could easily grasp the political and economic calamities (*huohuan*) threatening the country, they did not seem to be aware of this impending demographic one:

One only needs to look at today's educated youth. The men are afraid of the financial burdens of raising children. The women fear the pain of child-birth and so blindly advocate remaining single and practising birth control . . . Moreover, the educated do not give a thought to propagating [the race]. The result can only be a weak and diminished race [*minzu*] . . . We must advocate filial piety [*xiao*] because if there is *xiao*, everyone will feel there are advantages in having sons and daughters.[86]

Sun's irritation with educated young people went beyond mere annoyance at their political expressiveness or habits of faction and division. The May Fourth critique of patriarchy appeared to threaten both his style of leadership and his plans for mobilizing the people through communal rather than individual means.

   This tension between Sun's communal vision or 'narrative' of China as super-extended family and the challenge of a developing 'civil society'[87] appeared in the course of a student interview conducted with Sun in January 1924, shortly before he began the *Sanmin zhuyi* lectures.[88] His talent for provoking and persuading is also evident in what is an unusually complete record of both the content and style of Sun's rhetoric and the mixed reaction of his audience.

   Three Qinghua University students led by Xu Yongying, all bound for study in the United States, met Sun and discussed a range of issues, including the Nationalist Party's alliance with the Soviet Union and the prospects for success in the planned Northern Expedition. Sun began the interview with an explanation of why the reorganization of the Nationalist Party along Leninist lines was necessary. He stressed the importance of 'discipline' (*jilu*) and criticized party members who 'would not accept restrictions imposed by the party because they considered restrictive orders destructive to their freedom'.[89] For Sun, individual freedom was a principal obstacle to political and social mobilization. And, as Sun clearly implied, students, with their fractiousness and individualism, were the worst culprits in this regard. They failed to understand that the goal of the revolution ought to be freedom for the people, not for the individual. He went on to assert that, without a party able to subordinate individual freedom and will, the Soviet regime could not have survived Lenin's death on 21 January 1924. 'Therefore, with a party of extraordinary power and super-solid [*yichang zhi gu*] foundation, the death of a leader would not have the slightest effect.'[90]

   Sun suddenly asked the students: 'Why do Westerners struggle for freedom and the Chinese do not? Chinese not only do not struggle for freedom. Even the word [*ziyou*] acquired its current meaning only in the last ten or twenty years.' Xu and his classmates fumbled for answer because, as he later reported, they 'did not understand what he was getting at'. In response, Sun launched into a lecture on freedom that rehearsed what he would have to say about the topic in his second lecture on democracy two months later.

This is because Chinese have had too much freedom. Therefore, they did not even know they had it. If we think for a moment, what is the most important thing in our lives? Eating? No. It is breathing. How many times do we eat each day? Two or three times. At most four or five. But as far as breathing is concerned, each minute we take thirty breaths. We can stop eating for one, two, or three days without reaching the point of endangering our lives. But try stopping breathing one, two, or three minutes. You probably would not be able to do it. Doesn't this prove that breathing is more important than eating? When we ordinarily think about life, we are only aware of food, not air. That is because there is so much air.

We can use it as we please. We are not only unaware of its importance, we do not even consider the possibility of its absence.[91]

Sun abruptly interrupted his remarks to leave the room and conduct some business. As he left, 'at a goose step pace', he called to the students to wait for him to return.

When they were alone, one of Xu's companions, He Yongji, reacting to the way Sun marched out of the room, exclaimed: 'He is really too much!' Xu disagreed and defended Sun, saying that the way he walked must be natural for him and not something done just to impress his student visitors. Besides, 'Chinese who have this kind of vigour [*jingshen*] are too few and far between. When we see an old guy [*laotou*] of sixty like this, why make a big deal about that?'

Though separated generationally by decades, Sun's 'vigour', the elusive quality highly recommended by those offering advice to would-be public speakers, appealed to Xu Yongying. Later, on reflection and in his article, Xu admitted that there were aspects of Sun's manner that were unusual:

When Mr Sun spoke to us, he generally smiled and was unusually affable. But when, suddenly, his smile would disappear, his mouth would shut, and he would have this very serious look that you didn't dare cross. When he directed this expression toward us, we definitely could not speak freely. This is what he used towards those subordinate to him. With these two faces he could make you feel on intimate terms with him or in awe of him. This is clearly in tune with the times in so far as what it takes to become a leader. One kind of person can smile and grin. Another kind is severe-looking. [To have only one of these qualities] would be to be partial and incomplete.[92]

Xu's generous assessment of Sun and He's negative reaction suggest that Sun's mix of warmth and coldness, intimacy and aloofness as a speaker and propagandist might stir radically different reactions. On earlier occasions, Sun's use of a more diplomatic, affable approach had stirred criticism by those who wanted 'one or two words that hurt but also help in healing the nation's serious maladies' (lit., acupuncture or admonition *zhenbian*).[93] And in other meetings with May Fourth students Sun had accented his warmer side.[94] But here he weighs in with the grim determination of a Dr Stockmann prescribing bitter medicine. In one sense Sun appears extraordinarily impolitic in blaming students like Xu and his friends for the defeat of the revolution to date. Perhaps this helps account for He's exasperated comment. But Sun seemed determined to override group interests and affiliations to force unquestioning acceptance of himself and the revolution.

When Sun returned to the room, he calmly resumed his comparison between China and the West on the subject of freedom:

A person with air to breathe is not even aware there is such a thing as air. It is like a fish in the water not being aware of water. But take a fish out of water and put it on land. After half a minute, that fish will know what water is. If you shut a person inside a room and draw the air out with a pump, that person will know what air is. China does not know to demand freedom the same as the ordinary person does not think of demanding air. Westerners know the importance of freedom and struggle for it. This is because since the Middle Ages people's freedom has undergone severe repression, as if they were having the air sucked from them. They were just like fish on land. The freedom Chinese have had has actually been excessive. What Chinese require is discipline, not freedom.[95]

Whereas Lu Xun had famously imagined the Chinese people constricted and suffocating in an 'iron room', Sun is suggesting that Chinese have had too much room to breathe in. Implied is the need to 'pump' some of the air out, presumably through the kind of regimented party he was constructing in Canton. That some of those so affected might end up gasping like a fish without water or a person without air does not seem to trouble him.

When the students later discussed this meeting among themselves, He Yongji again criticized Sun, this time for making a 'false analogy' with his water and air examples. Xu Yongying was inclined to agree with him on that point. He also felt that Sun had overdone it in exerting himself so. It was a rather out-sized address for such a small audience—'a lengthy speech that was a tireless torrent [*taotao bujuan*]', as he put it.[96] But Xu also concluded that Sun's emphasis on discipline was 'naturally quite correct', and that the kind of theoretical and rhetorical misstep He objected to should not be held against Sun.[97]

The mixed reaction of the students to Sun's harangue about freedom and discipline is revealing. He Yongji, sounding like a liberal sceptic in the May Fourth tradition, was dismissive of the content of Sun's remarks and the artifice he employed. Xu, who joined the Communist Party in 1927 and was killed in 1933, was plainly impressed by Sun. That some of Sun's arguments were weak mattered less to Xu than Sun's 'vigour', the 'torrent' or words, and his insistence that China needed 'discipline' above all else.

For Xu, 'Big Gun' Sun, despite using a calibre of rhetoric a bit too large for the room, demonstrated his communicative skills. But in doing so he was working on another level of discourse than the more obvious one of argument. As Bruce Lincoln points out:

discourse is not only an instrument of persuasion, operating along rational (or pseudo-rational) and moral (or pseudo-moral) lines, but it is also an instrument of sentiment evocation. Moreover, it is through these paired instrumentalities— ideological persuasion and sentiment evocation—that discourse holds the capacity to shape and reshape society itself.[98]

Sun Yat-sen was able to overcome the weaknesses of argument and confusion that characterized his verbiage by appealing to sentiment. This was an aspect of modern political rhetoric that Sun and other Chinese had shown particular interest in: having the right 'look' (*zirong*) and generating sounds to 'stir the emotions'. Sun acted the leader, although he sometimes teetered on the edge of caricature. His call for discipline, along with his famous allusions to a 'plate of sand', effectively evoked the serious disorders of the period and the urgent need for a solution. Reading Sun's speeches for content alone, one may miss a measure of his appeal. As one historian has summed up Sun's strengths and weaknesses as a rhetorician, 'Lacking intellectual maturity and inner coherence, his writings [and, one might add, speeches] appear as conglomerations of unrelated facts and absurd inaccuracies, fuzzy reasoning and blatant distortion, interspersed, however, with emotional eloquence, high idealism, and flashes of genuine inspiration.'[99] Xu Yongying, and the larger audience of Sun's followers and sympathizers, responded to the eloquence and idealism and, often, forgave the inconsistencies.

Sun's Future China: Bodies and Machines

The content of Sun's political rhetoric reveals a mix of traditionalist and modernist elements. He looked backward towards the clan and family and forward towards a machine-based economy and a republican polity. He sought anchorage in the past for an ambitious programme of nation-building.

Sun also devoted much attention to the future at a time when utopian thinking gripped many Chinese. As Jiwei Ci has recently pointed out, the future was a new and potent force in twentieth-century China:

For a people accustomed to attach value to the past and not to think much beyond the present, utopianism enlarged the future in their consciousness and made it the purpose of their lives.[100]

What did not exist (an integrated nation, a technologically modern China, a well-fed and healthy citizenry) was as much the currency of politics as the tax receipts and weapons that did. Successful public speakers were supposed to have the capacity to see into the future through their 'power of imagination', as a 1912 commentary on the subject put it:

[to be able to] from things seen and heard think of things unseen and unheard, to infer the future from the present, to determine what kind of person someone is from that person's words and actions, to use the beauty and ugliness of customs to divine the rise and fall of nations, to take one word and understand the subtleties of human nature, one angle [and see] the expanse of the whole world.[101]

In the broadest sense, Sun sketched a picture of 'all Four Hundred Million being able to enjoy happiness and prosperity, with China a contented nation and a happy world . . . not just one generation of happiness, but generation after generation. This is the nation it will be: the future Chinese Republic.'[102] Once the Three Principles were carried out, 'the nation will become enormously rich. In the future, not only will all the common people be able to read, they also will all have enough to eat. Adults without a job will be given one in a state-run factory. The nation will take care of old people who cannot work or who do not have children to support them.'[103] Sun consciously adopted a strategy in his speeches of talking from 'what is near to what is distant'. For example, he might begin a lecture to students with remarks about their own school and then expand rhetorically to embrace the larger world and larger issues.[104] This approach made it possible for him to aim his audience towards a common goal and common future from the angle of their own concerns and interests.

Sun had an instinctive feel for the future and for a politics aimed at constructing it. He glorified the machine age with some of the same enthusiasm that animated contemporaries elsewhere, like the Italian Futurists with their rhapsodies about electricity and locomotives.[105] In his 1894 reform proposal submitted to Governor-General Li Hongzhang, Sun wrote that:

machines can excavate mines, can smash hard rock into powder, and dig the deepest spring wells. In this way, we can open up the hidden wealth of the earth. When we have machines for weaving, they can accomplish the work of a thousand workers in half a day . . . I cannot enumerate all the great uses for machinery.[106]

During his years of exile, Sun had witnessed rapid changes in cities like Tokyo brought on by the introduction of devices such as streetcars. Returning to Japan in 1905 after only a two-year absence, he declared that the Tokyo of his recent memory was 'already like [that of] a former age'.[107] He also observed that 'those who have machines grow richer by the day; those without grow poorer', and 'the economic power of those who have machines is sufficient to rule the world'.[108] Machines provided some of his favourite metaphors and analogies. For Sun the government was a 'machine',[109] and the nation (*guojia*) was an 'automobile' to be driven where you wanted it to go.[110] Sun himself was sometimes described as machine-like: 'When he spoke . . . there was a loud, resonant sound, like an electrical charge. Every sentence of what he said was true. Every word was fast, precise and pointed, as if fired from a machine-gun.'[111] Machines represented power and revolutionary change. Despite differences between human institutions and mechanical invention readily acknowledged by

Sun, the roles of inventor, builder, and engineer seemed closely to parallel the kinds of constructive challenges facing twentieth-century China.[112]

Sun saw himself as a political and social engineer or architect with plans for the 'construction' (*jianshe*)—a key and all-purpose word for him—of everything from railway lines and harbours to a political party and a new political culture. *Jianshe* has ancient origins as a word connoting the founding and defence of dynasties. By the turn of the century it was used to refer to both local developmental programmes and the larger project of building a strong China. When Sun helped inaugurate his journal *Jianshe* in 1918, he wrote in the first issue's preface that his purpose in 'inciting an ideological trend towards reconstruction' was to 'build the wealthiest, most powerful and happiest nation on earth'.[113] The magazine was given the translated English title of 'Reconstruction' in recognition of the need to *re*constitute the Chinese Republic in the aftermath of the fall of empire and the failure of the 1911 revolution. Although *jianshe* included things like building dams and harbours, the term drew its power from a broad conception of cultural and political renewal. The journal *Jianshe* accordingly included articles on politics, urban planning, psychology, communications, industrialization, and language reform. Reconstruction became a common trope in reformist and revolutionary writings. In this same spirit, Hu Shi advocated literary reform in a book entitled 'The Theoretical Bases of Literary Reconstruction' (*Jianshe lilun ji*).[114] The word flexibly applied to the entire country, as in Sun's plans for a nationwide railway system, and to particular provinces, cities, counties, and villages with plans for schools, roads, parks, or garden cities.

Jianshe represented one of the more positive and appealing aspects of Sun's leadership: the belief that a new China could be built from, or on top of, the old. Reconstruction touched a nerve with local reformers who imagined a school, factory, or railhead where there was none. But *jianshe* also took on a more destructive, even 'fatal' aspect in that it so often was used not just to chart the future as a step towards negotiating with localities over projects and plans, but also to obliterate any opposition in the name of the national interest in development.[115] Sun once related in a speech the objections of a friend to the destruction of traditional architecture of Guanyin Mountain in Guangzhou:

In the past [the friend] roamed about Guanyin Mountain and viewed those pagodas and pavilions. When he recently went again to take a stroll he came back and said to me, 'Why have those old buildings been torn down? Would anyone want to create this desolate tragedy? This is really lamentable!' I replied that this was [a part of] the New Plan of the municipal office to develop the whole mountain into an excellent new public park. Therefore, for the moment, they have created a scene of desolation. This isn't anything lamentable. Please next year go to

Guanyin Mountain and you'll realize what kind of new appearance the future will provide.[116]

Sun added that the 'circumstances of creating a nation-state [*guojia*] are the same' except that the process will take more than one or two years. Local leaders forced to bow to the logic of the *jianshe* imperative later warned against 'mistaking unity for uniformity' in the implementation of Sun's conception of national reconstruction.[117] Sun's heady vision of the future prefigured the giganticism of a five-year plan or a Three Gorges Project.[118] His tolerant approach to the 'desolation' and disruption wrought by such projects was understandable at a time when too little was being done by the state to confront the challenge of China's backwardness. But his enthusiasms for tearing things down in order to build the country up have lived on in the state's continued use of '*jianshe*' as a rallying cry for national development and a silencer of dissent. Controversies about the ecological, economic, cultural, and humanitarian costs of the Three Gorges high dam continue, while today at the site a huge sign proclaims: 'Reconstruct the Three Gorges and Develop the Yangzi River' ('*Jianshe Sanxia, kaifa Changjiang*').[119]

'*Jianshe*' as a slogan and concept fitted very well with Sun's determination to grasp and change China as one might manipulate a machine or any pliable object. Sun had spent so much time in exile outside the vast continental body of China that imagining it and planning its reconstruction had become an obsession. He was also fond of mapping out his military campaigns and development projects and acquired an intimate knowledge of the country through travel and study. A visitor to Shanghai in 1919 was struck by this dimension of Sun's continuing interest in the physical realities of China:

While a geographical map might seem dry and unstimulating to others, to him it was a most fascinating study and he could let his imagination roam over the map for hours tracing the railways that should be built, the ports located, the rivers trained, etc. He seemed to be familiar with the typographical characteristics of the whole country both from the viewpoint of industrial development and of military strategy.[120]

Sun's rhetoric exchanged and mixed metaphors to convey the plastic and dynamic qualities of *jianshe*. China was a taxi cab, a machine, a building. Through 'psychological reconstruction' (*xinli jianshe*), Chinese could be persuaded and stirred into action along the lines of development Sun had charted out. At the same time, China's state of civil war reflected a dramatic lack of unanimity on the question of how disparate social and regional elements were to be combined. China was not a single entity, much less a machine or a body, and as an audience was unpredictable in its reaction to even skilled speakers and propagandists like Sun. Not everyone and every place responded positively to Sun's rhetoric and his political touch.

On 14 January 1924, a week before beginning his Three Principles lectures, Sun gave a speech to a joint meeting of the Canton police force and the city's merchant corps (*shangtuan*). Sun was trying to build a national party, a government, and an army from a local, regional base in the South.[121] That effort required revenue, troops, and the popular support conducive to tax collection and enlistments. Some groups, like the working classes, were willing to support the Nationalists. Others, like merchants targeted for taxes, were unenthusiastic and finally hostile.[122] The 7,000-member merchant corps, organized originally 'to oppose the government and all buccaneers', was not favourably disposed towards what Sun was trying to accomplish by way of mobilizing southern wealth to accomplish his national objectives.[123] In fact, they may have been more sympathetic to Sun's local nemesis Chen Jiongming, a militarist skilled at putting the argument that unity need not mean uniformity and that the big projects such as national unification through military means might be destructive to local interests.[124]

Those in the hall heard Sun's promise that 'the revolution would certainly be successful in the end'.[125] He praised Canton as the birthplace of the revolution. He also confronted the awkward fact that his government did not monopolize armed force in the city: the armed police shared power with the armed merchants. Whereas in the lectures he was about to give the Chinese people appear as largely passive and A Dou-like, the well-organized and well-equipped merchants were a force to be reckoned with. Sun approached them gingerly:

You gentlemen of the merchant corps and the police have come together in one place in welcome. In the future the merchant corps and the police must work together to maintain order in Canton. The police are a government organ. The merchant corps is a civic organ [*renmin di jiguan*]. Today is the first day the merchant corps and the police have met formally face to face. That is, it is the first day the government and the people are joined. [applause] Gentlemen. Since this is the territory of the revolutionary government, both [parties] ought to enter into an open and honest [relationship]. [applause] The party of the revolution is using Canton as its fountainhead. As a new Chinese republic is constructed, the government and the people must work together. The people of Canton municipality must cooperate with the government.[126]

A few weeks later Sun, in a liberal turn, would lecture on a need for a proper 'balance' between the people and the government as essential to democracy.[127] But in a matter of months the negotiated, cooperative relationship between his government and the merchants of Canton would become unstuck. As the merchants continued to defy his authority and sought to acquire new arms, Sun, in August, contemplated shelling the merchant quarter of the city from gunboats. He was prevented from doing so only by counter-threats by French, Japanese, and British consular authorities.[128] An armed attack finally took place in October. The densely populated sections of the city where the Merchant Corps held fortified positions were taken with the use of considerable firepower followed by looting.[129] The attack left many Cantonese 'bitter and full of hatred' towards Sun and the Nationalist Party.[130]

For Sun, the state, and an 'all-powerful government' (*wanneng zhengfu*), was necessary if the nation, organized on the basis of communal solidarity, was to be preserved. He recognized that this act of preservation entailed violence. In explaining this joining of state and society, in a fashion that was perhaps franker than the bromide dispensed to the Canton merchant corps in January 1924, Sun drew elsewhere on the Chinese distinction between *wangdao* ('enlightened rule') and *badao* ('rule of force'):[131]

To speak of *wangdao* is to advocate benevolence and morality. To speak of *badao* is to advocate utility and power. Benevolence and morality means using justice to help change someone through persuasion. Utility and power means using guns and cannon to oppress people.[132]

Much of Sun's writings and speeches is devoted to the peaceful construction of government, economy, and society through constitutions, legal codes, and transportation systems. But what Michel Foucault has called the 'roar of battle' and the 'promise of blood' is never far from these constructions.[133] This was partly because Sun spoke, wrote, and organized in a time of war and violence and partly because of the rhetorical bridge that lay between the mechanistic strain in his thought, which has people and communities standing as objects of manipulation, and his calls for the deployment of the engines of war needed for the survival and growth of his regime.

Sun's focus on concentrating and acquiring power made him acutely aware of the 'state' (*guojia*) as an instrument of violence and 'top-down' control. He hoped that support for this enterprise would flow 'bottom-up' from the community. But the merchant corps uprising made it clear that he could, without hesitation, direct state violence against that same community. As a result, when Sun departed from Canton for the north in 1924, he left behind a bloody shambles in so far as 'state–society' relations was concerned.

In a 1916 speech in Shanghai Sun had spoken of the need to build a Chinese republic from the ground up based on a system of self-government.[134] In the speech, Sun played on differences in construction techniques in the West and in China. 'Chinese first hang the beam. Westerners first construct a foundation. Those who hang beams pay attention to the highest point. Those who construct a foundation look to the lowest point.'[135] Sun went on to argue that today statecraft follows architecture in this regard. As states get bigger, attention to the foundation is ever more important:

Whereas in the past there was a crude abode, today there is a lofty building. European and American skyscrapers have as many as fifty floors. There is no way you could hang a beam first. Therefore, you must build from the ground up. And not just on the surface. You must dig deep below to construct [the proper] foundation. Otherwise the building might fall down. Building a Chinese Republic today is not like [state-building] in ancient times. After it is established, it must never fall over. Therefore, it must be built on the body of the people [*bi zhu dipan yu renmin zhi shenshang*].[136]

The elegance of the analogy in reorienting the audience's perspective from top to bottom must have benefited from the context of Shanghai's growing line of skyscrapers along the Huangpu River. And Sun's interest in architecture dated back at least to 1892, when he designed a new house for the Sun family in his home village of Cuiheng which incorporated both Chinese and Western elements.[137] But one cannot help but think of what the implications of 'building on the body of the people' might be, especially if excavation proved necessary.[138] The lecture was given before Sun began his experiments in regime-construction in Canton and long before the attack on Canton's merchant quarter. The metaphor is of a piece with Sun's construction-minded orientation towards political development. When the Nationalists under Sun's guidance later adopted a multi-levelled, Leninist party model, Zou Lu described it as a 'pagoda-style organization with party branches as the foundation of the pagoda'.[139] It is a habit of mind and speech that is not inconsistent with his familial metaphors of Chinese society to the extent that family ties will turn sand to rock. But the flesh and blood of Sun's constituents and the complex, organic nature of the communities destined to support the modern political skyscraper seem at some considerable risk of rearrangement from this kind of *jianshe*. This somewhat strange phrasing offers a key to a contradiction between Sun's realism as a nuts and bolts state-builder and his romantic, even reactionary, impulses as a champion of community.

The looseness of Sun's language and his willingness to mix metaphors and draw 'false' analogies exposes contradictions that other tighter, more coherent, renditions of the state–society problem may conceal. In linguistic terms, Sun's political language resisted 'formalization' into a 'restricted code'.[140] Sun's manner of speaking suggests an instability and conflictedness that mirrored his predicament as an ideologue and politician. His mixing of metaphors and stretching for analogies helps us to locate points of tension in China's state-building and society-building projects. Specifically, the modernist, mechanistic, and violent model of state power Sun subscribed to did not sit well on the familial foundation he also promoted. When he brought the two together rhetorically, as in the state skyscraper erected on the body of the Chinese people, the effect was arresting and somewhat alarming. When he brought the two together in practice, as he did in Canton in 1924, the mixture of the local, 'civic' merchants corps and Sun's war-fighting and revenue-extracting machine was explosive.

The whole story of Sun's thought and action is of course more than a simple mismatch of visions or narratives. In fact, his sensitivity to a *Realpolitik* bordering on the nihilistic and to a crisis of local and national community bordering the revolutionary was remarkable. Sun understood the importance of establishing a connection between local society and the national polity and, in a larger sense, between state and society. Much of his theorizing about ascending levels of clan and locality sentiments was based on this recognition. But he had difficulty accepting any real differences between his national agenda and local interests and culture. And he hated being reminded of that fact, by May Fourth students in Shanghai or by 'local nationalists' in Canton.[141] The doubleness of Sun's 'faces', moods, imagery, rhetoric, and policy suggests that, whatever unique features the state–society interface in China may encompass, there is a binary, oppositional dimension to the relationship worth exploring.

Conclusion

Less than two months after Sun died, the May Thirtieth Movement broke out in Shanghai and spread rapidly to other cities and towns. In Beijing, on 10 June, during a huge protest rally outside of Tiananmen, a man named Chen Qianfu mounted a stage surrounded by tens of thousands of city residents representing more than five hundred groups such as guilds, unions, and professional associations. Chen gave a short speech which began: 'Foreigners insult us [by saying that] we are a plate of sand. They want to massacre us. We must be avenged!'[142] He then proceeded to cut one of his fingers and wrote on a white cloth with his own blood 'Save China or Die'. He went on to compose a longer statement of protest in blood (*xueshu*) and then, weakened by the ordeal, was removed from the platform. Sun Yat-sen was not the only prominent figure to use the phrase 'plate of sand'.[143] But he popularized the image through his writing and speaking and placed it in the public domain for use and further embellishment, here adding a theme of vengeance uncharacteristic of Sun. In comparable episodes, Sun's portrait was used as a shield to protect union-organizers.[144] Pilgrimages to his final resting place outside Nanjing were occasions of remonstration against the Nationalist government.[145] Sun's picture also graced Tiananmen and countless government offices and other public buildings all over China as a sign of statist ideology.[146]

For Chen and others like him, Sun and his words offered an 'angle' from which to envision the bigger picture, an image useful for signalling republican intentions and a rallying point for a continuing revolution from below and above. Sun had begun his career as a 'prophet without a people'.[147] He ended his life as a leader without a real regime. But the 'people' had begun to form in nationalist movements, strikes, and boycotts, and in the readerships and audiences courted by Sun and his contemporary allies and rivals. This new expanse of citizenry was coming to depend on ties to organizations like labour unions, chambers of commerce, and student federations, to governments like Sun's Canton experiment, and to leaders like Sun himself. The 'relationship between government and people' which he saw missing in the late imperial era, while still in its infancy as a nationwide phenomenon, had begun to take shape in the language of politics, the social dramas of protest and in a scattering of civil and military institutions waiting to be assembled. The full weight and significance of this relationship would emerge in later decades as strong leaders and states called for the construction of a new political order on the social 'body' of China. The reaction of that body, and the individuals, groups, and communities that composed it, has included both compliance and resistance. Calls for discipline have continued to stimulate both a popular appreciation of the value of a strong state and orderly society, and a persistent tendency to find other angles besides the statist one from which to view and comment on issues such as economic development, social policy, and political freedom.

NOTES

1. John Fitzgerald also makes this point in Fitzgerald, *Awakening China: Politics, Culture, and Class in the Nationalist Revolution* (Stanford: Stanford University Press, 1996).
2. The relational nature of leadership and the dependence of leaders on the predispositions of followers are explored in Georg Simmel, *The Sociology of Georg Simmel*, trans./ed. Kurt H. Wolff (Glencoe, Ill.: Free Press, 1950), 181–8; James M. Burns, *Leadership* (New York: Harper and Row, 1978), 19–20; and Garry Wills, *Certain Trumpets: The Call of Leaders* (New York: Simon and Schuster, 1994).

3. According to Alexander Woodside, 'the disappearance of formal hereditary political power meant that feudalism went underground. In compensation, it took the form of what one might call a spiritual micromonarchism, based upon families and big lineages': Woodside, 'Emperors and the Chinese Political System', in Kenneth Lieberthal, Joyce Kallgren, Roderick MacFarquhar, and Frederic Wakeman, Jr (eds.), *Perspectives on Modern China: Four Anniversaries* (Armonk, NY: M. E. Sharpe, 1991), 11.

4. *Sun Zhongshan pinglun ji* (Commentaries on Sun Zhongshan), Sanmin bianyi bu, comp. (Shanghai: Sanmin chuban she, 1925). The volume is a collection of death notices published in May, two months after Sun's demise.

5. ibid. 40. For background information on the *Shishi xinbao* (Current Events) and its ties to Liang Qichao see Fang Hanji, *Zhongguo jindai baokanshi* (A History of the Modern Chinese Press) (Taiyuan: Shanxi renmin chubanshe, 1981), ii.699.

6. *Sun Zhongshan pinglun ji*, 21; criticism of Sun reported in the *Hankou shisheng zhoubao* (Hankou Weekly City Voice).

7. For example, during Sun's struggles with Yuan Shikai culminating in the 'second revolution' of 1913, Yuan sponsored the publication of a 'Short History of Sun Wen' which charged Sun with everything from sexual peccadillos and cowardice to embezzlement and murder: *Sun Wen xiaoshi* (n.p., n.d.), carbon copy of handwritten version, Cornell University Library, Wason Collection on China and the Chinese. According to Hu Qufei, the work was done at Yuan's behest by a 'stupid literatus' (*wuliao wenren*) sometime in 1913 and several tens of thousands of copies were distributed throughout the country: see Hu Qufei, *Zongli shilue* (A Biographical Sketch of the President) (Taibei: Taiwan shangwu yinshuguan, 1971, first published 1936), 196.

8. Reported disapprovingly by Chen Duxiu, who took this as a sign of why Sun was worthy of respect: Chen Duxiu, 'Jinnian shuangshi zhongzhi Guangzhou zhengfu', *Xiandai zhoubao*, 133 (12 October 1925), 1216.

9. Sidney H. Chang and Leonard H. D. Gordon, *All Under Heaven: Sun Yat-sen and his Revolutionary Thought* (Stanford, Calif.: Hoover Institution, 1991), 51.

10. Sun, 'The Monetary Revolution', Shanghai, 6 December 1912, in Julie Lee Wei, Ramon H. Myers, and Donald G. Gillin (eds.), *Prescriptions for Saving China: Selected Writings of Sun Yat-sen*, trans. Julie Lee Wei, E-su Zen, and Linda Chao (Stanford, Calif.: Hoover Institution, 1994), 116.

11. Sun Yat-sen, *The International Development of China* (New York: G. P. Putnam, 1929, first published 1922).

12. *Sun Zhongshan pinglun ji*, 17–18. From *Guowen zhoubao* (Weekly News of the Nation). Shao Lizi was a left-wing member of the Nationalist Party, at the time also belonged to the Communist party.

13. ibid. 85.

14. Henrik Ibsen, *An Enemy of the people*, adapt. Arthur Miller (New York: Viking Press, 1951), 36.

15. *Sun Zhongshan pinglun ji*, 83.

16. ibid. 71, Guo Pinbo.

17. 'The Cause of [Sun's] Liver Cancer', *Sun Zhongshan yishi ji* (Collected Anecdotes of Sun Zhongshan) (Shanghai: Sanmin gongsi, 1926), 173–4.

18. *Sun Zhongshan pinglun ji*, 40; from the Shanghai *Shishi xinbao*.

19. Chen Jiang, 'Magua, qipao—Zhongshan zhuang, xizhuang' (From Mandarin Jackets and Cheongsam to Sun Yat-sen Suits and Western Clothes), in Xin Ping, Hu Zhenghao and Li Xuechang (eds.), *Minguo shehui daguan* (An Omnibus of Republican Society) (Fuzhou: Fujian chubanshe, 1991), 586. Sun adopted this uni-

form in 1912; while in exile he had worn a Western business suit. C. Martin Wilbur, *Sun Yat-sen, Frustrated Patriot* (New York: Columbia University Press, 1976), 15.

20. John Y. Wong describes how Sun became an early master of image-making through his understanding of the print media and public opinion: John K. Wong, *Origins of an Heroic Image: Sun Yat-sen in London, 1896–97* (New York: Oxford University Press, 1986).

21. Yang Manqing, 'Sun Zhongshan', *Beijing xinbao*, 2 September 1912, 1.

22. For example, a follower of Sun in Beijing cited two of his essays as 'books everyone knows of [but which] are extremely difficult to find' even in the city's many, well-stocked bookstores: *Sun Zhongshan pinglun ji*, 25; from the *Beijing yusu* (Beijing Discourse).

23. Shuang Lin, 'Sun Zhongshan zhi si yu Sun Zhongshan zhi di' (Sun Zhongshan's death and Sun Zhongshan's enemies), *Xiangdao zhoubao*, 107 (21 March 1925), 99–100.

24. Sun himself explained, 'Cantonese call me "*Dapao*", "Sun Dapao"': quoted in Tang Chengye, *Guofu geming xuanchuan zhilue* (A Sketch of the Guofu's Revolutionary Propaganda) (Taibei: Zhongyang yanjiuyuan sanmin zhuyi, 1985), 23.

25. The sobriquet apparently had to do with 'his frequent and overblown announcements of new military expeditions' (Howard L. Boorman and Richard C. Howard (eds.), *Biographical Dictionary of Republican China* (New York: Columbia University Press, 1970), 3, 185) and his 'being idealistic and impractical' (Wilbur, *Sun Yat-sen*, 4).

26. For example, Communist hard-liner and trouble-shooter Wang Zhen was so described. Wang Zhen (1909–93), who joined the Communist movement in the 1920s, was famous for the explosive vulgarity of his speaking style, a quality much admired by Mao who prized Wang for his political savvy: Zhong Yumin, 'Wang Zhen liqi faji mishi' (The Secret History of Wang Zhen's Bizarre Rise to Power), *Zhengming* (April 1993), 53.

27. Lyon Sharman, *Sun Yat-sen: His Life and Meaning: A Critical Biography* (Stanford: Stanford University Press, 1968), 271.

28. Yang Manqing, 'Sun Zhongshan', 2.

29. Bruce Lincoln, *Discourse and the Construction of Society: Comparative Studies of Myth, Ritual and Classification* (Oxford: Oxford University Press, 1989), 3–12.

30. *Guofu nianpu chugao* (Draft Chronological Biography of the Father of the Republic), ed. Lo Jialun (Taibei: Zhengzhong shuju, 1959), 650.

31. ibid. 644.

32. Tang Chengye, *Guofu geming xuanchuan shilue*, 14.

33. Sun Wen (Sun Yat-sen), *Zongli quanji* (Complete Collected Works of the President), ed. Hu Hanmin (Shanghai: Minzhi shuju, 1930) (hereafter *ZLQJ*), ii.568.

34. Tang Chengye, *Guofu geming xuanchuan zhilue*, 16.

35. Peter Bol, *'This Culture of Ours': Intellectual Transitions in T'ang and Sung China* (Stanford: Stanford University Press, 1992). Bol quotes Emperor Wen of the Wei: 'I would say that *wen-chang* is the enterprise of ordering the state . . . a splendor that does not decay' (p. 84). As Bol emphasizes, the question of what literary efforts of this kind could and could not accomplish and whether or not the consequences of such efforts were good or bad were enormously complex and controversial questions.

36. ibid. 96.

37. ibid. 84, referring to Tang scholars.

38. Joseph Esherick and Jeffrey Wasserstrom, 'Acting Out Democracy: Political Theater in Modern China', *Journal of Asian Studies*, 49:4 (November 1990), 850. Esherick

and Wasserstrom mention the *xiangyue* lectures on moral topics that were supposed to be delivered in local communities by the literati but note that 'this form quickly atrophied in the Qing, and never caught on in Chinese culture'. Speeches might take place in extreme situations in which officials or protest leaders might address a riotous crowd. See such tableaus as presented in Susumu Fuma, 'Late Ming Urban Reform and the Popular Uprising in Hangzhou', in Linda Cooke Johnson (ed.), *Cities of Jiangnan in Late Imperial China* (Albany, NY: SUNY Press, 1993). Fuma describes how an uprising leader, Ding Shiqing, 'is reported to have cried out to city residents' while manacled (p. 67), and how the official sent to suppress the uprising, Zhang Jiayin, spoke to a crowd of 2,000 Hangzhou residents from his sedan chair, listening to their complaints and urging them to disperse (pp. 68–9).

39. Esherick and Wasserstrom, 'Acting Out Democracy', 852. Sources like missionary preaching were very important in this process.
40. Sharman, *Sun Yat-sen*, 144.
41. Tang Chengye, *Guofu geming xuanchuan zhilue*, 99, in describing the activities of the 'Patriotic Study Society' in Shanghai in 1903.
42. ibid. 100.
43. ibid. Zhang Park was established in 1882 and became famous not only for its restaurants and theatres but also for the political activities that emerged there. See Yu Jianxin, 'Cong sijia huayuan dao gongyuan' (From Private Gardens to Public Gardens), in Xin Ping, Hu Zhenghao, and Li Xuechang (eds.), *Minguo shehui daguan* (An Omnibus of Republican Society) (Fuzhou: Fujian chubanshe, 1991), 959–60.
44. Tang Chengye, *Guofu geming xuanchuan zhilue*, 104.
45. *Sun Zhongshan yishiji* (Collected Anecdotes of Sun Zhongshan) (Shanghai: Sanmin gongsi, 1926), 11, 'Gaotan geming'.
46. Tang Chengye, *Guofu geming xuanchuan zhilue*, 108.
47. E. E. Sheng (pseud.), 'Yanshuo wei zuiyao zhi xuewen' (Public Speaking is a Most Important [kind of] Learning), *Aiguobao* (Patriotic Daily), Beijing, 8 August 1912, 1.
48. ibid.
49. Zhang Jianyuan, 'Dengtai yanshuo buyi', *Beijing xinbao*, 11 September 1912, 1.
50. Sheng, 'Yanshuo wei zuiyao zhi xuewen', 1.
51. Wilbur, *Sun Yat-sen*, 4.
52. Quoted in Tang Chengye, *Guofu geming xuanchuan zhilue*, 107.
53. ibid. 22.
54. Wellington Koo and Nathaniel Peffer, quoted in Wilbur, *Sun Yat-sen*, 3 and 5.
55. Sharman, *Sun Yat-sen*, 144, citing Ellis J. Barker, 'Dr. Sun Yat Sen and the Chinese Revolution', *Fortnightly Review*, 96 (November 1911).
56. Cited in Sharman, *Sun Yat-sen*, 92.
57. The lectures were given weekly from 27 Jan. to 2 Mar. (on the nation), from 29 Mar. to 27 Apr. (on democracy), and from 3 Aug. to 24 Aug. (on people's livelihood): *Sun Zhongshan nianpu* (A Chronological Biography of Sun Zhongshan) (Beijing: Zhonghua shuju, 1980), 33.
58. Wilbur, *Sun yat-sen*, 198.
59. *Sun Zhongshan xuanji* (Selected Works of Sun Zhongshan) (Beijing: Renmin chubanshe, 1981), 615.
60. Zou Lu, *Huigulu* (Reminiscences) (Nanjing: Duli chubanshe, 1946, 47; new edn, i.172). Zou recalled this statement of interest in popularization by way of defending the lectures against the charge that they were 'too easy to understand'.
61. ibid. 175.

62. *ZLQJ* i.117–18. The blackboard was used to display different models of equality and inequality, and a locust flower was presented to demonstrate how petals and leaves that look exactly alike (are 'equal') in fact under a microscope would reveal subtle differences.
63. *ZLQJ* i.177.
64. Lo Jialun (ed.), *Guofunianpu chugao* (Draft Chronological Biography of the *Guofu*) (Taibei: Zhengzheng shuju, 1959), 667.
65. *ZLQJ* i.105.
66. ibid. 122.
67. ibid. 103.
68. ibid. 111–12.
69. ibid. 115.
70. ibid. 107.
71. ibid.
72. ibid. 137, 145, and 161.
73. ibid. 185.
74. ibid. 160.
75. ibid. 164.
76. ibid. 167.
77. Sun saw the actions of rivals like Yuan Shikai and the revolts of former allies and subordinates like Chen Jiongming as evidence of the persistence of the 'mentality of wanting to be emperor': *ZLQJ* i.100–2.
78. ibid. 133.
79. ibid. 131. Sun's élitism seems to have been influenced both by the Chinese tradition of the scholar–official (*shidafu*) and by modern élitism; see Lu Fangshang, *Geming zhi zaiqi: Zhongguo guomindang gaizu qian dui xin si chao do huiying* (Rekindle the Revolution: The Kuomindang's Response to New Thought Before the Reorganization) (Taibei: Institute of Modern History, Academia Sinica, 1989), 112.
80. Wei Jieting, *Sun Zhongshan shehui shi guan yanjiu* (An Investigation into Sun Zhongshan's View of Social History) (Changsha: Hunan renmin chubanshe, 1986), 250.
81. *ZLQJ* i.130–1. Sun used the example of European workers who rejected in favour of men from their own ranks the leaders who had 'awakened' them in the first place. Sun saw this kind of independence as destructive and corrupting.
82. ibid. 167.
83. Gao Ru (pseud.), 'Sun Zhongshan daodi cha qiangren yi' (Sun Zhongshan is Certainly no Thug), *Huabei xinbao* (Tianjin) (20 January 1924), 2. It is significant that this essay both praises Sun's literary abilities (*wen*) and distinguishes him from *qiangren* (thugs or robbers), i.e. those who use violence.
84. *Funu ribao* (Tianjin) (4 January 1924), 2.
85. Herman Mast III, 'Tai Chi-t'ao, Sunism and Marxism during the May Fourth Movement in Shanghai', *Modern Asian Studies*, 5:3 (1971), 235. For a new, extensive account of the impact of May Fourth Movement on the Guomindang, see Lu Fangshang, *Geming zhi zaiqi*.
86. Zou Lu, *Reminiscences*, i.171.
87. For a discussion of the tension between narratives of community and civil society, see Partha Chatterjee, 'A Response to Taylor's "Modes of Civil Society"', *Public Culture*, 3:1 (Fall 1990), 119–32, and David Strand, 'Community, Society and History in Sun Yat-sen's *Sanmin Zhuyi*', in R. Bin Wong, Theodore Huters, and

Pauline Yu (eds.), *Culture and State in Chinese History: Conventions, Conflicts and Accommodations* (Stanford: Stanford University Press, 1996).

88. Xu Yongying, 'Jian Sun Zhongshan ziansheng ji' (An Account of Meeting Mr Sun Yat-sen), *Jindaishi ziliao* (Modern Historical Materials), 68 (Beijing: Zhongguo she-hui kexue chubanshe, 1988): 180–90; originally published in *Qinghua zhoukan* (The Qinghua Weekly), 308 (4 April 1924).
89. ibid. 183.
90. ibid.
91. ibid. 184.
92. ibid.
93. Yang Manqing, 'Sun Zhongshan', 1. Yang was reacting to a round of speeches that Sun was in the process of giving in Beijing.
94. See Chang Kuo-t'ao's (Zhang Guotao's) account of a meeting with Sun in the spring of 1920 with fellow student radicals Xu Deheng, Kang Baiqing, and Liu Qingyang also present. The students pressed Sun hard on various issues and at times he became 'agitated' or 'showed disapproval'. But he listened patiently, and Chang recalled that Sun's 'graciousness entirely transformed the atmosphere which . . . had been charged with antagonism [so that] everyone . . . wore a smile': see Chang Kuo-t'ao, *Autobiography*, i, *The Rise of the Chinese Communist Party, 1921–1927* (Lawrence, Kan.: University Press of Kansas, 1971), 78 and 80.
95. Xu Yongying, 'Jian Sun Zhongshan xiansheng ji', 185.
96. ibid.
97. ibid.
98. Lincoln, *Discourse*, 8–9.
99. Boorman and Howard, *Biographical Dictionary*, iii.189.
100. Jiwei Ci, *Dialectic of the Chinese Revolution: From Utopianism to Hedonism* (Stanford: Stanford University Press, 1994), 4.
101. Sheng, 'Yanshuo wei zuiyao zhi xuewen', 2.
102. *ZLQJ* ii.452, in a speech given on 4 April 1924.
103. ibid. 454.
104. Tang Chengye, *Guofu geming xuanchuan zhilue*, 81.
105. Charles Russell, 'The Poets of Time: Apollinaire and the Italian Futurists', ch. 3 in Russell, *Poets, Prophets, and Revolutionaries: The Literary Avant-Garde from Rimbaud through Postmodernism* (Oxford: Oxford University Press, 1985). Sun was significantly more critical and less manic in his appreciation of modernity than the Futurists.
106. Wei *et al.*, *Prescriptions for Saving China*, 9.
107. *ZLQJ* ii.70.
108. ibid. 449 and 253.
109. ibid. i.175 and 191.
110. ibid. 172.
111. Tang Chengye, *Guofu geming xuanchuan zhilue*, 78.
112. *ZLQJ* i.176–7. According to Sun, human institutions like 'administrative machinery' were harder to test and more resistant to change. In addition, 'no machine could last a hundred years', whereas the United States constitution, as a kind of machine, has continued to function despite its great age.
113. Quoted in Lu Fangshang, *Zhu Zhixin yu Zhongguo geming* (Zhu Zhixin and the Chinese Revolution) (Taibei: Sili dongwu daxue, 1978), 236.
114. Cited in John K. Fairbank and K. C. Liu, *Modern China: A Bibliographic Guide to Chinese Works, 1898–1937* (Cambridge, Mass.: Harvard University Press, 1961), 314.

115. R. R. Palmer uses the notion of 'fatal metaphor' to describe how 'gangrene' took on a destructive life of its own in the French Revolution once it came into common political use. 'This fatal metaphor of the gangrened limb spread like a contagion through French politics for five years. It was a commonplace for jacobin clubs, and it was the justification for the guillotine': Palmer, *Twelve Who Ruled: The Year of Terror in the French Revolution* (Princeton: Princeton University Press, 1941), 12.
116. *ZLQJ* ii.456.
117. See Guangxi governor Huang Xuchu, *Zhongguo jianshe yu Guangxi jianshe* (The Reconstruction of China and the Reconstruction of Guangxi) (Guilin: Reconstruction Book Company, 1939), 8.
118. For Sun's plan for development of the Three Gorges, see *ZLQJ* i.255.
119. The sign was visible during an August 1995 voyage past the site of the high dam. For controversies surrounding the dam see Shiu-Hung Luk and Joseph Whitney (eds.), *Megaproject: A Case Study of China's Three Gorges Project* (Armonk, NY: M. E. Sharpe, 1993).
120. Huie Kin, *Reminiscences* (Beijing: San Yu Press, 1932), 88–9. Sun was engaged at the time in writing *The International Development of China*.
121. Wilbur, *Sun yat-sen*, 167.
122. ibid. 168.
123. ibid. 169.
124. See Diana Lary, 'Regional Militarism and National Aspirations in Liangguang, 1917–1927', panel on 'Toward 1927: the Canton Decade in the Modern Chinese Revolution, 1917–1927', AAS Annual Meeting, Los Angeles, 26 March 1993.
125. *ZLQJ* ii.373–81. Also printed with applause markers in the *Guangzhou minguo ribao*, 23–5 and 28–30 January 1924.
126. *ZLQJ* ii.377.
127. Cited in Li Zehou, 'Lun Sun Zhongshan de sixiang' (On Sun Zhongshan's Thought), in Li Zehou, *Zhongguo jindai sixiang shilun* (A History of Contemporary Chinese Thought) (Taibei: Fengyun shidai chubanshe, 1990), 391. Li is particularly interested in the nature and limits of the 'liberal Sun'.
128. Wilbur, *Sun Yat-sen*, 251–2.
129. ibid. 262–3.
130. ibid. 263.
131. Quoted in Wei Jieting, *Sun Zhongshan*, 180.
132. Quoted in Li Zehou, 'Lun Sun Zhongshan', 382.
133. See James Miller's account of Foucault's 1976 lectures on the connection between violence and social order and the pervasiveness of a 'civil war' mentality in modern politics: Miller, *The Passion of Michel Foucault* (New York: Anchor, 1993), 286–91.
134. *ZLQJ* ii.164–72.
135. ibid. 165.
136. ibid. 166.
137. Li Fan, *Sun Zhongshan quanzhuan* (A Biography of Sun Zhongshan) (Beijing: Beijing chubanshe, 1991), 26.
138. The word 'on the body' (*shenshang*) suggests a physical presence even when the meaning is more figurative, as in the stock phrase, 'our hopes are placed on the young people' (*xiwang jituo zai qingnian shenshang*).
139. Zou Lu, *Zhongguo guomindang shi lueyice* (An Outline History of the Chinese Nationalist Party) (Shanghai: Shangwu yinshuguan, 1945), 118.
140. Michael Schoenhals, *Doing Things with Words in Chinese Politics* (Berkeley: Institute of East Asian Studies, 1992), 1.

141. The term 'local nationalists' is from Lary, 'Regional Militarism'.
142. Yang Yicun, 'Beijing renmin aiguo fandi de yizi zhuangju wusan yundong Tiananmen dahui' (A Glorious Beijing People's Patriotic, Anti-Imperialist May Thirtieth Movement Tiananmen Rally), *Wenshi ziliao xuanbian* (A Compendium of Historical Materials), 31 (Beijing: Beijing chubanshe, 1986), 106–9.
143. For example, Lu Xun saw the 'crabbed, archaic' nature of China's literary language as obstructing communications among Chinese: 'Hence our people, unable to understand each other, are like a great dish of sand.' See Lu Xun, 'Silent China', *Silent China: Selected Writings of Lu Xun*, ed./trans. Gladys Yang (New York: Oxford University Press, 1973), 163–4.
144. A union organizer marched into a Beijing match factory in 1928, held up a portrait of Sun, and proceeded to rally the workers to establish a union on the spot: David Strand, *Rickshaw Beijing: City People and Politics in the 1920s* (Berkeley: University of California Press, 1989), 231.
145. In 1931 students invited to Nanjing by Chiang Kai-shek to pay their respects at Sun's tomb used the opportunity to protest against Chiang's government: see Jeffrey Wasserstrom, *Student Protests in Twentieth-Century China: The View from Shanghai* (Stanford: Stanford University Press, 1991).
146. On Sun's portrait hanging on Tiananmen, see Linda Hershkovitz, 'Tiananmen and the Politics of Place', *Political Geography*, 12:5 (September 1993), 404.
147. The phrase is from William Theodore de Bary, *The Trouble with Confucianism* (Cambridge, Mass.: Harvard University Press, 1991), 102.

3

The Essence of Contemporary Chinese Bureaucracy: Socialism, Modernization, and Political Culture

Ryosei Kokubun

Chinese Perspectives on the Problem of Bureaucracy

The study of administrative management (*xingzheng guanlixue*) is currently receiving much attention from Chinese academics,[1] even taking priority over research on the political system *per se*. In effect, this consists of research into what the Chinese bureaucratic system should ideally be.

In China, the term 'bureaucratism' (*guanliaozhuyi*) (which shares the same meaning that the cognate term *kanryoshugi* has in Japanese) is frequently used; however, perhaps because of its association with 'bureaucratic capital' (*guanliao ziben*), which refers to the imbrication of the state and financial cliques in the Nationalist period, the terms 'bureaucracy' (*guanliaozhi*) and 'bureaucrat' (*guanliao*) are almost never employed formally. As for the so-called *yamen*, which constituted the basic administrative unit of imperial China, the term is of course no longer used in the present despite the institution's long existence. The English word 'bureaucracy' is sometimes translated as *guanliao zhengzhi* in Chinese, but once again this term is never employed when referring to the political organs of the present Chinese state.[2] In the place of such terms, such concepts as 'bureaucracy' (*guanliaozhi*), 'administrative organization' (*xingzheng jigou*), 'government organization' (*zhengfu jigou*), and 'bureaucrat' (*guanliao*) are expressed by formulations such as 'administrative cadre' (*xingzheng ganbu*), 'state cadre' (*guojia ganbu*), and 'government employee' (*zhengfu zhiyuan*).

In any event, there is essentially no real difference between such labels as 'administrative organization', 'government organization', and 'administrative cadre', terms that are employed in the Chinese administrative management literature, and what we ourselves call 'bureaucracy' and 'bureaucrat'. This is due to the fact that in China the existence of both a vast organizational structure for the purpose of ruling the nation and a myriad of government officials who operate within it is regarded as an inevitable development. In particular, the role of the bureaucracy has definitely tended to increase in tandem with the launching of the reforms and the opening of China to the outside world in the 1980s. As symbolized by the charismatic leadership of Mao Zedong himself, Chinese politics in the Maoist period witnessed a large role being granted to individuals and factions in the determination of policy, compared with which the bureaucracy has only limited functions, mainly as an organ of implementation for matters decided at rather high levels.

Of course, this situation has not altered in its essentials during the subsequent era of Deng Xiaoping. It is impossible to gainsay either Deng's personal power or his special role in policy decisions. However, more important are the changes in the structure and functions of the bureaucracy that have begun to occur in tandem with the extension of the state apparatus, resulting from the modernization policies that sprang from the opening to the external world. As the research of Lieberthal and Oksenberg has demonstrated clearly, there has been no essential change in the importance of the 'human' factor in such areas as the dynamics within and between organizations.[3] Despite the continued importance of personal ties and connections, it is nevertheless a fact that the bureaucracy itself has begun to change into a more meaningful element in the power structure. Indeed, the flourishing of the study of administrative management has precisely these circumstances as its background. As Vivienne Shue has proposed in her effort to stir debate on these issues, in comparison with the loose institutionalization that characterized the Maoist period, the Dengist era offers an indication that the actual political dominance of the state has been expanded and reinforced.[4]

Premised on the recognition of such trends, this essay constitutes an effort to examine the formation and the development of the bureaucracy in China since 1978 from three standpoints: (1) the bureaucracy and socialism; (2) the bureaucracy in the process of modernization; and (3) the bureaucracy viewed from the standpoint of Chinese political culture.

The Bureaucracy and Socialism

Why was it that the bureaucracy, which Marxism–Leninism had imagined would be eliminated with the arrival of socialism, marched off in the diametrically opposite direction and became even more bloated and powerful? The growth of the bureaucratic apparatus occurred in three stages. First, in order to realize a planned socialist economy, the state monopolized the means of production as well as all powers of management and rule over them. Thus, a stratified order with the state at its apex was formed. Secondly, in order to manage and control this stratified order in an efficient manner, a bureaucracy was formed from its top to its bottom, and absolute one-party dominance of this apparatus was accomplished through the agency of the Communist Party in its guise as the 'nucleus of leadership'. Thus, creative capacities of the lower levels of the system were ignored by the upper ones, producing social stagnation and a profound lack of information about what was really happening at lower levels of society. In the final stage, the Communist Party itself came to possess a vested interest in the bureaucratic apparatus, and thus the protection of the system became an important goal in its own right. In this fashion, the Communist Party was transformed into a vast 'new class', the trend towards excluding all other social forces from entry to the apparatus was strengthened, and the party thereby ended up creating a hotbed of corruption.

Mao Zedong, the founding father of the People's Republic of China, was the person who possessed the highest degree of vigilance against such trends in the Chinese Communist Party (CCP). The Great Proletarian Cultural Revolution had as its background just such a virulent critique of Soviet society. If one focuses on the ideas behind the Cultural Revolution, one finds in them an expression of consciousness of crisis on Mao's part towards the degeneration of China into a 'state of bureaucratic privilege' through the agency of the CCP, in the same manner as occurred in the Soviet Union. As evidence of this, we have the so-called 'Sixteen Points' passed by the Eleventh Plenary Session of the Eighth Central Committee of the CCP in August 1966, which described the political form of the Paris Commune as the Cultural Revolution's political ideal. However, history provided an ironic conclusion to this episode. Mao, who confronted the confusion and disorder of the Cultural Revolution, drew back from the idea of the Paris Commune, and in order to suppress the movement he injected the military into the situation. Later, in planning the reconstruction of the party, Mao accepted a revival of CCP dominance. The critique of the party's proxy rule thus wound up with the reassertion of its strength.

When we reach the Dengist period, under the slogans of reform and opening to the outside world, the leadership indeed began to engineer a shift from the former socialist economic system with its highly centralized power structure to a more diversified distribution of economic power, and at the same time began to open up the previously closed economic and social systems to the outside world. By so doing, both economy and society gradually began to move from the previously monist system to a more pluralist one. However, compared with these trends, the pace at which the structure of political rule underwent a similar pluralization was quite slow. In other words, on the political front, adherence to the 'Four Cardinal Principles' (the socialist road; the dictatorship of the proletariat; the leadership of the CCP; and Marxism–Leninism and Mao Zedong thought) continued to serve as a fundamental premise of the system as a whole. Moreover, as time passed, the leadership of the CCP became established as the most important of these principles.

Thus, a contradiction arose between the reform of the economic system, which continued unabated, and the political system. In other words, although authority for economic decisions was increasingly granted to the lower levels of society as a result of the reforms, in practice, because of the presence of Communist Party members posted in each unit (*danwei*) at the local level, the scope of the authority of these units did not actually expand. Deng Xiaoping himself raised this issue at that time in the following manner:

Many problems concerning the improvement of Party leadership remain to be solved. For instance, we have said all along that in a factory the director should assume overall responsibility under the leadership of the Party committee, in an army unit the senior officers should do so, and in a school the principal. If these systems are to be continued in the future, is it necessary for the committees of general Party branches to lead work in the workshops and for party branches or groups to lead the work teams and groups in factories? Likewise, is it necessary for the committee of general Party branches to lead the individual university departments? Is this form of leadership beneficial to the functioning of factories and universities?[5]

Put differently, in order to advance the economic reforms in an efficient manner, the question arose of how the CCP in particular should cast its own role.

The lack of clarity in the respective roles of the political organization and the party organization also became a problem. All along, it had been common in the Chinese political structure for cadres occupying important posts in the party to 'double' by occupying similarly important positions in the government. Because of this, it was almost never expected that governmental organs would come to play an independent role. In other words, the principle of CCP leadership was accomplished via this overlapping of posts. As everyone is aware, this outcome was in fact fated from the very foundation of the People's Republic of China (PRC), since there were established in the central government organs so-called 'leading groups' (*dangzu*), which functioned as organizations for the leadership exercised by the party.[6] Thus, during the 1980s the necessity of political reforms, which included such matters as the division of the roles to be performed by the party and the government and the pros and cons of the continuance of the leading groups, came to the fore as a topic for discussion.

Moreover, a principle such as that concerning the absolute leadership of the party could become an important factor in such problems as the bureaucratism and corruption of party officials. And, these problems were linked with others, such as the measures for preferential treatment and the perquisites that cadres were granted not only on the political front but also in their private lives. Specifically, cadres were able to read important documents and internal materials with restricted distribution, and also to attend important meetings. As far as their private existence was concerned, they received special allowances as part of their salaries, were given preferential treatment in such matters as housing and medical treatment, and were similarly granted preferential treatment in such areas as lodgings and use of transportation facilities when they undertook trips. Moreover, all of these privileges were recognized by detailed regulations which governed them.[7] As far as the children of such cadres were concerned, it was common for them too to enjoy a wide variety of special privileges in such areas as entering schools, finding work after graduation, and studying abroad. The system of nomenclature, which was often underscored in studies of the bureaucratic apparatus of the former Soviet Union, was not foreign to the operation of the Chinese system either. Once again, Deng Xiaoping often called for attention to these kinds of problems. In his own words:

As you know, one of the chief subjects of conversation among the masses recently has been precisely the pursuit of personal privileges by cadres. This, I am afraid, pertains mainly to senior cadres. Of course, I am not saying that all senior cadres are like that. Many, in fact live very simply. However, there are indeed some whose addiction to personal privileges is rather serious. That is also true of some cadres at the middle and lower levels . . . It has become a general tendency in our society—a social problem.[8]

From these sorts of angles, the necessity for reforms of the political system was repeatedly raised, particularly as it concerned the question of what the 'leadership of the CCP' should consist of, as China passed through the 1980s. As a first step, Deng delivered a report entitled 'On the Reform of the System of Party and State Leadership' at the enlarged meeting of the Politburo in August 1980. In it, he issued an appeal to the effect that rectifying the above-mentioned problems of cadres entailed introducing reforms in a number of other areas as well, such as an over-concentration of power, the prevalence of cadres holding two or more posts concurrently or holding too many deputy posts, the confusion of the responsibilities of the party with those of the government, and the lack of a mechanism for leadership succession.[9] Following up on these proposals by Deng, in 1982 administrative reforms aimed at ameliorating the problem of the bloating of the apparatus, particularly that of the government, began to be implemented; yet reforms concerning the leadership of the party were never launched in a large-scale manner. At this stage the campaigns against 'bourgeois liberalization' and 'spiritual pollution' were launched, and one can infer that the considerable resistance to the reforms relating to the leadership of the party, which was symbolized by these campaigns, still probably exists within the party.

As regards the need for reforms of the political system including the matter of the leadership of the party, a debate on the topic was begun in earnest only in 1986. This was due to the fact that, even though the first phase of the economic reforms had drawn to a close, in order for there to be a further breakthrough on the economic front, a partial review of such things as the system of party committees and of party groups had become necessary. The prime instigator behind this drive for political reform was once again Deng Xiaoping, who delivered a long series of speeches on the issue:

If we do not carry out reforms of the political system, then it will be difficult to accomplish our reforms in the economic sphere. If we attempt to separate the party from the government, this will then carry over into reform of the political system. Well then, what should be done with regard to the party committees? The party should deal only with large problems, should not involve itself with small ones.[10]

The debate concerning reforms of the political system had thus at this stage reached a rather audacious point. Among the questions raised, the ultimate objective of the political reforms was seen to lie not only in their capacity as accessories to economic reform but also in democratization itself. There even were heard voices calling concretely for the introduction of a system of checks and balances *vis-à-vis* the expansion of political participation and power.[11] However, the long and short of this episode is that, as a result of the fall from power of Party General Secretary Hu Yaobang, who had garnered strong sympathy concerning political reforms, in January 1987, the movement for reform suffered a temporary setback.

Nevertheless, the drive for reforms of the political system was revived soon afterwards at the Thirteenth National Congress of the CCP in the autumn of 1987 with Zhao Ziyang playing the central role. Moreover, at this congress a concrete programme concerning political reforms was proposed formally, and was divided into seven points: (1) separating party and government; (2) delegating authority to lower levels; (3) administrative reform of the government; (4) reforming the personnel system relating to cadres; (5) establishing a system of consultation and dialogue; (6) improving a number of systems relating to socialist democracy; and (7) strengthening the socialist legal system. The central theme out of these seven elements was indeed the first one, separation of party and government. In sum, the following policy was hammered out in relation to this issue:

The executive organ of the party committee should be smaller but more efficient, party departments that overlap their counterpart government departments should be abolished, and the administrative affairs they are now managing should be transferred to competent government departments. The present practice in government departments of making leading Party members' groups responsible to the Party committees of the next higher level which have approved their establishment is not conducive to unity and efficiency in government work; such groups should therefore be gradually abolished.[12]

However, the actual launching of this programme was marked by serious difficulties. The largest obstacle was, as might be expected, the opposition of party cadres, who were unwilling to relinquish their vested interests, and there was additional concern over the weakening of the party's leadership role which would accompany the separation of party and government and the separation of party and enterprises. As a result, when it began to be revealed that these political reforms had come to a standstill, the disappointment over the gradual transformation through administrative reform spread rapidly among students and intellectuals. The demand for democracy triggered by the death of Hu Yaobang occurred in such an atmosphere; however, it ended in the tragedy known as the Tiananmen Square Incident in 1989.

Since that time, China has been witness to the dissolution of both the Communist Party of the former Soviet Union and the former Soviet federation, and thus has become dead-set on preserving at all costs the leading character of the CCP. With this goal in mind, reforms of the political system, which put the separation of party and government and of party and enterprises at the top of the list, have been shelved. The collapse of the Communist Party in the former USSR was caused chiefly by the separation of the party and the government; this proved that the separation of party and government under a one-party dictatorship leads to self-destruction.

Accordingly, to date, reforms on the political front, beyond the fact that administrative reform has become an issue, have not made any headway, a matter that stands in direct contrast with the state of the economy, where reforms aimed at establishing a 'social market economy' continue to progress. At the Fourteenth National Congress of the CCP, which was held in October 1992, the hall resounded with such slogans as 'Strengthen the Communist Party!' and 'Raise the Level of Leadership of the Communist Party!'—perhaps with the negative example of the Soviet

Union as a backdrop.[13] Together with the development of a market economy, it is probable that the privatization of state-run industries will also progress further. If the leadership attempts to promote the respective roles of the party and the market economy at the same time on parallel tracks, this will certainly result in the further imbrication of party and enterprises and thereby worsen the problem of corruption.

As far as additional problems faced by China today are concerned, although there is talk of strengthening the leadership role of the CCP, in reality the results of the division of authority stemming from past reforms are that the party organization has gradually lost the cohesion it previously possessed. Thus, in order to compensate for these circumstances, it is inevitable that the party will rely on the coercive force of such organizations as the armed forces and the Bureau of Public Security. Perhaps as a reflection of such considerations, the preparedness and strengthening of the armed forces and the guiding nature of the CCP regarding them was repeatedly emphasized at the Fourteenth Party Congress.[14]

In sum, if the party hopes to resolve in a fundamental way the contradictions inherent in a socialist bureaucratic apparatus, the solution will inevitably be tied up with the party's capacity to cleanse itself, particularly as concerns the reduction of its own vested interests. Here we encounter two separate but related analytical issues. The first involves the establishment of democracy outside the party. This concerns the question of whether or not the party possesses sufficient patience to tolerate external criticisms of it as well as the willingness to establish systematic guarantees assuring potential critics that they will not be subject to reprisals. In other words, this question concerns the creation of a mechanism of checks and balances outside the party proper. The second issue involves the establishment of democracy inside the party. The largest problem with this consists of the often observed fact that political dominance in China is exercised by well-connected individuals, and in particular by party elders, in a manner surpassing the formal structure of the political system. At the same time a systematic mechanism for the cultivation of political successors has still not been firmly established. As long as these matters remain unclear in their fundamentals, the socialist bureaucratic order under the leadership of the party will continue to contain the contradictions described above for the foreseeable future.[15]

The Bureaucracy and Modernization

In those cases where the growth of the bureaucratic apparatus in China has been interpreted as one of the processes stemming from modernization, it is possible to examine the question from the following two standpoints. The first, which derives from the writings of Max Weber, regards the bureaucracy as a component of the process of the evolution and development of the forms of domination undergone by modern societies. The second, which is found in modernization theory literature, views the bureaucracy as part of the process of 'institutionalization' which is undertaken with a view towards securing political stability by developing countries that are in the process of political development.

Max Weber developed the following typology of the forms of legitimate domination: (1) traditional; (2) charismatic; and (3) legal–rational. According to Weber, it is this last form of legal–rational domination that in fact characterizes bureaucracy in modern society. In other words, with the appearance of modern society, politically neutral departments exercising control over a large number of administrative affairs become necessary. In such departments, officials will see to their responsibilities on the basis of an objective sense of duty which excludes from consideration the importance of 'personality', and officialdom will possess such characteristics as a hierarchical system of posts, special powers according to one's post, and specialization in the allocation and performance of tasks. Moreover, legal–rational bureaucracy is characterized by the facts that the disposal and administration of tasks of all kinds are carried out in accordance with written documents, and that a multitude of organizations will be established in which the people populating them will receive a fixed salary for their work.

As noted above, in the case of China, in order to demarcate the new regime clearly from the 'bureaucratic capitalism' of the past, and moreover to distinguish itself clearly from 'bourgeois nations', the leadership almost never employed the term 'bureaucracy'. Nevertheless, when faced with the task of building a new state, the leadership did not display any reluctance to construct a massive bureaucratic apparatus for the purpose of ruling over a vast and diverse territory and society. However, the class bases that supported the Communist regime differed fundamentally from those that underlay the previous Nationalist government; from the pride it took in the fact that China had shifted to a regime based on the 'people', the leadership either adopted an exceedingly optimistic view concerning the actual development of the bureaucratic system under which its rule was carried out, or intentionally steered away from discussing the subject.[16] In particular, in the first half of the 1950s, the Soviet-style socialist political and economic system ordered along Stalinist lines and involving a concentration of power was introduced without any dissent, and under the name of 'people's government' a powerful bureaucratic apparatus was firmly established.

As a reaction against this, during the Cultural Revolution the destruction of the bureaucratic structure was carried out at Mao's initiative. The
Cultural Revolution witnessed a particular antipathy to bureaucracy, but
if we position the Maoist period according to Weber's typology, then it is
no exaggeration to describe it as an era of *charismatic* domination. The
cult of personality that developed around Mao, who was the overwhelming leader of the CCP, was formed socially, and nourished by the repeated
political mobilizations of Chinese society. However, when we enter the
subsequent period of Deng Xiaoping, even though Deng's personality and
prestige was no less vast than were Mao's, the conditions that might have
brought about a personality cult around Deng no longer existed, given the
increased pluralization of society. Voices critical of Deng could actually be
heard throughout Chinese society.

Above and beyond the creation of a personal charismatic character,
Deng Xiaoping concentrated his efforts on laying a foundation for his
power and prestige in the existing organization. In late 1970s he repeatedly
emphasized: 'the realization of ideological line and political line must be
assured by organizational line'.[17] With this in mind, Deng set about the
reconstruction of bureaucracies in various parts of the state in an aggressive manner. Consequently, if one looks for example at the total number
of organizations in such parts of the state apparatus as the departments
and committees of the State Council, one finds that they grew rapidly from
a figure of 52 in 1975, at the end of the Cultural Revolution, to 76 in 1978
and to 100 in 1981. However, this increase was not necessarily carried out
according to a plan. The organizations that enjoyed the most rapid growth
in number during this period were those related to the economy, a fact that
may reflect the swift advance of both the economic reforms and economic
modernization: of the total figure of 52 organizations for 1975, 32 were
economic departments (61 per cent), compared with 46 out of 76 (66 per
cent) in 1978 and 66 out of 100 for 1981.[18]

Such a rapid hypertrophy of governmental organs was a result of the situation that then existed in China, in which no one in authority seemed to
have any clear notion that the gaps in the organizations that had been
destroyed during the Cultural Revolution ought to be filled in. Therefore,
the hypertrophy was for securing employment for the rehabilitated and
newly recruited cadres, not in order to promote a more specialized division
of labour. Once again, Deng Xiaoping interpreted this rapid swelling of
the state as a serious problem:

Streamlining organizations constitutes a revolution . . . If we fail to carry out this
revolution, if we let the present overstaffed and overlapping Party and state
organizations stay as they are—without clearly defined duties and with many
incompetent, irresponsible, lethargic, undereducated, and inefficient staff mem-

bers—we ourselves will not feel satisfied and we will not have the support of the lower cadres, much less of the people.[19]

Following these reductions in the number of organizations, adjustments in governmental personnel were carried out resolutely in 1982; yet, owing to the further modernization and advance of reforms, China once again ended up on the road to bureaucratic hypertrophy.

Despite the fact that the Chinese bureaucracy hardly conforms to Weber's legal–rational ideal type, Deng insisted that the organizational management had to be based on the specialization of work, the division of labour, and structural and functional institutionalization. However, old-fashioned Stalinist cadre management, especially the administrative reform under one-party dictatorship of the Communist Party, made difficult the establishment of an independent, politically neutral, Weberian-type bureaucracy.

Faced with the repeated failure of administrative reform, the CCP began to propose the drastic reform of the old-fashioned cadre management system. At the Thirteenth National Congress of the CCP, Zhao Ziyang summarized the system's deficiencies in the following terms:

The concept of a 'state cadre' is too general and lacks a scientific classification; the power of cadre management is over concentrated and the people who handle personnel affairs lack professional knowledge; the methods are outdated and simplistic, which hinders the intellectual growth of talented people; the management system is flawed and there are no laws governing the way personnel are used.[20]

The establishment of a new, more professionalized civil service seemed to have faltered following the Tiananmen Square Incident in 1989. However, it was experimented with at some local government levels and agencies. As a result of these experiments, the 'Tentative Regulations of the State Public Servants' was promulgated in August 1993.[21] Although the promulgation can be taken as major progress, there remain many problems in its execution. The major problems are the handling of existing cadres who resist giving up their vested interests, and the harmonizing of the system for the state public servants and the fundamental principle of the leadership of the CCP. In other words, there still exist obstacles concerning the establishment of politically neutral bureaucracy that may not be affected by the power struggles within the party.

Next, let us consider the Chinese bureaucratic order as an element of the process of 'institutionalization' in the political development of developing countries. In general, developing countries are threatened by the constant prospect of political instability. Chiefly because of poverty, such countries are continually exposed to internal and external pressures. Thus, in order to escape from these circumstances, developing countries generally make the modernization of the state a paramount objective. However, in the process of modernization, conflicts inevitably arise with the traditional value system. Even so, there are often instances where the traditional value system, instead of appearing to be something to be overcome through modernization, can be seen to harmonize with the new society as modernization proceeds. On this point, one can say that modernization involves not so much the question of how to *eliminate* tradition as of how to *recast* it so that it fits with modern society.

Since China is one such developing country, it has encountered many obstacles in the process of its bureaucratization. As noted above, Deng Xiaoping himself recognized the existence of such problems; yet even in the 1980s the Chinese bureaucratic apparatus was immature in terms of its division of functions, and moreover the division of powers between officials remained unclear owing to the random proliferation of organizations. As for the bureaucrats themselves, their knowledge was insufficient, their degree of specialization was inadequate, and there spread throughout the apparatus a tendency towards irresponsibility on their part.

The scholar who interpreted the process of modernization in developing countries with a view towards the establishment of political stability is Samuel Huntington. According to him, for the political stability of such countries the most necessary condition is the establishment of political order. This in turn is connected to the so-called institutionalization of a wide variety of fields—in other words, the bureaucratization of society. According to Huntington, the greater the degree to which organizations are characterized by adaptability, complexity, autonomy, and coherence, the more modern a society will become.[22]

China has come to employ Huntington's argument both publicly and privately. This is due to the fact that his theory concerning the need for institutionalization to achieve political order has come to serve as a theoretical endorsement for delaying democratization. The Chinese edition of Huntington's *Political Order in Changing Societies* was published in 1988, but even before this date his argument had exercised considerable influence over Chinese researchers. An early example of this came in the spring of 1986, when Zhang Bingjiu, then a graduate student at Beijing University, developed the following typology of the stages of political development: (1) a political system with concentrated power; (2) a political system with semi-concentrated power; and (3) a political system with a division of power. Zhang argued that, since China's commodity economy was still immature at its present stage of development, the country had no room for a breakthrough to democratization, and he therefore proposed that China should instead adopt a political system with semi-centralized

power. In this type of approach, one can indeed sense the influence of
Huntington.[23]

Another example is Liu Junning of the Political Science Research
Institute of the Chinese Academy of Social Science, who has published a
series of essays in the journal *Zhengzhixue yanjiu* (Studies in Political
Science) with such titles as 'Political Stability in the Process of
Modernization' and 'From the Actual Situation of Idealization to the
Order of Institutionalization: A Discussion of the Connections between
Democratic Government and Industrial Society'. In these essays,
Huntington's arguments concerning political stability and institutional-
ization cast a heavy shadow.[24]

The most conspicuous employment of Huntington's theory of political
development in China came at the end of 1988 and the beginning of 1989,
when the so-called 'theory of new authoritarianism' came to the fore. As
a background to the emergence of this theory, there was an attempt to
reconstruct the political system with centralized power on the part of
Zhao Ziyang and his brain trust. This was done in order to revive Zhao's
own power and prestige, which had begun to slide since he was deemed
responsible for the overheating of the economy in 1988.

According to Wu Jiaxiang, a research worker at the Department of
Investigation and Research of the Central Office of the CCP, the new
authoritarianism took as its model the example of the newly industrialized
economies (NIEs) in neighbouring Asian countries, which, in order to
achieve rapid economic growth, maintained a strong centralization of
political power. Wu noted that the concept of new authoritarianism
derived from the works of Huntington. Moreover, according to Wu, the
reason why the word 'new' had been added was because, whereas previous
authoritarian regimes had suppressed individual liberties, in China state
authority existed in order to protect such personal freedoms.[25] Whatever
the truth or falsehood of these suppositions overall, the basis of this viewpoint was the hope that an institutionalized framework could be constructed through an adjustment of the bureaucratic apparatus with a
policy bifurcation into 'hard' politics and 'soft' economics. Included in
this plan was the further hope that, through such means, policy formulation based on personal prestige could be made into a more systematic
affair.

Perhaps because it is viewed as a product of the preceding era of Zhao
Ziyang, the term 'new authoritarianism' is no longer employed in China
in the post-Tiananmen Incident period. Nevertheless, it is still clear that
China is attempting to overcome its present situation with precisely
this form of political system. By looking at the development strategy of
China in the 1990s, it seems that the developmental model that Deng had

envisioned was the state-led (party-controlled) model that can be seen in the process of economic development in NIEs such as South Korea, Taiwan, and Singapore.

In East Asia, the state designed and implemented industrial policy and accumulated the foreign currency by shifting competitive goods to the export market. This policy had been supported by a superior bureaucratic system and an authoritarian regime. As a result, democratization as a political agenda was ranked after economic growth. It seems that Chinese developmental strategy under the leadership of Deng and the Communist Party is a state(party)-led, economic development based on the presumption of an efficient and powerful bureaucracy.

The problem here resides in the fact that, since leaders who possess as much personal authority as Deng Xiaoping will pass from the scene in the post-Deng era, and because of the weakening of the central government resulting from the distribution of power to local governments, the leadership will increasingly have to rely on the coercive powers of such agencies as the armed forces and the Bureau of Public Security, in addition to strengthening the bureaucratic apparatus under the party's guidance, in order to buttress the party's authority and actual power. Up to the present time in China, the power of the party and the military have been intertwined as a result of the existence of political stability. It appears likely that fundamental political reform of the existing regime, namely democratization, would be necessary for achieving real political stability which does not require the military support.

The Bureaucracy and Political Culture

Wang Yanan, a Marxist scholar known as the translator of Marx's *Das Kapital* into Chinese, published an important work entitled Research on Bureaucratic Politics in China (*Zhongguo guanliao zhengzhi yanjiu*) in 1948, just before the establishment of the People's Republic of China. In this book, Wang summarizes the characteristics of bureaucratic politics in traditional China in three concepts: (1) continuity; (2) inclusiveness; and (3) thoroughness. The concept of continuity refers to the fact that the bureaucratic system possessed a permanence that rivalled that of traditional Chinese culture. Inclusiveness alludes to the fact that bureaucracy possessed intimate and harmonious relations with such social and cultural phenomena as ethics, religion, arts, law, and property relations. Finally, thoroughness refers to the profound influence that China's bureaucracy exerted even in such areas as the modes of thought and world view of the Chinese people.[26]

After analysing the class basis supporting the bureaucratic politics of traditional China, Wang in his capacity as a Marxist thinker offered the following conclusion concerning the means for eliminating such a system of rule:

It is necessary to liquidate the feudal order which has served as bureaucracy's social base, and to sweep away the social status relations which set in opposition officialdom and the people. Moreover, we must make the workers and peasants continuously stand up in a conscious manner, make them participate in movements for political reform, and thereby make them the main leadership. In this manner for the first time in our history bureaucratic politics will confront the era of its demise.[27]

Indeed, the era of the 'people' under the guidance of the Chinese Communist Party did subsequently arrive. Yet, as history has shown, even though the ideology that supports the political system has been replaced, one can argue that the present bureaucratic apparatus of China still seems to possess the characteristics of continuity, inclusiveness, and thoroughness.

The historian Etienne Balazs also positioned Chinese bureaucracy in the category of a 'permanent characteristic' of that country. One can summarize the peculiarities of the structure of the Chinese bureaucratic order that Balazs pointed out as follows. First, China historically was a society with a vast peasant base; moreover, because the merchant class which lacked autonomy was looked down on, power was consistently in the hands of a part of officialdom. Second, Chinese bureaucrats were specialists in dealing with human beings. Moreover, in society there existed a terroristic political system which employed mutual supervision among the members of society. In other words, traditional Chinese politics possessed a totalitarian nature and was averse to any innovative change because of its conservative character. Third, the practice of avoiding and shifting responsibility on the part of Chinese bureaucrats has traditionally been strong. Finally, Chinese officials adopted Confucianism as their state ideology. Confucianism teaches respect and submission towards one's elders, and thus through this dogma a kind of class order was erected, which in turn corresponded well to the order of rule exercised by the bureaucracy.[28]

If one examines the premisses of Balazs's argument from the standpoint of today's China, one can see numerous commonalities between the historical bureaucratic system and that of the CCP. In the first place, China is fundamentally a peasant society, and formerly under the socialist economic system private enterprises and merchant businesses were not fostered. Furthermore, as far as the structure of political rule is concerned, as noted above, the system of authoritarian rule under the auspices of the

CCP has been maintained for a long time. Second, with a CCP committed to the 'Four Cardinal Principles', hostility towards a pluralistic system of values is extremely strong. Third, the modern Chinese bureaucracy is a pyramidal structure under the leadership of the CCP, and bureaucrats more often than not will sound out the opinions of upper-level leaders and party elders concerning final decisions; in other words, the tendency towards avoidance of responsibility remains strong. And finally, the ideology that supports the Chinese bureaucracy today is Marxism–Leninism, an ideology that, like Confucianism, legitimizes domination by a monist hierarchical order.

Recently, an interesting argument has been advanced by Jin Guantao and Liu Qingfeng of the Chinese Academy of Science concerning the historical deep-rootedness of bureaucracy in China. Jin and Liu interpret the historical stagnation of Chinese society as a product of the great stability present in the social structure itself, a phenomenon which they term *da yitong*. According to them, what maintained Chinese feudal society for such a long time was the existence of a fusion of the political order and ideology. In other words, because Confucianism served as the ideology of the state, politics and culture were united.[29] Although the two authors do not directly discuss modern China, from this kind of argument one naturally associates the Chinese Communist Party with the traditional political structure, and 'socialism' with the traditional ideology of Confucianism.

Much of the research that interprets the modern socialist bureaucracy of China from the standpoint of political culture chiefly explains the historical continuities of such problems as venality and corruption in the ruling apparatus as being due mainly to such things as bureaucratism and 'personal rule' (*renzhi*). Once again, Deng Xiaoping himself recognized the sources of bureaucratism as the dual product of history and the contemporary system in the following terms:

In addition to sharing some common characteristics with past types of bureaucracy, Chinese bureaucracy in its present form has characteristics of its own. That is, it differs from both the bureaucracy of old China and that prevailing in the capitalist countries. It is closely connected with our highly centralized management in the economic, political, cultural and social fields, which we have long regarded as essential for the socialist system and for planning.[30]

Although Deng Xiaoping interpreted bureaucratism from the basis of the two separate factors of history and the system itself, one should probably concede that the socialist order under the leadership of the CCP wound up harmonizing rather closely with traditional Chinese political culture.

The problem of 'personal rule', raised repeatedly in the Dengist era, can be traced to the Maoist period. The role of Mao Zedong in all kinds of policy decisions was absolute and transcended the confines of the political system and the legal framework. Owing to the fact that no fixed age for retirement existed, it was a general practice for CCP cadres to occupy their important posts for their entire lives. And the well-known case of Lin Biao, who came to the fore during the Cultural Revolution, showed how violent and ruthless the politics of personalism could become. Lin attempted a *coup d'état* by organizing a group of followers composed of his family members and adherents in 1971, and after the coup failed they met a pitiful fate. The Li Yizhe group of Canton harshly criticized the symbolism of this incident in a wall newspaper in November 1974, at a time when it was still being concealed from the public, in the following terms: 'The vices of dictatorship and arbitrary action have sunk their roots deeply not only among the broad masses but also in the minds of the general party membership.'[31]

It might have been expected that Deng Xiaoping would take the Maoist period as a negative example. Indeed, following the Maoist era, measures for abolishing the lifetime occupancy of posts by cadres were ordained. However, in reality, the political élite to whom these measures have not been applied remains numerous. Moreover, even though Deng Xiaoping himself did not possess any formal title in his final years, no one raised an objection to his actual position as 'supreme influence wielder'. There is the famous story of how, during Zhao Ziyang's meeting with Gorbachev in May 1989, it was revealed that in all important matters the leadership continued to defer to the guidance of Deng.

After the Tiananmen Incident and the dissolution of the Soviet Union, a vigorous argument was advanced in China for a time which held that, in order for China not to follow the Soviet Union's lead, it ought to select successors with resolute political consciousness. At this time, there appeared a new term: *taizidang*, or 'party of the crown princes'. This term referred to the mentality and behaviour of high-level cadres, who, in order to protect their vested interests, attempt to pass on their power to their children. Of course, though there are plenty of opposing opinions on this score, if one examines the issue in the light of Chinese political culture it is an extremely interesting phenomenon. Kazuko Mori has compared the modern system of perquisites with that of the various special privileges accorded to the children and blood relatives who continuously succeeded their fathers in the civilian bureaucracy of traditional China, and points out that there are striking similarities between the two.[32]

Needless to say, 'personal rule' breeds corruption. From the commencement of the Deng Xiaoping period matters took a rapid turn for the worse, and the connection between personal corruption and the reforms of the economic system is quite close. Even though reform measures have been implemented in the areas of separation of powers and a market economy, the political authority of cadres in the party and the government remains just as strong as before. In addition, it has become possible for the cadres to squeeze profits out for themselves from the commercial activities of others and to transform themselves into businessmen and reap immense profits (*guandao*). Earlier in the autumn of 1988, the problems of corruption surrounding the Kanghua Company, which was run by Deng Xiaoping's own son, were for a time exposed by the authorities, but then the pursuit of this issue was suddenly dropped before being resolved.[33]

In order to forestall such incidents, policies for the separation of party and enterprises will become increasingly important; and yet, as described above, these too have been shelved in deference to the principle of the leadership of the CCP. Furthermore, at the Fourteenth National Congress of the CCP it was decided to implement a 'socialist market economy' under the major premiss of the 'leadership of the party'; thus, it is possible to imagine that henceforth, with the advance of marketization, party cadres will 'retire' to lucrative posts within enterprises. One can conclude that the danger that this will produce an upsurge of corruption is exceedingly high, given the fact that from the outset their 'pipeline' of connections to politics will be thick. This is why China continues to call for a campaign to prevent corruption.

Meanwhile, the bureaucratic structure has tended to become ever more bloated as the organizations of each section grow in size in response to needs arising from the economic modernization policies and the systemic reforms. In particular, in order to promote 'greater efficiency' and 'democratization' in the determination of policies, such organizations as policy think-tanks and research institutes have proliferated in a wide variety of governmental bodies since the 1980s. The 'necessity' for specialization and efficiency, understood within a Weberian framework, has thus, paradoxically, expanded the field for the corrupt practices as described above.

However, at the same time, these new structures and research institutes are characterized by elderly cadres being in charge of such posts as director and trustees. Thus, it seems as if these places have been established as spots for the 'retirement' of those elderly cadres who have been forced unavoidably into withdrawing from the political stage owing to such policies as the abolition of the lifetime occupancy of posts. Perhaps as a reflection of this state of affairs, in 1984 Deng Xiaoping went so far as to make the following statement:

We must persuade elderly cadres to vacate their leadership posts. Otherwise there are no posts for younger cadres. While the current situation is on the whole one of stability and unity, a matter which still leaves a rather unpleasant feeling is this particular problem, and the thing which we must skilfully resolve is once again this problem.[34]

Furthermore, in the Chinese bureaucratic apparatus, although the creation and abolition of a variety of organizations is of course fraught with policy meaning, at the same time it is common, on another front, for such organizational changes to be the direct expression of power struggles. In other words, bureaucratic organization is extremely important for political leaders as their power base. An example of this in recent years is the case of Zhu Rongji, the former mayor of Shanghai, who is viewed as a member of the reformist camp. Immediately upon assuming office as a vice premier in April 1991, Zhu established in the State Council an Office of Production, of which he became the director. This was one of a series of measures aimed at creating a base for himself, because Zhu had no personal bureaucratic foothold for those people he wanted to place in posts in the central government.

Zhu Rongji was originally deputy director of the State Economic Commission, and he became mayor of Shanghai after this commission was absorbed by the State Planning Commission in 1988 as a result of the administrative reforms. This absorption of the former by the latter was due to the recognition that the former was no longer needed since, owing to the advance of reforms, only macro management of the economy was deemed necessary, and the Economic Commission was in charge of micro management. Zhu Rongji's establishment of the Office of Production may be viewed as an effort to check the Planning Commission, which has served as the stronghold of the conservatives, or as an attempt to abolish the Planning Commission and revive the powers of the Economic Commission.[35]

As evidence of this, in June 1992, before Zhu's elevation to the Standing Committee of the Politburo at the Fourteenth National Congress of the CCP, the Office of Planning was eliminated at the same time as Zhu came to the fore, and an Office of Economics and Trade under the directorship of Zhu was established. Zhu thus saw the scope of his authority expanded beyond the field of production to include that of the departments concerned with commerce. He then succeeded in developing this section into the State Commission for Economics and Trade through the institutional reform in March 1993. However, it became difficult for the State Commission for Economics and Trade to stand over the State Planning Commission, because of the criticism against Zhu Rongji from the conservatives about economic management, especially on the issue of the state enterprises.

In any case, when viewed from the standpoint of the reformist camp, such actions on the part of Zhu Rongji conflict with the reformers' stated goal of a more rational civil service free of political meddling. In Chinese politics such examples are too numerous to list. In general, such cases indicate that, whereas the tendency of the bureaucratic apparatus in China to create 'people' (*ren*) has continued to increase steadily with the construction of a modern system, at the same time the tendency of 'people' (*ren*) to create bureaucracy in that country remains just as strong as before.

As a final remark, when considering the question of the bureaucratic apparatus from the standpoint of Chinese political culture, it will not do to forget the tendencies that arise from the above discussion of China as a developing country. In other words, in general developing nations experience conflicts between the process of modernization and such things as tradition and historical peculiarities, and the mutual relations between these two sets of factors becomes a major factor influencing the course of modernization. Such is particularly true when it comes to bureaucracy, which cannot help but become the locus of the most fierce conflicts between the old powers and the new. Nevertheless, in the case of China, the history of its bureaucratic order is so overwhelmingly long in comparison with that of other developing countries that it should be stressed all the more that 'the weight of history' is a 'Chinese characteristic' (*Zhongguo de tese*).

Conclusion

The Chinese bureaucratic order can be viewed from the three angles discussed above, i.e. socialism, modernization, and political culture. While the Deng era reforms clearly advocated the norms of efficiency, rationality, and specialization found in Weber's ideal-type, the combined impact of the socialist and late imperial bureaucratic traditions has been dominant.[36] Poor political communications from one administrative level to another have fostered a heavy reliance on the medium of individuals (*ren*) rather than on any impersonal system (*zhidu*).[37] Formal, unchecked power and readily available personal networks have encouraged cadre corruption, especially in the context of market reforms which have made 'renting out' government authority and discretion on economic matters extremely lucrative for officials. While democratization and rule of law present themselves as logical remedies, the hardening of commitments to monist CCP leadership since 1989 among the politically privileged élite has made even administrative and managerial reforms painful to contemplate and difficult to accomplish.

NOTES

1. The formal establishment of the field of administrative management in China was in October 1988. However, as a precursor, a preparatory office for a learned society for administrative science had already been set up in the middle of the 1980s, and at the same time the monthly journal *Zhongguo xingzheng guanli* (Chinese Administrative Management) began publication. Recently the related field of personnel management has also flourished in China.
2. See *inter alia* Miao Changqing, 'Lun "guanliao zhengzhi" gainian de hanyi' (On 'Bureaucratic Politics': the Meaning of the Concept), *Xueshujie*, 2 (1992).
3. Kenneth Lieberthal and Michel Oksenberg, *Policy Making in China: Leaders, Structures, and Processes* (Princeton: Princeton University Press, 1988).
4. Vivienne Shue, *The Reach of the State: Sketches of the Chinese Body Politic* (Stanford: Stanford University Press, 1988).
5. Deng Xiaoping, 'The Present Situation and Tasks', in *Selected Works of Deng Xiaoping: 1975–1982* (Beijing: Foreign Languages Press, 1984), 255–6.
6. Concerning leading groups, see the detailed discussion in Tang Liang, 'Chugoku no gyosei kikan ni okeru to guruppu' (The Party Groups in the Administrative Organs in China), *Ajiya Kenkyu* (Asian Studies), 38:2 (December 1991).
7. For example, see Zhao Qizheng (ed.), *Ganbu renshi gongzuo shouce* (Handbook of Cadre Personnel Activities) (internal publication) (Shanghai: Shanghai renmin chubanshe, 1986), ch. 11.
8. Deng Xiaoping, 'Senior Cadres Should Take the Lead in Maintaining and Enriching the Party's Fine Traditions', in *Selected Works of Deng Xiaoping*, 209.
9. Deng Xiaoping, 'On the Reform of the System of Party and State Leadership', in *Selected Works*.
10. Deng Xiaoping, 'It is Essential to Have a Blueprint for Reforms of the Political System', in *Gendai Chugoku no kihon mondai ni tsuite* (On the Fundamental Problems in Contemporary China) (Beijing: Foreign Languages Press, 1987, Japanese edn), 259.
11. See *inter alia* 'Woguo de zhengzhi tizhi gaige yu zhengzhixue de fazhan' (China's Political Structural Reform and the Development of Political Science), *Zhongguo she-hui kexue*, 4 (1986), and 'Zhongyang dangxiao zhaokai "zhengzhi tizhi gaige lilun yan-taohui"', *Guangming ribao*, 19 July 1986.
12. Zhao Ziyang, 'Report Delivered at the 13th National Congress of the Communist Party of China', *Beijing Review* (9–15 Nov. 1987), 38.
13. Jiang Zemin, 'Report Delivered at the 14th National Congress of the Communist Party of China', *Beijing Review* (26 Oct.–1 Nov. 1992), 9–32.
14. ibid. For a work that argues that the internal functions of the Chinese bureaucracy have increasingly tended towards 'dispersal' since the commencement of reforms and opening to the external world, see Kenneth Lieberthal and David Lampton (eds.), *Bureaucracy, Politics, and Decision Making in Post-Mao China* (Berkeley: University of California Press, 1992).
15. Uehara Kazuyoshi has sparked an interesting debate with his view that the sources of bureaucratism in the Chinese polity reside in the contradictions of socialism itself which outweigh factors rooted in China's traditions. See his essay 'Gendai Chugoku kenkyu no kadai' (Issues of Contemporary Chinese Studies), *Kokumin Keizai Zashi* (National Economic Journal), 166:3 (1992).
16. See Ryosei Kokubun, 'Chugoku fukkoki ni okeru keizai kanryosei' (Economic

Bureaucracy in China's Reconstruction Period of the Early 1950s), *Hogaku Kenkyu* (Journal of Law), 60:1 (January 1987), 272.

17. Deng Xiaoping, 'The Realization of Ideological Line and Political Line Must be Assured by Organizational Line', in *Selected Works*, 269–74.
18. On the pace of administrative reforms in China, see Ren Xiao, 'Zhongguo xingzheng gaige de dongli yu jincheng (1982–1988)' (The Momentum and Process of China's Administrative Reform), *Zhengzhixue yanjiu* (Studies in Political Science), 6 (1989).
19. Deng Xiaoping, 'Streamlining Organizations Constitutes a Revolution', in *Selected Works*, 374.
20. Zhao Ziyang, 'Report Delivered', 40.
21. *Renmin ribao*, 19 August 1993.
22. Samuel Huntington, *Political Order in Changing Societies* (New Haven: Yale University Press, 1968).
23. Zhang Bingjiu, 'Jingji tizhi gaige he zhengzhi tizhi gaige de jincheng yu xietiao' (The Process and Coordination of Economic and Political Structural Reform), in Liu Jun and Li Lin (eds.), *Xin quanweizhuyi: dui gaige lilun gangling de lunzheng* (Neo-Authoritarianism: Debates on the Theoretical Framework of Reform) (Beijing: Beijing jingji xueyuan chubanshe, 1989).
24. Liu Junning, 'Xiandaihua jinchengzhong de zhengzhi wending' (Political Stability of the Modernization Process), *Zhengzhixue yanjiu*, 6 (1987), and the same author's 'Cong lixianghua de shiti dao zhiduhua de chengxu' (The Reality of Idealization to the Process of Institutionalization), *Zhengzhixue yanjiu*, 3 (1988).
25. Wu Jiaxiang, 'Xin quanweizhuyi de shuping' (A Critique on Neo-Authoritarianism), *Shijie jingji daobao* (The World Economic Herald), 16 January 1989.
26. Wang Yanan, *Zhongguo guanliao zhengzhi yanjiu* (The Study of China's Bureaucratic Politics) (Beijing: Zhongguo kexue chubanshe, 1981, 2nd edn, part 3, 'Zhongguo guanliao zhengzhi de zhu teshu biaoxiang' (Some Specific Phenomena of China's Bureaucratic Politics)).
27. ibid. 195.
28. Etienne Balazs, 'China as a Permanently Bureaucratic Society', in his *Chinese Civilization and Bureaucracy* (New Haven: Yale University Press, 1964).
29. Jin Guantao, *Zai lishi de biaoxiang beihou: dui Zhongguo fengjian shehui chao wending jiegou de tansuo* (Behind Historical Appearances: an Exploration of 'Super-Stability' in Decentralized Chinese Society) (Sichuan: Renmin chubanshe, 1983).
30. Deng Xiaoping, 'On the Reform of the System', in *Selected Works*, 310.
31. Zhi Hao and René Viénet, *Ri Ittetsu no Daijiho* (The Wall-poster of Li Yizhe) (Japanese edn, Nitchu Publishing Co., 1977), 65.
32. Mori Kazuko, 'Chugoku seiji ni okeru "kanbu" mondai' (The Cadre Problems in Chinese Politics), in Eto Shinkichi (ed.), *Gendai Chugoku seiji no kozo* (Structure of Contemporary Chinese Politics) (Tokyo: Nihon Kokusai Mondai Kenkyujo, 1982).
33. *Yomiuri Shimbun*, 8 October 1988; *Asahi Shimbun*, 16 October 1988.
34. Deng Xiaoping, 'Address to the Third Plenary Meeting of the Central Advisory Committee', in *On the Fundamental Problems in Contemporary China*, 148.
35. *Yomiuri Shimbun*, 19 June 1992; *Asahi Shimbun*, 18 July 1992. In addition, Zhu Rongji assumed a variety of key posts which Zou Jiahua, Director of the Commission for State Planning, had held up to that point, such as Director of the Commission for National Security and Production, Director of the Commission for the Management of National Wireless Network, and Chairman of the Small Leadership Group for Large-scale Technical Equipment of the State Council, by June 1991: *Chugoku naigai soko* (Inside and Outside Trends of China) (11–20 June 1992), Radio Press, p. A4. In

addition, hints to this effect were made to the author concerning economic bureaucrats in the course of interviews carried out in Beijing in March 1992.
36. Since the Tiananmen Incident, the strength of political culture has often been underscored in analyses of Chinese politics. Most of these discuss the relation between state and society, and argue that China lacks a mature civil society and individuality. On these questions, see *inter alia* Lucian W. Pye, 'The State and the Individual', *The China Quarterly* (September 1991); and Elizabeth J. Perry and Ellen V. Fuller, 'China's Long March to Democracy', *World Policy Journal* (Fall 1991).
37. Hong Yung Lee has argued that an imbalance between the immense party–state system and the deficiency of the process of institutionalization have brought about the hypertrophy of the political élite, and points out that this élite is today in the process of becoming 'bureaucratic technocrats': see Hong Yung Lee, 'From Revolutionary Cadres to Bureaucratic Technocrats', in Brantly Womack (ed.), *Contemporary Chinese Politics in Historical Perspective* (Cambridge: Cambridge University Press, 1991).

4

Control as Care: Interaction between Urban Women and Birth Planning Workers

Cecilia Milwertz[1]

In China, according to the Law of the People's Republic of China on the Protection of Rights and Interests of Women passed in 1992, 'Women have the right to child-bearing in accordance with relevant regulations of the state as well as the freedom not to bear any child.'[2] The 'relevant regulations' of the state are defined within the framework of the national population policy. The main objective of the post-Mao population policy is to limit population growth rates and ultimately to stabilize population at zero growth. The main remedial measure for reaching these targets has been to lay down a fertility limit of one child per couple. Although, especially since 1984, this limit has been revised so that the rural majority of the Chinese population are permitted to give birth to two children per couple when the first child is a girl, the fertility limit in cities, and especially among state employees, has consistently been one child per couple.

These limits are in direct conflict with international human rights conventions. Internationally, the right of individuals to determine in a free and responsible way the size of their family was recognized at the International Conference on Human Rights held in Teheran in 1968 to mark the twentieth anniversary of the Universal Declaration on Human Rights.[3] Subsequently, the concept of family planning as a human right has been further developed to embrace concepts of reproductive health, reproductive rights, and reproductive self-determination.[4]

An evaluation of the Chinese one-child family policy based on the definition of family planning as a human right inevitably reveals that the direct intervention of the Chinese leadership in the fertility decisions of the individual and the family amounts to a violation of basic human rights. In conventional human rights issues, such as protection against torture or prohibition of disappearances, much has been done to expose and oppose violations. However, monitoring governmental compliance with population-related human rights has yet to be introduced. One reason for the paucity of international attention to violations in the area of population policies may be the fact that victims are women and that protection of human rights of women lags far behind that of men.[5] Similarly, very few China scholars have directly condemned the Chinese population policy as violating basic human rights.[6] The Chinese leadership maintains that the population policy adheres to a principle of voluntary acceptance, meaning that, in cases of conflicting interests between the state and the individual, the latter is expected to accept voluntarily that the interests of the state take precedence over the interests of the individual.[7] None the less, it has been acknowledged that coercion does take place, and the Chinese leadership has assumed responsibility for local-level coercion in policy implementation.[8] But such violation of human rights is not, as the leadership would have it, merely an episodic or local phenomenon: on the contrary, coercion and violation of human rights are implicit in the policy itself in so far as the leadership has set a fertility limit.

The objective of this paper is to present an understanding of the cultural meanings inherent in the concept of acceptance at the micro level of society by examining the interaction of urban birth planning workers and women. During the process of interviewing one-child women in China, I gradually came to realize that the assumption that human rights violations are inherent in the one-child family policy was not shared by the women I was interviewing. While the notion of universal rights has broad appeal and obvious utility in raising and maintaining global standards of freedom and personal security, the responses of women underline the cultural and historical origins of the rights themselves. In pointing this out, my aim is not to justify the Chinese population policy, nor to support the way in which Asian political leaders have co-opted the anti-colonial analysis of feminists in Asia towards Western market-oriented economic development models. (These leaders have also warned against the dangers of Westernization and argued that feminism and reproductive rights are mere importations by upper-class Asian women and thus alien to the traditional Confucian ideal of a docile, quiet, and all-sacrificing woman.[9]) However, unless one grasps the cultural basis of acceptance of birth control among urban women, their behaviour and perspectives cannot be fully understood.

The data derive from a study, based on the experience of one-child mothers, of costs and consequences of the demographically successful population policy in urban China. A survey of 857 state and collectively employed women and qualitative interviews with forty of these women were carried out in city districts of the municipality of Beijing and the provincial capital Shenyang of Liaoning province over a period of seven months in 1991 and 1992. Cities in China are administratively divided into urban, suburban, and rural districts. Inhabitants are registered as either agricultural (*nongye*) or non-agricultural (*fei nongye*). High one-child rates are found in the city districts where the population is mainly non-agricultural and is employed in state and collective enterprises.[10] The women studied were born between 1953 and 1967, which means that their number of children was influenced by the one-child policy. This paper is based on the qualitative interviews as well as on interviews with birth planning workers at the levels of city district birth planning committee and street committee birth planning office as well as with birth planning cadres and propagandists at two factories in Beijing and one in Shenyang. About half of the women interviewed were employed in these three factories.

The interviews indicate that urban women perceive of controls designed to avert the birth of a second child not only as control, but also as concern and care. This is the case even though they are well aware that the main objective of the measures implemented by birth planning workers is to secure policy adherence. Control is perceived as care even though 52 per cent of the women studied indicated two children as their preferred number. In fact, the desire for two children is probably much larger since, in response to an additional question on the preferred number of children, 72.5 per cent indicated that the ideal number of children in a family was two, while 82.8 per cent thought that it would be beneficial for their child to have a sibling. None the less, even though it may disturb the Western feminist and/or human rights advocate, the majority of the city-district one-child women studied do not perceive the one-child policy in itself, or the implementation of the policy, as other than voluntary. Even in cases where the policy is termed coercive by some urban women, they none the less accept the control exercised by birth planning workers to ensure that they follow the policy.

Policy Implementation

The three main measures applied in order to implement the one-child family norm and reach the demographic policy target are ideological education (*xuanchuan jiaoyu*),[11] which is given the highest priority, and administrative and economic measures. The essence of ideological education is that leading cadres and birth planning workers explain the policy to the people in the context of the national economic situation and the requirements of the national modernization programme. Presuming that leaders and officials do their job well, the people will 'definitely and immediately accept the programme for control of the population growth'.[12]

Former PRC programmes leading to considerable social reform[13] have been initiated by nationwide propaganda explaining the need for the programme, the problems it was addressing, and the value to the nation as a whole.[14]

In carrying out these programmes of social change, the state has made use of coercive measures, but education and persuasion have been seen as the more important factors in bringing about compliance. The practice has been to distinguish between the uninformed, uneducated, and unwilling, who are assumed to be susceptible to propaganda, and a small group of those in actual opposition. In the case of one-child family policy implementation in the countryside, it has proved exceedingly difficult, in view of the magnitude of rural opposition, to identify a small group of transgressors.[15] Ideally, the majority of the populace will be persuaded by ideological education alone to adhere to the policy of one couple, one child. When ideological education is not sufficient to persuade them to follow the policy, economic measures in the form of penalties are resorted to. It was initially stressed that birth planning work should rely primarily on ideological education and encouragement, and that economic penalties were to be applied only to a minority of the populace who after such education were still not willing to adhere to policy fertility limits. The aim, as expressed by the official terminology, is to educate people to follow the policy, and to ensure that the policy, which is based on the interests of the state and the people, is not violated.[16] Economic measures also include incentives, primarily in the form of a one-child certificate, which carries with it a range of financial and educational benefits.

In contrast to rural China, the group in active opposition in the city districts of urban China has been relatively small. Birth planning workers found that only the first years of implementing the policy were really difficult. Following ideological educational work, the urban populace proved willing to follow the policy. According to one district-level birth planning cadre in Beijing, there have been only rare cases of opposition because, as she says:

The state call for one couple one child is advocated by way of voluntary acceptance. The policy is based on everyone understanding the benefit of the policy for the nation and understanding the burden being placed on society. Also the policy is based on everyone deciding on their own fertility according to their own interests.[17]

In other words, in the city districts, ideological education as the main remedial measure has been more or less sufficient towards all but a relatively small group in opposition.

The Structure of the Birth Planning Institution

The highest level of the birth planning institution in Beijing and Liaoning is the Family Planning Commission, placed directly below the municipal and provincial government.[18] Beneath this level, the birth planning institution is divided into two parallel vertical systems based on area of residence and work unit, with the institution being represented at each of the subsequent administrative levels.[19] At the lowest levels of both the residential area and the workplace, birth planning cadres and propagandists work in direct contact with women.

The district factory in Beijing employs 469 staff and workers, of which 307 are women. Of the 307 women, 216 are women of reproductive age, meaning they are married but have not reached the age of 50. The factory has one part-time birth planning cadre and eight propagandists—one in each of the six production workshops and two who are responsible for the administrative personnel. The propagandists serve as assistants to the part-time birth planning cadre who assigns them specific tasks.

The birth planning cadre at the Shenyang factory has worked full-time on birth planning since 1982. She is responsible for birth planning at the factory, which employs 1,300 workers and administrative personnel, and supervises the eight birth planning propagandists at the four workshops and four departments of the factory. When she has been to a meeting at a higher birth planning institutional level concerning policy implementation or instructions concerning the speech of a leader, she passes on the messages to the eight propagandists, who then convey the information to the women in their respective departments. Each of the workshops is further organized systematically into smaller birth planning groups. One spinning workshop of 400 employees has four birth planning activists. At the Beijing factory, the union representatives in the workshops also act as birth planning propagandists.

The work unit and the residential area birth planning institutions work together in a system of 'combined line and area' (*tiao kuai jiehe*),[20] in which the work unit provides vertical control from above to below while the residential area provides overall daily surveillance of residents. Although the residential area birth planning institution does not have as much control over the lives of its residents as the vertical work unit system, it works in close cooperation with work units and is able to report to the work units if there are aspects of their lives that residents are attempting to conceal.

Persuasion

The rare problems encountered in the city district work units are usually related either to the older generation's insistence on having a grandson to carry on the family line, or to second marriages. However, while these are the main problem areas within the work unit, private entrepreneurs and the so-called floating population of migrants from rural areas are the more serious urban problem groups. The floating population is difficult to control as these migrants are not registered at the main birth planning control posts—the work unit and the residential area. The effect of economic penalties levied on private entrepreneurs has been eroded as they are often able to pay the sizeable sums they are fined. In 1992 the fine for having a second child in Beijing was between 5,000 and 50,000 yuan and for a third child, between 20,000 and 100,000 yuan.[21] These are quite substantial sums compared with an ordinary monthly salary of approximately 200–300 yuan.

In order to resolve the problems related to desire for a grandson or to a second marriage, birth planning workers will visit the homes of people to conduct their ideological work and to persuade them to follow the policy.[22] Any person or group that does not feel immediately obliged to follow a given policy after receiving the preliminary ideological education is subjected to 'persuasion'. Whereas ideological education is aimed at large groups in society, 'persuasion' takes place in direct personal meetings between the birth planning worker/workers and the person/persons unwilling to follow a given policy. The susceptibility of the unwilling person/s to persuasion depends on the nature and context of the issue in question. The example cited below illustrates a case of relatively uncomplicated persuasion.

Supplementary to ideological education/persuasion and the system of economic incentives and penalties, the third birth planning policy measure is the administrative use of a national quota for the number of annual births. Birth planning cadres at the level of the work unit and the residential area manage the distribution of the annual quota of births to women in their jurisdiction. Before she becomes pregnant, a woman must apply for a share of the quota in the form of a birth permit. Births following granted permission are registered as planned births (*jihua nei*, literally 'within the plan'), while births that have not been permitted are registered as unplanned births (*jihua wai*, literally 'outside the plan'). When in the Beijing city district in 1988 a surge of women in the 1960s were applying for birth permits, the women were asked to queue according to their age. The birth planning cadre explains:

We let the eldest, the 28–27–26 year olds, give birth first, and persuaded the 24 and 25 year olds to wait for two years. After we persuaded them, they agreed to wait and we did not give them a permit. If, for example, we have three women applying for a birth permit but we have a quota of only two, we will persuade the youngest woman to wait until next year. We discuss the situation with her taking her personal situation into consideration, saying for example: 'You are still at school, or you have just started working, so you need to make a special effort at school or at work. Don't you agree?' And she will agree to wait another year. This is the way we persuade. We make everyone understand, make them support and agree to the policy. We do not apply force.[23]

Cadres will continuously visit a reluctant person who is not immediately susceptible to being persuaded, to explain the reasons why it is necessary to adhere to the policy in question until the person is prepared to accept.[24]

Preventing the Birth of a Second Child

The duty of birth planning cadres and propagandists is mainly to carry out ideological education work and to do practical work directed at married women of reproductive age with a view to promoting policy implementation. Birth planning workers are responsible for the first procedures of registering women for permission to marry, for permission to give birth, and for application for one-child certificates.

The most important part of birth planning work starts following the birth of the first child, and this is to make sure that women do not have a second child by ensuring that once they have given birth they use contraceptives, and apply for a one-child certificate, and to control and monitor their contraceptive practice constantly.[25] This is where the propagandists in every workshop play a role. If a woman is pregnant, they will notice and they will inform the birth planning cadre, who will then contact the woman and make sure she has an abortion as soon as possible.

The most frequently used form of contraception is the IUD.[26] At the district factory, 170–180 of the 216 married women of reproductive age were using an IUD or had been sterilized, while about ten women were using contraceptive pills. A worker at the Shenyang factory who gave birth to her daughter in 1986 said:

I use, the habit in China is to use, an IUD. After giving birth to a child you go to have an IUD inserted. The IUD is a good contraceptive method that safeguards the health of women. The work unit makes arrangements for an annual X-ray check-up at the hospital, which is quite convenient. All the women using IUDs go along. Everyone uses an IUD. After the birth of one child nearly everyone uses an IUD and there are no side effects.[27]

The birth planning propagandist at the Shenyang factory confirms that the most used contraceptive after first birth at the factory is the IUD. As she says:

The objective is to ensure that every couple has only one child, not to let anyone have a second child. Usually no one wants a second child. There is no problem. Sometimes, however, the contraceptives fail. But everyone quite willingly has an abortion. I do not have to convince them.[28]

Birth planning workers prefer the long-term IUDs because they need to be checked only once or twice a year. Birth planning workers at both the residential area and the work unit make sure that women do have IUDs inserted. At a Shenyang residential area, birth planning workers visit women about six months after they have given birth to check up on their contraceptive practice. At the Shenyang factory, birth planning workers make sure the woman starts using contraceptives when she comes back to work following her 150 days of maternity leave. Sometimes it is necessary to do ideological work, although, according to birth planning workers, most women do not have to be persuaded. The hospital that inserts the IUD issues an IUD certificate which the woman must show birth planning workers at both the residential area and the work unit, as both keep an account of the contraceptive practice of the women of reproductive age in their jurisdiction.

One of the reasons for registration of contraceptive practice at the Beijing factory is that if a woman who is using an IUD becomes pregnant there are no repercussions, as an IUD is considered a long-term contraceptive; if the woman has not been using an IUD and becomes pregnant, her bonus will be deducted during the sick leave following the abortion and her medical expenses will not be reimbursed. At another Beijing work unit there are no penalties for the first abortion for a woman who is using an IUD, whereas a second abortion, along with any abortion that is due to lack of IUD use, results in bonus reductions.

Although penalties for not using an IUD are not applied at the Beijing factory until the woman without an IUD becomes pregnant and has to have an abortion, the birth planning cadre does advocate the use of IUDs. Employees at the Beijing factory as well as other women confirm that birth planning workers 'handle birth planning work relatively severely', and 'that they request that you use a contraceptive method so that you will not give birth to a second child', that women of reproductive age who have given birth 'must be sterilized or use an IUD; usually they don't let you use contraceptive pills; usually women use an IUD', and that 'use of an IUD is voluntary'. In sum, women who have given birth to their first child must use some form of contraceptive method and the IUD is advocated. Most women agreed to have an IUD inserted 'because abortions are so painful' and 'because the woman herself will suffer if she does conceive'.[29]

Contraceptive use after the birth of the first child is compulsory, but there is a limited extent of freedom of choice as to which contraceptive method to use. Women are encouraged, by way of incentives and the threat of penalties should they become pregnant without an IUD, to choose an IUD. There are, however, some work units where women definitely do not have a choice of contraceptive method, as their bonus is deducted if they do not have an IUD inserted following the birth of their child. Some women cannot use an IUD because of heavy bleeding or other side effects; in such cases it is the duty of the birth planning cadre to help them choose a more suitable contraceptive method. The birth planning cadre at the Shenyang factory confirms the opinion of Beijing birth planning workers that contraceptive pills and other forms of contraceptives are acceptable if a woman is unable to use an IUD, though in her opinion contraceptives other than IUDs have a tendency to give rise to unplanned pregnancies. For this reason, she says, pills are not good for the health of the woman because she will have to have an abortion.

The argument of birth planning workers is thus that women must use an IUD to protect their own health, as an abortion is a disturbing and painful affair. Their reasoning takes as its point of departure the assumption that the population policy measure of only one child must be followed, starting at the point where women must as a matter of course adhere to the policy. Within the assumption that the policy advocated by the leadership must be followed, the health of the woman is in fact best protected if she does use an IUD subsequent to the birth of her child. In this way, the role of birth planning workers is not only to ensure that the policy measure of one child per couple is not violated, but also, within the limits set by the policy, to care for the women under their control. Not only do birth planning workers perceive of their duty as caring for women, but women themselves experience the work of the birth planning workers as care, as is illustrated by the words of a Beijing woman:

When you become pregnant, you cannot have the child and must have an abortion. Many abortions are not good for women's health. The birth planning workers are caring (*zhaogu*) for women by applying a method of supervision and urging. They supervise and urge you to use a certain contraceptive method to avoid injuring your health. They are showing concern (*guanxin*)[30] for women by continuous urging. When you have one child and have a one-child certificate they help you to find a safe contraceptive method to save you from enduring hardship.[31]

The merging of control and care, through which coercion and control become care, operates in relation to several spheres of duties of the birth planning workers and is an integral part of the tight control system as well as of residential area and work unit cooperation. It is also part of the basis from which control is established by the birth planning institution. Interlinking ideological education with providing a service to people is, according to a 1990 article by Shen Guoxiang, Director of the State Family Planning Commission Ideological Education Department, a new development within recent years in the sphere of birth planning ideological education work. The birth planning service should not only ensure that women give birth according to the policy requirements, but should also, for instance, care for the physical and mental health of women and children and for the welfare of the elderly. The objective is to make people realize that birth planning as required by the policy is in accordance with their personal interest.[32]

The 'Five Visitings and Five Inquiries' are one of the forms of combining ideological education with providing care. The 'Five Visitings and Five Inquiries' include 'visiting couples who, after giving birth to one child, do not request to be permitted second children; visiting family planning role models and active elements; visiting comrades who have undergone birth control surgical operations; visiting comrades who, for all sorts of reasons, have been subjected to punishment; visiting newlyweds; inquiring about people's conditions in the winter, when it is cold, or when it is very warm; inquiring after the health of the mother and her daughter or son; inquiring about the financial difficulties in the family; inquiring about people's opinions on the work that is being done'.[33]

Care and control is combined when the birth planning worker from the work unit visits a woman who has been on sick leave for some time in her home to bring her medicine and 'to keep an eye on things'. Once they have given birth, women are visited in their homes both by work unit and residential area birth planning workers at varying intervals. At the Shenyang factory a birth planning propagandist says that when a woman in her workshop has given birth she will call on her in her home to convey greetings to her, because 'To give birth is a big event in a woman's life, so we must call on her as representatives of the factory to express our concern.'[34]

Women are of course well aware that the visits to their homes by birth planning workers are part of the work to ensure policy compliance; this is particularly apparent as one objective of many visits is to fill in forms on the contraceptive practices of women. However, they also perceive of the visits as expressions of care and concern. As women see it, the birth planning worker visits once or twice a year not only to check on whether or not the woman is using the contraceptive method she is registered as using, but also to check up on her health in general, just as the birth planning worker is concerned with the health of the child. The annual or bi-annual, depending on the economic capacity of the work unit, gynaecological check-ups for married women of reproductive age who have given birth are also perceived of as an expression of the care that the nation, the work unit, and the birth planning workers extend towards women, although it is obvious that the primary motive underlying the organization of the check-ups is to avoid the birth of second children by making sure the IUDs are in place and that women are not pregnant.

Thus, the control implemented to avert the birth of second children is perceived by women not only as control, but also as concern and care, even though they are well aware that the main objective of the measures implemented by birth planning workers is to secure policy adherence. However, the role of birth planning workers is not only to ensure that the policy is adhered to by women within their jurisdiction, but also to implement the policy based on the interests of women within these limits. It is not in the interest of women to have one or more abortions; therefore the main contraceptive method is the IUD, which is advocated at some work units and compulsory at others. Control is care. Control is an aspect of concern, or concern is an aspect of control—the two merge and are part of, or perhaps the very essence of, a reciprocal control system. Providing care is an integral aspect of the work to ensure policy adherence, in the sense that the primary motive for providing care is to ensure policy compliance. The work unit supplies care, and as employees are dependent upon and subordinate to the work unit in exchange for care, compliance is expected and control is accepted.

The Cultural Meaning of Acceptance

The tight net of control exercised at work units as well as in the residential areas and strengthened by their cooperation indicates the importance of control for the demographic success of the urban one-child policy. The cultural meanings that support compliance are constructed within the framework of control as care. Urban state enterprise employees are, as Andrew Walder has described, subject to a relatively high degree of dependence upon their workplace because employment plays a welfare role. The state workplace is politically and economically organized to satisfy a broad range of the needs of employees. The needs that are satisfied (or potentially satisfied) at the workplace include not only the money wage, but also the satisfaction of other economic and social needs such as health insurance, medical care, pensions, housing, and childcare. Dependence is further strengthened by the scarcity of alternatives for satisfaction of these needs.[35] Notwithstanding a recognition of the significance of economic as well as political control exercised by the workplace and the subsequent dependence of employees, an insight into the structure of control mechanisms does not sufficiently explain why women are accepting control to such a degree that they perceive of control not as coercion but, on the contrary, as care.

The following four features constitute the perception of control as care. First, control and monitoring is taken for granted as a basic element of everyday life. Second, the women being controlled are aware that birth planning workers are themselves subject to control—they are just doing their job. Third, control as care is based on cultural assumptions of reciprocity: as long as the work unit satisfies the needs of employees, they will in return follow the requirements of the work unit. Fourth, women and their families are willing to act contrary to fertility preferences in following the one-child requirement on the condition that the policy requirement is applicable to all urban residents. Together, these four interlinked features shape the pattern of the perception of control as care.

The perception of control as care was expressed by a Beijing woman, who said:

There are unplanned births in Beijing, although very few. There was a woman at my work unit who left to become a private entrepreneur. Her first child was a girl, and I have heard that she has already given birth to three girls. They have money enough. If there are economic penalties, they just pay however much they have to. They are private entrepreneurs, and they want a son who can inherit their property, so she has given birth to several children without permission. I don't know whether the nation has any measures towards this kind of people. If there are not any special measures, then, as far as I can see, people who have the economic means can have as many children as they like as the economic penalties do not bother them. From my point of view the nation should apply measures to prevent this. They have money and they don't care about penalties. The nation ought to ensure that, even though they have money, they should not have as many children as they please. They should understand that this is not their personal concern, this is the concern of a whole people, of a whole nation. There are many private entrepreneurs, and if they all act like this it will amount to only us ordinary people complying with the call of the nation as we don't have the money to do otherwise.

Implementation of the policy is voluntary, but if we compare with them—they also live on the land of this nation, they ought also to observe the policy of the party. They should not have as many children as they please just because they have the economic means to do so. From the point of view of the nation, coercive measures ought to be applied towards them. Even though they have money, they should follow the call of the nation. The problem is not only the private entrepreneurs in the cities but also the rural population.

If I, as an employee in a state enterprise, give birth to a second child, I will be fined maybe 5,000 yuan. I couldn't pay that much money in a whole year. At present, the coercive measures work only with employees in state and collective enterprises. At the shop where I work I would be fired immediately if I gave birth to a second child. This is what the penalty would be. I have only my basic salary, so even though in our hearts we might want another child we do not dare to. I have to protect my job. If I am fired I wouldn't have the money to support the child, so I would not dare to have another child. This is a form of coercion that does not exist towards private entrepreneurs. It is possible to control staff and workers in state and collective enterprises relatively severely. You can have a child if you want, but if you do, you will be fired.[36]

This woman quite precisely conveys the core of acceptance of the policy. Acceptance is voluntary in the sense that she chooses to follow the requirement of only one child regardless of her fertility preference. She chooses to keep her job in view of the consequences of living without the welfare provided by the work unit. The Shenyang factory, which has improved working conditions at the factory as well as wages and subsidies during the past ten years and has established a system of a monthly five-yuan pension supplement for one-child parents, has achieved 100 per cent one-child implementation since 1983. It is part of a cultural assumption of reciprocity that the work unit has the right to control the people within its care. Women perceive of the policy as voluntary in the sense that, as long as they remain within the structure of the work unit and the work unit welfare system, they must also accept control as they are indebted to the work unit.

Indebtedness, as described by Lung-kee Sun, is central to the pattern of control as care. Following Sun's analysis, in the Chinese culture a person is motivated to serve and make sacrifices out of a sense of indebtedness.

If, as a Western philosopher points out, reciprocity is a matter of returning good 'in proportion to the good we receive', and of making 'reparation for the harm we have done', then what amounts to 'sacrifice' is a form of compensation for a beneficence one has already received. In other words, so-called sacrifice is a matter of mutual benefit in a relationship based on 'reciprocity'.[37]

Sun further emphasizes that, not only is reciprocity in the Chinese culture institutionalized as a formal obligation, in contrast to for instance American society, where reciprocity is also a social reality, but also, inherent in reciprocity is the implication of expectation and control.[38]

Women do not find having to apply for permission to give birth at all peculiar or offensive. When a critique of the quota system is voiced, it is not the system as such, but rather what is perceived as an unfair implementation of the system that is protested. For example, the system was perceived of as unfair in the case where a woman who married a divorcee, who already had a child from a previous marriage, could not obtain a first-child birth permit. In another case, a Beijing woman was obviously angry on behalf of her friend at what she perceived as the unfairness of policy implementation. Her friend was a 40 year old unmarried woman who wanted to adopt her brother's child so that he and his wife could then have her share of the birth plan quota. As an unmarried woman, however, she was not eligible for a share of the quota, so she had no share to give away.[39]

Women do not question the structure of policy implementation itself. The only possible way of avoiding control is to leave the work unit. Control and monitoring are an integral part of everyday life, which women do not question, and with which they are familiar as the tight system of control from above to below and upwards again in the form of reporting on colleagues and neighbours is a reproduction of the overall political organization at the workplace.[40] Women felt that birth planning work was being handled 'relatively severely' and 'very severely' both at residential areas and at work units. However, they were also aware that birth planning workers were merely doing their job according to orders they had received from higher levels. Responding to the question of what she thought about the visits in her home to monitor contraceptive practice, one Beijing woman said: 'I do not have any opinion. Usually I am quite cooperative, as this is just routine business.'[41]

The system of penalties is not questioned either. Penalties are accepted as a logical consequence of the overall policy requirement of having only one child, and as the overall policy framework is accepted unquestioningly, so is the system of penalties. Just as women choose to stay within the work unit, and therefore to accept the control that is part of work unit care, they choose to use an IUD in view of the consequences of not following the advocacy of birth planning workers. Women do not question the system of penalties; they adapt their actions to fit the system in the sense that if a woman wants to avoid penalties she must use an IUD.

Control as care is a reciprocal relationship. The employee is dependent upon the work unit and therefore is culturally obliged to be compliant. The functioning of the reciprocal relationship is dependent not only on the work unit supplying care, but also on a perception of equity, implying that as long as control is universal the reciprocal system is accepted. Sulamith Heins Potter and Jack M. Potter write of policy implementation in the village of Zengbu that

no one should receive an unfair advantage. This is a crucial element of the villagers' definition of justice. They will accept an unpopular policy if the hardship appears to be equally shared. However, if they think that some people are receiving privileges denied to others, they will resent it so much as to threaten the possibility of enforcing the policy.[42]

In this context it is significant that birth planning workers are themselves the mothers of only one child, as women would be unlikely to accept being controlled by someone who had not herself had to comply to the policy.

On the other hand, there is little sympathy with those women who attempt to have a second child. When private entrepreneurs are able to have more than one child, not only because they have the economic means to pay the economic penalties, but also because they are not subject to a reciprocal relationship with a work unit, the result is dissatisfaction among those who are subject to these limits. The ultimate consequence is that they will feel released of their cultural obligation of reciprocity. Control is therefore practised not only to ensure that the individual woman does not give birth to more than one child, but also to avoid the risk that others will follow the example of the couple who does have a second child, and to prevent those with only one child from becoming dissatisfied with having to follow the policy while others are exempt from it. In this way the control being exercised is also an expression of state and work unit care towards employees, because tight control ensures that everyone is subject to the policy fertility limit. Furthermore, tight control and the insurance that everyone is subject to the policy limit is a prerequisite for the functioning of the cultural assumption of reciprocity.

Conclusion

The majority of women are not happy with the one child limit—they would prefer two children. However, they give birth to only one child and they accept implementation measures. There are, however, some exceptions. One woman at whose work unit IUD insertion was compulsory after the birth of one child was explicitly resentful that she could not herself decide what kind of contraceptive method she wished to use. In her opinion, it should be up to her to decide as long as she did not give birth to a second child, which, she said, she had absolutely no intention of doing. At another work unit women had been required to take a test on their knowledge of the one-child family policy, and they had been required once again, as they had already signed a one-child certificate, to sign a declaration stating that they would not give birth to a second child. These women do not question the one-child policy itself; they do, however, question the way in which it is being implemented at their particular workplace. They express resentment and indignation that they are being controlled, as they have already pledged to have only one child. They feel capable of keeping the pledge themselves, and regard the control, in the form of compulsory IUDs, tests, and pledges, as unnecessary. The woman

at whose unit IUDs are compulsory had no means of avoiding the requirement, just as the women who were given a test did not have the option of
not handing in completed forms. They had protested against the test by
letting one woman in their office fill in the test forms of all eight women.
A similar form of silent protest by non-action was practised by a woman
who deliberately has avoided taking part in the annual gynaecological
check-ups for two years. She does so simply by ignoring the request of the
birth planning worker that she take part. She does not say that she is
unable to take part or that she does not intend to: on the contrary, she
assures the birth planning worker that she will attend. Not only does she
not take part in the annual check-ups, she is not using an IUD, although
birth planning workers have tried to make her use one and have repri-
manded her. In her present job, she is is not often present at the work unit,
so as she remarks: 'Nobody keeps an eye on me. I have not taken part in
the check-ups these past two years because I don't feel I have any health
problems. Also, sometimes I am busy working, so who cares.'[43] The two
years in which she has not taken part in the check-ups correspond to the
two years she has had her present job, in which her work does not take
place at the unit itself. She has thus been out of the reach of the daily work
unit birth planning control system.

There are very few means of evading the control system. One of them is
to be, like this Beijing woman, physically out of the sight and reach of daily
work unit control; another is to evade the annual check-ups. Other women
who did not articulate their antipathy as precisely as this woman were
probably also evading control when they did not attend the check-ups, just
as physiological reasons were certainly used as an excuse not to use an
IUD, in the context that no other exception to its required use was made
by birth planning workers.

In these examples of (1) resenting the compulsory IUD use, (2) protesting against the population policy knowledge test, (3) avoiding having an
IUD inserted, and (4) avoiding the gynaecological check-up, women are
silently protesting at being controlled and are applying a strategy of avoidance (non-action). However, it is not the policy itself or the policy requirement of one child that is being contested. Just as the leadership has
criticized coercive practices that take place locally from time to time in
implementing the policy, women are criticizing not the policy itself but
local-level implementation practice. In these examples, contrary to the
experience of the majority of women, control is viewed as control, not as
care.

The cultural meaning of acceptance—of control as care—with which
the majority of the urban women studied perceive of policy implementation, differs fundamentally from the human rights definition of family

planning as an individual right. However, although the protest that women do express, in a silent form of avoidance, is aimed at the implementation level of population policy rather than at the policy itself, the reactions of these few women, for whom control is not viewed as care, suggests that a change is taking place in the cultural assumptions within which women perceive of control. This might be an indication of the cracks that, according to Lucien Pye, are appearing both in the public's awe of state authority and in the general hostility towards individualism.[44]

Coercion becomes care; strict control of only one child per couple has become quite natural, and is taken for granted in the context that control is universal. The women whose children are about 10 years old or older would not be likely to have a second child even if a change of policy did take place, whereas many of the younger women whose children are small would have a second child if it were possible. One woman estimates that 85 per cent of women at her workplace would prefer two children, and the Beijing factory birth planning cadre says that sometimes women jokingly whisper to her that if the policy is relaxed to allow for the birth of a second child, she must let them know first. The importance the nation attaches to the population policy is recognized, and the necessity of the policy is accepted by women. None the less, as one woman remarks: 'If birth planning workers don't keep a strict eye on the signing of one-child certificates and contraceptive practice and you yourself are not quite attentive, it is easy to become pregnant.'[45]

National interests and the population policy are accepted only in so far as the state, represented by the work unit and residential area control network, is strong enough to ensure that the policy is followed. Until recently—from as far back as the Beijing factory birth planning cadre remembers up until 1990—confirmation from the work unit that a woman had reached the age of late marriage was sufficient for the street committee office to issue a birth permit. However, restrictions are now more severe. One of the reasons for tighter control is that some people would pretend to be ignorant of the rules and, for instance, a woman who was marrying for the first time would not inform birth planning workers that her husband was marrying for the second time and already had a child from the previous marriage. Now, with the new rules on tighter control, both the woman and her future husband must obtain certificates from their work units specifically indicating whether or not the marriage in question is a first marriage. As the Shenyang factory birth planning cadre noted, the control system is effective because there are no leaks. However, as soon as there is a weakness in the system, a leak or a crack through which someone manages to pass, others will follow, because the basis for the culturally assumed reciprocity will then have been undermined.

NOTES

1. This paper is based on a chapter in the author's Ph.D. dissertation, 'Accepting Population Control: the Perspective of Urban Chinese Women on the One-Child Family Policy', University of Copenhagen, October 1994, now published as *Accepting Population Control: Urban Chinese Women and the One-Child Family Policy* (Richmond, Surrey: Curzon Press, 1997). My thanks to the Nordic Institute of Asian Studies and the Curzon Press for permission to incorporate this material.

2. *Zhonghua renmin gongheguo funü quanyi baozhang fa* (Law of the People's Republic of China on the Protection of Rights and Interests of Women), ch. VII, art. 47. Adopted at the Fifth Session of the Seventh National People's Congress on 3 April 1992.

3. *Proclamation of Teheran on Human Rights* (New York: UN Office of Public Information, 1968). The Proclamation stated that 'parents have a basic human right to determine freely and responsibly the number and spacing of their children' (para. 16). This definition of family planning was included in the revised Charter of Human Rights in 1968. Subsequently the statement, with the substitution of 'individuals and couples' for 'parents' and the addition of the important phrase 'and to the information and the means to do so', was reaffirmed by, among others, the World Population Conference in 1974, the International Conference on Population in 1984, and the Conference on the Decade for Women in 1985: UNFPA, *The State of World Population* (New York: UN Population Fund, 1991), 10. The Convention on the Elimination of all forms of Discrimination Against Women (CEDAW), the platform from which the 1995 Fourth World Conference on Women was held, also includes the statement.

4. For an elaboration on the concepts of reproductive rights, reproductive health, and reproductive self determination, see Betsy Hartmann, *Reproductive Rights and Wrongs* (New York: Harper & Row, 1987) and Ruth Dixon-Mueller, *Population Policy and Women's Rights: Transforming Reproductive Choice* (Westport, Conn.: Praeger, 1993).

5. Katarina Tomaševski, *Human Rights in Population Policies* (Lund: Swedish International Development Agency (SIDA), 1994), 7–8.

6. See John S. Arid, *Slaughter of the Innocents* (Washington: AEI Press, 1990) and Judith Banister, *China's Changing Population* (Stanford: Stanford University Press, 1987).

7. Chen Muhua, 'Shixian sige xiandaihua, bixu you jihua de kongzhi renkou zengzhang' (Planned Control of Population Increase is Necessary for Realization of the Four Modernizations), *Renmin ribao*, 11 November 1979, translated and commented by Pichao Chen in *International Family Planning Perspectives*, 5:3 (September 1979), 92–100. See also *Human Rights in China* (Beijing: Information Office of the State Council of the People's Republic of China, 1991).

8. See Tyrene White (ed.), 'Family Planning in China', *Chinese Sociology and Anthropology*, 24(3) (Spring 1992), 36.

9. Sylvia Estrada-Claudio, 'Strengthening Women's Voices in Southeast, East and North Asia', Keynote Address to the First Organizational Meeting for a Woman and Health Network in the Southeast, East and North Asian Region', 1–5 December 1993, Los Banos, Philippines.

10. In the five city districts of Shenyang, the percentage of first-child births in 1988 was 98.03, 98.54, 97.74, 98.20 and 98.54. Permission was given for less than 200 second-child births, and only 17 children were born without permission. See *Laioning sheng renkou tongji nianjian 1988* (Population Statistical Yearbook of Liaoning Province,

110   *Interaction between Urban Women and Birth Planning Workers*

1988) (Liaoning, 1989). In the city district studied in Beijing, in the early 1980s there was already a high rate of first births. In 1981 there were 197,562 women of reproductive age: of these, 187,859 did not give birth. Of the 9,703 births, 9,463 were first births, 232 were second births, seven were third and one was a fourth birth: *Beijing sishi nian 1949–1989* (Beijing Forty Years, 1949–1989) (Beijing: Zhongguo tongji chubanshe, 1990).

11. Literally, *xuanchuan jiaoyu* means propaganda education, i.e. education via propaganda.
12. Chen, 'Shixian sige xiandaihua'.
13. These programmes include the 1950 Marriage Law, the law regarding labour insurance, the effort to outlaw the use of opium and suppress prostitution, programmes of social assistance as well as efforts to improve health and offer universal education: see Joyce K. Kallgren, 'Politics, Welfare, and Change: The Single-Child Family in China', in Elizabeth J. Perry and Christine Wong (eds.), *The Political Economy of Reform in Post-Mao China* (Cambridge, Mass.: Harvard University Press, 1985).
14. For a discussion of the campaign to implement the one-child family policy as a continuation of the pre-1978 political practice of mobilization of the party and mass organizations to take a lead in implementation, as well as the skilful and massive use of the propaganda apparatus, see Tyrene White, 'Postrevolutionary Mobilization in China: The One-Child Policy Reconsidered', *World Politics*, 43:1 (October 1990), 53–76.
15. Kallgren, 'Politics, Welfare, and Change', 134–5.
16. Wang Nairong, 'Wo guo kongzhi renkou zengzhang zhengce de jige wenti' (Some Questions related to the Policy of Controlling Population Increase), *Renkou Yanjiu*, 2 (1981), 51–5.
17. Interview with Beijing birth planning cadre, 13 July 1991 (BIO.001.130791). (Interview codes: B = Beijing or L = Liaoning; I = birth planning institution official or W = woman; O = officially arranged interview; 001 = interview number which may be prefixed by J = residential area or F = factory; 130791 = interview date.)
18. For an account of the structure and work of the Beijing Family Planning Commission in implementing the one-child family policy in the early 1980s, see Elisabeth Croll, 'The Single-Child Family in Beijing: A First-Hand Report', in Elisabeth Croll, Delia Davin, and Penny Kane (eds.), *China's One-Child Family Policy* (London: Macmillan, 1985). I would prefer to translate the Beijing Family Planning Commission (*Beijingshi jihua shengyu weiyuanhui*) as the Beijing Birth Planning Commission, not only because birth planning is the literal translation of *jihua shengyu*, but mainly because the term 'family planning' as a human right is not compatible with the Chinese concept of birth planning. I have, none the less, followed the practice of applying the official Chinese translation in order not to create confusion. For lower levels of the birth planning institution I have used 'birth planning' for *jihua shengyu*.
19. See Li Muzhen, *Zhongguo renkou: Beijing fence* (China Population Series: Beijing volume) (Beijing: China Financial and Economic Publishing House, 1987), 412.
20. See also Hong Yung Lee, *From Revolutionary Cadres to Party Technocrats in Socialist China* (Berkeley: University of California Press, 1991), 359–60.
21. Interview with Beijing birth planning cadre, 8 June 1992 (BIO.F01.080692) and personal communication from Chinese scholar, 1992.
22. The Chinese word *dongyuan* is translated 'to persuade'. *Zuo gongzuo*, which literally means 'to do work', is translated 'to convince'. *Zuo sixiang gongzuo*, literally 'to do thought work', is translated 'to do ideological work', which also means 'to convince'. *Dongyuan*, *zuo gongzuo*, and *zuo sixiang gongzuo* all designate 'to cause or

induce someone to have a certain belief', or 'to cause or induce someone into a certain action'.

23. Interview with Beijing birth planning cadre, 13 July 1991 (BIO.001.130791).
24. This form of persuasion is not an innovation of the new order, but rather a traditional process. For a description of how persuasion was used in a village during the collectivization process, see Sulamith Heins Potter and Jack M. Potter, *China's Peasants* (Cambridge: Cambridge University Press, 1990), 65.
25. None of the birth planning workers mentioned that their work was in any way aimed at male employees or residents, just as the women themselves generally took it for granted that they alone were responsible for not becoming pregnant.
26. In 1981, 69.46% of women of reproductive age in China were using contraceptives. Of these 50.20% were using the IUD, while 25.40% had been sterilized (tubal ligation). In 1987, 71.21% of women of reproductive age were using contraceptives, with 41.48% of these using an IUD and 38.24% having been sterilized. The percentage of men who were sterilized (vasectomy) was 10% in 1982 and 10.99% in 1987: Zhu Chuzhu, 'Gaige beijing xia de Zhongguo nüxing renkou' (China's Female Population During the Reforms), in Wu Cangping (ed.), *Gaige kaifang yu renkou fazhan* (Reforms and Population Development) (Shenyang: Liaoning Daxue Chubanshe, 1990), 272–83.
27. Interview with Liaoning worker, 3 April 1992 (LWO.F04.030492).
28. Interview with Liaoning birth planning worker, 2 April 1992 (LIO.F01.020492).
29. In connection with the concern that women should not be subjected to abortion, it is worth noting that abortion is often performed without the use of anaesthetics. The birth planning cadre at the Beijing factory does not know why anaesthetics are not used. She assumes, however, that the reason is that the pain is not unbearable, as an abortion, in her opinion, is less painful than delivery. Interview with Beijing birth planning cadre, 8 June 1992 (BIO.F01.080692).
30. *Zhaogu* and *guanxin* both mean care. *Guanxin* is translated as 'to be concerned with, show solicitude for; to be interested in; to care for': *Hanying Cidian* (Chinese-English Dictionary) Beijing: Beijing Waiguoyu Xueyuan, Yingyu Xi, 1981). *Zhaogu* is translated as '(1) to give consideration to; to show consideration for; to make allowance(s) for, or (2) to look after; to care for; to attend to': *Hanying cidian* (1981), 881. The distinction between the two forms of care and concern is that *zhaogu* involves a more practical form of care whereas *guanxin* is primarily verbally expressed concern. To distinguish between the two forms, *zhaogu* is translated as 'care', *guanxin* is translated as 'concern'.
31. Interview with Beijing woman, 18 May 1992 (BWO.J02.180592).
32. Shen Guoxiang, 'Jinyibu fahui xuanchuan jiaoyu zai jihua shengyu gongzuo zhong de zhongyao zuoyong' (Further Promote the Important Role of Ideological Education Within Birth Planning Work), in Zhang Pei and Chen Manping (eds.), *Zhongguo jihua shengyu de weida shijian* (Beijing: Zhongguo renkou chubanshe, 1990).
33. Translated from Document no. 7 in White, *Chinese Sociology*, 38.
34. Interview with Liaoning birth planning worker, 2 April 1992 (LIO.F01.020492).
35. Andrew G. Walder, *Communist Neo-Traditionalism* (Berkeley: University of California Press, 1986).
36. Interview with Beijing woman, 18 May 1992 (BWO.J04.180592).
37. Lung-kee Sun 'Contemporary Chinese Culture: Structure and Emotionality', *Australian Journal of Chinese Affairs*, 26 (July 1991), 1–41.
38. ibid.
39. Interview with Beijing woman, 16 May 1992 (BWO.J02.160592).
40. For an account of the political control system at the workplace, see Walder,

Communist Neo-Traditionalism, 19. Walder also writes about how work unit political control has changed from the Mao era to the reform era: Andrew G. Walder, 'Workers, Managers and the State: The Reform Era and the Political Crisis of 1989', *The China Quarterly*, 127 (September 1991), 465–92. Although political control mechanisms have changed, the basic structures of control are still being used within birth planning work.

41. Interview with Beijing woman, 18 May 1992 (BWO.J03.180692).
42. Potter and Potter, *China's Peasants*. The significance of the equity issue has been mentioned in quite a different context by Andrew Walder. One of the factors that gave rise to worker support of the 1989 student movement was that workers were dissatisfied because they felt that other groups—private entrepreneurs, suburban peasants, and cadres and their families—had better work, better wages, and more benefits than the average worker: see Walder, 'Workers, Managers and the State'.
43. Interview with Beijing woman, 18 May 1992 (BWO.J03.180592).
44. Lucien W. Pye, 'The State and the Individual: An Overview Interpretation', *The China Quarterly*, 127 (September 1991), 443–66.
45. Interview with Beijing woman, 18 May 1992 (BWO.J04.180592).

5

Ownership and Community Interests in China's Rural Enterprises

Susan Young[1]

Introduction

The pressing contrast between state and non-state performance in China's economic reforms, against the background of the proposed wholesale dismantling of the state economy in the former socialist countries of Eastern Europe, made ownership reform an inescapable issue for China by the late 1980s. Unavoidably, much of the debate was informed by the stark progression in economic performance from state enterprises, which responded only sluggishly to reforms, to the dynamic rural collective enterprises, to the newly revived private sector, which showed the fastest growth of all. When all is said and done, the ongoing efforts to reform state enterprises have basically centred around the problem of how to make them behave as much like private enterprises as possible, without actually privatizing them.

China, nevertheless, insists that it is not going down the capitalist road. What looks like capitalism is in fact 'socialism with Chinese characteristics'. Even when China had abandoned the idea that central planning should steer the economy and officially espoused the aim of developing a market economy, this was still 'market socialism' and not to be confused with privatization. It was argued that things which capitalism had long claimed for its own—a market-regulated economy, private ownership, exploitation of labour, stock markets, rampant consumerism—either were neutral techniques which were the common inheritance of all humanity, or were rendered neutral by the dominance of the socialist system.

It is easy to be cynical about these claims. There is, surely, little room for the expression of socialist goals in a collectively owned enterprise handed over to a private individual for rent. Bosses who earn forty times what they pay their employees look pretty much the same under an avowedly socialist government as under any other. And as for the wholesome influence of the socialist state, the Chinese state has been having enough trouble controlling the supplies, prices, and taxation of state enterprises, let alone exerting effective control over the non-state sectors. On another level, some observers have seen these very phenomena as signs of the growing strength of market forces, which, once allowed to take root in the economy, inevitably exert pressures for further progression (and I use the word advisedly) towards something like a Western-style capitalist system. Victor Nee's analysis of the forces at work in reforming rural China argues that the market economy demands a rationalization of economic administration,[2] while many analysts, including Brødsgaard and Gold in this volume, see the market economy and private entrepreneurs as forces for the potential creation of civil society.

In the literature on the problem of the transition away from Soviet-style central planning, extensive privatization has generally been seen as fundamental to the successful establishment and operation of a market economy.[3] The kind of system envisaged in China's goal of 'market socialism'—dominated by state ownership and yet still market-led—is seen as unsustainable and inimical to genuine market reform. This school of thought, heavily influenced by the work of Janos Kornai, argues that state-owned enterprises will not be effectively market-oriented because they will remain burdened by the external interests of the state and, in return, cushioned by the state's willingness to bail them out of financial difficulty.[4] Another factor is the association of the soft budget constraint with rent-seeking by officials in predominantly state-owned economies, which adds weight to the argument that privatization is absolutely vital for effective market reforms.[5] In keeping with an economic ideology that goes all the way back to Adam Smith, not only Western and Eastern European analysts but also the Chinese reformers themselves see the clarification of property rights and the removal of government officials from direct involvement in economic enterprise as fundamental requirements of improved efficiency.

And yet, in China's dynamic rural industrial sector, although private investment and management have played a significant role, the various experiments in reforming economic management in rural enterprises are far from constituting privatization as it is commonly understood. Even private enterprises, an increasingly important part of the rural economy, are very different from those in capitalist systems. Local government officials, far from having to be prevented from obstructing enterprises' interaction with market forces, have positioned themselves precisely where enterprises and markets meet. They are the brokers between enterprises and the world of wider opportunities, assisting enterprises in reaching new markets, obtaining funds, key raw materials and premises, and improving technology. Ownership rights in enterprises are far from being either clarified or guaranteed, and the formal ownership status of an enterprise may bear little relation to the real conditions of its operation. This is partly because of centrally directed political and regulatory constraints, but more intrinsically not so much because of socialist regulation, but because of a lack of it. In the poorly regulated, highly personalized environment of the reforms, ownership is less important than control, and rights less important than obligations.

The policy changes and fiscal reforms of the 1980s gave rural adminis-trations, especially at township and village level, extensive new freedoms to manage their own economies. At the same time as restrictions on entre-preneurial activity were reduced, the wide price gap between raw materi-als and processed goods and the abundance of cheap labour provided numerous opportunities to develop rural industry. For political and logis-tical reasons, however, official policies and regulations could not keep up with the rapid changes in the rural economy, and therefore local officials used the discretion given to them by reform policies to work out a variety of ways of harnessing economic forces. The increased localization of economic decision-making, in the context of China's closely knit rural communities, has given local officials opportunities both to bend reform policies to serve local community goals (or their own, personal goals), and to exert extensive influence over the operation of enterprises of all owner-ship types.

The following discussion illustrates this by looking at a variety of enter-prise types in rural China. It is based mainly on material from interviews in China in early 1992 and late 1993. The 1992 trip included visits to a vari-ety of enterprises in three rural counties—Xindu, Anyue, and Dazu—in Sichuan province, concentrating on one village or township in each county and interviewing enterprises' managers and officials at county, township, and village level. Although some of the interviewees were personal con-tacts and were very helpful, the time spent in each county was only a few days, and it is impossible to reach any firm conclusions on the basis of the few examples seen. In any case, conditions in China are so varied from one region to another that it is dangerous to rest all such conclusions on local-ized research, however exhaustive. In the context of a wider view of the reform process in China, however, even superficial studies can provide valuable insights into the problems and prospects of China's development.

How 'Private' is Rural Private Enterprise?

According to official statistics, the acknowledged private sector has played an important role in the development of China's rural industry and commerce. Although around 90 per cent of rural enterprises are registered as privately owned, they are mostly small household concerns and produced only 27 per cent of the total gross output value of rural enterprises in 1993.[6] Their sheer number, however, means that they provided 47 per cent of jobs in non-agricultural enterprises in 1994,[7] and are of key importance in distributing both productive and service-related industry much more widely than would otherwise occur. Furthermore, investment in fixed assets by the rural private sector was only some 26 per cent less than by rural collective enterprises in 1994, and was climbing at a faster rate.[8]

The official statistics are certain to be understating the volume of business handled by private businesses: most are small and difficult for authorities to monitor, and there are strong incentives for under-reporting both by private businesses and by local governments themselves, which can still access unreported profits through unscheduled, off-budget charges.[9] There are also many temporary or unlicenced private businesses which do not get into the statistics; on one occasion just such an enterprise, unregistered even though it had an established workshop and machinery and had been operating for several months, was included by officials themselves on the list we were to visit. This was in Dazu county's Longshui district in 1992, where a rapid revival of the traditional local industry of knife-making could be seen in action in virtually every doorway and courtyard. Faced with this phenomenon, local officials were far more concerned with how to encourage and strengthen it than how to count it.

Throughout the 1980s, the attitude of the Chinese Communist Party (CCP) to the developing private sector remained equivocal, and this had a profound effect on the pattern of private entrepreneurship and the ways in which it was incorporated into the reforms.[10] In the case of rural China, private operators in sectors such as commerce, transport, and construction were a significant force in spreading the impact of the household responsibility system beyond the relatively developed, accessible areas more easily served by collective enterprise. Private, household operation was an obvious way of mobilizing investment for the small-scale, low-capital ventures that formed the basis for further development in many areas and which made up the majority of new businesses as the reforms took effect. On the other hand, the CCP had just spent over thirty years working to eradicate the 'petty peasant proprietorship' that Lenin had warned against and to establish a collectivist, egalitarian ethos in its place.

Hence, although in many places rural private business actually developed faster, and was more readily accepted, than in the cities, its emergence in publicized policy was slowed. The State Council regulations on urban household businesses (*getihu*) issued in 1981, which allowed private non-agricultural businesses with up to seven employees, applied in principle to rural businesses also.[11] It was not until 1984, however, that regulations were issued specifically for rural *getihu*.[12] Key rural policy documents in 1984 also acknowledged the existence and economic contribution of private businesses exceeding the seven-employee limit (they had in fact appeared in academic and policy discussions as early as 1981), but these were not to be formally regulated for until 1988.[13] This did not mean that private enterprise was not developing in rural areas, but that it had to be accommodated informally, amid continued uncertainty about its political and administrative status. This meant that, in addition to the private businesses which, whether licenced or unlicenced, were acknowledged to be private, a great deal of private entrepreneurship (in the sense of investment by individuals of personal funds for private profit) was included, one way or another, in the 'collective' sector. Oddly enough, this covert development pattern actually contributed to the successful utilization of private investment in rural China, in the political conditions prevailing at the time: since it did not have to be acknowledged as 'private' , it could be allowed to go ahead long before the CCP's formal ideology had adjusted enough for its open acceptance.

The first avenue for this to occur was within the household responsibility system itself. Here the development of 'specialized households' (*zhuanyehu*)—households in which alternative business activities replaced agriculture as the main source of income—provided a less controversial space for developing private business, since *zhuanyehu* were still considered to be 'a management level within the cooperative economy'.[14] The same kind of fudging of the ownership issue occurred in the case of joint enterprises between two or more households (*lianhu*). In such enterprises the ownership and control of the assets and profits after tax obligations were held privately by the joint investors, and if such an enterprise were to employ over seven people it would also fit the definition of a private enterprise in the 1988 regulations. But from another point of view, *lianhu* can be seen as cooperative ventures between villagers. This has enabled local officials, if they wished, to treat such enterprises as part of the collective sector in matters such as new business approvals, loans, and the like. For example, in Longshui, where small-scale businesses had been very important to local economic growth, forming a *lianhu* by taking on a sleeping partner enabled private operators to expand and, especially, take on more employees without confronting the constraints aimed at limiting private enterprise growth.

In theory, *lianhu* were subject to restraints on their management such as having to reinvest at least 60 per cent of profits in the enterprise; but the accounts of most of these enterprises were far from reliable, and it was clear that in Longshui they were still allowed a great deal of freedom. With limited resources, the township government would have had difficulty in monitoring and regulating its many small enterprises in accordance with central regulations, but it chose not to let this delay their development. It is important to note, however, that the freedom and degree of ownership autonomy allowed these enterprises was not held as a right, but was given by the local government at its own discretion, because this suited its priorities at the time.

Some of the other ways for private entrepreneurs to obtain collective-sector status again placed them at the mercy of local officials. Some paid an 'administration fee' to a state or collective enterprise, township, or village, and used its name to be registered as being township or village-run. In the late 1980s there was much discussion of this in terms of private entrepreneurs running 'fake collectives' and thereby unfairly taking advantage of tax relief and other benefits aimed at developing the collective sector. Such enterprises were targeted as part of the clean-up campaign aimed at increasing central control over economic administration and improving tax collection which was launched in late 1988, but as far as clarifying their ownership registration went it was not very effective.[15]

A more subtle method of obtaining collective status—sometimes adopted in order to ward off the threat of expropriation by the local government—has been to add 'collective' features to the enterprise's operation, most commonly by issuing 'shares' to employees. In several enterprises I visited in Sichuan in 1988 and 1992, the owners had made a small issue of non-voting, non-transferable shares to staff, and used this to justify their claim to collective status. In effect, the shares were simply an entitlement to year-end bonuses tied to profits, in some cases based on a contribution paid by new employees in order to obtain the job in the first place, as was also a common practice in enterprises genuinely run by the township or village.[16] These enterprises clearly had the cooperation of local authorities in maintaining their collective registration. They were relatively large, successful enterprises contributing significantly to the local economy, and it was easier to support them if they had collective status. Enterprises that have instituted some sort of share system are not seen as 'fake' collectives, but they are also different from the traditional collective-sector enterprises owned by villages or townships. At the discretion of local officials, they may or may not be required to conform to regulations stipulating, among other things, the proportions of after-tax profits to be invested in production and staff or community welfare, but they do not hand over profits directly to the township or village. Politically, they are part of the collective economy; how much a part of it they are administratively is very much dependent on local officials.

Collective status is important not only for political reasons. Larger enterprises nearly always need local government backing to get the land, equipment, supplies, finance, contacts, and approvals they need to operate. In these matters, openly 'private' enterprises have been subject to discriminatory practices aimed at maintaining the dominance of the public sector. (For example, their access to limited goods and bank loans is usually restricted, and wholesale and import opportunities, released only slowly to the private sector in the first place, were quickly revoked in the effort to strengthen state economic control in 1988–9.) In a system where markets have not fully replaced the state distribution network, at least some direct administrative cooperation is usually necessary to do business on a large scale. One entrepreneur interviewed in 1992 said that this was changing as market forces were strengthened in China, and that, whereas he used to have trouble doing business because his was a private enterprise, now 'Never mind about socialism, whether you are a socialist enterprise or not. What people really care about is money.' Nevertheless, his was still a 'share' enterprise (in which the shares were owned by relatives), so that it was formally regarded as collective.

The support of local governments, and cooperation in collective registration, is not given without strings attached. As Jan Winiecki points out, the widespread opposition and obstructive behaviour of officials in reforming Soviet-style economies that attempt to promote a private sector is not solely, or even mainly, about ideology: it is about control.[17] Even small-scale private businesses, by providing their operators with an alternative source of income and their customers with alternative sources of goods and services, present an undeniable challenge to the systems for official rent-seeking and socioeconomic control established within the public sector. But in rural China under the post-Mao reforms, the combination of pressing economic imperatives and increased administrative discretion gave local officials another option: instead of opposing private business as a threat to their collective-sector fiefdoms, they could, if they chose, use the chronically uncertain position of private enterprise to enhance their power over it and co-opt it into serving their ends.[18]

Although some private enterprises are able to operate successfully while remaining registered as such, very few are able to grow significantly without local government and community support, and to get this they must be seen to contribute to the community. Of course, they may do this simply by providing employment, paying taxes, and enhancing local economic growth; but the pressure generated by their political position also causes many entrepreneurs to make more visible contributions as well. Not only direct pressure from local officials, but also community opinion and the desire to improve their standing, leads private entrepreneurs to donate large sums towards improving local welfare. Common examples cited in the press include donations to schools and environmental improvement programmes, although it must be said that these press reports are aimed as much at encouraging more private entrepreneurs to donate as at reporting on those who already have. Donations to such projects are not always exactly spontaneous; when I asked one private entrepreneur in Sichuan, in the presence of local officials, whether he felt pressured to make such contributions, he scarcely had the chance to reply before an official jumped in with the statement that local entrepreneurs were all so public-spirited that township officials had merely to mention a project in need of funds, and the entrepreneurs would do the right thing.

The pressure can also extend to the internal management of private enterprises, which, like their collective-sector counterparts, may be pressured to provide jobs or free goods and services either to poorer villagers or to officials' relatives, or to provide training so that others in the community can get rich too. Ole Odgaard, for example, describes several instances of private entrepreneurs being forced by community pressure—including direct action such as vandalism and theft—to adopt a more public-spirited business style that shared some of the gains from entrepreneurial success.[19] Collective-sector registration does not in any way alter these obligations. In my experience, all enterprises started and operated by private individuals or partners are referred to locally as private (*geti* or *siying*) enterprises: their formal collective or cooperative status merely denotes a closer relationship with local government, with attendant constraints as well as advantages.

Indeed, the reliance of such arrangements on the goodwill of local officials gives them a further source of leverage over these enterprises. Some private entrepreneurs who obtained collective registration for their enterprises have found themselves required to live up to it by handing over a percentage of gross profits, or have even been forced to hand over the whole enterprise when local governments decided to claim real ownership.[20] Although both openly private and 'fake collective' private entrepreneurs generally still retain the bulk of profits for themselves, their contribution to the local community can sometimes be on a very similar scale to that formally required of township and village enterprises.[21] For local governments, there are actually certain advantages to having private enterprises contribute on an informal basis, since such contributions will generally not appear in budgets handed to higher levels. This is another aspect of the control issue in connection with the development of private enterprise: local governments have been able to use the powers handed to them by the reform process to generate particularistic relationships with private entrepreneurs on their own terms, not necessarily those of central regulations. In late 1988 and 1989, the central government made an effort to gain more control over this situation by launching a drive to clear up ownership registration and, in particular, force private enterprises to register as such. When officials in Longshui were asked how this work was progressing, however, they professed complete ignorance of the finer points of ownership and spoke as if it were simply not an issue. The State Bureau of Industry and Commerce (ICB), the organization responsible for the registration drive, had a more limited role in Longshui than in many places: even the getihu paid their administration fees (if they paid any) to the Township and Village Enterprise Bureau, and the ICB was largely restricted to administering the area's important wholesale markets.

Separating Ownership and Management: How 'Collective' are Collective Enterprises?

At the same time as the private sector was developing and being absorbed into the rural collective network, the nature of this collective sector was also changing. In spite of their theoretical status as the collective property of the residents of the township or village, township and village enterprises are effectively owned by local governments at these levels: they are in fact local state enterprises.[22] If rural township and village enterprises are lumped together as part of 'the state sector', however, it is easy to downplay the importance of these enterprises in providing local governments with increased independence from higher levels of 'the state'.[23] Although they do not have anywhere near the same level of direct social welfare obligations to their employees as do those labelled 'state' enterprises in the Chinese terminology, township and village enterprises are never the less vitally important to community welfare, both as providers of better-paid jobs and as a source of revenue for local government. During the 1980s reformers, influenced both by Western economic theories and by the history of government involvement in industry in China, advocated increased separation of enterprise management from governments. Just as the household responsibility system was providing a way of introducing what was essentially private management without formally privatizing land ownership, various forms of contracting and leasing of collective enterprises were introduced to do the same in enterprises.

The aim of contracting or leasing enterprise management to individuals or worker groups was to 'prevent the enterprise from being a branch of politics, which helps increase the enterprise's vigour and deal with the problems of enterprise autonomy and responsibility for profits and losses'.[24] But the whole point of collective enterprises is to serve community interests, and the specific arrangements made have varied according to how those interests are perceived in different communities and with respect to different enterprises within a community. In some cases enterprises have been virtually privatized, and leasing has been an important source of starting capital for private entrepreneurs.[25] Interviews in Sichuan suggested that this was more commonly the case with smaller enterprises, typically former production team enterprises that were contracted out to the people who had started them up in the first place. These would be the subjects of 'one big kick' contracting (*yi jiao ti*), which was actually renting or even, in terms of the end result, renting-to-buy. In other cases, particularly with larger enterprises, local governments have been unwilling to hand over management rights in any meaningful way.

From the mid-1980s onwards there was an extensive debate in China about whether or not individual contracting would lead to privatization, especially since in some cases contract managers went on to invest their profits in the same enterprise.[26] It was a difficult problem: if enterprise operators were successful enough to accumulate funds and felt secure enough to invest them in the enterprise, surely this was a good thing for local economic growth. On the other hand, weren't these very funds capital accumulated at the expense of the collective—indeed, at the expense of employees who were theoretically the part-owners of the enterprise?

As with most of these thorny ideological questions, in practice it was easier just to skirt around the issue and let economic considerations guide decisions. In fact, it is rare for a contract manager formally to sever relations with the collective. More often, the enterprise retains its official, advantageous 'collective' status while the rights to its ownership and management become extremely unclear, a matter of informal understandings reached over the years rather than what is written down on paper. An example is an enterprise visited by the author in Sichuan in 1992. The enterprise was introduced by our hosts, the township enterprise office, as a village-run enterprise. It had been founded in 1973 by several production-team members as a small furniture workshop, the premises being the current manager's private house. (In another era, this would have been called a private business.) In 1982 the brigade invested some 300 yuan to upgrade it to a production workshop making folding furniture. In 1983 it employed eleven people and had an output value of 100,000 yuan. In 1984 the manager contracted to run the enterprise, and by 1992 he paid the village an agreed rent of 5,000 yuan per year and ran the enterprise independently. Since 1984 he had built up fixed assets worth at least 400,000 yuan, including a foundry making rail trucks for the local coal-mining industry, but at this point in our interview the narrative became very obscure and he did not want to reveal an exact amount. On the question of profits, he claimed, amid disbelieving laughter from the assembled officials, who thought he was understating the case somewhat, that his 1991 profit on a gross output value of 860,000 yuan was 20,000 yuan.

The question of ownership of this now thriving enterprise would be difficult to resolve, and it is one that both the manager and the village preferred to set aside for the time being. The manager was in a position to make sure that he and his family could appropriate a large part of the profits, but it was also clear that he felt secure in investing them in the enterprise. The enterprise was located in his house and all management personnel were family members, making the enterprise difficult to expropriate successfully. Another important factor in the manager's sense of security was his own role as a major village personality involved in many village projects, which also made any outright appropriation of the enterprise by the village unlikely. The manager confidently spoke of his son 'inheriting' the enterprise upon his retirement.

In many other contracted enterprises, however, the lack of clear ownership rights has led to problems such as the running down of collective assets, short-term planning, and at the same time a lack of real managerial independence. Managers have complained that, while they must suffer the consequences of poor performance, they do not have the right to make key decisions affecting performance, particularly in matters such as staffing and new investment.[27] The experimental nature of contracting and the lack of a legal foundation has meant that the situation is very changeable, and it was common in the 1980s for the rental and management arrangements to be changed arbitrarily, especially when local governments found that they had underestimated the profitability of an enterprise.[28] In the early 1990s contracts were becoming clearer (for example, including a three-year time limit before rents could be altered), but important questions concerning what management rights were being handed over were usually settled in an *ad hoc* manner as specific issues arose, and the manager's standing in the community and relationships with key cadres were usually far more important than the formal contract.

Thus, contracting and leasing ran into very similar problems to those encountered in the household responsibility system in agriculture. These problems stem from a lack of clarity in property rights, which itself stems from the fact that China, at both the theoretical level and the level of local practice, has not decided how much private enterprise it really wants. It is, apparently, not generally acceptable to township and village administrations to have larger-scale, high-impact enterprises developing outside their influence; but at the same time, spurred on by the effective economic incentives instituted by the fiscal reforms of the mid-1980s, they have been extremely creative in finding flexible ways to facilitate the personal investment and entrepreneurial skills of individuals within the existing regulatory framework. That is, they want the benefits of private entrepreneurship, but they want to be able to ensure that it benefits the collective community. Therefore, they have used the initiative handed to them by reform policies to develop a private sector which need not be always private, and to make room, in a variety of ways, for individual entrepreneurship in the collective sector.

Shareholding Enterprises: The Answer to Ownership Confusion?

The rapid growth and successful economic performance of many private, contracted, or leased enterprises, long before the theoretical issues were adequately resolved, shows the wisdom of the feeling-for-stones approach. The particularistic relationships and opaque property rights that characterize this solution, however, make it difficult to reconcile the various interests in an enterprise to the satisfaction of all parties. This is a problem not only at the level of the enterprise itself or between the enterprise and local government, but also between local government and higher levels. Therefore since the second half of the 1980s there has been continued discussion of the need to clarify property rights in rural enterprise, not only to improve incentives, reduce transaction costs, and simplify and encourage new business relationships, but also to facilitate more effective regulation and macroeconomic control.

In the early 1990s shareholding enterprises, which had appeared in various forms in rural enterprises from the early 1980s onwards, began receiving much attention. They are seen as a way to concentrate capital, but also as a solution to the problem of ownership definition. Potentially, shareholding offers a means for the various interest groups associated with all rural enterprises above a certain size—be they nominally private or collective—to articulate their interests with more efficiency and fairness than the interplay of informal, often even unstated, bargaining positions that emerged under the forms allowed. Formally expressing these interests as shares, and formulating procedures for decision-making and allocation of responsibilities to shareholders, directors, and managers, offers a way of stabilizing the parameters of enterprise operation and regularizing the relationship between local government and enterprises. In China, it has also been important that shareholding can also be seen as offering an ideologically acceptable means of separating enterprises from direct government management without resorting to outright privatization: so long as the concentration of share ownership is avoided, shareholding can be seen as a form of collective ownership which nevertheless mobilizes the profit-seeking self-interest of individuals or institutional owners. At an ICB conference on the rural shareholding system in late 1993, it was suggested that in some cases, for example commonly in Wenzhou, shareholding was merely a collective-sounding cloak for private partnerships,[29] but in many other cases, as will be discussed below, there are strong pressures for at least some degree of genuinely collective character based either on staff shareholding or on community rights.

The shareholding system regarded as appropriate for rural enterprises is the *gufen hezuozhi*, or cooperative share system, with which the best-known experiments have been in Wenzhou, Zhibo in Shandong, and Fuyang in Anhui. This should not be confused with the experiments in changing state-owned enterprises to joint-stock ownership, which have been the subject of a series of increasingly detailed regulations and policy documents in recent years. In rural enterprises, the evolution of share-holding has occurred largely as a way of concentrating capital and over-coming a range of ideological, procedural, and regulatory barriers, and the specific arrangements vary widely. The great advantage of sharehold-ing in rural areas, apart from some of the efficiency and incentive benefits it could provide, was that, while share enterprises were administratively considered to be part of the collective sector, they could actually encom-pass all or any of the formal ownership categories. They could be formed by associations of individuals or enterprises of the same or differing own-ership, by government bodies at various levels, or by a combination of all of these. Because rural shareholding is seen as being at an early, experi-mental stage, and because many rural enterprises are small and not very advanced in their management methods, attempting to regulate them in a detailed manner is considered impractical and counter-productive.[30] This has meant that, as with other rural reforms, their nature is strongly influ-enced by local pressures.

Rural shareholding developed both through the formation of new enter-prises, in which shares would be held by the founders, and through the transformation of existing enterprises, frequently as a means of clarifying the complex ownership situations arising from contracting and leasing. When an enterprise transfers to a share system, it is generally valued and divided into shares which are allocated to those who have contributed to its development. Rural collective enterprises are typically divided into some combination of a 'collective' shareholding, personal shares for staff or local residents, legal-person shares held by other enterprises if they invest in the enterprise, and the 'enterprise share', a device for ensuring that some profits are allocated to maintenance and development. This share can also be a handy way of preventing the overt privatization of a contracted enterprise in which the contractor has invested. For example, an agricultural machinery plant on the rural outskirts of Shenyang, which had been contracted to an individual for a flat rent of 20,000 yuan per year from 1982, had grown in seven years to include six factories and two shops. The original plant was valued at 70,000 yuan, which was designated the village's collective share. The remaining 190,000 yuan of fixed assets represented by the other factories and shops was designated the contractor's individually owned share, but from this he contributed 90,000 to be the 'enterprise' share, also under collective ownership. In addition, another 190,000 yuan worth of shares, at 1,000 yuan per share, was bought by enterprise staff. Thus, if staff shares are included as collective ownership, the new share enterprise was more than three-quarters collectively owned.[31] In most such enterprises each type of share is subject to different conditions regarding transferability, inheritability, voting rights, and so on, and these rights vary among different enterprises and localities. In 1992 this system began to be actively promoted by all levels of government, with provinces organizing conferences and pilot projects from which guidelines for applying the system were to be developed. Sichuan, which had had a small number of rural share enterprises since the early 1980s but no outstanding 'model' areas, produced an initial set of guidelines in October 1992.

Xindu, being close to the provincial capital and having a relatively well developed collective enterprise sector, began to develop shareholding enterprises from around 1983 and has quite a number of them, but they vary quite a lot in their real nature. Without the backup of an established legal framework, the ownership rights set up in the shareholding agreements are not necessarily effective. The majority of enterprises claiming to be shareholding enterprises (*gufen qiye*) when shareholding became fashionable in the early 1990s did not even have agreements that set out these rights clearly. In a 1988 survey in Xindu, 80 per cent had no clear organizational structure, only 8 per cent had a formal charter.[32] What happened instead was typically that the enterprises drew their character from the organizations and power structures that had been instrumental in their formation. While the shareholding system was proving useful in improving incentives and providing capital for expansion or new ventures, it was not always so effective in increasing the separation between enterprises and government, which has also been seen as desirable in order to free enterprises from directly serving political interests.

For example, the enterprises we visited in 1992, which were joint ventures between different levels of government, or between a state enterprise and a township, were little different from ordinary state or collective enterprises. A drill-bit factory set up by a state company in Chengdu and a township in Xindu had its managerial personnel, and production targets, sent down from the Chengdu company. The management were on state-enterprise employment conditions, and worked under the state-enterprise contract responsibility system rather than the more independent contracting forms used by many township and village enterprises. The manager complained of constant restrictions by the parent company. What the Chengdu enterprise really wanted was just a branch factory set up to use cheap rural land and labour, but the structure of collective ownership in the rural economy meant that, in order to obtain the land and favourable operating conditions, it had to set up the joint venture with the township itself, leading to numerous conflicts of interest between the two shareholders.

Another shareholding enterprise was a furniture factory set up as a joint venture between the supply and marketing company under the Sichuan township and village enterprise bureau and a village in Xindu county. The factory's board of directors consisted of three representatives from the provincial company, the head of the village committee, and the factory manager, who was also a member of the village committee. Forty per cent of profits went to the enterprise, while the remaining 60 per cent was divided 50–50 between the provincial company and the village. Basically, the provincial company provided assistance with raw materials and the marketing of the high-quality furniture produced, and the village was responsible for production. The enterprise still contracted management and production targets with the village and fulfilled other community obligations such as providing direct subsidies to agriculture and employing needy villagers to do quite unnecessary jobs. Typically of share enterprises in Xindu, the factory's targets were contracted not between the manager and the directors, but between the manager and the village committee. The manager stated that contractual and other obligations were actually not very formalized, but were more a matter of personal discussion within the village committee.

Even an enterprise which, on the face of it, was entirely owned by private shareholders, was found to be subject to a very complex and apparently binding set of unwritten obligations to the collective. This was the Chengdu Health Products Factory, which had received considerable press coverage as a success story. It made mainly pillows, quilts, and pads for various parts of the body which were filled with medicinal herbs. Housed in a set of large, new, freshly painted buildings, its tall white chimney stack dominated the flat landscape, just as the enterprise itself dominated the village economy.

In 1985 Ma Liuwen, a former 'barefoot doctor', had already successfully set up two enterprises, one making the Chinese medicine *huangliansu* and the other making fibreglass-reinforced plastic. Both were profitable, but both also had problems, as the former competed with state enterprises for raw materials and the latter used raw materials inefficiently. When he happened to read a newspaper article about some medicinal pillows, Ma decided that this was the product he was looking for. He set up a deal with a nearby medicinal research institute to provide research and development and guarantee raw material supplies, and persuaded some 80 households to put up an average 2,000 yuan each to start the factory. In a village of some 400 households with a per capita annual income of approximately 400 yuan at that time, this was quite a feat. But in fact Ma himself, and indeed the entire board of directors, were also on the village committee, and it was really as much a village project as a private one. The result was an enterprise that was a sort of hybrid of private ownership and public obligation, an example of how, in the unregulated reform environment, a community can control new developments to its advantage.

The enterprise charter makes no mention of any community obligations, but clearly sets out the management structure and the rights and liabilities of the shareholders. Each shareholder is entitled to one job for a family member as well as interest and dividends on the shares, and can vote at the annual meeting of shareholders to elect the board of directors and ratify its choice of manager (still Ma Liuwen, so far). In 1985 the village provided the initial land parcel for the enterprise free of charge; in return for its status as a 'village-run' collective enterprise, the factory paid only an administrative charge set at 0.2 per cent of annual gross output value (waived for the first two years), although the charter also stated that if the factory were to close all its buildings would become the property of the village.

The enterprise did very well, and by 1992 was the second largest enterprise in Xindu. By this time the original 0.2 hectare land parcel had been supplemented by a further 3 hectares, for which the enterprise paid rent set at the cash equivalent of 1,000 *jin* of rice. What would happen to the new buildings on this land in the event of failure remains unclear. In 1991 Chengdu Health employed 680 people (more than 300 of whom were travelling salespeople) and had fixed assets valued at 4 million yuan plus over 10 million yuan in circulating capital; its 1991 profit was 2.36 million yuan. But none of the shareholders had taken anywhere near the dividends to which they were entitled from such success. This was partly because they had chosen to leave the money in the factory, so that the enterprise maintained a large amount of circulating capital which helped it to weather the credit squeeze after 1988. Another reason cited for the shareholders' reticence, however, was that it just wouldn't be proper to make so much more money than neighbours who were not shareholders. Instead, some of the factory's profits had been distributed so that they benefited the whole community. Electricity had been provided to every household; a village health clinic, primary school, and recreation centre had been built. Other enterprises in the village were subsidized in that the village's entire tax quota was paid by this enterprise alone. Farmers received assistance for machinery purchases. In addition, Chengdu Health naturally contributed to the normal local yearly charges or one-off collections for fertilizer subsidies, road-building, agricultural education, land improvement, and whatever else came up. (The provisional regulations on rural cooperative shareholding enterprises passed in 1990 do specify that 60 per cent of after-tax profits should be reinvested and a maximum of 20 per cent issued as cash dividends, the remaining 20 per cent to be put towards 'collective welfare, staff bonuses, and so on', but also that the precise proportions should be decided not by the shareholders, but by each locality.[33]) Over the years, the composition of both the board of directors and the village committee had changed, and there was no longer a correspondence between the two (although this was partly because some village leaders now worked full-time for Chengdu Health). But the factory's local obligations were as strong as ever, and it continued to pour funds into local projects. This single enterprise had had an enormous impact on the welfare of the whole village, in fact making far larger contributions than many traditionally formed collective enterprises do.

In spite of such success stories, there are serious problems with such a model. Its reliance on a particular community spirit and a set of personal relationships may undermine its long-term stability as economic growth itself changes rural villages, and the need for an exceptional entrepreneur to have the right idea and the right connections at the right time precludes it from becoming typical. In less propitious circumstances such an enterprise would likely never get off the ground, or could only do so by serving particular interests. Like all of the informal arrangements described in this paper, it is also one that works for profitable enterprises in a rapidly expanding economy, but would be much harder to sustain if conditions were tighter—in enterprises that cannot afford to contribute more than they are obliged to and need to know how much that is, or that fail and become a tangle of undefined liabilities. The direct provision of public welfare by the enterprise is ominously reminiscent of the system that has caused so much inefficiency in the state enterprise sector, particularly when the village economy becomes dependent on a single enterprise. Then, in the event of the enterprise running into trouble, it is likely that there would be strong political pressures for government assistance.

Cooperative shareholding has been promoted by central authorities as a step towards clarifying interests in rural enterprises, which would help to regularize administration and facilitate effective monitoring and macro control. But the shareholding systems being implemented in rural areas are developing within the context of the highly particularistic, *ad hoc* administrative style which has characterized the rural reforms as a whole, and which gives local governments and entrepreneurs the flexibility they need to cope with a rapidly changing economic and regulatory environment. Consequently, as illustrated in the examples above, they have not replaced the action of informal interests, but merely added a new field for their operation. Of course no one, least of all Chinese administrators, would expect the administration of China's rural enterprise sector to become regular and formalized overnight; but if the shareholding system is to add clarity to enterprise operation rather than yet another layer of complexity, it will have to take informal local interests into account.

This can be seen in the negotiation process for transforming a collective township or village enterprise into a cooperative share enterprise. Once the problem of valuing the enterprise has been dealt with (and this in itself is no easy matter), the various interested parties each fight to stake their claim upon it. One important issue being discussed during the early 1990s was whether or not tax concessions granted to enterprises when they were starting up should be seen as an 'investment' deserving of a share in the enterprise. Most of the academics involved in the debate—who generally believed in the importance of separating government from enterprises— said they should not, but the local governments which used their discretion under the fiscal contracting system to grant the concessions contested this. Obviously other assistance, from land allocations to technical assistance to help with marketing or locating raw materials, also had to be considered. Under the system of local obligation established in the 1980s, such help from cadres was all part of the currency of informal but binding understandings which made enterprises part of the local community. Local cadres did not want to lose these understandings in a more formalized system.

The competition for power between central and local governments is an important dimension of the drive to institute the shareholding system. Formalization of any sort is seen as conducive to increasing local accountability to higher levels and discarding the outmoded ownership categories which shaped enterprise administration and registration, and taxation in the 1980s is an important step towards rationalizing economic administration. As explained above, much of the freedom of action achieved by local governments in relation both to higher levels and to enterprises was derived from the informal arrangements necessitated by the gap between ownership regulations and practical economics, and narrowing this gap also narrows the field for informal administration. In the longer term, it is also possible that the share system itself may be used as a direct path to increased central state control. At township level, a formal local government share in an enterprise would technically be seen as owned by the *state* (headed by the central government), which might seek to use such ownership to regain some of the local-level control it relinquished in order to stimulate growth in the 1980s. For example, it might seek eventually to bring all such shareholdings under the purview of the Bureau for the Administration of State Assets, which has been formed to control the state share in former state enterprises changing to a shareholding system. The cooperative share system has intentionally been promoted in a flexible and not very regulated way, in order to make it adaptable to the wide variety of local conditions in rural China, but there is also a tendency to see the cooperative share system as a stepping-stone to the more formalized structure of the limited liability company, for which a complicated and detailed range of state regulations is being developed.

Therefore, the biggest problem in transforming enterprises to the cooperative share system is what to do with the 'collective' share. In many cases this is managed by township governments or by enterprise management committees set up by them, which may merely perpetuate the informal arrangements already in force, depending partly on whether shares held by individual villagers have voting rights attached or only rights to income. In village enterprises the retention of the collective share by village committees was not such a problem, because village committees officially represent the village rather than the state. There is a danger in either case, however, that control of the enterprise will not be clarified effectively if, as in the health products factory discussed above, the share distribution does not reflect the real interests involved in the enterprise. The convention of the 'enterprise share' is also problematic: putting the basic financial needs of the enterprise in terms of a 'share' of existing assets leaves the problem of management rights, and of liability in the event of failure, partly unresolved, for who is responsible for the 'enterprise's' share? The cooperative share system is considered appropriate for the initial reform of rural enterprise ownership precisely because it demands less clarity and is therefore more easily adaptable than the more formal share systems being tried in urban enterprises, but this means that some problems have to be shelved for the time being.

Cooperative shareholding, then, has not yet provided the clarification of interests that reformers and higher-level government bodies would like to see, although it does provide a framework for their more formal expression, and as the market economy becomes more developed there will be increasing incentives for this to occur. What it has done is provide a more flexible, more open structure for overcoming barriers to further development of rural enterprises. For example, in some relatively developed areas in Guangdong and Shenzhen, shareholding of this kind has been a way of dealing with the problem of how to distribute collective income fairly as industry replaces agriculture as the main generator of income and land allocation according to the household responsibility system becomes problematic. Instead of particular enterprises, the entire enterprise sector of the village has been incorporated as a share enterprise, with shares sold and/or allocated to villagers in ways that take into account seniority, labour contributions, and so on. Similar systems are also being tried in agriculture, in order to allow for agglomeration of the many small plots while still recognizing collective land rights.[34] As suggested by some of the examples above, shareholding enables rural enterprises to cross administrative lines of both ownership type and location, allowing combined investment from different ownership sources and, importantly, facilitating investment in rural areas by urban enterprises and further development of the rural enterprise sector.[35] Rural communities close to cities are already becoming increasingly urbanized, and there is now not only a flow of labour into the cities, but also a small flow in the other direction, especially of technically qualified personnel. Chengdu Health Products, for example, employed two Master's graduates (in economics and administration) and three ordinary graduates. Shares are a common way of enticing urban talent out to rural townships, and in the longer term might also offer a way of resolving the conflicts arising from the increased mobility of labour. The collectivist, community-based nature of the rural economy is an equalizing factor worth maintaining if China retains any pretensions whatsoever to socialist goals, but market pressures will require it to become more flexible. Arrangements could be made for permanent migrants to buy into a community, and for departing residents to be paid off, similar to those arrangements made in cooperative enterprises both in China and elsewhere, without resorting to a capitalist stock market system.

Conclusion

The interaction of market reforms and bureaucratic powers obtaining in the 1980s enabled local administrations to establish a range of informal, but binding, controls over enterprises of all nominal ownership types. With the further development of the rural enterprise sector, there is pressure to develop a more formalized system. The central government seeks to regulate the economy more effectively. Entrepreneurs, as they seek to expand into national and international markets and attract capital from a wider base, can also benefit from more clarity in ownership and less reliance on local relationships. Local governments (which in many ways are themselves the entrepreneurs) also have the same incentives as their local economies become more developed. Indeed, this very development, itself facilitated by informality in the uncertain ideological climate of the 1980s, is likely, as rural–urban and inter-rural barriers break down and small towns grow larger, to erode some of the cohesiveness of local communities that made informal administration work so well.

But any attempt at formalization, if it is to succeed, will have to be flexible, and will have to represent effectively the real interests in rural enterprises. Case studies of enterprises of a variety of ownerships—individual, joint, township-run, shareholding—reveal an even greater range of management realities. With some exceptions, in general the only really 'private' enterprises are the small individual or family types, as enterprises that expand beyond this size tend to need support from collective authorities which comes weighted with reciprocal obligations. Reformers, seeking to establish a more standardized environment in order to improve the efficiency of the market and to facilitate macroeconomic control, have made much of the need to separate government from enterprises and to clarify ownership and management rights. However, ownership reform itself is an experimental process, and the key role of local governments in any new policy or administrative change means that they are in an ideal position to make sure new developments still work to their advantage. The smallness and cohesion of many rural communities has also been a factor in pressuring enterprises to contribute directly and visibly to local welfare. The ability of local government and community interests to influence all types of enterprise suggests that any attempt to clarify ownership relations will have to take them into account. Thus, if the centre is to achieve its goal of formalizing economic administration, it will also have to formalize the articulation of local and private economic interests, in relation both to one another and to higher levels of 'the state'.

NOTES

1. This is a revised and expanded version of a paper, 'Ownership and Obligation in China's Rural Enterprises: Community Interests in a Non-legalistic Environment', first presented at the 5th annual conference of the Chinese Economic Association, University of Adelaide, Australia, November 1992. Proceedings of the conference were edited by Wu Yanrui and Zhang Xiaohe and published in a volume, *Chinese Economy in Transition* (Canberra: National Centre for Development Studies, Australian National University, 1994).

2. Victor Nee, 'Peasant Entrepreneurship and the Politics of Regulation in China', in Victor Nee and David Stark (eds.), *Remaking the Economic Institutions of Socialism: China and Eastern Europe* (Stanford: Stanford University Press, 1989), 169–207.

3. See e.g. Hans Blommestein and Michael Marrese (eds.), *Transformation of Planned Economies: Property Rights Reform and Macroeconomic Stability* (Paris: Organisation for Economic Cooperation and Development, 1991); Jeffrey D. Sachs, 'Privatization in Russia: Some Lessons from Eastern Europe', *American Economic Review*, 80 (May 1992), 43–8.

4. Janos Kornai, *The Socialist System: The Political Economy of Communism* (Princeton: Princeton University Press, 1992).

5. Jan Winiecki, *Resistance to Change in the Soviet Economic System* (London and New York: Routledge, 1991), esp. ch. 3.

6. *Zhongguo xiangzhen qiye nianjian 1993* (China Township and Village Enterprise Yearbook 1993) (Beijing: Nongye chubanshe, 1993), 147.

7. *Zhongguo nongcun tongji nianjian 1994* (Rural Statistical Yearbook of China 1994) (Beijing: Zhongguo tongji chubanshe, 1994), 338.

8. *Zhongguo tongji nianjian 1995* (Statistical Yearbook of China 1995) (Beijing: Zhongguo tongji chubanshe, 1995), 137.

9. See Susan Young and Yang Gang, 'Private Enterprises and Local Government in Rural China', in Christopher Findlay, Andrew Watson, and Harry X. Wu (eds.), *Rural Enterprises in China* (Basingstoke and London: Macmillan, 1994), 24–39; Ole Odgaard, *Private Enterprises in Rural China* (Aldershot: Avebury, 1992), esp. ch. 6.

10. See Susan Young, *Private Business and Economic Reform in China* (Armonk, NY: M. E. Sharpe, 1995).

11. 'Guowuyuan guanyu chengzhen fei nongye geti jingji ruogan zhengcexing guiding' (Certain Policy Regulations of the State Council on the Urban Non-Agricultural Individual Economy) (7 July 1981), in (no eds. given) *Siying he geti jingji shiying fagui daquan* (Complete Laws and Regulations for the Private and Individual Economy) (Beijing: Renmin chubanshe, 1988), 61–4.

12. 'Guowuyuan guanyu nongcun geti gongshangye de ruogan guiding' (Certain Regulations of the State Council on Rural Individual Industry and Commerce) (27 February 1894), in *Renmin ribao*, 12 March 1984.

13. In March 1988 the Constitution was revised to allow specifically for larger private enterprises, and in June the State Council issued a set of three regulations for the formation of *siying qiye* (private enterprises) and the taxation of the income they produced. These regulations were published in *Renmin ribao*, 29 June 1988. The implications of rural policy in the mid-1980s for private enterprises are discussed in Young and Yang, 'Private Enterprises and Local Government'.

14. Li Chengxun and Zhao Zhixiang (eds.), *Zhuanyehu jingying guanli shouce* (Handbook of Specialized Household Management and Administration) (Beijing: Beijing chubanshe, 1987), 298.

15. Young and Yang, 'Private Enterprises and Local Government', 34–5; Young, *Private Business*, 141–2.

16. This practice is discussed in Jean C. Oi, 'The Fate of the Collective after the Commune', in Deborah Davis and Ezra F. Vogel (eds.), *Chinese Society on the Eve of Tiananmen* (Cambridge, Mass.: Harvard University Press, 1990), 15–36; 32.

17. Winiecki, *Resistance to Change*, 9–12.

18. This is not to say that the first option disappeared, and there were many cases of officials discouraging the growth of private business in order to protect collective enterprises from competition. See Young, *Private Business*, 49–50; Ole Odgaard, 'Collective

Control of Income Distribution: A Case Study of Private Enterprises in Sichuan Province', in Jørgen Delman, Stubbe Østergaard, and Flemming Christiansen (eds.), *Remaking Peasant China* (Aarhus, Denmark: Aarhus University Press, 1990), 106–21.

19. Odgaard, *Private Enterprises*, 176–7 and 215; see also Oi, 'The Fate of the Collective', 31.
20. Odgaard, *Private Enterprises*, 215–17; *Jingji cankao* (Economic Information), 9 December 1990, 1, and 16 December 1990, 4.
21. *Nongmin ribao* (Peasants' Daily), 16 December 1988, 2; Hu Guohua, Liu Jinghuai, and Chen Min, *Duo sediao de zhongguo geti jingyingzhe* (The Many Colours of China's Individual Business Operators) (Beijing: Beijing jingji xueyuan chubanshe, 1988); He Wenfu, 'Siying qiye fazhan mianlin de wenti' (Problems for the Development of Private Enterprises), *Sichuan jingji yanjiu*, 1 (1989), 53–4; *Zhongguo gongshang bao* (Chinese Industry and Commerce), 12 August 1993, 3.
22. Andrew Walder points this out in an analysis that includes rural 'collective' (township and village) enterprises in the state sector, but disaggregates state ownership into different levels of government to analyse the different constraints and freedoms affecting the relationship between enterprises and government at each level. See Walder, 'Local Governments as Industrial Firms: An Organizational Analysis of China's Transitional Economy', *American Journal of Sociology*, 101:2 (September 1995), 263–301.
23. Scott Rozelle discusses rural enterprises from this angle in 'Decision-Making in China's Rural Economy: The Linkages between Village Leaders and Farm Households', *China Quarterly*, 137 (March 1994), 99–124.
24. *Renmin ribao*, 19 June 1987, 2.
25. See e.g. Liu Wenpu, 'Lun nongcun jiti qiye siyinghua wenti' (On the Privatization of Management of Rural Collective Enterprises), *Nongmin ribao*, 21 September 1988, 3; Li Gourong, 'Siying jingji: geti jingji fazhan de disan tiao lu' (The Private Economy: The Third Road for the Development of the Individual Economy), *Caijing yanjiu*, 7 (1988), 25–30; Zhongguo shehui kexueyuan nongcun fazhan yanjiusuo siying jingji yanjiuzu, 'Wei siying qiye wending, jiankang fazhan chuangzao lianghao de shehui jingji huanjing' (Creating a Good Socioeconomic Environment for the Stable and Healthy Development of Private Enterprises), *Zhongguo nongcun jingji*, 3 (1988), 49–56.
26. e.g. Liu Wenpu, 'Lun nongcun jiti qiye siyinghua wenti'; Li Gourong, 'Siying jingji'; *Jingjixue zhoubao*, 28 February 1988, 6.
27. *Jingji cankao*, 26 January 1988, 1. See also Oi, 'The Fate of the Collective', 23–9.
28. The same problems occurred in Poland when leasing was tried in the 1970s, and the lack of legal guarantees meant that leaseholders frequently had to bribe administrators if they wished to retain their leases once they had made the enterprises profitable. See Anders Åslund, 'The Functioning of Private Enterprise in Poland', *Soviet Studies*, 36:3 (1984), 427–44, 438.
29. *Zhongguo gongshang bao*, 27 November 1993, 1.
30. See e.g. Dai Suli, 'Guanyu xiangzhen qiye shixing gufenzhi de diaocha baogao' (Report on an Investigation of the Implementation of the Share System in Township and Village Enterprises), *Qiye suzhi yanjiu*, 2 (1989), 2–4, reprinted in Zhongguo renmin daxue shubao ziliao zhongxin (eds.), *Fuyin baokan ziliao, F22: nongcun qiye guanli* (Reprints from Newspapers and Periodicals, F22: Rural Enterprise Administration), 4 (1989), 64–6.
31. ibid. 66.
32. Hu Jueqiang and Luo Zuming, 'Dui xian jieduan xiangzhen qiye gufenzhi de fenxi yu sikao' (Analysis and Consideration of the Current Shareholding System in Township

and Village Enterprises), *Nongjing lilun yanjiu*, 1 (1989), 35–7; reprinted in Zhongguo renmin daxue shubao ziliao zhongzin (eds.), *Fuyin baokan ziliao, F22*, 3 (1989), 46–8.

33. Ministry of Agriculture, 'Nongmin gufen hezuo qiye zanxing guiding' (Provisional Regulations on Peasants' Cooperative Shareholding Enterprises) (12 February 1990), in *Jingji ribao*, 13 March 1990, 3. See also Ministry of Agriculture, 'Guanyu tuixing he wanshan xiangzhen qiye gufen hezuozhi de tongzhi' (Notice Concerning the Promotion and Improvement of the Cooperative Share System in Township and Village Enterprises), 24 December 1992, in *Zhongguo xiangzhen qiye nianjian 1995*, 134–6.

34. These experiments are detailed in Zhejiang sheng nongyanshi fu Guangdong kaocha zu, 'Guangdong nongcun gufen hezuo jingji kaocha Gaogao' (Report on an Investigation of the Rural Cooperative Share Economy in Guangdong), *Nongcun gongzuo tongxun* (Zhejiang), 8 (1993), 2–14.

35. The development of a more flexible ownership framework is thus another factor that will tend to break down the barriers between the urban and rural sectors, with beneficial effects on the rural sector. Other barriers and their erosion are discussed in Zhang Xiaohe, Christopher Findlay, and Andrew Watson, 'Growth of China's Rural Enterprises: Impacts on Urban–Rural Relations', *Journal of Development Studies*, 31:4 (1984), 567–84.

II
CIVIL SOCIETY

6

Reconstructing Society: Liang Shuming and the Rural Reconstruction Movement in Shandong

Stig Thøgersen

The Rural Reconstruction Movement (RRM) initiated by Liang Shuming stands out as an ambitious and visionary alternative to more bureaucratic government-sponsored modernization drives, as well as to the Communist revolutionary model for social change. The RRM and its work in Zouping county, Shandong province, between 1931 and 1937 was just one expression of the growing attention paid to the villages by Chinese reformers and revolutionaries from the later half of the 1920s.[1] What makes Liang's experiments particularly relevant for the discussion of the relationship between state and society in the modern transformation of China, however, is his firm belief in the potentials of rural society, and his articulate aversion to state intervention and coercive measures. Liang conceived of the drama of modernization and rural reconstruction as a triangular relationship between village communities, intellectuals, and the state. His aim was to reconstruct rural society through the establishment of village schools (*cunxue*) which should play the double role of administrative organs and community centres. The state should only accept and assist this process, not dominate it, while the intellectuals should contribute with new ideas and knowledge. The implementation of these ideas in Zouping was no unqualified success, however, and even before the Japanese invaded the area in 1937 Liang was forced to admit that village China resisted this remodelling more than he had imagined.

Western presentations have analyzed the RRM primarily as a manifestation of Liang Shuming's ideas.[2] This paper will examine the experiences of the RRM from a different angle, focusing on the interaction between the movement and local society, particularly in the field of educational reform. the RRM represented an attempt to reconstruct society through the establishment of institutions and procedures that were intended to strengthen local society *vis-à-vis* the state. Such reconstruction, however, meant the demolition of existing social and educational structures as well as the building of new ones. In the context of the ongoing debate on civil society in China, this offers an interesting example of the difficulties involved in understanding movements of intellectual activists like the RRM, and the type of social engineering they stood for, inside a state–society framework. Using Liang's own state–society dichotomy to describe what went on in Zouping appears misleading and even mystifying. Rather than defending the 'good' society against the 'evil' state, the interventions of the RRM zigzagged across the blurred division line between them.

The paper starts with an introduction to Liang Shuming's thoughts on education and rural reconstruction which provided the ideological basis of the RRM. Then follows an outline of education in Zouping before 1931 in order to set out the changes brought about by the Movement. The bulk of the paper deals with three aspects that are relevant, in different ways, to the themes of this volume: the remodelling of rural social structures; the redefinition of knowledge and of the relation between knowledge and power; and the diffusion of modern values through the school system.

Liang Shuming's Thoughts on Education and Rural Reconstruction[3]

Liang Shuming (1893–1988) gained national fame after the publication in 1921 of a series of lectures titled *Eastern and Western Cultures and Their Philosophies*.[4] This book introduced Liang's personal brand of Confucianism based on the belief that Chinese culture held the answers to the fundamental moral questions facing mankind, not only in China but all over the world. While the Western spirit could solve man's material problems, the Chinese, according to Liang, could solve the social and ethical ones and create personal and social harmony.

Liang saw education, and particularly spiritual perfection, as the key to the rebirth of China, and through the 1920s and early 1930s he developed the basic ideology behind the educational aspects of the RRM experiment. His starting point was his work on the difference between Eastern and Western cultures, which he saw reflected also in the field of education. Western education, he said, emphasized knowledge about concrete matters, as for example in the natural sciences, while Chinese education had its strong point in the teaching of moral and ethical principles.[5] The Western attitude had led to the accumulation of human experiences in systematic categories and disciplines, which facilitated the transmission of knowledge from one generation to the next. The Chinese, on the other hand, depended much more on intuition and personal experience. He used the example of Chinese medical doctors, who relied almost totally on their personal clinical experience rather than on a systematic knowledge about pharmacology or other disciplines of the Western medical profession. In this respect, China had much to learn from the West.

Seen in a wider perspective, however, the Chinese were on the right track when accentuating the teaching of emotions and ethics, because emotions were the inner nature of life, while knowledge was only a tool in the service of life itself. In the tradition of Mencius and the Ming dynasty philosopher Wang Yangming, he held that a child was born with all the right emotions or instincts, and that the main task of education was to protect this inborn moral goodness from the perversions brought upon it by its surroundings. The problem with the Chinese educational tradition was therefore not that it gave priority to ethics, but rather that the methods it used suited the transmission of knowledge rather than the cultivation of moral qualities. These methods, said Liang, were dry and boring and detrimental to their own goals. A long, tedious lecture on filial piety was unlikely to strengthen the ties between children and parents, for example. Instead, he recommended the discourse (*jiangxue*) model, where a closely knit group of students together with a teacher formed a collective which was in charge of its own daily life and moral development. He emphasized the close personal ties inside such groups, wherein teachers and students should be friends, and teachers should always be aware of any problems, intellectual or psychological, that their students might have. Self-study should to a large extent replace lectures, and the use of rewards and punishments should be banned, as such methods were detrimental to the very goals of education. Though moral development should be the heart of all studies, modern subjects should dominate the curriculum.

From the late 1920s, Liang, like so many others tried to adapt his theories on education to the realities of rural China. In 1929 he visited prominent experiments with rural reconstruction and mass education, such as one of Huang Yanpei's vocational education projects in Jiangsu, Tao Xingzhi's school complex in Xiaozhuang, James Yen's Ding county, and the more bureaucratic Shanxi programme initiated by the provincial governor Yan Xishan.[6] In 1931 the governor of Shandong, Han Fuqu, invited Liang to become leader of the Shandong Rural Reconstruction Institute which was set up in Zouping county. Liang accepted, and until 1937, when the Japanese invasion army arrived, Zouping was the scene for the realization of Liang's vision of a new village China based on Confucian values.[7]

There were several reasons why the village population came to play a crucial role in Liang's image of a revitalized and modernized China. He saw agriculture as the foundation of all economic activities in China, where the cities, as opposed to urban centres in the West, were consuming more goods than they were producing. The whole population was therefore living off the villages, and the intellectuals in particular were 'eating the blood and sweat of the peasants',[8] so China's economic reconstruction had to start in the countryside. The fact that this was also where the overwhelming majority of the population lived made the villages politically vital as well. Most importantly, however, in the rural areas there were still traces of life in those superior cultural values which would, in the final analysis, save the Chinese nation and all mankind.

Originally, claimed Liang, before the West had forced China to change its ways, the villages had been peaceful and prosperous, small stable societies governed by mores and customs rather than by law. He described this traditional Chinese culture, still alive in the memories of some old folks, as an ancient tree whose roots spread out deep under the villages. Though the leaves and branches of the tree were dead, new sprouts could spring from those roots, and under careful protection grow into a new culture.[9]

Although Liang recognized that the villages were not socially homogeneous, he maintained that they held no class contradictions in the Marxist sense, but only differences in occupation and wealth. There was therefore no need for further disruptions of the social structure in the shape of a violent revolution. The problem was rather that the villages were culturally 'dead', their organic social structures and fine moral codes were smashed, and they lacked the internal strength to bring about their own spiritual awakening.

For this reason, the villages had to be not only modernized but also revitalized, and because the need for change had been brought about by contacts with the West rather than grown out of Chinese society itself, it was up to the urban intellectuals, and particularly those who were well versed in Western culture and science, to carry out the necessary transformation. Intellectuals of a new variety, fundamentally different from the parasitic and impractical types normally trained in Chinese schools, should be the 'new elements' in rural society, who would revive the village communities by bringing local leaders and ordinary peasants into closer contact with each other, organizing meetings and introducing new technologies.[10] The task of these intellectuals, though, was only to be the nipple through which the peasants could suck the spiritual nourishment prepared at Liang's Research Institute in Zouping.[11] The food should not be forced down their throats. This was exactly what Liang felt made his strategy superior to the bureaucratic reform measures taken by the government, to Yan Xishan's programme in Shanxi, and to the rash and arrogant manners of some young reformers with Western ideas.

Rural reconstruction and education was thus a matter between the villagers and this new type of intellectual, while the state should play only a minor role. In Liang's opinion, the reason for violence, and other social evils was that the state, whose power in the final analysis rested on violence, governed education rather than the other way round.[12] Liang's ideal society should be created through educational means. First, the school system should shift its focus from the cities to the rural areas. Western culture had always been based on handicrafts and commerce and Western education therefore had an urban orientation. During the preceding decades, China had copied this feature from the West when it started building 'new schools' in the Western style. Therefore, claimed Liang, 'the result of thirty years of "new education" has been that group after group of village sons have been lured and driven into the cities', where they had nothing to do except sponge off the villages.[13] His alternative to urban, Western-style education was rural education organized by the village communities and adapted to local needs.

Liang found support for his resistance to state dominance over education primarily in the experience of the Danish folk high schools, which were simultaneously educational institutions and community centres. They were established on local private initiative, recruited young adults rather than children, taught general rather than vocational subjects, and aimed at generating a nationalist revival through informal training centred on discussions, all in perfect harmony with Liang's own visions.[14]

Liang realized that the weak point in this construction was the local communities, because China lacked a sense of organization and collective discipline just as much as it lacked Western technology. The re-creation of active and independent rural communities was therefore crucial for all rural reconstruction. At the organizational level, this meant the establishment of village and township schools as nuclei for educational activities as well as for communal life.

Such were the visions Liang wanted to implement in Zouping after 1931, but his ideal school system was not constructed in a vacuum. Like other rural counties, Zouping already had well established ways of transmitting knowledge, including a school system supported by a combination of state and local efforts.

Education in Zouping before 1931[15]

Prior to the arrival of the rural reconstructionists, there were two types of primary school in Zouping: the traditional private schools (*sishu*), and the modern government schools, officially called 'new schools' (*xin xuetang*) but known among the villagers as 'foreign schools' (*yangshu*).

Private school education had been available for centuries. A village, lineage, or family would invite a teacher to instruct those local boys whose parents were willing to disburse his moderate fee which was normally paid in kind. The curriculum consisted of literacy training and Confucian morality, and the teaching materials were those in general use all over China: first *The Three Character Classic*, *The Hundred Family Names*, *The Thousand Character Text*, and sometimes other primers; later *The Four Books*.[16] Other skills, such as the use of the abacus, were sometimes added to this curriculum on the parents' demand or on the teacher's own initiative. The students were not divided into classes but were taught individually, according to their age and ability. They were expected to memorize the assigned texts, and any failure to do so, as well as any breach of discipline, would make the teacher hit the palms of their hands with his ruler, or their heads with his pipe. Some *sishu* teachers were local intellectuals of some status, traditional doctors, or former merchants with wide social experience, while others had a low level of learning and a dubious reputation. In all cases the fate of the school, and of its teachers, depended on the people of the village or neighbourhood that financed it. During the Ming and earlier phases of the Qing dynasty, the lineages played an important role in providing this type of schooling to their members, but around the turn of the century, and certainly by Republican times, the lineage schools appear to have lost importance and been replaced by schools set up on the initiative of the teacher and based on an agreement between him and the village élite. Traditional primary education was thus a central field of intra-village cooperation alongside with crop-watching and religious ceremonies.

From the beginning of the century, these *sishu* had competition from state-promoted schools offering a modernized curriculum. The modern vernacular gradually replaced the classical language, arithmetic was taught with arabic figures instead of the abacus, and nationalist ideology came to permeate the textbooks. At the formal level, the state now played a more important role in education, as the establishment and curriculum of the modern schools was the result of government directives, and the state tried in numerous ways to gain control over the training and appointment of teachers. Still, many things remained unchanged in Zouping schools because the county-level authorities there, as elsewhere in China, had very limited funds; they financed and controlled a few higher and complete primary schools, a vocational school in the county seat, and a teacher training school, while the remaining schools were established and controlled either by members of the traditional local élite, or by young intellectuals who returned to Zouping after graduating from institutions in Jinan or elsewhere. In either case, educational funds came mainly from fees paid by the students' families, land endowments, and local surtaxes. The didactic principles of the modern schools (memorization of texts and harsh discipline) were not substantially different from those of the traditional ones, partly because many 'modern' teachers were former *sishu* instructors.

In 1931 these two types of school still co-existed in the county, and it was probably not until 1928 that the modern schools outnumbered the traditional ones. Right up to 1950 children were sent to modern schools only when the pressure from outside authorities (typically the county magistrate) was strong enough. When the villages were left more or less to their own device, typically during periods of civil war and social disorder, the *sishu* popped up again.[17] The teachers were by and large the same, and in some cases the children had both sets of textbooks, but used the modern ones only when representatives from the higher levels came on inspection.

To understand the real importance of the modern schools, however, one has to consider their political role. During the Republican period schools were the principal media for promoting nationalism in Zouping and other rural areas. Nationalist values were preached in the classrooms, and students and teachers were the driving force behind most political manifestations, such as the local repercussions of the May Fourth Movement. When the rural population learned about events at the provincial and national levels, it was often through students studying inside or outside the county. Zouping had no post-primary schools before 1931, but many higher primary students were in their late teens or even older, and they locally played a role similar to that of the more advanced students in urban centres.

The modern schools, like their traditional counterparts, primarily transmitted general qualifications: they created in their students a set of modern values and ideas supporting the nationalist endeavour, and a strong sense of political mission and superiority in relation to the 'backward' rural environment. In fact, the students of Chinese rural and middle and higher-level schools generally saw themselves as beacons of enlightenment in a sea of feudal darkness. In contrast to their political importance, the impact of these schools on economic life was quite restricted, as the skills and knowledge necessary to sustain life were almost always acquired directly through participation in work. This was true not only for manual workers such as farmers, blacksmiths, and carpenters, but even for shopkeepers, traditional doctors, and pharmacists.[18] Training in such trades and crafts had originally taken place in relatively formal apprenticeships, but in the Republican period was often carried out in a more casual way, with a boy following a master for a couple of years until they both felt he knew the trade. The master would in most cases be the boy's father or another close relative. Generally speaking, the transmission of economically useful skills was thus controlled by the lineage or family, while ideological instruction (Confucian or Nationalist), and the teaching of basic literacy took place in schools (traditional or modern), which were the concern of the village community as a whole with some assistance from the county-level administration, the local representative of the state. The three types of training (*sishu*, modern school, and apprenticeship) were, to a large extent, supplementary: a boy would often go to *sishu* for one or two seasons, followed by a few years in a government school, and would then start his training as, say, a blacksmith when he was physically strong enough. After the abolition of the imperial examination system in 1905, modern schooling was the most evident path to upward social mobility, but the flexible and decentralized enrolment procedures of the middle schools made it possible for *sishu* students also to be enrolled.

A household survey conducted in 1935 by the RRM provides material for an estimate of the achievements of the pre-1931 educational system.[19] Out of a total population in Zouping of 165,543 people, 85 per cent were illiterate (defined as having gone through neither traditional nor modern schooling), less than 9 per cent had been to a traditional school, 7 per cent had attended a modern primary school, and only 0.3 per cent had been to middle school. The literacy rate for the male population over the age of 40 was around 24 per cent, with only insignificant differences between those over and under 60, while it was 30 per cent for those in the 26–39 age group.[20] The establishment of modern schools, together with the continued existence of many traditional ones, had raised the literacy rate to 40 per cent for the 20–25 age group and to 47 per cent for teenage boys (age 13–19). Less than 2 per cent of the women had gone to school, most of them very young, and even when we look at girls aged between 13–19, a group that might have been expected to profit from the more positive Republican attitude to girls' education, we still find that in 1935 less than 2 per cent had received any schooling at all.

The educational realities facing Liang Shuming and the rural reconstructionists when they embarked on the reform process were thus characterized by a strong community and family involvement in education and training, and a trend towards growing enrolment rates in primary school, at least for boys. It was true that the modern schools had been forced upon the villages by the state, but the local élite was deeply involved in their promotion, and between them the new and old schools and the apprenticeship system provided a broad variety of knowledge and skills, as well as opportunities for upward social mobility. Zouping education was in no way a blank sheet of paper for the RRM to write a new story on. Still, the existing structures attracted little attention from Liang Shuming. He apparently ignored the *sishu* as well as the apprenticeship system and was highly sceptical about the modern schools, particularly their social role. Instead, he and the RRM activists set out to create a new educational and social system, and in the process intervened deeply in the life of the Zouping villages.

Adult Education and the Remodelling of Social Structures

The village communities were the building blocks of Liang's revitalized China, and the all-important interface between an ideal, distant state and the rural dwellers. In this he differed both from Sun Zhongshan, discussed by David Strand in Chapter 2 above, who focused on families and lineages at one end of the scale and on the state at the other, and from Mao Zedong, who made the villages go through the purgatory of violent class struggle before they were resurrected as cooperatives and work brigades. Considering Liang's Confucian background, the family played a surprisingly insignificant role in his rhetoric. In a speech to Zouping schoolteachers, he used families and lineages, together with religious congregations, secret societies, etc., as examples of the apparent, superficial existence of organization (*zuzhi*) in China. Such organs still belonged to the old, closed society, he claimed, where people could live all their lives without even visiting the neighbouring village. They did not match the modern world, and they offered no solution to China's 'plate of sand' syndrome.[21] The closed social space of the family and lineage would, in fact, have left little room for the operations of the intellectual activists. With the village, and in particular the village school, the reconstructionists created a stage for themselves, a public sphere where they could interact with the farmers.

Liang's followers apparently had a variety of different visions of the non-state, non-traditional social structures they wanted to establish. Yang Xiaochun, probably the most influential educational reformer in Zouping, clearly saw the village schools as embryonic forms of democratic institutions which resembled and could stand in for organizations characteristic of Western civil society. According to Yang, who was a disciple of Tao Xingzhi and was influenced by his progressive educational ideas, the Chinese lacked not only discipline, but also 'the ability to organize, so that when many people are together they can discuss and solve problems'. He found it problematic that, while Chinese history could boast many excellent and noble men, the country had never produced any stable and influential collective organizations such as the political parties or the religious and academic associations of the West. In his presentation, the new organizations should above all be such collective bodies, expressing the will of the rural population.[22]

Other RRM activists preferred to emphasize the schools' role as manifestations of state power in the villages. According to Li Nai, for example, the Chinese state had never been able to control the rural areas directly but relied instead on the local gentry and other intermediaries. In this way the responsibility for tax collection, law and order, and other public and communal affairs had fallen into the hands of individuals who often used their authority to exploit and suppress the population. The task of the new system for adult education was therefore to train a group of cadres who could take over these functions and collectively play the role of local representatives of the state, thereby strengthening the administrative efficiency of the county government. Only civil associations (*shehui tuanti*) such as the RRM could handle the task of educating the rural population, Li found, and the government would therefore have to transfer authority and money to such groups.[23]

Whatever the end goal of the village schools was, the procedures for establishing them seem to have been rather uniform.[24] When the RRM activists came to a village, they would first investigate local conditions, and then appoint to the board of trustees a group of men who had a high status among the villagers. One of these was chosen as the director, who would perform many of the same administrative tasks as the former village head had done.[25] Above the director was the school principal, who should be a generally respected gentleman of high morality and would serve as supervisor, mediator, and a last court of appeal if there were complaints against the director or the board. It was considered important that the school principal kept a neutral position in all conflicts. All other villagers, regardless of age and gender, were named the 'students' (*xuezhong*).

In this way, social relations in the village were inscribed into an educational metaphor which was well established in Chinese culture. The school principal and director would exercise their power not as representatives of state power, but as teachers, with all the traditional status attached to this position. The peasants were reduced to the role of students who were to obey both the local élite (the school board) and the urban intellectuals (the RRM), not because of the power or wealth of these people, but because of their superior knowledge and higher moral awareness.

The members of the school boards were always selected from the existing village élite. Practically all of them were male farmers over the age of 30 with considerable land holdings and former leadership experience. This was the conscious policy of the RRM, and its distinctive feature compared with, for example, Tao Xingzhi's movement in Xiaozhuang, which to a much larger extent was oriented towards the lower social strata of rural society. The RRM did not believe that reforms could be implemented without the active support of the people they saw as possessing almost all material, intellectual, and organizational resources in the villages.[26]

The old élite thus kept its position, but the content of its leadership role was challenged by the newcomers, the teachers trained by the RRM. As explained by one of the leading figures in the Zouping experiment, the traditional village leaders should handle most of the daily affairs, but it was only the teachers who could and should point out the direction of the reform process:

What is the direction? What are the methods? The original village leadership cannot know that, because this direction and these methods all relate to the larger, external society, to national affairs, to the international situation, and to the actual changes in Chinese culture. You cannot just haphazardly come up with suggestions. The teachers have gone through new [i.e., modern] training and received new enlightenment; they know a bit about the new trends . . . and have ample support and help behind them, so they can present opinions and find solutions. The task of reforming this village-level society . . . rests on their shoulders.[27]

Some RRM-sponsored initiatives which the village leaders in the school boards were expected to support fell clearly within the traditional role of the 'enlightened gentry', such as campaigns against 'unhealthy' plays and operas, foot-binding, and crime. In other fields, the movement transgressed existing borderlines between state and villages, and was subsequently met with resistance. One such case was the introduction of a household registration system in 1935. The system was rooted in national legislation, but in few places was it implemented as vigorously as in Zouping, where it was combined with a social survey which should have provided the reconstructionists with reliable data for their future work. The survey implied, among other things, that every household should be registered with a number placed on a plate outside its main gate (*menpai*), quite similar to the plates found in Chinese residential areas nowadays. The villagers were very sceptical about the whole exercise, as we can see from the following excerpt from the diary of Li Jialin, one of the activists:

There is no school in Guzhuang [a village in Qingyang township], no students from the Institute have lived here, and no propaganda has been carried out about the survey, so the masses mostly just find us meddlesome, and many even mistakenly think that we are out to find soldiers for conscription, or illegal landplots, so they don't dare to tell us the truth. This is probably a common malady of small, closed villages . . .

[In Qingyangdian, the largest village in the township] we were just going to have breakfast when the head of the town turned up . . . He complained that the weather was bad, and apparently wanted to postpone [the survey], but teacher Ru struck first and scolded them severely because our guide had run away yesterday and the door plates had been torn down, and suddenly they were at our beck and call. Then teacher Ru said a few nice words to them.

The people in charge of this village are really awful, they can't even write a door plate correctly . . . Haven't they got anyone who can read around here. I guess they deliberately ignore their public duties, following their natural tendency to muddle through their work.

Before the survey, the township director and teacher Ru . . . repeatedly told them about the survey so that they could do propaganda for us and make it known to the masses. But eight or nine times out of ten, when we come to someone's door they ask us: 'What? A population survey? What on earth is a population survey?' Does this not clearly show that the village head and director have not lived up to their responsibilities? No one in the smaller villages dares to come up with such absurd tricks.[28]

The quotation indicates that at least in some contexts local people saw the RRM as just a new way for the authorities to extract from the villages what they always came for: taxes and soldiers. It also shows that some of the activists behaved just as paternalistically as previous representatives of state power had done. But above all, the whole registration process represented an unprecedented penetration of rural society: never before had so many details about Zouping villagers, their age, education, and family conditions been known to outside authorities.

The RRM also clashed with rural society when it started to establish a local militia. This was an essential component of the rural reconstruction programme, partly because banditry was a major problem in the area, and partly because military training was perceived as a key tool for transforming the 'scattered and disorganized' village youth into a 'disciplined and organized collective'.[29] For these reasons, military training played a dominant role in the adult education programme of the RRM. In 1933, two young men from each of Zouping's fourteen townships were trained for four months at the RRM headquarters and then sent back to their local township schools to work as militia group instructors. By demanding that all instructors should be at least higher primary school graduates, the RRM again aimed at recruiting the local élite for these posts. Besides organizing military training, the instructors were expected to maintain law and order in their districts, and to keep an eye on the usual suspects: vagrants, the unemployed, drug dealers, gamblers, actors, those who wanted to undermine 'original Chinese good manners and propriety' (probably leftist activists), and militiamen who abused their power.

The selection and training of this batch of future leaders proceeded rather smoothly, but some months later the RRM decided to expand the programme dramatically and enrol 1,200 new militiamen. The new recruits were to come from respected land-owning families, and their local communities should pay their expenses during the two-month course in the county seat, and provide each of them with a rifle. This new move was met with distrust and outright hostility in the villages, where it was seen as a trick for conscripting soldiers to a warlord army, a practice with which the villagers were only too familiar. In order to escape this destiny, the first group of conscripts tried to avoid the draft by all means; some hired replacements, some fled the county, and some openly resisted the authorities. In the end, the county government had to drag their new recruits to the training ground by force. When students were recruited for the second and third groups in 1934, the villagers' attitude had become more positive, as they had seen that the first group actually returned after the course, and so gradually it became easier for the RRM to collect money for buying weapons.

Still, a certain scepticism on the part of traditional village society was not unjustified, as one explicit purpose of the adult education programme was to break down traditional bonds and loyalties and establish new ones. 'We all know', said one RRM writer, 'that in Chinese society today the "family" and the "lineage" are serious obstacles for the progress of new [forms of] organizations.' The recruits were therefore divided into groups according to their height so that men from the same village would be trained in different groups in order to 'effectively demolish their concepts of family, lineage and village'. Only later, when they had been instilled with new collective values, were they regrouped into township detachments and put under the command of their local instructors.[30]

Besides military drills, the recruits attended lessons on the ideology of the RRM and of the Nationalist Party, and on the role of the militia, the cooperatives, etc. In spite of this spiritual training, however, the RRM soon found that the recruits developed an intolerable arrogance: they started wearing leather shoes and Western clothes, and demanded still more pocket money from their village elders to sustain their expensive new habits. It is interesting to note how even the modest level of education achieved through the militia course apparently was enough to engender such a feeling of superiority among the students.

The RRM responded by decentralizing the training of subsequent classes to the township and village levels, where the students could be directly supervised by their elders. Concurrently the programme was extended to all young men between 15 and 25 years of age, first in one district, but from 1935 throughout the entire country. The course was compulsory and consisted of one hour of military training and one hour with general subjects every day for three months. Absentees were threatened with severe punishment, but in reality the RRM could do little about the numerous tricks and excuses used to escape attendance. More than 8,000 men took part in the course, which was, however, cut down to one month, officially because the county needed the young men as manpower for a water regulation project, but probably also because of local resistance.[31]

From 1936, adult education was organized directly by the village and township schools, and again the construction of village communities was a central task. At meetings organized at the township level, students from different villages wore different uniforms, or at least different colours, to distinguish them from the others, and villages competed against each other in military exercise, singing, general knowledge, and public speaking. A panel of judges gave prizes to the best performing villages rather than to individuals. In this way the RRM tried to make the farmers identify more with their villages and less with their families and lineages.[32]

In spite of the relative organizational success of adult education, however, it fell short of Liang's ideals, particularly because the RRM still had to use coercive measures to make the villagers attend. The tone was now very different from the first years, when euphoric descriptions of old and young flocking around the schools to benefit from the new knowledge were the rule. By 1936 the following picture was more common:

We maintain the viewpoint of Mr Wang Bingcheng [an RRM leader]: 'When we tell them to attend they must attend, and they should not leave before we allow them to.' The course is compulsory for everyone, because the village population is lazy and sloppy, without organization or will. We can compare them to stones: a little wind and rain will not move them an inch. If it was voluntary to attend, maybe nobody would turn up. If they could leave when they wanted to, maybe nobody would be left [in school]. In the present difficult situation for our country, we cannot go on running the schools as if they were tea houses![33]

Liang Shuming himself was deeply disappointed with the results of the adult education and social transformation his movement had initiated. The peasants, he said in late 1935, were still only the *object* of the transformation process, while the intellectuals in the movement were the active *subject*. The rural population was generally indifferent or even hostile to the intellectual activists. If given the choice, the rural population simply did not want any changes at all. They refused to be budged by his movement. According to Liang, this was the case not only in Zouping but in rural reconstruction programmes all over China.[34]

Knowledge and Power

While the RRM did not touch the formal power of the village élite, they did challenge existing conceptions of knowledge and power. Up to 1931, the transmission of practical and professional skills had been left to the families and rural communities, as mentioned above, while the role of the state and the school system by and large had been restricted to the field of general cultural knowledge. The RRM made economically relevant information one of the cornerstones of their adult education programme, and they vastly expanded the number of fields in which the village population was expected to learn new and modern techniques. The slogan of 'teaching for life', which Yang Xiaochun and other of Tao Xinzhi's students brought with them to Zouping, expressed the ambition that all aspects of human existence should be included in a flexible, non-formalized curriculum. For example, the men should learn how to use new crops and pesticides, how to hold meetings, and how to dig wells, while the women should even be trained in skills formerly considered strictly as part of the family sphere, such as child care, cooking, and sewing.[35]

Behind this enormous increase of what should and could be taught lay the belief that 'modern' learning was superior to traditional knowledge in all fields and should replace it. Liang Shuming's cultural conservatism and anti-urbanism was not matched by any very deep respect for the cultural practices or intellectual capacity of the rural population. In his opinion, even the most incompetent intellectuals could serve as the peasants' ears, eyes, and tongues by teaching them a few characters and by speaking out for them about their sufferings, and the better qualified could provide the peasants with what they needed most: a brain.[36] Though Liang's ultimate aim was the unification of the intellectual 'brain' and the peasant 'body', so that '[i]n the end there will be no difference between the two, and China's problems will be solved', there was little doubt in his mind about who were going to do the thinking on the road to this distant goal.[37]

Based on these ideas, Liang advocated a traditional Confucian rule of the wise and worthy. Although everyone should take part in the discussions held at the village schools, matters should not be settled through majority decisions, as this Western type of problem solution would be incompatible with China's traditional respect for seniority and wisdom. This was meant not just as a temporary measure; Liang believed that the more technologically complicated society got, the wider the gap between specialists and commoners would become, and the more essential, therefore, it would be that the ignorant followed the directions of the educated.[38]

The redefinition of knowledge also implied a transformation of the role of the teacher. In traditional private schools and academies, as well as in the earlier Republican schools, the teacher was primarily a transmitter of knowledge embedded in textbooks. This was most obvious during the first years in school, when students were simply taught to memorize texts without explanation, but even the later stages of the learning process were highly text-based. The teachers trained in Zouping, and the young urban intellectuals who joined the RRM, were given a more central role in the learning process, as the harbingers of modernity. Rather than teach a fixed curriculum, they were supposed to change the basic attitudes of their students through numerous different activities: speeches, exhibitions, meetings, campaigns, etc. The curriculum was now deposited in the minds of the teachers rather than in the books.

The didactic process, which now covered much broader areas of rural life, was still conceived as one-way communication running from the RRM to the villagers. The activists wanted to integrate the villagers into the world of modern learning, and to establish a less authoritarian relationship between teachers and students, but they were convinced that they had the answers while the villagers had only the questions, even in fields such as agriculture, where many peasants had a lifetime of experience. This relationship between movement and population was expressed as in the following typical presentation at the Peasants' Science Hall in Zouping:

In earlier days the school was separated from the village by high walls, and neither intervened in the other's affairs. The school was, of course, unconcerned about the difficulties and problems facing the village, and the peasants had no way of knowing what was being studied in the school . . . We think this is wrong and intend to change it. We will put school and village in touch with each other. When there is a problem in the village, we should find out about it, and find a way for [the villagers] to solve it. Once we find a way of solving it, we should tell them . . . Their problems are our problems; as we live in the same place, we should be concerned about the same problems.[39]

It is obvious that Liang Shuming, in spite of his veneration for the villages, did not share the idea found for example in Maoist thought that the accumulated work experience of the peasants represented a type of learning superior (or at least supplementary) to the 'foreign' or 'theoretical' knowledge of the intellectuals. Neither did he feel any need for the type of detailed socio-political analysis of rural conditions which Mao carried out in Hunan and Xunwu through interviews with local people.[40] The social surveys carried out in Zouping came too late to have any real influence on Liang's blueprint, and they focused more on quantitative data than on soliciting the opinions of the peasants. Liang sometimes mentions in his speeches that he is not very familiar with the situation in Zouping, does not know much about the local lineage structure, and has never lived for longer periods of time in a village.[41] Such phrases should, perhaps, be taken just as polite figures of speech, but they probably also reflect the deeper reality that Liang, like the traditional literati and, one could add, many present-day Chinese intellectuals, did not believe that what the peasants could tell him would be of much interest.

Although the RRM generally paid little attention to local knowledge, there was an interesting exception which was related to the idea of reconstructing village society. The RRM did introduce specific information about the Zouping area into the curriculum. Traditional teaching materials were designed to provide a common basic knowledge of Chinese culture and history. As elementary education was the first step on the way to mastering a culture that saw itself as valid globally, the question of local relevance never arose. The categorizations used in *The Three Character Classic*, for example, were studied universally throughout China, and children memorized the names of the same six kinds of grain and the same six types of domestic animal no matter which crops and beasts were actually found in the fields around their village. During the Nationalist era the standardizing function of the educational system was equally crucial, now as part of the building of a nation state, and the idea of a nationally unified curriculum was generally accepted, though the provinces had some leeway for introducing minor changes. National symbols, national heroes, and knowledge about Chinese history and geography were essential for the creation of a national consciousness, while localized knowledge was often perceived as irrelevant or even detrimental to this project. The education programmes of the RRM, however, rehabilitated a knowledge of local affairs, at least as a didactic device to give the villagers a better grasp of the national situation. The purpose of the course in history and geography for militiamen, for example, was to 'give [the students] a clear understanding of local geography and of changes in the local area since the Opium War, and of the changes in the general situation in China'.[42] Similarly, the Teacher Training School organized the publication of a book series on local affairs including titles such as *A Guide Book of Zouping, Songs from Zouping*, and *Zouping Peasant Proverbs*.[43]

Childhood Education and the Diffusion of Modern Values

Liang Shuming's educational strategy focused on the adult population, and the development under the RRM of the regular village primary schools was not too impressive. The total number of school-aged children in the county was around 20,000–25,000 during the 1930s,[44] and in 1931 the 282 village primary schools existing at that time enrolled around 8,000 students. By 1937 the number of schools was down to 272 while the number of students approached 9,000. Though this figure was not low by the standards of the time, the development in the 1930s did not even keep up with the speed of the years before the arrival of the RRM, when the number of students had risen from more than 3,000 to more than 7,000 between 1921 and 1930.[45] By 1937, however, an additional 5,000 children were taught by other children in informal groups (*gongxuechu*), where one regular primary school pupil gathered a small number of friends around him for training in basic reading and calculating skills. Education for girls continued to develop rather slowly, although the number of female students in the regular schools doubled between 1932 and 1934, and their share of the places rose from 6 to 12 per cent.

Although the quantitative growth of primary education was limited, the flagship of the RRM's educational efforts, the combined teacher training school and experimental school in the county seat of Zouping, became the centre for the first radical reforms of teaching methods in the history of the area. The transformation from traditional to modern schools in the beginning of the century had modernized and diversified the curriculum, and changed the method of instruction from an individualized approach to one of class teaching, but the role of the teacher and the reliance on rote learning and recitation had not changed. The two men who introduced new concepts in this field to Zouping were Yang Xiaochun and Zhang Zonglin, who had both been working with Tao Xingzhi in Xiaozhuang and had been recommended by him to Liang Shuming.

Zhang Zonglin, who was appointed headmaster of the Zouping teacher training school in 1935, was a specialist in pre-school education, and he broke radically with Chinese traditions in his recognition of the individuality and personal rights of children, and in his redefinition of the role of the teacher. According to Zhang, the typical Chinese primary schoolteacher was a merciless tyrant, killing every sprout of joy and curiosity in the children:

Sitting on a tiger skin, a cane in his hand, with the cold expression of a judge, putting on sullen and nauseating airs, and scaring innocent and lively little children out of their wits as if they were devilish offenders, that is the awe-inspiring power of ordinary primary schoolteachers.[46]

Parents and teachers alike thought that they were serving the children's best interests by forcing them to study the prescribed textbooks, claimed Zhang, but after a few years 'the children's backs are hunched, their hands are weak, their feet cannot run, and their eyes are near-sighted'.[47] Such critiques of China's rural education have regularly been heard in the media throughout the twentieth century, but Zhang Zonglin's was more radical in his suggested solution than its present-day echoes: 'The purpose of education is not to give the children a lot of knowledge, but to nourish in them the ability to solve the problems in life.'[48] The best way to do this was to encourage students to ask questions and let the pedagogical process be guided by these questions rather than by curriculum guidelines: 'The question method fundamentally does not recognize the existence of curriculum subjects: all questions arise, fresh and lively, from life itself. Can children's lives be restricted by subjects in a curriculum?'[49] Zhang did, in fact, often sound directly opposed to schooling in his rhetoric: 'Why must children in primary school learn arithmetic which has nothing to do with them? Why force them to read about "the big dog barks, the little dog jumps"? Why not let them out into the merry world of nature?'[50]

The teacher should carry out the question-guided teaching with a smile on his face, addressing the children (called 'little friends') politely and in a soft voice, although he should not give in to unreasonable whims and demands.[51]

Zhang Zonglin stayed in Zouping for less than a year. It is ironic that this prophet of flexible and non-authoritarian schooling was expelled from Zouping because of his connections to the CCP, which in the 1950s introduced curriculum guidelines and teaching plans as rigid as anything China had ever seen. When Zhang organized a demonstration to demand that the Guomindang government stop fighting the Communists and instead resist the Japanese, he was expelled by the county magistrate in early 1936. Still, although his ideas were never fully implemented in Zouping, he made a deep impression on many people who later became teachers in the area.[52] One informant who had attended Zhang's course remembered him very clearly because Zhang, unlike the other teachers, never gave lectures, but actually talked to the students and discussed things with them, often organizing them to work in groups to seek their own answers to the questions he asked. He also encouraged the future teachers to do away with the squared writing paper normally used for character practice, and instead let the children write the characters as large or small as they wanted to. While this may seem to be an insignificant detail, it was symbolic of his break with the mimetic approach so dominant in the Chinese didactic tradition, where students were always taught to reproduce the model exactly.

With Zhang Zonglin, the radicality of Liang Shuming's social reforms were extended to the sphere of teaching practice. Zhang's view of children, their individuality, and the role of the teacher were a clear break with the past inspired by Tao Xingzhi and contemporary Western ideas, but the goals he set were so high that they contributed to a feeling of frustration among his followers. Two of the experimental school's leaders, for example, were forced to recognize that their experiments had helped to show only that nothing could be accomplished within the framework of the present school system, with its curriculum guidelines and timetables, and that they as teachers were actually 'ruthlessly grasping the children's fragile throats with ice-cold iron fists, while on the other hand hypocritically shouting out to them "be spontaneous, get organized" '.[53]

While most village schools were left practically untouched by Zhang's radical ideas, the children who lived close to the experimental school felt that something new was going on, and many parents in this area even started to send their girls to school.[54] The teaching became more varied, with singing and drawing lessons, military training, etc., and the pedagogical ideas of the teachers were advanced even by international standards. However, even in the experimental school, it is doubtful how many of these ideas were actually implemented. The school enjoyed considerable prestige in the area, but when former students think back on it now they tend to praise its high academic standards rather than its radicalism: the teachers had a good educational background as graduates from modern schools; they came from several provinces, bringing with them news from a wider world; and the school offered a sound preparation for going on to middle school, for example mission schools in nearby Zhoucun or in Jinan. What the students and their families appreciated, in short, were those features that pointed *up* the social ladder and *out* from the narrow village world. They responded positively to the access to modernity offered to them, rather than to Liang's visions of a re-traditionalized 'rural' social order.

Concluding Remarks

Although Liang's ideas on rural reconstruction differed in several respects from those of his contemporaries, the actual policies of the RRM were not so distinct. Face to race with rural realities, Liang became more of a prototype modernizer and less of the anti-state protector of village China whom we meet in his writings. The RRM penetrated rural society and opened it up for nationalist mobilization and the ideology of modernization by trying to break down existing social structures and build up alternative organizations. These new organizations, the village schools, were not democratic in the Western, liberal, sense of the word, but they still represented an attempt to integrate the rural population more actively into the local political process, and some of the activists, at least, hoped they would develop into organs that could truthfully reflect local demands.

This was no easy process, however. To the RRM, the existing social infrastructure of the villages did not qualify as an alternative to state dominance. Liang Shuming demanded a double set of qualities from the new types of organization, which often seem to be imminent also in present-day discussions of the organized expressions of civil society: they should be voluntary, independent, and indigenous, while at the same time being modern, progressive, and socially (or even globally) responsible. In the eyes of Liang and the RRM, only associations like their own, which combined formal independence from the state with the ideology of modernization, could fully embody 'society'. In the course of the reforms, however, it became increasingly clear that the function of the RRM was that of a mediator between the Chinese state and a rural hinterland which had so far been almost inaccessible to state officials. This role had earlier been played by the village élite, and the RRM consistently tried to find allies among this stratum. However, the urban intellectuals in the movement were fully aware, and were constantly reminded, that their ideas and values were far removed from those of the rural population. In this sense, the image used by the two Zouping school leaders about the relationship between teachers and children could also describe the general dilemma of the RRM: they were shouting for self-organized grass-root activities while clutching the villagers' throats to keep them from returning to their original 'backward' ways. To the people of Zouping, the distinction that Liang Shuming found so important between state-directed reforms and an 'NGO' like his own movement must have been vague indeed.

A particular problem was the inability of the RRM to integrate traditional and modern knowledge systems, or at least to recognize some value in the learning and experiences of the rural population. In spite of their general good intentions, the reformers seem to have lacked respect for the villagers, and showed little curiosity about their world. These problems were not unique for the RRM, or even for China, but it is remarkable that a movement that directed so much attention to them still was so far from solving them.

It appears that the RRM got the best response from the villages when it was most 'state-like', as was the case in the reforms of primary education. Perhaps the experimental school became popular in Zouping mainly because it qualified its students to other schools at higher levels, and thereby to social advancement and, ultimately, to urban careers. With its diverse and academically qualified teaching staff and its novel ideas of freedom and individuality, however, it also introduced Zouping to the modern world and changed the sultry air in the classroom. The repercussions of this modernization were felt for decades, while the village schools themselves broke down the moment the Japanese moved in.

NOTES

1. For a full discussion of this phenomenon, see Charles W. Hayford, *To The People: James Yen and Village China* (New York: Columbia University Press, 1990).
2. Guy S. Alitto, *The Last Confucian: Liang Shu-ming and the Chinese Dilemma of Modernity* (Berkeley: University of California Press, 2nd edn, 1986).
3. For more information on Liang Shuming's life and philosophy, see Alitto, *The Last Confucian*.
4. *Eastern and Western Cultures* is discussed in detail in Alitto, *The Last Confucian*, 75–134. For the text in Chinese see Liang Shuming, *Zhong-xi wenhua ji qi zhexue* (East–West Culture and Philosophy), in *Liang Shuming quanji* (Liang Shu-ming's Collected Works, hereafter *LSMQJ*), i (Jinan: Shandong renmin chubanshe, 1989), 319–547.
5. Liang Shumin, 'Dong-xi-ren de jiaoyu zhi bu tong' (Differences in the Education of Easterners and Westerners) (1922), in *LSMQJ* iv.655–9.
6. Liang's own account of his tour can be found in 'Beiyou suo jian jilüe' (Record of What I Saw During my Travels to the North) (1929), in *LSMQJ* iv.874–904.
7. The rest of Liang's career is only of marginal interest here, and I will just briefly mention that he came to terms with the CCP after the establishment of the People's Republic, and, though he was severely cricitized in the 1970s, his biographer, Guy Alitto, found him to be very satisfied with life when he met him in 1980 and 1984. Right until his death in 1988, Liang stuck to those views on Confucianism and Chinese culture which he had held through most of the 20th century.
8. Liang Shuming, 'Zhongguo jingji jianshe du luxian' (The Road to Economic Construction in China) (1937), in *LSMQJ* v.984–96, quotation from p. 988.
9. Liang Shuming, *Xiangcun jianshe dayi* (The Gist of Rural Reconstruction) (1936), in *LSMQJ* i.599–720, particularly 611–15.
10. Liang Shuming, 'Xiangnong xuexiao de banfa ji qi yiyi' (The Methods and Purpose of Rural Schools) (1933), in *LSMQJ* v.347–56.
11. Liang Shuming, 'Cunxue xiangxue shiyi' (Explaining the Meaning of Village Schools and Township Schools) (1934), in *LSMQJ* v.438–47.
12. Liang Shuming, 'Shehui benwei de jiaoyu xitong cao'an' (Plans for an Educational System Based on Social Ethics) (1933), in *LSMQJ* v.393–410, quotation from 397.
13. Liang Shuming, 'Danmai de jiaoyu yu women de jiaoyu' (Danish Education and Our Education), in *LSMQJ* vii.653–84, quoted from 678.
14. ibid. I have discussed Liang's relation to the folk high schools in Stig Thøgersen, 'Liang Shuming and the Danish Model', in Søren Clausen, Roy Starrs, and Anne Weddell-Wedellsborg (eds.), *Cultural Encounters: China, Japan and the West* (Aarhus: Aarhus University Press, 1995), 267–88.
15. The information in this section is based on *Zouping xian jiaoyuzhi* (A Gazetteer of Zouping Education) (Zouping: Shandong sheng chubanzongshe Huimin fenshe, 1990), and on a number of interviews which I conducted in Zouping in 1992 and 1993.

16. For a traditional elementary education in China see Evelyn S. Rawski, *Education and Popular Literacy in Ch'ing China* (Ann Arbor: University of Michigan Press, 1979); and Sally Borthwick, *Education and Social Change in China: The Beginnings of the Modern Era* (Stanford, Cal.: Hoover Institution Press, 1983), particularly 1–37.

17. I even met a man in Zouping who had attended *sishu* with his grandfather as late as in 1961, after he had finished agricultural middle school.

18. The only important exception to this rule are the schoolteachers, who were gradually required to go through professional training after the turn of the century.

19. Wu Guyu (ed.), *Zouping shiyanxian hukou diaocha baogao* (Report from Household Survey in Zouping Experimental County) (Shanghai: Zhonghua shuju, 1936). The survey offers information on the general educational level in the county, as well as on the distribution of education according to gender, age, and geographical place. It is therefore possible to extract information on the pre-1931 cohorts.

20. There may have been some under-reporting of reading skills gained from traditional schools, as such schools were illegal during certain periods.

21. Liang Shuming, *Xiangcun jianshe dayi*, 625–8.

22. Yang Xiaochun, 'Zhongguo nongcun fuxing yu jiaoyu gaizao' (The Revival of China's Villages and Educational Reform), *Jiaoyu zazhi* (China Education Review), 24:1 (1934), 81–5.

23. Li Nai, 'Zouping er nian lai de xiangcun qingnian xunlian zhi wo jian' (My View on the Training of Rural Youth in Zouping During the Last Two years), *Xiangcun jianshe* (Rural Reconstruction), 5:10 (1936), no pag.

24. The following paragraph builds on the recollections of Xu Shuren, who served as county magistrate of Zouping for two periods while Liang was there. See *Zouping wenshi ziliao xuanji* (Collected Materials on Zouping's Culture and History), 4 (1988), 115–48. See also Alitto, *The Last Confucian*, 248–53. Liang Shuming has described his vision of how the schools should work in detail in 'Cunxue xiangxue xu zhi' (What Ought to be Known About Village and Township Schools) (1934), in *LSMQJ* v.448–65.

25. From 1933 Zouping received the status of experimental county. This gave the RRM a free hand to establish administrative procedures that did not follow national regulations.

26. A detailed argument for this strategy, together with a description of the social background of the leadership of one village school, can be found in Gong Zhuchuan, 'Benyuan Cuijiapo shiyan minzhong xuexiao de banfa ji qi yiyi' (The Methods and Purpose of Our Institute's Experimental Popular School in Cuijiapo), *Xiangcun jianshe*, 5:27–9 (1933), 10–26.

27. Li Xingsan, 'Zouping shi-yi shi-er xiang xiangxue xinde gongzuo fadong zhi di-yi feng xin' (First Letter on the Initiation of New Work in the Township Schools of the Eleventh and Twelfth Townships), *Xiangcun jianshe*, 5:6 (1935), no pag.

28. In Wu Guyu, *Zouping shiyanxian hukou diaocha baogao*, 50.

29. Li Nai, 'Zouping er nian lai de xiangcun qingnian xunlian zhi wo jian'.

30. ibid.

31. ibid.

32. Han Shao, 'Zouping di shi xiang chengnian jiaoyu shishi' (The Implementation of Adult Education in Zouping's Tenth Township), *Xiangcun jianshe*, 5:13 (1936), no pag.

33. Song Leyan, 'Zouping de chengnian jiaoyu' (Adult Education in Zouping), 2, *Xiangcun jianshe*, 6:16 (1937), no pag.

34. Liang Shuming, 'Women de liang da nanchu' (Our Two Big Difficulties) (1936), in *LSMQJ* ii.573–85.

35. Yang Xiaochun, 'Xiangnong xuexiao de xuetuan bianzhi' (The Formation of Study Groups in the Peasant Schools), *Xiangcun jianshe*, 2:22–3 (1933), 8–16.

36. Liang Shuming, 'Shandong xiangcun jianshe yanjiuyuan sheli zhiqu ji banfa gaiyao' (Outline of the Objective and Methods of the Establishment of the Shandong Rural Reconstruction Research Institute) (1930), in *LSMQJ* v.222–39, quotation from 227.

37. Liang Shuming, 'Zhongguo wenti zhi jiejue' (The Solution to China's Problems) (1930), in *LSMQJ* v.206–20, quotation from 218.

38. Liang Shuming, *Xiangcun jianshe dayi*, 657, 698–9, 710.

39. Zhang Boan and Zhu Baojian, 'Women de nongmin kexueguan' (Our Peasants' Science Hall), *Xiangcun jianshe*, 5:8–9 (1935), no pag.

40. Mao Zedong, 'Report on an Investigation of the Peasant Movement in Hunan', in *Selected Works of Mao Tse-tung* (Peking: Foreign Languages Press, 1967), i.23–59; Mao Zedong, *Report from Xunwu*, trans. and with an intro. and notes by Roger R. Thompson (Stanford: Stanford University Press, 1990).

41. Liang Shuming, *Xiangcun jianshe da yi*, 625, 632.

42. Li Nai, 'Zouping er nian lai de xiangcun qingnian zhi wo jian'.

43. 'Xiang-shi bianyin ertong duwu ji minzhong duwu' (The Rural Teacher Training School Publishes Reading Materials for Children and the Masses), in *Xiangcun jianshe*, 5:6 (1935), no pag.

44. The figures in this paragraph are, unless otherwise indicated, from *Zouping xian jiayuzhi*, 345–65.

45. ibid. 131–3.

46. Zhang Zonglin, 'Dadao shi wei' (Down with the Teacher's Power) (1931), in Zhang Lu (ed.), *Zhang Zonglin youer jiaoyu lunji* (Zhang Zonglin's Selected Works on the Education of Children) (Changsha: Hunan jiaoyu chubanshe, 1985), 830–4.

47. Zhang Zonglin, 'Jiefang ertong' (Liberate the Children) (1930), in ibid. 820–3.

48. Zhang Zonglin, 'Jiefang ertong de kou' (Liberate the Children's Mouths) (1931), in ibid. 824–9.

49. ibid.

50. Zhang Zonglin, 'Jiefang ertong'.

51. Zhang Zonglin, 'Xiaoxue jiaoshi dui ertong de taidu' (The Attitude of Primary School Teachers Towards Children) (1930), in ibid. 735–9.

52. Wang Jingwu and Song Yiping, 'Huiyi Zhang Zonglin xiaozhang zai Zouping xian-li jianyi xiang-shi de shiji' (Director Zhang Zounglin's Achievements at the Zouping County Simple Rural Teachers Training School), in ibid. 7–12.

53. Zhang Boan and Liang Junda, 'Women de xiaoxue jingyan jingguo' (The Results of Our Experimental Primary Education), in *Xiangcun jianshe*, 5 (1935): 8–9.

54. This paragraph is based on interviews conducted in Zhongxingcun, Zouping, in 1992 and 1993.

7

Bases for Civil Society in Reform China

Thomas Gold[1]

The popular demonstrations of 1989 revealed a number of things about the Chinese people, or, more specifically, about many urban Chinese. They exposed the depth of frustration with the slow pace of political reform, with the corruption of the élite, and with the loss of many of the certainties of the old system, such as fixed prices and the iron rice bowl. The demonstrations also made clear to the world, and to the Chinese people themselves, that the people were not, as commonly assumed, mere passive objects of party policy, but were capable of acting as subjects, as agents of historical change, organizing on their own without party mediation, and articulating their grievances in public.[2]

Obviously, the Communist Party did not sanction this autonomous organization and expression of opinion, no matter how small a percentage of the population actually joined in. But it occurred anyway, in urban areas throughout the country, as well as some rural locations. Paralysed for more than a month by factional struggles, the party could not act to stop or co-opt it, and the movement spread and grew.

In the view of many analysts, the growth of the movement and autonomous organizations revealed that, in spite of four decades of pervasive Communist Party political hegemony over society, something comparable to what is called 'civil society' in the West and in Eastern Europe had started to emerge, and from a variety of different social bases.

In this chapter, I will first discuss the meaning, significance, and problems with the concept of civil society, and then speculate, as much from imagination as from hard evidence, about possible bases for the emergence of civil society in China, in spite of the 1989 crackdown. In the final section, I will address issues of facilitating and constraining factors in the emergence and consolidation of civil society in China. I hope that this will go some way towards clarifying the concept, generating empirical research, and helping us understand the process of reconstruction underway in China.[3]

Civil Society

It is no mean task to come up with a definition of civil society that will receive universal acceptance, even (or especially) within the China field, or agreement of its relevance for the study of China.[4]

I use 'civil society' to mean the realm between society and the state, where associations of autonomous individuals, participating voluntarily, enjoy autonomy to establish themselves, determine their boundaries and membership, administer their own affairs, and engage in relationships with other similar associations. 'Civil society rests first of all on the idea of the autonomous individual and the terms of association, trust, and mutuality between these individuals articulated on general, universal principles (principles whose first stage of realization must be in the classical idea of citizenship)'.[5] The existence of civil society can be certified by the appearance of a variety of associations engaging in public contestation on their own account, meaning not as agents of the state or Leninist party, although, as I will argue later, they may in fact be organs of the party–state in a Leninist system. The degree of formal organization of these associations is not set—what end up as organizations often originate as social movements.[6]

The autonomy of elements constituting civil society is not absolute, and varies widely along a continuum within and among different political systems and traditions. The fact that an organization registers with the state and is thereby subject to legal limits on its activities does not automatically mean that it lacks 'true' or 'real' autonomy[7] and is thereby disqualified as one element making up civil society. The same goes for a *de facto* autonomously operating association which 'hangs on to' (*guakao*) an official organization for protection. Owing to historical and cultural factors, there is no reason why in practice civil society in Communist China should look like civil society in post-communist Hungary or post-authoritarian Taiwan, but there will be enough commonalities that one can, with some confidence, certify the existence of civil society there.

Civil society is not the same as 'society'.[8] The latter is a realm made up primarily of individuals, the family, particularistic ties, and unorganized and unregulated informal activities. It is the realm of the private. For heuristic purposes, if we think of 'society' as the largest of a series of concentric circles, then 'civil society' is a more narrow aspect of society, a sphere where individuals, often from very diverse backgrounds, come together on their own and in groups, to pursue interests that in some way address public (community) affairs, including those of the state. This does not include taking over the state: that is the arena of a still narrower subset that grows out of civil society, namely, political society. Ideal-typical civil society includes such things as the media, religious organizations, labour unions, schools, think tanks, philanthropic and other community-oriented bodies such as foundations, and voluntary associations based on common interests or characteristics—private individuals coming together in the *public sphere*[9] to pursue individual and group interests. Although some of these interests and activities are certainly more weighty than others, in a system where the political authority attempted to eliminate literally all non-party-led associations, any autonomous organization takes on political significance, proof of which can be seen in the ruthlessness with which the authorities attempt to stamp them out.

The innermost of these concentric circles is the state—the sum of organizations of administration, coercion, adjudication, defence, welfare, and so on. In liberal democracies, its makeup and policies reflect the balance of power among more or less organized groups and classes in civil society.

Groups in civil society may be quite anti-democratic, and may try to form parties or movements to eliminate other groups, rather than to engage them in competition for influence in civil society and/or the state. The idea of 'civility' is important here, meaning a code of manners (probably derived from the bourgeoisie-dominated urban areas (*civis*) which gave 'civil' society its name) according to which organs of civil society should treat each other.[10] Civil society without any supervising agency runs the risk of degenerating into a Hobbesian nightmare of the war of all against all—*luan* in Chinese. This implies the need for a state that legitimates and protects individual autonomy, and sets guidelines and institutionalized means for forces in civil and political society to compete.[11] As Chamberlain writes, 'Although civil society is a relatively autonomous entity, distinct from both state and society, it nevertheless partakes of both, and faces and constantly interacts with both.'[12]

In a recent formulation, Juan Linz and Alfred Stepan propose five interrelated arenas necessary for a consolidated democracy, each of which has its own organizing principle which reinforces the arenas. The authors distinguish among civil society, political society, the rule of law, state apparatus, and economic society. Clearly, in this view, the state guarantees and enforces the freedoms necessary for civil society to exist.[13]

The metaphor of a competitive market is important, and reflects the role of the bourgeoisie in creating civil society in the first place. Marx and Engels, basing themselves on Hegel, defined civil society as 'embrac[ing] the whole material intercourse of individuals within a definite stage of the development of productive forces. It embraces the whole commercial and industrial life of a given stage'.[14]

So, in analysing the existence and nature of civil society. I see it not as a matter of *either* civil society *or* the state, but rather as a fluid relation wherein the state establishes rules but permits autonomous groups to exist and compete for influence. At the same time, the state itself must be subject to laws and institutions: it cannot enjoy unlimited power.

In an ideal-typical Marxist–Leninist system ('totalitarianism'), civil society is by definition non-existent.[15] In such a system, as part of its revolutionary transformative mission (and the practical need to eradicate opponents), the communist party tries to reshape society from without and within, eliminating whatever civil society might have existed and preventing its (re-)emergence. It tries to atomize individuals, shattering the type of trust essential, in Seligman's analysis cited above, for civil society. It removes autonomy, forbidding individuals from coming together on their own in non-supervised associational life, including such traditional forms as extended kin and personal networks.[16] As a result, there is 'society' as defined above; however, the sort of organizations or even movements I listed as comprising *civil* society may have names indicating autonomy, but in reality would be cells of the corporatist body, all infiltrated and dominated by agents of the communist party–state, intentionally designed to prevent autonomous activity.[17] In this type of system, the party and state are indistinguishable in practice; the state is little more than the executive arm of the party. There is no institutionalized 'political society', as no other parties or social movements can contend for power over the state.

The concentric circle image needs to be reconceptualized in a two-part, three-dimensional way as a party–state both above and imbricating society. Were the autonomous elements characteristic of civil society to coalesce, a form of zero-sum game (at least in the party's perception) would ensue, in that it would compel the party–state to withdraw from penetration and dominance of some organizations and activities, and the party–state would also be compelled to lay down some rules for emerging civil society. This means the party–state would set out the parameters of a public sphere in which groups, through various means and media, could debate issues, jockey for influence, and make their existence and positions known. The components of civil society would not necessarily be interested in establishing political parties or taking over the state, just in attaining some control over their activities. However, because of the totalitarian impulses of a Marxist–Leninist system, any of these activities takes on political significance and, as has been seen in practice in Eastern and Central Europe, can function as an opening wedge to weaken the party–state's control over society. In a plausible scenario, the state above society would retract back towards and into society, withdrawing its tentacles, and undergoing restructuring to reflect the new situation.

Ascertaining the existence of civil society—that is, operationalizing and measuring this dependent variable—in a Marxist–Leninist system is problematic. Is there some threshold of group numbers or media presentations which, when crossed, indicates that a viable civil society has emerged? Does one autonomous group a civil society make? Does the knowledge of secret underground churches and labour unions mean that civil society exists? Do formal constitutional provisions guaranteeing the right of assembly and organization, even though they are never implemented in practice, indicate civil society? Does an article in the media critical of the party prove independence? This is a grey area. I would have to argue that the answer to the threshold question is a weak yes, meaning that, if groups commonly thought of as comprising civil society have emerged in fact, we can at the very least speak of nascent or incipient civil society, but the answer would be a strong yes if the state then permitted them to carry on with their affairs, openly, and over time.[18]

The pervasiveness of the party in all associations makes it difficult to gauge the degree of actual autonomy of action. For instance, a newspaper's journalists may engage in some sort of street protest or publicize their autonomous position different from the party's in its pages, as happened in Beijing in 1989. The party cadres in the paper may approve and even lead this action but it may be part of a factional power struggle within the party. It thus has one foot in autonomous participation in the public sphere, but the other still caught in the totalitarian system.

As noted earlier, there is controversy surrounding the applicability of the term 'civil society' to a study of contemporary China. This is because the concept originated in studies of the very different historical trajectory of Europe, and was revived (some would argue distorting the original meaning) in the early 1980s to discuss the breakdown of European Marxist–Leninist totalitarian regimes.[19] However, in my view, 'civil society' is a useful concept for the study of China for several reasons. First, structurally, Communist China shares essential features with the former Soviet Union and its bloc—not surprisingly, given their role in creating communist institutions in China. Second, although the historical legacies and recent processes may differ, the phenomenon of autonomous associations materializing and challenging party–state monopoly over society is comparable. For both of these reasons, adding the comparative case of China can help us to understand the diversity of structures and processes, causes and outcomes, in reforming communist systems. Third, we are prisoners of language: since this is the term being used in this discourse, we should use it to bring China into the discussion, even as we remain sensitive to its problematic nature. Finally, the term is being employed by Chinese dissidents at home and abroad as an essential piece of their activist strategy and a blueprint for a post-communist China. It thus has a very real-world relevance which needs to be considered.

In the next section, I will distinguish what I see as potential bases for civil society grounded in the specific institutions of communist China.

Bases for Civil Society in Reform China

This is not the place for a detailed review of the reforms initiated in China after the landmark Third Plenum of the Eleventh Central Committee of the Communist Party in December 1978. I will single out aspects of the reforms relevant for the discussion of potential bases for civil society. The gist is that the reforms have unleashed a number of interactive economic, social, cultural, legal, and political forces which are impacting on China's institutional structure in such a way as to create the possibility of the emergence and consolidation of civil society and a possible democratic transition.

1. *Economic* 'Open to the outside world, enliven the domestic economy', the watchword of the reforms, has brought in foreign investment and enlarged foreign trade. In the autumn of 1992, the official line became the intentionally vague 'socialist market economy'. As the role of the market has expanded and that of the plan shrunk, enterprises have been compelled to compete and take responsibility for their own profit and loss at the risk of bankruptcy. This includes schools, think tanks, and cultural troupes. The collective, private and foreign-invested sectors have grown much faster than the state-owned sector. Collective and small state-owned enterprises have been subcontracted to individuals and operated on a quasi-private basis, and many state-owned enterprises are listed on stock exchanges in China and abroad. Agriculture has been decollectivized and farmers encouraged to undertake sideline activities. As a result of these reforms, more and more valuable resources are passing from government control into the hands of private and quasi-private interests, including foreign ones. A labour market has replaced the job assignment system for most urbanites. Local governments compete with each other to provide incentives for local and foreign investors. The tourist and service sectors have exploded, with most of the country now open even to foreign visitors.

2. *Social* The party now tolerates, even encourages, inequality of income and diversity of life styles. People have the chance (which many do not want) to make their own way in the world and take responsibility for their personal achievements and failures. Subsidies and entitlements are being commoditized. There are new opportunities for geographical, occupational, and class mobility. The status of private business people has risen

significantly. The explosion of the consumer economy has dramatically changed the quality of life and expectations. Minority nationalities have more freedom to maintain their unique features and manage their own affairs. Public opinion polls publicize and legitimate differences in positions and attitudes, as well as making citizens aware of the fact that there are others who feel the way they do about issues, ways that might be at odds with the official line. Professional and personal contact with foreigners is less curtailed. Individuals have begun to claim more of a private sphere of friendship, romance, family life, and taste outside of official control.

3. *Control* Popular culture has been dramatically de-ideologized, artists enjoy broader freedom of artistic expression, and foreign culture has entered the market in a big way. Popular culture of all kinds from Taiwan to Hong Kong is especially prevalent. Performers, creators and publishers are all responsible for their economic fate, increasing the commercialization of culture. There is a legitimization of leisure time and the role of entertainment. The teaching and promulgation of communist ideology have been radically curtailed. Religious institutions have been reopened and expanded along with revived ties with foreign religious bodies and figures. Intellectuals are more free to study and discuss foreign philosophies and intellectual trends among themselves and with foreign counterparts.

4. *Legal* Criminal, economic, and civil codes, as well as laws of procedure, have been promulgated and massively propagandized. Foreign experts have been involved at many stages. Law schools have been expanded. Laws and the constitution have been amended to improve the business environment and formally codify the reform institutions. Some of this has been done for the sake of foreign investors and Hong Kong and Taiwan citizens concerned about future reunification. Legally binding contracts have begun to define the relations among economic units, even state-owned ones. Citizens have tentatively begun to sue each other and official organizations.

5. *Political* Although the Communist Party does not tolerate challenges to its monopoly of power, it has upgraded the stature and role of the People's Congresses, People's Political Consultative Conferences, and democratic parties, while also bringing new blood into them. The Ministry of Civil affairs has begun to experiment with free, though non-partisan, elections for village leaders. The party has defined with greater clarity its role in the political sphere. The civil service is more professional and staffed by more technocrats.

These forces and trends have not impacted on all of China's diverse regions, peoples, and organizations in the same way, of course. Aggressive promotion, deliberate obstruction, local traditions, and geographical location have all played additional roles.

I now turn to elements in China which I believe, in particular circumstances, could function as bases for civil society, that is to say, could either free themselves from direct party control or establish themselves outside party leadership, in order to manage their own affairs and, in time, gain the legitimacy and protection of the state.

Enterprises

China's economic system comprises state, collective, private, and foreign-invested enterprises, as well as joint ventures across types.

State enterprises are still very much part of the party-dominated system.[20] They have party secretaries and are subject to bureaucratic intervention. None the less, there have been many changes which make it conceivable that they could function autonomously and become a base for civil society. The reforms have reduced the role of the plan and the dependence of state enterprises on the state. Instead of subordinate vertical ties to ministries and bureaus, they now operate through horizontal contractual relations with other enterprises in the state, collective, private, and foreign sectors. They are permitted to file suit against other enterprises for breach of contract. The state is trying to separate ownership (by the 'whole people', i.e. the state) from management by professionals. The scope of the plan has been drastically reduced, so the enterprises are responsible for their own profit and loss. This means that the workers' well-being is more directly tied to the economic performance of the enterprise. This may raise their sense of empowerment *vis-à-vis* how the enterprise is run, and compel beleaguered managers to lobby on behalf of their firm in the public sphere, through whatever means are available. Managers have more choice over whom they hire, and workers have more employment options as well.

Collective enterprises are even more subject to the market and increased labour mobility, although they too—the larger ones at least—continue to have party leadership, and are vulnerable to political and personal manipulation. But, as Mayfair Yang shows, they foster a sense of corporate identity on their members, which may bring them into conflict with the state.[21]

In parts of the countryside, entire villages are being reinvented as 'enterprises' (*shiye gongsi*), where the party branch secretary becomes the general manager or chairman of the board. These bodies very definitely foster a corporate identity among their members, and on occasion can act against the state.[22] They represent 'new organizations of an associational character', between state and society, protecting 'an increasingly atomized

population' both from the 'still relatively monolithic state' and 'the insta-
bilities, insecurities and inequalities of the market'.[23]

What is more, some villages have begun to experiment with free, though
non-partisan, elections for their own leaders, with candidates appealing
for votes on the basis of their ability to lead economic development as well
as serve the interests of the villagers.[24]

Private enterprises, both small individual households (*getihu*) and
larger private firms (*siying qiye*), are the most integrated into the market.
They need to deal with enterprises in the other sectors, as well as the
bureaucracy. Although marginal in terms of their legitimacy in a still
self-styled socialist country (albeit now watered-down to 'market socialism', whatever that is), they have become a significant force in the economy and society through employment and satisfaction of many essential
needs.[25]

Foreign-invested enterprises also need to be considered a potential base
for civil society. They and their employees enjoy a certain amount of protection from the Chinese system. Foreign investors, including lawyers,
have been very influential in pressuring the state to introduce and implement laws and procedures to improve the investment climate. This has
included some degree of impartiality in arbitration of business disputes,
clarifying the duties and obligations of all signatories to a contract, and
forcing party officials and party organizations out of enterprises.

The picture that is forming bears resemblance to Marx and Engels's
conception of civil society, an objectively functioning realm of industry
and commerce mediated by the market and subject to various institutions
and laws. Even enterprises that are part of the state now must compete in
this market.

*Units (*danwei*)*

The basic cell of urban Chinese society is the unit, or *danwei*. The business
firms just discussed are examples, but so are schools, hospitals, government offices, theatrical troupes, and so on. In addition to providing work,
they perform a variety of costly functions, such as, housing, health care,
child care, elder care, education, allocating rationed items, recreation, etc.,
for employees and their families. For those who do not work, their place
of residence is their *danwei*.

In an effort to lighten its own burden, the state is trying to commoditize
many welfare benefits, but units balk at implementing such an unpopular
move, and the urban dwellers do not support the smashing of their rice
bowls, something they had believed was a concrete manifestation of the
superiority of socialism. The state is urging members of non-business

units, such as schools and think-tanks, to go into business (*xiahai*, literally go into the sea), but this is not universally popular either.

So here again, the leaders of units need to represent their increasingly dissatisfied constituents in making their case to the authorities, and in competing with other units for funds and favours. Although much of this goes on in private, the media periodically describe the situation in particular units. China's media are organs of the party–state, so decisions to do this are not independently taken, and are most likely weapons in a power struggle. But the message gets out into the public sphere, even though the party dominates this as well.

Professional and Occupational Associations

As part of the corporatist system, the communists established and dominated a range of associations based on one's profession, from writers to workers to capitalists. They functioned both as another means of control and supervision and as 'transmission belts', linking the party and people. Under the nominal rule of 'the mass line', it was important that policy decisions be shown to result from consultation between the masses and leaders, not as commandist fiat from above.

In practice, these organizations generally have not enjoyed the autonomy to actually represent the interests of their constituents as determined through democratic means, but rather to convey the thinking of the élite and ensure compliance. None the less, research has demonstrated that on numerous occasions these associations have asserted themselves politically on behalf of their members in protest at the party's policies. In the case of workers, the most sensitive class in a state putatively under the rule of the proletariat (or at least of its agent, the Communist Party), the 1989 demonstrations marked 'the fifth time that a portion of the Chinese working class (at times led by the official trade unions) had asserted itself politically', although few Chinese were aware of this fact.[27] Following prior practice, the party has established new associations to absorb new social forces, such as self-employed entrepreneurs, private businessmen, and even foreign enterprises which have emerged in the course of reforms.[28]

One professional group which definitely bears watching is the new cadre of lawyers. Many work closely with foreign business interests. As China promulgates reams of new laws governing civil as well as criminal activity, the role of lawyers, as advocates of clients even against the state, will increase. In 1989, lawyers and legal scholars played an influential role.[29]

Intellectuals

Considered as a separate category, and based on East European experience, intellectuals need to be seen as a potential base for civil society through the various units in which they work and interact. In Eastern Europe, intellectuals on their own, and through solidarity with other social forces, such as workers, played a central role in establishing civil society in the face of party opposition. Certainly in China in the 1980s, emboldened intellectuals began to be more outspoken in class, seminars, salons, and publications. Intensified linkages with foreign intellectuals and media strengthened them and, to a degree, protected them. Although most did not make the step from speech to street action, their impact on those who did was enormous.[30] Intellectuals belong to many cross-cutting extra-*danwei* and attend seminars bringing together people from many different units and locations, which can facilitate their ability to link up, share ideas, and plan strategies. These include domestic and international professional associations and alumni associations, many of which also have members who live abroad or in other Chinese societies, such as Hong Kong and Taiwan.

Mass Associations

In addition to occupation-based associations, beginning in the 1950s the communists also herded citizens into party-controlled ascriptive characteristic-based organizations such as peasant associations, women's federations, Communist Youth League, Young Pioneers, student and youth federations, and so on. These represented one more unit in the cross-cutting network of supervision and control, and, as with the occupational groups noted above, on occasion they have lobbied for their constituents; an example would be women's federations arguing for special treatment for women. At times these actions occur in private meetings, but, for women in particular, the case has been pressed in the media. As something of a subset of cells of the corporatist body, we might also consider the National People's Congress and Chinese People's Political Consultative Conference, at all levels, as potential bases for civil society. The petition drives of 1989 and later by some members of the NPC are an example of an effort to act autonomously in the public arena.[31] The same goes for the so-called democratic parties, should their members speak out independently on issues.

Mass associations can be positive for civil society because, like religious organizations, they bring together people from many different otherwise circumscribed *danwei* for extended contact. They provide another form of identification.

Religion

Religion, as a community of faith and trust with an institutional form, provides a potential base for civil society which cuts across individual *danwei*, geographical locales, and professions.

Religious activity in China has risen dramatically for several reasons, and participation is a matter of choice by autonomous individuals. The de-ideologization and loosening of control over cultural life and individual belief has opened the previously tightly shut door for religious adherence. The political, social, and ideological turmoil in China over the past decades has created a great deal of anomie, an admitted 'crisis of faith', which has had a push function useful for religion. Impressionable Chinese see the important role that religion plays in modern countries, and join up to appear sophisticated.

In Poland the uniting of workers, intellectuals, and the Catholic Church into the Solidarity Movement paved the way for civil society. In China the party has tried to keep organized religion well within its corporatist system. The Three-Self Patriotic Movement and the Chinese Catholic Patriotic Association are examples of institutions for co-opting believers and closely managing their activities, especially contacts with foreign co-religionists. But that does not remove the potential for acting autonomously. It is well known that, in addition to official religious bodies, there are numerous underground churches and mosques. 'Superstitious cults built around charismatic figures, such as *qigong* masters and rural shamans, have sprung up in many places'.[32]

In some areas religion overlaps with minority nationality. For instance, within the Xinjiang Muslim community, the party–state tried to regulate the appointment of mullahs, and to prevent their becoming autonomous figures such as the Ayatollah Khomeini who brought down the Shah of Iran. It also hopes to prevent linkages with co-religionists or nationals in other countries.[33] Tibet is another area where religion and nationality are inextricably intertwined. The Panchen Lama who died in 1989 remained effectively under the party's thumb, but the Dalai Lama, of course, is a severe headache which refuses to go away. Beijing's clumsy efforts in 1995–6 to block the Dalai Lama's choice of a reincarnated successor to the Panchen Lama and select its own illustrates its continued fear in this area. In Xinjiang and Tibet, Beijing faces actual resistance movements, both of which can draw on many kinds of support from beyond the PRC's borders.

Secret Societies and Criminal Networks

One hates to include such groups in civil society, but they should not be ignored. With closer contacts between Hong Kong and the mainland, there are frequent reports of activities by Hong Kong-based Triads on the mainland, especially across the border in Guangdong province. They could gain control over business enterprises, media, or some of the associations listed above, such as those for private entrepreneurs.

Criminal gangs have been operating not only in Guangdong, but in other areas as well. There are reports of mounted armed bands holding up trains. Often the police and other officials collude with the criminals. On the other hand, Operation Yellowbird, which has helped Chinese dissidents flee the mainland, is also closely allied with the Hong Kong underworld.[34]

Clans and Guanxi Networks

In some parts of China, again most commonly in the south, large clans and lineages have begun to revive, controlling substantial resources. Somewhat comparable to the corporate villages cited above, although further unified through common ancestry, and often based in temples, these bodies can increasingly govern their own affairs, even in policing, brazenly resisting efforts of the party–state to control them. On a larger, not necessarily kin-based, scale, the continued prevalence of networks based on any number of particularistic ties provides the means to accumulate the 'social capital' necessary for the associations at the base of civil society.[35]

Social Movements

The student movement of 1989 is a very good example of a protest-based spontaneous association acting autonomously in the public sphere. Students were not the only participants, as workers, peasants, and other citizens organized autonomous associations, commonly across units, to participate.[36] Another example with potential is the environmental protection movement, especially centred around the Three Gorges project.[37] Secessionist movements in Tibet and Xinjiang are further examples. There are constant rumours of a large underground network of anti-party organizations throughout China. When Tiananmen activist Shen Tong returned in 1992, he went with the purpose of establishing links with these groups.[38] The estimated 130 million members of the 'floating population', although not sharing a common ideology or goal, could, under certain conditions, coalesce as a social movement.[39] Certainly, the emergence of self-administered migrant communities such as Beijing's Zhejiang Village indicates the potential for autonomy and resistance to the party–state.

Media

The Communist Party quite clearly sees the media as an integral part of its movement, playing an important role in conveying information the leadership deems necessary and suitable for the common folk to know, as well as clues on what it means.

If we broaden our definition of media to include big character posters, then the 1988–89 Democracy Wall Movement illustrated the use of media by masses. In 1989 official organs of the propaganda system strove for independence and the ability to make their voices heard autonomously in the public sphere. Potentially, the media could function quite literally as a mediating institution between some elements in emerging civil society and the public sphere, drawing attention to their agendas. The explosion of cable television, with broadcasts from Taiwan and Hong Kong, and increased access to foreign-language publications (including some translated into Chinese) have made the Chinese media field increasingly complex and hard to micro-manage.

Non-governmental Organizations

The reform period has witnessed the emergence of a range of 'non-governmental organizations' (NGOs), many established on government initiative, which enjoy varying degrees of autonomy to address particular issues in Chinese social life. These include charity and philanthropy, disaster relief, underdeveloped regions, protecting cultural relics, environmental protection, education, and so on. These foundations control financial and social resources, which in some cases include assistance from abroad.

As in traditional China, these organizations can supplement the work of the overstressed government and may or may not have another agenda. However, intentionally or not, they do comprise an alternative base of resources and activity cutting across *danwei*, classes, and regions that could quite easily assert themselves against the party–state.[40]

Chinese Abroad

There are now tens of thousands of PRC citizens living abroad. Some are avowedly apolitical, concentrating on research, studies, or business.

Others are determinedly political. Both kinds have established numerous organizations. There are professional associations, such as economists, political scientists, and scholars of women's studies; there are numerous social groups; then, there are dissident organizations, such as the US-based Chinese Democratic Alliance and the Paris-based Front for a Democratic China. All types publish newsletters and journals and hold conferences, while the political groups also lobby politicians and work with foreign media as part of civil society in their new homelands.[41] There is an extensive electronic mail network, easily and rapidly drawing together Chinese worldwide, frequently to share information about China, debate political issues, and plan activities.

During the Qing Dynasty, Sun Yat-Sen relied on the support of similar groups in his revolutionary quest. Comparable associations played a major role in pushing forward the reluctant democratization by the Kuomintang regime in Taiwan. With the support of wealthy Hungarian–American financier George Soros, who has quite consciously funded the creation of civil society throughout Eastern Europe,[42] American-based dissident Liang Heng attempted to do the same for China. Soros created the Fund for the Reform and Opening of China, with Zhao Ziyang's blessing, providing financial support for autonomous intellectual and artistic activity. Liang arranged to have his journal *The Chinese Intellectual* (Zhishifenzi) published twice in Beijing before the 1989 crackdown. This was the boldest step in linking Chinese associations abroad with civil society at home, and demonstrated both its feasibility and its vulnerability. The journal continues to be a major forum for discussing issues of civil society and democracy.

This is an admittedly sketchy list, but the purpose was to identify some social actors who might act in such a way that they could function as a foundation for civil society in China. As we saw in 1989, some previously non-existent groups, such as the Autonomous Students Federation, emerged to do just that, but some organizations which are integral parts of the system, such as unions, *danwei*, neighbourhoods, the media, and the mass and professional associations, also acted autonomously in the public sphere, in disregard of party policy and threats.

Constraining and Facilitating Factors

The previous section has singled out some possible bases for civil society, but what factors might influence their chances of succeeding or failing to evolve into a full-blown institutionalized civil society?

First in the constraint category are central elements of China's histori-cal legacy. There is an ongoing debate over whether or not China had something resembling Europe's civil society or public sphere in late impe-rial and/or Republican times.[43] Much of Chinese tradition was undeniably antithetical to the values of autonomy, privacy, and public expressions of heterodoxy, especially by the masses of common people. The individual was seen not as an autonomous actor protecting his sacred rights against an encroaching state (elements at the root of Seligman's definition cited above), but rather as a node in a network with duties and obligations to the larger community.[44] To some analysts, the Chinese face great problems in building trust among non-kin or non-network persons; this works against creating and maintaining large-scale organizations, for business or other purposes, which is fundamental for civil society.[45]

Cities were not bastions of autonomy as in the West, but were either administrative locations or commercial centres under close bureaucratic supervision.

Although we can identify a range of associations that might have become the functional equivalents of bases for civil society—guilds, native-place associations, religious organizations, voluntary associations, etc.—they did not engage in the sort of competition in the public sphere which is the hallmark of civil society. They did not utilize whatever auton-omy or resources they had to challenge the state: rather, they saw them-selves as performing functions on behalf of the short-handed and often financially strapped authorities.

Similarly, intellectuals did not perceive of themselves as independent judges of society and politics; rather, the purpose of getting an education was to sit for civil service exams and enter the bureaucracy in service to the regime. Although there was a legacy of remonstration by stalwart scholar–officials who saw themselves as protecting the common people suf-fering under a corrupt regime which risked losing the Mandate of Heaven if it did not rectify itself, here again, this was done in service to the state, not as part of a sense of autonomous expression of interests or as part of a legit-imate, institutionalized sphere for public debate. Remonstrating scholar-officials hoped that they could become insiders, replacing others they deemed corrupt, incompetent, or simply rivals. They did not intend to mobilize the common people to assume an active role in political life.[46]

As Andrew Nathan has argued, 'democracy', even as advocated by twentieth-century liberal reformers, meant the opportunity for broader participation in strengthening the state, not consolidating an autonomous civil society.[47]

How much, in the end, does the historical legacy matter? While it can-not be ignored, I would argue that it should not be reified into an insuperable barrier. First, although one can find many examples of factors inhibiting civil society, there were others that could have served as 'functional equivalents' for it, given different historical trajectories. For example, William Theodore de Bary notes Zhu Xi's use of community compacts (*xiangyue*) as a type of mediating institution for 'promot[ing] community spirit and a sense of shared responsibility for the community welfare—in effect a meeting place for the discussion of local needs and problems'.[48] Looking at other neighbouring societies with a similar legacy, most notably Taiwan,[49] as well as those that lived under communism for longer than China, the conclusion must be that this legacy can be overcome. To be sure, efforts to establish civil society can be premature—one of the lessons of 1989 Beijing and the ongoing turmoil in the former Soviet Union, in my judgement. And historical trajectories and cultural legacies will make 'civil society' vary in appearance and action across societies. On the other hand, so much has happened in China to overcome the anti-democratic legacy and introduce a foundation for civil society that the situation has changed dramatically. The process is still very much in the early stages, something impatient politicians and journalists in the United States in particular have trouble accepting.

Although we can trace some beginnings of civil society in the Republican era, the combination of repression by the centre and local warlords plus unending civil war and foreign invasion prevented its flourishing. However, the potential for civil society was demonstrated, and this should not be overlooked.[50]

If China's pre-communist legacy were not negative enough, the establishment of the totalitarian regime eradicated whatever tendencies there might have been to institutionalize civil society and the idea of a public sphere.[51] The sorts of groupings that are commonly associated with civil society were either destroyed or brought under party control; new ones could not form. Adults were remoulded and supervised, and children were socialized to accept the legitimacy of all-round party control, and not even to conceive of acting autonomously. Control over residence, occupation, and access to rationed necessities, especially in the urban areas, gave a material basis to this.[52]

We must also not overlook factors such as China's giant physical size, complex geography, ethnic mixture, and uneven levels of development, all of which militate against building a unified nationwide movement. In all, there are still no viable alternatives on a national level to the Communist Party.

Over the course of reforms, new social forces have emerged, such as private entrepreneurs and the floating population, while others, such as students, peasants, and intellectuals, have gained a measure of freedom unknown before.[53] However, the party organization (and the People's Liberation Army—PLA) is not dead, and even though the centre has shifted power downward, this does not necessarily translate into a tremendous scope of action for common people. In fact, freed from close supervision, many local cadres are strengthening their grip over people under their jurisdiction, flouting the law. This combination of coercion, cooptation, and corruption, added to the communists' inherent reluctance to legitimize a sphere for autonomous activity, works against civil society.[54]

Finally, there is the trauma of the 1989 massacre and subsequent witch hunt. As a corollary, there is the cautionary ongoing socio-political chaos and economic collapse in the former Soviet Union and the resurgence of communist parties there and elsewhere in the region. This has given pause to people who might otherwise have continued to demand more freedom. University students today channel their energies into strategies for going abroad or getting good jobs in foreign-invested enterprises, not into changing the world.

Turning to factors that might facilitate the emergence of civil society, the pre-massacre 1989 events showed that, given a conducive environment, Chinese urban-dwellers can organize autonomously. They know how to articulate their viewpoints and know how to do this publicly. To a large degree, Chinese learn how to participate in group life. Although they are not instructed on how to set up voluntary associations and elect leaders democratically,[55] they do tend to think in terms of organizations and division of labour. With the breakdown of societal order in the Cultural Revolution, youths in particular, who had not known any other system, translated the skills taught them by the party into the formation of groups of Red Guards, competing for resources, attention, power, and basic survival. Despite the difference in time and environment, the demonstrations and organizations of 1989 showed that the youth of the 1980s apparently preserved these talents.[56]

Beyond this, the highly organized nature of Chinese urban society also facilitated the emergence of collective action out of the *danwei* and other institutions in which social life is embedded.[57]

The trends listed above as resulting from the reforms need to be considered as facilitating forces. In particular, opening to the outside world and marketization have introduced, perhaps unintentionally, an unprecedented amount of diversity and information about the rest of the world into China. Direct-dial private telephones and fax machines played a critical role in the 1989 movement; since 1995, electronic mail has become increasingly widespread as another source of information and tool of communication and liaison. Foreign influence includes the idea of a legitimate private realm. The state has increasingly legitimated this, promulgating some rights to privacy, both economic and social.[58] Although many people seek primarily a haven from party-dominated social life rather than an opportunity to organize, the fact that they can opt out, can hold divergent beliefs (as revealed in state-sponsored public opinion polls), and can associate with whomever they please, including (though with some limits, to be sure) foreigners, is an important foundation for civil society. The autonomy of units, whether actively sought or reluctantly accepted, can facilitate civil society as well, as they need to compete for a wide range of commodities and influence, through whatever means at their disposal.

The knowledge of what happened in the rest of the socialist world from 1989 to 1991 is of acute relevance for the Chinese. Besides these institutionally similar societies, there is knowledge of democratization in the culturally similar referent societies of Taiwan and South Korea and the people's power movement in the Philippines. The formation of 'Greater China', and the pervasive presence of Chinese from Hong Kong and Taiwan throughout the mainland, provide fluid access to information about the situation in those offshore Chinas.

It is not useful to weigh positive versus negative factors and come up with a prognosis. As 1989 showed, the critical factor is a conjuncture of forces. The history of Communist China has repeatedly shown that when there is liberalization[59] citizens have taken advantage of it to further their own causes, and this is conducive to civil society. In the current environment, mobilized citizens may take the initiative to press for more liberalization without waiting for a party-granted opening or a crisis. Given the two decades of reforms, increasingly complex society, a visionless and factionalized non-monolithic decentralized party–state, and lessons of failure and success at home and abroad, there is every reason to think that a future conjuncture of events—deaths of leaders, rise of charismatic politicians, reticence to crack down by the forces of coercion, economic crises, external setback (such as a declaration of independence by Taiwan), environmental crisis, dissemination of information, and incitement by mass media—might provide the fertile soil for another burst of autonomous action that will push forward the idea of a legitimate public sphere and civil society.[60]

Conclusion

In this chapter I have speculated about potential bases for civil society in China. I want to reiterate, in closing, that, while civil society and democracy can emerge with little historical or cultural foundation,[61] they are not the only potential outcomes of the rise of market society and the collapse of Marxism–Leninism.[62]

We need to avoid imposing our ethnocentric assumptions on the Chinese. Although Western values and behaviour have penetrated parts of the country, we cannot assume *a priori* that a significant number of Chinese desire the sort of autonomy we in the West prize so highly. It is not a core value in Chinese tradition or modern practice. Seeing their world collapse, a majority might prefer to opt for a person or organization offering community and stability, not 'freedom'. Given China's long tradition of seeking alliance and incorporation with the state, people may organize in the hope of achieving protection, not independence. In 1989 students, workers, and others called their associations 'autonomous' (*zizhi*) to stress their independence from the party–state, though their ultimate understanding of 'autonomy' is unclear. But surely some of them did not desire incorporation into the élite. Certainly, based on the Taiwan experience, we have seen Chinese establish autonomous associations of all stripes which seek to challenge or capture the state, not be folded into the current powers.

Even were incipient civil society to take root, it might not lead to democracy. It could result in chaos, and bring on fascism. The Beijing Spring of 1989 witnessed the creation of a community of trust and civility among urban citizens, at least for a time. It is unclear, if it recurred, how long it could be sustained by grass roots efforts, or whether it might be co-opted by a fascistic demagogue or criminal elements.

Conceivably, the best chance for civil society might lie within the corporatist system itself. Leaders and rank and file supportive of civil society might have more room to manoeuvre and crack the system from within than poorly organized challengers from without. This might evolve into civil society and the mediating institutions of a public sphere for discussing issues, without bringing about a pluralistic political system. The line between state and society would not be as clearly drawn as it is in the West.

If the party–state continues to lose legitimacy, organizational effectiveness, and strength, it may not be able to enforce the rules of the game necessary for healthy civil society and its evolution towards democracy. The experience of the former Soviet Union offers little consolation. Many people there and in China yearn for the certainties of the old party-led system.

It took a crisis to draw attention to the emerging of something resembling civil society in China. Activists and analysts fear getting caught unprepared a second time. Clearly, there have been fundamental changes in China's social and institutional structures, and the party–state's grip has

relaxed tremendously. But in understanding this and predicting consequences, there is another risk: mislabelling activities and trends as leading
to civil society or democracy as we in the West conceive and value them.
It will be a difficult task to ensure the positive development and understanding of such activities and trends.

NOTES

1. The original paper was also presented at seminars at the Center for Pacific Asia
   Studies, University of Stockholm, and the Center for Chinese Studies, University of
   Hawaii at Manoa. I would like to thank the participants at those seminars for their
   comments, and also Wm. Theodore de Bary, Marc Garcelon, and David Strand for
   additional comments.
2. It would be worthwhile to research the role the international media played in China in
   1989, especially the meeting of the Asian Development Bank and the Gorbachev visit,
   in helping to empower urban Chinese, give them ideas, and fan the flames of their frustrations. In this sense, China has become an actor in the global public sphere.
3. This chapter represents a retreat from my earlier assertions about the re-emergence of
   a previously existing civil society in China, in Thomas Gold, 'The Resurgence of Civil
   Society in China', *Journal of Democracy*, 1:1 (Winter 1990), 18–31, and 'Party–State
   versus Society in China', in Joyce K. Kallgren (ed.), *Building a Nation-State: China
   after Forty Years* (Berkeley: Institute of East Asian Studies, China Research
   Monograph, 1990), 125–51.
4. An indication of the problem can be gleaned from the special issue of *Modern China*,
   19:2 (April 1993), 'Symposium: "Public Sphere"/"Civil Society" in China?' For a
   Chinese view of the Western debate, see Gu Xin, 'A Civil Society and Public Sphere in
   Post-Mao China? An Overview of Western Publications', *China Information*, 8:3
   (Winter 1993–4), 38–52. For Chinese views, see Shu-Yun Ma, 'The Chinese Discourse
   on Civil Society', *China Quarterly*, 137 (March 1994), 180–93. Ma traces the origins of
   this discourse to 1986 and examines the discourse both within China and among dissidents abroad. For a discussion of whether or not the term should be used at all, see
   Krishnan Kumar, 'Civil Society: An Inquiry into the Usefulness of an Historical
   Term', *British Journal of Sociology*, 44:3 (September 1993), 375–95.
5. Adam Seligman, *The Idea of Civil Society* (New York: Free Press, 1992), 179. I will
   address the question of 'the autonomous individual' below.
6. This is argued by E. J. Perry and E. V. Fuller, citing David Strand, Elizabeth J. Perry
   and Ellen V. Fuller, 'China's Long March to Democracy', *World Policy Journal* (Fall
   1991), 663–85 at 666.
7. Dorothy J. Solinger, 'Urban Entrepreneurs and the State: The Merger of State and
   Society', in Arthur L. Rosenbaum (ed.), *State and Society in China: The Consequences
   of Reform* (Boulder, Colo.: Westview Press, 1992), 121–41.
8. This argument draws on Heath B. Chamberlain, 'On the Search for Civil Society in
   China', *Modern China*, 19:2 (April 1993), 199–215; Marc Garcelon, 'The Shadow of
   the Leviathan: Public and Private in Communist and Post-Communist Society', in Jeff
   Weintraub and Krishnan Kumar (eds.), *Public and Private in Thought and Practice*
   (University of Chicago Press, 1997), 303–22, and discussions with Larry Diamond of

the Hoover Institution, including his summary comments at the conference on 'Economy, Society and Democracy', Washington DC, 6–9 May 1992.

9. See Jurgen Habermas, *The Structural Transformation of the Public Sphere* (Cambridge, Mass.: MIT Press, 1989); also, Craig Calhoun, 'Introduction: Habermas and the Public Sphere' and Jurgen Habermas, 'Further Reflections on the Public Sphere', in Craig Calhoun (ed.), *Habermas and the Public Sphere* (Cambridge, Mass.: MIT Press, 1992), 1–48 and 421–61 resp.

10. This 'civility' is a central part of Anne Thurston's discussion in 'Waiting for Deng: Chinese Society Uncivil and Civil', paper presented at the Fourth US–Japan Symposium on China, Tokyo, July 1995.

11. Neither is civil society neutral. Just as the structure of the state reflects the balance of power among classes within society, so will this be reflected in civil society as well. See Antonio Gramsci, *Selections From the Prison Notebooks*, ed. and transl. Quintin Hoare and Geoffrey Nowell Smith (New York: International Publishers, 1971).

12. Chamberlain, 'On the Search for Civil Society', 207.

13. Juan J. Linz and Alfred Stepan, 'Toward Consolidated Democracies', in Larry Diamond, Marc F. Plattner, Yun-han Chu, and Hung-mao Tien (eds.), *Consolidating Third Wave Democracies: Themes and Perspectives* (Baltimore and London: Johns Hopkins University Press, 1997), 14–33. On the continuing need for the state, see also Michael Walzer, 'The Idea of Civil Society: A Path of Social Reconstruction', *Dissent* (Spring 1991), 293–304, esp. 301–2.

14. Karl Marx and Frederich Engels, *The German Ideology* (New York: International Publishers, 1970), 57.

15. For a discussion of the fundamental institutions of a communist system, see Andrew G. Walder, 'The Decline of Communist Power: Elements of a Theory of Institutional Change', *Theory and Society*, 23 (1994), 297–323. Walder argues that the phenomenon of civil society challenging the communist state needs to be situated in 'a broader and more consequential set of changes set into motion by departures from central planning under communist party rule' (p. 315).

16. This is the core of the argument in Ezra Vogel, 'From Friendship to Comradeship: The Change in Personal Relations in Communist China', *China Quarterly*, 21 (1965), 46–60. Also see my update, 'Thomas Gold, 'After Comradeship: Personal Relations in China Since the Cultural Revolution', *China Quarterly*, 104 (December 1985), 656–75.

17. On the relevance of the concept of 'corporatism' to Marxist–Leninist systems, see Daniel Chirot, 'The Corporatist Model and Socialism', *Theory and Society*, 9:2 (March 1980), 363–81; and Jonathan Unger and Anita Chan, 'China, Corporatism, and the East Asian Model', *Australian Journal of Chinese Affairs*, 33 (January 1995), 29–53.

18. This reminds me of the old Soviet joke: 'We have freedom of speech; we just don't have freedom after speech.'

19. There is now quite a literature on this. Influential works include: Andrew Arato, 'Civil Society against the State: Poland 1980–81', *Telos*, 47 (Spring 1981), 23–47; Andrew Arato, 'Empire vs. Civil Society: Poland 1981–82', *Telos*, 50 (Winter 1981–2), 19–48; Timothy Garton Ash, *The Uses of Adversity* (New York: Vintage Books, 1990); Z. A. Pelczynski, 'Solidarity and "The Rebirth of Civil Society" in Poland, 1976–81', in John Keane (ed.), *Civil Society and the State* (London: Verso, 1988), 361–80.

20. Andrew G. Walder, 'Local Governments as Industrial Firms: An Organizational Analysis of China's Transnational Economy', *American Journal of Sociology*, 101 (1995), 263–301.

21. Mayfair Mei-hui Yang, 'Between State and Society: The Construction of Corporateness in a Chinese Socialist Factory', *Australian Journal of Chinese Affairs*, 22 (July 1989), 31–60.
22. The best example is the village of Daqiuzhuang near Tianjin. (For a detailed study to 1992, see Nan Lin and Mai-Shou Hao, 'Local Market Socialism: Reform in Rural China', unpubl.) The residents have become quite wealthy, but the strongman ran it as a private fief, and kept the Tianjin police out when they attempted to investigate a murder: Lincoln Kaye, 'Ugly Face of Reforms', *Far Eastern Economic Review* (22 April 1993), 19. In Guangdong, villages have literally battled each other over economic issues.
23. Gordon White, 'Prospects for Civil Society in China: A Case Study of Xiaoshan City', *Australian Journal of Chinese Affairs*, 29 (January 1993), 63–87 at 68. See also works by Jean Oi, e.g. 'Fiscal Reform and the Economic Foundations of Local State Corporatism in China', *World Politics*, 45:1 (October 1992), 99–126.
24. Kevin J. O'Brien, 'Implementing Political Reform in China's Villages', *Australian Journal of Chinese Affairs*, 32 (July 1994), 33–59; Zhongguo jiceng zhengquan jianshe yanjiuhui (China Research Association on Establishing Basic Level Political Power), *Zhongguo nongcun cunmin weiyuanhui huanjie xuanju zhidu* (Study on the Election of Villagers Committees in Rural China) (Beijing: Zhongguo shehui chubanshe, 1993).
25. For a range of views on the role of the private sector in social change, see Thomas B. Gold, 'Urban Private Business and Social Change', in Deborah Davis and Ezra F. Vogel (eds.), *Chinese Society on the Eve of Tiananmen: The Impact of Reform* (Cambridge, Mass.: Harvard University Press, 1990), 157–78; David L. Wank, 'Bureaucratic Patronage and Private Business: Changing Networks of Power in Urban China', in Andrew G. Walder (ed.), *The Waning of the Communist State: Economic Origins of Political Decline in China and Hungary* (Berkeley: University of California Press, 1995), 153–83; and Ole Bruun, 'Political Hierarchy and Private Entrepreneurship in a Chinese Neighborhood', in Walder, *Waning*, 184–212.
26. On the *danwei* system, see Yang, *Between State and Society*; and Gail Henderson and Myron S. Cohen, *The Chinese Hospital* (New Haven: Yale University Press, 1984); Andrew G. Walder, *Communist Neo-Traditionalism: Work and Authority in Chinese Industry* (Berkeley: University of California Press, 1986), and Andrew G. Walder, 'Factory and Manager in an Era of Reform', *China Quarterly*, 118 (1989), 242–64.
27. Anita Chan, 'Revolution or Corporatism? Workers and Trade Unions in Post-Mao China', *Australian Journal of Chinese Affairs*, 29 (January 1993), 31–61 at 32.
28. David L. Wank, 'Private Business, Bureaucracy, and Political Alliance in a Chinese City', *Australian Journal of Chinese Affairs*, 33 (January 1995), 55–71; Margaret M. Pearson, 'The Janus Face of Business Associations in China: Socialist Corporatism in Foreign Enterprises', *Australian Journal of Chinese Affairs*, 31 (January 1994), 25–46; Christopher Earle Nevitt, 'Private Business Associations in China; Evidence of Civil Society or Local State Power', *The China Journal*, 36 (July 1996), 25–43, and Jonathan Unger, ' "Bridges": Private Business, the Chinese Government and the Rise of New Associations', *China Quarterly*, 147 (1996), 795–819.
29. Mark Sidel, 'Dissident and Liberal Legal Scholars and Organizations in Beijing and the Chinese State in the 1980s', in Deborah S. Davis, Richard Kraus, Barry Naughton, and Elizabeth J. Perry (eds.), *Urban Spaces in Contemporary China: The Potential for Autonomy and Community in post-Mao China* (Cambridge: Woodrow Wilson Center Press and Cambridge University Press, 1995), 326–46.
30. Michel Bonnin and Yves Chevrier, 'The Intellectual and the State: Social Dynamics of Intellectual Autonomy during the Post-Mao Era', *China Quarterly*, 127 (September

1991), 569–93; Merle Goldman, 'The Intellectuals in the Deng Xiaoping Era', in Arthur Lewis Rosenbaum (ed.), *State and Society in China: The Consequences of Reform* (Boulder, Colo.: Westview Press, 1991), 193–218; David Kelly, 'Chinese Intellectuals in the 1989 Democracy Movement', in George Hicks (ed.), *The Broken Mirror: China after Tiananmen* (Harlow, Essex: Longman, 1990), 24–51; Orville Schell, *Discos and Democracy: China in the Throes of Reform* (New York: Pantheon, 1988).

31. Matt Forney, 'Don't Hold Your Breath', *Far Eastern Economic Review* (7 March 1996), 24–8; Hu Shikai, 'Representation without Democratization: The "Signature Incident" and China's National People's Congress', *Journal of Contemporary China*, 2:1 (Winter–Spring 1993), 3–34.

32. Nancy N. Chen, 'Urban Spaces and Experiences of *Qigong*', in Davis *et al.*, *Urban Spaces*, 347–61.

33. Clement C. Yang, 'China and the Central Asian Nightmare', *Journal of Contemporary China*, 5 (Spring 1994), 88–95.

34. Melinda Liu, 'Still on the Wing', *Newsweek*, 1 April 1996, 44–5; Ma Shu-yun, 'The Chinese Discourse on Civil Society', 189–90, and fns. 58–61.

35. Robert P. Weller, 'Horizontal Ties and Civil Institutions in Chinese Societies', paper prepared for the Working Group on Civil Society and Civil Culture, Boston, 28–9 1995; Mayfair Mei-hui Yang, *Gifts, Favors, and Banquets: The Art of Social Relationships in China* (Ithaca, NY: Cornell University Press, 1994), esp. ch. 8.

36. Craig Calhoun, *Neither Gods nor Emperors: Students and the Struggle for Democracy in China* (Berkeley: University of California Press, 1994); Clemens Stubbe Ostergaard, 'Citizens, Groups, and a Nascent Civil Society in China: Towards an Understanding of the 1989 Student Demonstrations', *China Information*, 4:2 (Autumn 1989), 28–41; Jonathan Unger (ed.), *The Pro-Democracy Protests in China: Reports from the Provinces* (Armonk, NY: M. E. Sharpe, 1991); Andrew G. Walder and Gong Xiaoxia, 'Workers in the Tiananmen Protests: The Politics of the Beijing Workers' Autonomous Federation', *Australian Journal of Chinese Affairs*, 29 (January 1993), 1–29.

37. In April 1993, the San Francisco-based Goldman Foundation awarded the journalist Dai Qing a prize for her advocacy of environmental protection, in particular her criticism of the Three Gorges Project. There has been speculation about where 'China's Chernobyl' will be, and the consequences for protest movements.

38. Ross Terrill, 'Return to Tiananmen Square', *San Francisco Examiner Image*, 4 April 1993, 6–13. See also Patrick E. Tyler, 'Chinese Dissident, Unbroken, Greets Freedom Cautiously', *New York Times*, 21 September 1993, p. A1 for some additional examples.

39. Dorothy J. Solinger, 'The Floating Population in the Cities: Chances for Assimilation?' in Davis *et al.*, *Urban Spaces*, 113–39.

40. John W. Cook *et al.*, *The Rise of Nongovernmental Organizations in China: Implications for Americans* (New York: National Committee on US China Relations, China Policy Series No. 8, 1994). Liang Congjie, the grandson of democratic forerunner Liang Qichao, has been active in an NGO, The Friends of Nature. This group took on Hong Kong investor Li Ka-shing's gargantuan Oriental Plaza complex, which would have overshadowed the Forbidden City in violation of Beijing zoning laws. Liang embarked on a speaking tour abroad in 1994 to criticize the project and the Beijing government's malfeasance. The Chinese government's fear of NGOs, and especially the role of foreigners in them, was clearly revealed in the Public Security Bureau's clumsy unannounced shutdown of a charity banquet in Beijing on 30 March 1996: see Patrick E. Tyler, 'Chinese Halt Fund-Raiser By Foreigners for Orphans', *New York Times*, 1 April 1996, p. A7.

41. Geremie Barme, 'Traveling Heavy: The Intellectual Baggage of the Chinese Diaspora', *Problems of Communism*, 40:1–2 (January–April 1991), 94–112; Shu-yun Ma, 187–92.
42. Connie Bruck, 'The World According to Soros', *The New Yorker*, 23 January 1995, 54–78; Michael Lewis, 'The Speculator', *The New Republic*, 10 and 17 January 1994, 19–29.
43. For a review of the literature as well as recent contributions to the debate, see the special issue of *Modern China*, 19:2 (April 1993), entitled, 'Symposium: "Public Sphere"/"Civil Society" in China? Paradigmatic Issues in Chinese Studies, III'. See also two essays by Martin King Whyte: 'Urban China: A Civil Society in the Making?' in Rosenbaum (ed.), *State and Society in China*, 77–101, esp. 80–3; and 'Prospects for Democratization in China', *Problems of Communism*, 61:3 (May–June 1992), 58–70.
44. See the special issue of *Daedalus*, 'The Living Tree: The Changing Meaning of Being Chinese Today', 120:2 (Spring 1991), esp. articles by Tu Wei-ming and Ambrose Yeo-chi King.
45. Francis Fukuyama, *Trust: The Social Virtues and Creation of Prosperity* (New York: Free Press, 1995).
46. Events in 1989 did little to illustrate much change. See Barme, 'Traveling Heavy', and Perry and Fuller, 'China's Long March'.
47. Andrew J. Nathan, *Chinese Democracy* (Berkeley: University of California Press, 1985).
48. Wm. Theodore de Bary, *The Trouble with Confucianism* (Cambridge, Mass.: Harvard University Press, 1991), 95. Huang Zongxi likewise 'gave much thought . . . to the public roles of schools and academies . . . It is significant that in Korea the community compact associations, originally inspired by the writings of Chu Hsi and his leading Korean interpreters, served as the organizational base for popular political movements and uprisings in the nineteenth century' (p. 99). See also de Bary, 'China, Confucianism and Civil Society', *Newsletter of the 'State and Society in East Asia' Network*, 2 (May 1993), 2–17.
49. See Thomas Gold, 'Taiwan: Still Defying the Odds', in Diamond *et al.*, *Consolidating Third Wave Democracies*, 162–91.
50. See two works by David Strand, *Rickshaw Beijing: City People and Politics in the 1920s* (Berkeley: University of California Press, 1989), and 'Protest in Beijing: Civil Society and Public Sphere in China', *Problems of Communism*, 39:3 (May–June 1990), 1–19.
51. Whyte, 'Prospects for Democratization'; Thomas B. Gold, 'Party–State versus Society'.
52. Walder, *Communist Neo-Traditionalism*, and 'Decline of Communist Power'.
53. Ostergaard, 'Citizens, Groups'.
54. See works by Solinger and Wank cited above.
55. These are, of course, elements singled out by de Tocqueville in his analysis of democracy in America.
56. Memoirs of 1989 illustrate this: e.g., Shen Tong, with Marianne Yen, *Almost a Revolution* (Boston: Houghton Mifflin, 1990); and Thomas B. Gold, 'Youth and the State', *China Quarterly*, 127 (September 1991), 594–612. Although youth attracted the most attention, other elements of society, such as workers and urban dwellers (*shimin*), also organized themselves: see Andrew G. Walder, 'City People in the 1989 Democracy Movement: Popular Mobilization and Political Penalties', paper presented to the Regional Seminar, Center for Chinese Studies, University of California, Berkeley, 27 April 1991.
57. See Walder and Gong, 'Workers in the Tiananmen Protests'; and Xueguang Zhou,

'Unorganized Interests and Collective Action in Communist China', *American Sociological Review*, 58:1 (February 1993), 54–73.

58. Shaoguang Wang, 'The Politics of Private Time: Changing Leisure Patterns in Urban China', in Davis *et al.*, *Urban Spaces*, 149–72.

59. I have discussed the dichotomy between forces of *shou* (restriction) and *fang* (liberalization) in Gold, 'Party–State versus Society'. Liberalization here does not mean the same as that discussed by Guillermo O'Donnell and Philippe C. Schmitter in *Transactions From Authoritarian Rule: Tentative Conclusions about Uncertain Democracies* (Baltimore: Johns Hopkins University Press, 1986): 'making effective certain rights that protect both individuals and social groups from arbitrary or illegal acts committed by the state or third parties' (p. 7). It refers to a selective loosening of control by the party.

60. In the Maoist spirit of 'one divides into two', it must be noted that these crises could also result in efforts by the party–state to reassert tighter control, as happened during the Taiwan crises of 1995–6 under the pretext of an external security threat. But the ability to carry this off successfully will be compromised by the factors noted above.

61. Marcia A. Weigle and Jim Butterfield. 'Civil Society in Reforming Communist Regimes', *Comparative Politics*, 25:1 (October 1992), 1-23. The authors distinguish between defending civil society and civil society's emergence.

62. See the interchange between Gordon White and Barrett L. McCormick in *Australian Journal of Chinese Affairs*, 31 (January 1994), 73–110.

8

State and Society in Hainan: Liao Xun's Ideas on 'Small Government, Big Society'

Kjeld Erik Brødsgaard

In connection with the establishment of Hainan as a new province and a special economic zone in 1988, a series of economic, political, and social reform proposals were advanced under the concept of 'small government, big society'. The concept constitutes one of the clearest examples of how social and economic change during the Deng period has stimulated new thinking about the relationship between state and society in China and how new conceptions often are developed locally before having a national impact.

The idea of 'small government, big society' and its theoretical and practical implications were originally worked out by Liao Xun, a young research fellow in the Chinese Academy of Social Sciences. In 1987 he became a member of a working group, headed by CASS vice-president Liu Guoguang, which was to develop a plan or blueprint for the future economic, political, and social setup of the new province. The group embraced Liao Xun's ideas and as a consequence the final report has 'small government, big society' as one of its overarching themes. The political leadership of the new province received the report with enthusiasm and appropriated 'small government, big society' as a key concept in its reform work. Liao Xun himself was in 1988 appointed vice-director of the new provincial government's Centre for Research on Social and Economic Development.

Liao Xun's ideas on 'small government, big society' are of great importance. They constitute the first major effort by a Chinese intellectual and scholar working within the system to elaborate a fundamentally reformed political system since Liao Gailong put forward his famous *gengshen* reform in 1980.[1] If fully implemented 'small government, big society' will create the foundations of the kind of civil society that has been so vigorously researched and discussed in the China field since 1989. However, it will be a kind of civil society implemented from above and not from below, as was originally thought would be the case in China. Liao Xun's ideas are also important in that they appear to indicate that the Chinese political discourse is developing concepts and notions, which may stimulate Western political thought, *in casu* the civil society debate.

Liao Xun wrote his first work on the concept of 'small government, big society' in July 1986 in the form of a paper entitled 'Marx and Engels's Thought on "Small Government" and the Current Economic Reform'. This paper was subsequently expanded and revised and published in 1988 as a book with the same title.[2] The book argues that the most important question concerning socialist reform is to radically cure (*genzhi*) the 'bureaucratic sickness' of the traditional Soviet model. In order to do this, it is necessary to reject the big governmentism of the Soviet model and reconstruct the concept of 'small government' originally elaborated by Marx and Engels and implemented during the Paris Commune.

As mentioned above, in 1987 Liao Xun became involved in the reform work in Hainan Island. In connection with this work, he solidified his views and ideas on 'small government, big society' in a number of articles and reports. A selection of the most important of these are contained in his 1991 book.[3] It is in these papers that Liao Xun outlines his vision of a new political, economic, and social system on Hainan. In December 1993 Liao Xun published his third book pertaining to the theme of 'small government, big society'.[4] More recent essays can be found in *Hainan Tequ Bao* (Hainan Special Zone News), a Haikou-based newspaper which comes out twice a week.

In the following pages Liao Xun's reform programme will be presented and discussed. This will be followed by an attempt to relate the concept of 'small government, big society' to the ongoing civil society debate. Finally, the paper will examine whether Liao Xun's proposals actually have been followed by the political leadership of Hainan Island. Here the focus will be on issues related to the expansion of the private sector and the emergence of new social organizations.[5]

Small Government

In November–December 1987 Liao Xun wrote an important report on the reform of the political system in Hainan. The report was entitled 'Hainan jingji fazhan zhong de zhengzhi tizhi wenti' (Questions Concerning the Political System in Hainan's Economic Development).[6] In this report Liao Xun gives a detailed description of how he envisages the introduction of 'small government, big society' in the new province. The basic theme is that one must do away with the principle of big government and instead create a small government which will give room for a big society—a form of civil society (*shimin shehui*).[7]

In Liao Xun's opinion, the new political system and new administrative setup encapsulated in the notion of 'small government' entail that the government uphold or take care of only a few, but very important, functions which the individual persons, enterprises, organizations, or social associations do not have the capacity to cope with. These functions are grouped in four basic systems and the new government is to be structured according to these four systems.[8]

The first is a political guarantee system (*zhengzhi baozhang xitong*), which includes courts of law, police, matters concerning staff, personnel, overseas Chinese affairs, etc. The second system, the social service system (*shehui fuwu xitong*), concerns health, education, matters concerning the minorities and social welfare, etc. The third system, the economic development and organization system (*jingji fazhan zuzhi xitong*), is supposed to deal with matters in agriculture, industry, transport, communication, and science and technology. Finally, Liao Xun's plans involve the creation of an economic control and coordination system (*jingji jiandu xietiao xitong*), to manage economic planning and control, taxes, and environment issues.

Specifically, Liao Xun suggests the establishment of a department (*ting*) for each of these functions. Altogether he proposes seventeen *ting*:

- Political Guarantee System
    1. General Department
    2. Administrative Supervision
    3. Personnel
    4. Law Department
    5. Overseas Chinese Affairs
- Social Service System
    6. Labour Welfare
    7. Physical Training and Public Health
    8. Education and Culture
    9. Minorities and Religious Affairs
- Development and Organization System
    10. Trade and Industry
    11. Transport and Resources
    12. Agriculture
    13. Scientific and Technical Development
- Economic Supervision and Coordination System
    14. Economic Supervision

15. Economic Planning
16. Finances and Taxes
17. Urban and Rural Resources and Environment

In addition to these seventeen government departments, Liao Xun envisages the creation of two semi-governmental organs which will be subject to the dual leadership of the provincial government and the Standing Committee of Hainan People's Congress: a provincial People's Bank (*sheng renmin yinhang*), dealing with issues concerning macroeconomic regulations and control, and a Statistical Office (*sheng tongji shu*), which would gather information in order to facilitate society's supervision of the government's economic work.[9] Liao Xun argues that, since Hainan province is China's largest special economic zone, the bank should have a relatively independent status. The head of the bank should be someone nominated (*timing*) by the governor subject to ratification by the Standing Committee of the People's Congress, and, in order to ensure stability, the tenure of office should alternate (*jiaocuo*) with that of the governor. The head of the Statistical Office should be elected in a similar way.

The establishment of the above-mentioned seventeen *ting* and the two semi-official organs imply a reduction of the administrative structure of the former administrative district (*qu*). Compared with other market economies, there are still too many organs, according to Liao Xun. However, in the future, when the economy of Hainan has become marketized, urbanized, and more pluralistic, it will be possible to further reduce the number of government organs.

The core of Liao Xun's notion of small government is to change government functions. This means that the functions of consultancy (*zixun*), policy-making, and execution should be separated and be relatively independent.[10] Thus, government policy-making should first pass through the stage of expert deliberation in consultancy organs, to be followed by government initiative in the decision-making process; finally, relevant organs and personnel should take care of policy implementation. This will turn policy-making into a more scientific, democratic, and orderly process.

In order to attain such a situation, Liao Xun proposes that a clear system for selecting and evaluating cadres and government officials be implemented. In choosing leaders from vice-department leader on down, one must observe the principles of strict examination and impartial competition, and appoint (*xuanba*) people according to their qualifications (*zeyou luyong*). Liao Xun suggests that a selecting committee (*pingxuan weiyuanhui*), consisting of some of the cadres and responsible persons involved in establishing the province and some experts and a few retired cadres, should be formed to decide a method for relevant political and professional examination and proper evaluation procedures. At the final stage of its work, the committee should elect the new leading personnel by secret ballot (*wu jiming toupiao*).

Concerning the selection of the top leaders of the province, Liao Xun advises that the first governor be nominated by the State Council and approved by the Standing Committee of the National People's Congress.[11] The vice-governor and the principal (*zhengzhi*) heads at *ting* level should be nominated by the governor and approved by the Standing Committee of Hainan's National People's Congress. After the province has been established, it will be possible to practise an even more democratic method of electing the governor.

Big Society

The crux of the notion of 'big society' is independent, autonomous self-management. While reducing government functions, readjusting government organs, and simplifying government bureaucracy, full scope will be given to the autonomous functioning of society and a great number of social and economic undertakings will be handed back to individuals, enterprises, and social institutions and other social organizations in society. Liao Xun mentions that in the past there had been many attempts to reduce the size of government and to decentralize power, but none achieved any substantial results. The more the organs were simplified and cut (*kan*), the bigger they became; the more the staffing was reduced (*cai*), the more it grew. To him the reason is that there was no corresponding expansion of social functions. The reform experiences of other socialist countries show that government organs can be cut back provided the functions of social self-rule are expanded and the functions of the government system are reduced. Liao Xun explains:

If you do not change the functions of government and society and do not decentralize from the centre to the local arena, government organs will be overstaffed. Put the other way around—if you want to reduce organs, you must disperse power and reduce government functions. If you want to reduce government functions, you must expand the functions of society. If Hainan were to cure the root of the bureaucratic sickness, it would be necessary to fundamentally change the old system where the individual depends on the enterprise and the enterprise depends on the state, and instead bring forth the pluralistic interests of society.[12]

Liao Xun emphasizes that his ideas concerning the system of 'big society' involve a number of issues. First of all, it would be necessary as early as possible to affirm (*queren*) and ensure the economic decision-making power of the individual. According to Liao Xun, the individual citizen is the real building block (*xibao*) of society's economy. Not only is s/he the owner of personal consumption material and labour power, but s/he can be partly or fully the owner of certain production materials. Citizens should have the right freely to choose not only their consumption in a free market, but also their education or occupation; to decide whether they will participate in or withdraw from any enterprise, no matter what the ownership form, and to decide whether to open an individual or private enterprise. As consumers, the citizens should have the freedom to consume; as labourers, they should have the freedom to choose their occupations; as owners of property, they should have the freedom to invest.

In Liao Xun's mind, the right of enterprises to handle their own affairs should also be guaranteed. Hainan province should realize the free co-existence of many economic components, and all kinds of ownership, including state-owned, locally owned, and collective enterprises; joint ventures and new forms of jointly run enterprises; private enterprises (including individual enterprises, private enterprises with internal or foreign capital such as Hong Kong, Macao, or Taiwan capital). Thus, they should deliver taxes in a similar way and receive the same legal protection.

Enterprises and Social Institutions

Liao Xun realizes that there are problems concerning the efficiency and productivity of state-owned enterprises and that they are not as dynamic as private and collective enterprises. In order to remedy this situation, he suggests the implementation of the share-holding system. This would put the publicly owned enterprises in a better position in terms of attracting investment and human talents. He also advances the idea that state-managed enterprises should be independent (*duli zizhu*), should assume sole responsibility for their profit and losses (*zifu yingkui*), should take responsibility for their own risk and have the power to decide investment and to hire and fire workers, and should have the power to merge and split. As long as they do not infringe upon the law, government should not interfere.[13] State-owned enterprises should be led by enterprise-level boards of directors. The board should be composed of the party secretary, some representatives for state capital, representatives for staff and workers, and representatives for the private stockholders. It should have responsibility for overall policy-making and for electing or appointing the factory director or manager. The tenure of office for the factory director should be directly determined by the board of directors and not be the responsibility of the department in charge.

Liao Xun is also concerned with the role of social institutions. Their independence should be affirmed and guaranteed, and although such institutions need state financial funds and subsidies, they are not government units but relatively independent social units.[14] Those institutions in which intellectuals are in the majority ought to practise a kind of self-rule. The party secretary, some intellectuals held in high esteem, and other intellectuals should form school, university, or research institute committees or similar organs of self-rule. The leaders, elected or appointed, should be reported to the relevant government organs for approval of their appointment. Those institutions that have the capacity to be independent should be encouraged to form boards of directors (*dongshihui*) and in a proper way to strengthen the representation of state (or local) capital and private capital and to implement business management. If possible, all institutions ought to issue shares and actively absorb non-government (*minjian*) capital.

'Small government, big society' involves the reform of existing trade union organizations, and Liao Xun stresses that it is necessary to clarify the rights and powers of staff and workers' committees. At the same time, the organization of local trade unions at province, city, and county level under the new system must fully reflect the interest of enterprises of different economic elements, different areas, different branches, and the different interests of workers and staff.[15] All workers and staff committees and labour associations should independently perform various activities. In order to formalize their independent position, all mass organizations should provide for their own funds.

The enterprises as such should have the right to establish and participate in branch societies (*hangye gonghui*). They should have the authority, on a voluntary basis, to decide to participate, withdraw or not participate in a branch society organization. After having reached internal unanimity, they can represent the common interest of the enterprises in the branch and conduct a dialogue with the government or negotiate on important issues.

Finally, Liao Xun argues for the establishment of a new association of industry and commerce in order to make it possible for private enterprises and foreign enterprises to have their interests represented.

Social Associations

The most important and inventive part of 'small government, big society' concerns the establishment of various forms of social associations (*shetuan*) and various non-government organizations.

This aspect of Liao Xun's programme entails not only the establishment of a consumer organization to protect the interests of the consumers and to supervise the market behaviour of the enterprises, but also the formation of a friendship association of fellow provincials (*tongxiang lianyi zuzhi*). This organization should be open for the many 'mainland volunteers' that flocked to Hainan after the establishment of the new province, and it should represent their interests *vis-à-vis* the provincial government.

Liao Xun envisages the creation of private legal consultancy/advisory organizations and private law offices. He says:

Hainan not only should greatly develop state and collective legal consultancy organizations and law offices, but also should allow the establishment of private legal consultancy organizations and law offices. No matter whether it is a publicly administered organization or a privately administered organization, no matter whether it is a Chinese or a foreign lawyer, they should all be equal before the law.[16]

Other non-state organizations that should be established as part of 'small government, big society' include accounting firms (*kuaiji shiwusuo*), employment bureaus (*zhiye jieshaosuo*), and marriage introduction service centres (*hunyin jieshaosuo*). Their objective is to service enterprises, social institutions, government organizations, and individuals in both the state and non-state sector.

Liao Xun also deals with bank, finance, and insurance organizations. These are special institutions which ought to have the same powers, rights, and obligations as other enterprises. In his opinion, the financial market of Hainan should be completely opened, which means that foreign banks with foreign or overseas Chinese capital should be encouraged to establish offices or branches in Hainan. It is also important to encourage or stimulate the development of financial credit organizations of collectives and private people. In addition, Hainan should actively prepare to open a stock market (*gupiao shichang*).

Liao Xun is much concerned with democracy at the grass-roots level. He feels that every locality should try out or popularize the social autonomous organizations of villages and towns in order to promote the process of democratization of political power in these communities. The autonomous political power of villages should be represented in a committee elected by the village congress. The committee would elect a chairman. The tasks of the committee would include managing local finance, public construction, the streets, and health facilities and maintaining public order in the local area.

Liao Xun is also convinced that in Hainan's countryside independent organizations should be developed and supported in their efforts to elect local-level political leaders and perhaps effect a merger (*ronghe*) of basic-level political power and autonomous social organizations.

In Liao Xun's view, the above-mentioned 'restoration and perfection of social autonomous functions' will mean that more and more public tasks will be handled in an effective way. This will not only 'greatly reduce the burdens of government, but will also greatly reduce the moral responsibility of government'.

In general, the new system of 'small government, big society' requires that government and society establish a brand new (*zhanxin*) relationship. It also requires that the organs of local power in Hainan province, e.g. the People's Congress of Hainan Province, truly reflects the plurality of interests in Hainan. A step in this direction would be to introduce path-breaking direct elections:

We claim that the People's Congress of Hainan ought to be a step ahead of the National People's Congress and at a suitable time [ought to] begin to implement direct elections.[17]

Stages of Political System Reform

The reform of the political system, which is a necessary part of the implementation of 'small government, big society', can be divided into three stages. The first stage Liao Xun calls the preparation stage (*zhunbei jieduan*). Important tasks during this stage include drafting a 'basic law for promoting and developing Hainan', designing a political system specifying the limits and powers of authority of government at different levels, and establishing social organizations. During this phase, which should last no more than three years, the mass media should be fully used in order to promote and spread the new ideas.[18]

The second stage in Liao Xun's scheme is called the test-run stage (*shi yunxing*). During this stage the new system will start to operate and will be continuously improved on the basis of the experience gained. Liao Xun stresses that the test-run phase should regularize policy measures in the form of law, and he further states that 'from now on we must walk the path of the rule by law'.[19] Moreover, it would be necessary to continue to strengthen theoretical mass media propaganda work. The test-run stage will last four to five years.

The third stage is called the stage of normalizing operation. Liao Xun argues that the tasks of this phase are difficult to foresee. However, a major task would be to correct problems that have cropped up during the first two stages. During this stage it is also important to uphold the close connection between political and economic reform. Liao Xun is quite emphatic on this point:

Political system reform is the basic guarantee for economic system reform and the development of the economy. We will absolutely not allow anyone with any pretext to put an end to political system reform.[20]

Lai Xun's reform proposal is well argued and comprehensive in scope. It is remarkable in stressing in unequivocal terms that political reform is a precondition for the successful implementation of economic reform. But perhaps more important in this context, Liao Xun's reform proposal is a unique example of a Chinese discourse on establishing the foundations of a civil society in the form of intermediate organizations and associations and a developing market economy. Moreover, there is a pronounced emphasis on the role of the individual, which is rare in contemporary Chinese political writings.

Liao Xun and the Concept of Civil Society

Liao Xun's thinking can be related to three different discourses on civil society: the classical–liberal, the Hegelian, and a newer, Havelian, discourse which takes its inspiration in the East European and Soviet transition to post-communism.[21]

In the classical–liberal discourse, John Locke's *The Second Treatise on Civil Government* assumes paradigmatic importance.[22] Locke maintains that all people are equal and free and that they own the results of their own labour. The transition from 'the state of Nature' to 'political society' is not, as Hobbes argued, based on the abolition of the principle of equality. Neither does the individual resign his freedom or property rights. The transition to political society is predicated on the individual's transfer to the state of his or her rights to implement the laws of nature. Says Locke:

Whereever, therefore, any number of men so unite into one society as to quit every one of his executive power of the law of Nature, and to resign it to the public, there and there only is a political or civil society. And this is done whereever any number of men, in the state of Nature, enter into society to make one people one body politic under one supreme government . . . And this puts men out of a state of Nature into that of a commonwealth, which judge is the legislative or magistrates appointed by it.[23]

Locke identifies civil society with political society: '[The people] could never be safe, not at rest, nor think themselves in civil society, till the legislative was so placed in connective bodies of men, call them senate, parliament, or what you please, by which means every single person became subject equally, with other the meanest men, to those laws, which he himself, as part of the legislative, had established.'[24]

However, although civil society is based on government and political society, Locke emphasizes that absolute monarchy 'is indeed inconsistent with civil society'. In fact, political society is 'nothing but the consent of any number of freemen capable of a majority, to unite and incorporate into such a society'.[25] In political society, the state has no rights, only obligations. These obligations are primarily to protect the rights of the citizens.

Liao Xun is also of the opinion that the state should serve the individual and should not interfere in everything. In fact, one could imagine that the state in the future would serve three main functions: as a 'soccer referee' (*zuqiu caipan*), as 'traffic police' (*jiaotong jingcha*), and as a 'fire fighter' (*xiaofang duiyuan*).[26] In the first function the state would issue a set of rules, and it would interfere only when citizens intentionally 'bumped' into each other or were guilty of 'offside'. In the second function the state should 'clear the streets and bridges' and create conditions for the orderly flow of transport and communication. Finally, in the third function the state would intervene in case of fire or disaster which necessitated relief work.

In general, Liao Xun favours a state construction that is reduced as much as possible, and on several occasions he approvingly quotes Thomas Jefferson saying, 'The best state is the state that governs as little as possible' (*guanli zui shao de zhengfu, jiu shi zui hao de zhengfu*).[27] Liao Xun also states that he subscribes to the theory that the individual should be considered the basic cell of society.[28]

Here again, there are obvious parallels to the classical–liberal discourse, *in casu* John Stuart Mill. In his essay *On Liberty*, where the central position of the individual is stressed we read that:

the only purpose for which power can be rightfully exercised over any member of a civilised community, against his will, is to prevent harm to others . . . The only part of the conduct of any one, for which he is amenable to society, is that which concerns others. In the part which merely concerns himself, his independence is, of right, absolute. Over himself, over his own body and mind, the individual is sovereign.[29]

Mill lists three reasons why it is essential to limit government interference. The first is that the thing to be done is likely to be better done by individuals than by government. The second is that, although the individuals may not 'do the particular thing so well, on the average, as the officers of government, it is nevertheless desirable that it should be done by them as a means to their own mental education'. Third, one should not make government work too attractive since,

if every part of the business of society which required organized concert, or large and comprehensive views, were in the hands of the government, and if government offices were universally filled by the ablest men, all the enlarged culture and practised intelligence in the country, except the purely speculative, would be concentrated in a numerous bureaucracy, to whom alone the rest of the community would look for all things: the multitude for direction and dictation in all they do; the able and aspiring for personal advancement.[30]

In short, the term 'civil society' began as an affirmation or recognition of the human need and capacity to create political institutions as distinct from a state of nature, but later came to be used to emphasize private goals and interests as distinct from public order or control.[31] The inalienable rights of the free individual constituted the red thread in this process. The economy was based on the presupposition that no extra-economic agency interfered with the transactions in the market, thereby ensuring everyone's welfare and justice in accord with the individual's capacity to perform. Liao Xun draws on this liberal tradition when he emphasizes the central position of the individual and the reduced role of the state as a 'soccer referee' and a 'fire fighter'.

The Hegelian and Marxian Discourse

There is another strand in Liao Xun's thinking, which links him to the Hegelian discourse. For Hegel civil society and the state were separated, and he viewed civil society as a realm of intermediary institutions and associations between the individual and the state. Hegel's analysis of civil society consists mainly of a discussion of the guilds and corporations, the estates and classes, and the associations and local communities that constituted the structure of the German society in which he lived. Unlike Locke, Hegel did not believe that the state was composed primarily of individual citizens. In his view the individual must be mediated through a series of corporations and associations in order to obtain the full status of citizenship in the state.[32]

The creation of a range of various intermediate associations is an important part of Liao Xun's vision of 'small government, big society'. These take the form of branch societies, associations of industry and commerce, consumer associations, associations of fellow provincials, etc. As in the Hegelian discourse, these intermediate associations are positioned between the individual and the state. In the 'small government, big society' discourse, they are not only intermediate (*zhongjian*), but also non-government (*minjian*). Liao Xun is rather specific about how these associations should be formed and whom they should represent.

Marx identified civil society with bourgeois society and the capitalist state.[33] His idea that civil society belongs to the capitalist stage implies that civil society is relative to a particular historical period. Therefore the concept becomes associated with private property, with exploitation of the immediate producers, and with market competition. On this basis, the Marxian discourse cannot hold the notion of a *socialist* civil society.

Liao Xun seems to disagree with Marx on this point. To Liao Xun the elements of 'small government, big society' are to be found in different historical periods and in different political–economic systems. Liao Xun refers to the liberalism of the nineteenth-century United States, the NEP policies of Lenin, and the economic reforms of Eastern Europe as periods of time and social experiments in which sprouts of 'small government, big society' can be located.

The East European Discourse

When the discourse of civil society was reinvented in Poland in the 1970s, it was used to describe the autonomous spheres of activities that were emerging.[34] The most notable of course was the independent trade union Solidarity, but this was only one example of a number of networks that emerges creating a new public discourse beyond the control and limits of the party–state.

In the East European version, the use of the concept of civil society refers to the organization of a plurality of interests outside the state and party in an increasingly independent or autonomous social sphere. Formulated in another way, civil society is envisaged as a sphere of social and cultural space to be carved out of an all-encompassing matrix of a totalitarian communist party–state by the social action of conscious workers and intellectuals.[35]

Liao Xun does not define his concept of 'small government, big society' in opposition to the existing orthodoxy. In fact, he takes great pains to underline that his formula will make the system work better and will serve the interest of the party. However, in reality, if successfully introduced, 'small government, big society' will create a society characterized by civic initiatives and a vibrant associational life and it is difficult not to see obvious parallels to the East European situation.

The Habermasian Discourse

The civil society debate has been much influenced by Jürgen Habermas's theories on the public sphere.[36]

It is Habermas's contention that the public sphere emerged in Europe in the seventeenth and eighteenth centuries in the coffee shops of London, the salons of Paris, and the *Tischgesellschaften* of Berlin. Together with the medium of the press, they formed a public sphere in which people engaged in a rational–critical debate.[37] This public sphere arose in the broader sphere of the bourgeoisie as an expansion of the intimate sphere of the conjugal family.

In the Habermasian discourse, the existence of a public sphere is an important prerequisite for talking about a civil society. It is true that there is no indication that Liao Xun has ever read any of Habermas's works. However, the Hainan reformer is much concerned with the public sphere. He is a prolific writer in one of Hainan's major newspapers, *Hainan Tequ Bao*, which since February 1994 has twice weekly carried a front-page column by him entitled 'Tianwa shiping' (Commentary on Current Affairs in Hainan) in addition to regular longer essays on basic issues pertaining to the Hainan reform process.[38] These public writings for a wider audience is a reflection of his conviction that it is the duty of intellectuals to take part in public debate. In fact, many of Liao Xun's ideas have been put forward first through the newspapers, and one can often find others picking up on the theme in the media in Hainan.

In stressing individual initiative and autonomy, the importance of intermediate bodies beyond the individual, the importance of public discussion, and so on, Liao Xun's thinking is connected to some of the central discourses in the Western civil society debate. However, when Liao Xun developed his basic ideas in the 1981–91 period he was apparently not aware of this debate. So what appears to have happened is that Liao Xun's views developed primarily from within the Chinese discourse itself in the same way as Liao Gailong's reform programme from 1980 followed logically from the political reform proposals discussed at that time. Thus, one could argue that Deng's reforms carry 'liberal' ideas in a negative, but logical, fashion.

Only in 1993 did Liao Xun become aware of the Western discourse on civil society. He realized that the central concerns of this discourse in many ways were similar to his own, and in 1994 he published a major article explicitly linking his own thinking to the civil society debate.[39] This essay is important since it gives us an idea of the intellectual influences that Liao Xun himself determines to be of importance for his ideas.

As in Liao Xun's other writings, most of the references in this article are Marxian, and it is Stalin and Soviet Marxism that are rejected most clearly. However, there are also a number of references to Thomas Jefferson and Hegel. This is important, since it shows that Liao Xun is aware of liberal thinking as well as Hegel's philosophy. In fact, the main emphasis in the essay is on the need to establish more intermediate organizations in the Hegelian sense in order to create a civil society: 'Civil society is the goal, and the state is only an instrument of civil society.'[40]

In sum, although Liao Xun was unaware of the debate concerning the concept of civil society while first developing his thinking on 'small government, big society', he provides what is possibly the most comprehensive and detailed mainland Chinese exposition on the subject. Moreover, it is possible to relate his line of thought to three different discourses on civil society (the classical–liberal, the Hegelian–Marxian, and the East European). Liao Xun's thinking appears to have taken its starting point in Chinese realities, but its affinity to widely discussed Western concepts shows its more global significance.

The Hainan Reform Process

Turning to the actual situation on Hainan, I will first address the issue of whether Liao Xun's ideas on reducing the government and expanding society actually have been implemented. Have government organs actually been cut, and do we find an increase in various intermediary associations and organizations? Second, I will take a closer look at the expansion of the private sector in Hainan, since the assumption is that the development of private economic activity and marketization will contribute to the creation of autonomous activities and a social space independent of the state. Third, I will consider the important issue of social associations (*shetuan*) and their role in Hainan.

Reform of the Administrative Structure

Immediately after the establishment of the new province on 1 January 1988, the planned streamlining of the administrative structure was implemented, and as a consequence the number of administrative organs at provincial (former administrative district) level was reduced by 37 to 48.

Originally Liao Xun had suggested nineteen department (*ting*)-level organizations, including a provincial-level People's Bank and a Statistical Office. All these *ting* were established in the beginning of 1988, with the exception that the Department of Physical Training and Public Health was split into two: the Public Health Department (Weisheng ting) and the Department for Culture and Physical Training (Wenhua tiyu ting) (later renamed the Department of Culture, Broadcasting and Physical Training, Wenhua guangbo tiyu ting). Although the Department for Labour Welfare (Laodong fuli baozhang ting) was not established as envisaged, this did not mean a reduction in the number of organs, since a number of new ones were created: the Department for Public Security (Gongan ting), State Department for Public Security (Guojia gongan ting), Department of Enterprise Law (Sifa ting), Department of Civil Affairs (Minzheng ting), Department of Construction (Jianshe ting), Department of Economic Cooperation (Jingji hezuo ting), Office for Port Administration (Kuoan guanli bangongshi), and, finally, the Research Centre for Economic and Social Development (Shehui jingi fazhan yanjiu zhongxin).

There were two reasons why it was difficult to reduce the administrative structure further. As mentioned by Liao Xun, in the past there had been attempts to reduce the size of government, but often the result was more bureaucracy and red tape rather than less. This pattern is also recognizable on a wider national scale; for example, the administrative reforms in 1982 and 1988 were both halted by the system's immanent tendency to bureaucratic hypertrophy. Moreover a reform process produces new tasks and problems which have to be solved, and as the old organs often are incapable of handling the problems new organs are created, resulting in a renewed swelling of the bureaucracy.

The other reason why it was difficult to reduce the administrative structure any further was that, even though Hainan reformers at the local level might escape the logic of bureaucratic hypertrophy so characteristic of centrally based systems, new problems would arise. The main problem stems from the *duikou* or 'connector' factor. This is related to the fact that because of the administrative reform Hainan often no longer possesses organs on a similar level to government agencies on the mainland. For this reason central agencies sometimes have difficulties connecting (*duikou*) with the provincial organs on Hainan. This creates problems when funds and resources are transferred from central sources or when Hainan has to deal with other provinces.[41] Because of this problem, it has been necessary to re-establish a few of the old administrative structures. An additional difficulty is that administrative reform has not yet reached the lower county (*xian*) level, and therefore the new provincial-level government organs in Hainan have become sandwiched between a central level and a local, county level, neither of which has as yet experienced similar administrative reforms.

The 1994 *Hainan Nianjian* lists 20 departments (*ting*), 3 offices (*bangongshi*), 2 committees (*weiyuanhui*), 1 branch (*fenhang*), and 24 bureaus (*ju*). Of the 24 *ju*, 17 are also listed as companies (*gongsi*); this is because they have been subject to an attempt to change them from administrative organs to social enterprises, which in theory should be independent from the government. Liao Xun himself admits that the present administrative structure is 'fatter' than originally envisaged, but this is due to the fact that the above-mentioned administrative problems have arisen.

The Development of the Urban Private and Individual Economy

As illustrated in Table 1, in 1993 the private sector contained 3.2 per cent of Tianjin's urban workforce and 3.6 per cent of Beijing's, but constituted 11.4 per cent of Fujian's, 13.9 per cent of Guangdong's, and 16.0 per cent of Hainan's. Thus, the development of private business appears to have gone farther in Hainan than in any other province in China.

TABLE 1   Relative Size of the Urban Private Sector in China, 1993

Province/ city	Urban workforce (1)	Private workforce (2)	(2) as % of (1) (3)
Tianjin	3,032,000	98,000	3.2
Beijing	4,832,000	173,000	3.6
Jiangsu	9,540,000	371,000	3.9
Liaoning	10,983,000	707,000	6.4
Zhejiang	5,538,000	515,000	9.3
Fujian	3,894,000	445,000	11.4
Guangdong	10,222,000	1,423,000	13.9
Hainan	1,216,000	194,000	16.0
National	159,640,000	11,160,000	7.0

Source: *Zhongguo Tongji Nianjian 1994*, 84–5.

Hainan's percentage of the employed workforce in the private sector of the urban workforce was already higher than the national average in 1979 and more than twice as high in 1993. The greatest yearly growth took place in 1991, when the private urban workforce grew from 77,000 to 129,000 or by 68 per cent (see Table 2). In 1993 there was a further rapid expansion of the private sector in Hainan: the privately employed work-force in the cities increased from 137,000 to 223,500, or by 63 per cent.

About 66 per cent of urban private business in Hainan is located in the three cities of Haikou, Sanya, and Danzhou.[42] Haikou in particular has experienced a blooming of the private sector. As in the rest of Hainan, there was some stagnation in 1989 and 1990, but from 1991 the develop-ment of private enterprises accelerated. In 1990 the number employed in the private sector in Haikou was 14,838; one year later it had increased about 300 per cent to 47,743 (see Table 3). In 1992 the urban private work-force in Haikou grew by an additional 20 per cent to 57,531; however since the total labour force of Haikou had grown by 59,000 people, the private labour as a percentage of total labour force actually fell. In 1993 Haikou's private sector experienced a new surge: the number of people employed in that sector increased by 97 per cent to 112,814, which equals almost a third

TABLE 2   The Development of the Urban Private Sector in Hainan, 1977–1993

	Urban workforce (1)	Private urban workforce (2)	(2) as % of (1) (3)
1977	804,400	900	0.1
1978	798,400	n.a.	n.a.
1979	832,400	7,100	0.9
1980	854,500	13,200	1.5
1981	911,300	21,800	2.4
1982	956,100	15,600	1.6
1983	946,300	20,600	2.2
1984	983,700	29,200	3.0
1985	1,025,300	45,400	4.4
1986	1,047,800	47,500	4.5
1987	1,057,600	55,600	5.3
1988	1,101,700	75,300	6.8
1989	1,116,300	76,400	6.8
1990	1,133,200	76,800	6.8
1991	1,210,500	129,000	10.6
1992	1,255,500	137,000	10.9
1993	1,334,100	223,500	16.8

Source: *Hainan Tongji Nianjian 1994*, 43.

of the city's total labour force. As there is still in China in general a tendency to under-report private economic activity, the real share must be assumed to be considerably higher.

This not only makes Haikou an important case study in researching the patterns and processes of current private enterprise development in China,

TABLE 3   Private-Sector Proportion of Total Labour Force in Haikou City, 1989–1993

	Total labour force (1)	Private labour force (2)	(2) as % of (1) (3)
1989	195,500	15,055	7.7
1990	212,500	14,838	7.0
1999	260,668	47,743	18.3
1992	319,018	57,531	17.9
1993	386,348	112,814	29.2

Sources: *Hainan Tongji Nianjian 1990*, 90; *Hainan Tongji Nianjian 1991*, 26; *Hainan Tongji Nianjian 1992*, 70; *Hainan Tongji Nianjian 1993*, 59; *Hainan Tongji Nianjian 1994*, 44.

but it also illustrates that an important part of the 'small government, big society' is in fact being realized.

Originally statistics did not distinguish between employment in the so-called individual economy and employment in the private economy. However, from the beginning of the 1990s the Hainan authorities started to release figures which makes it possible to form an impression of the relative size of the two forms of private economic activity (see Table 4). Thus, according to *Hainan Nianjian 1992*, in 1991, of the 47,743 engaged in the private sector, 27,392 were in the individual economy and 20,351 in the private; in 1992 these figures increased to 28,450 and 29,081 respectively. Although private businesses (*siying qiye*) employed only about five hundred more people than individual businesses (*getihu*), in terms of investment and size of the registered capital, *siying qiye* by far exceeded *getihu*. At the end of 1992 the registered capital of the *getihu* in Haikou amounted to 22,036,000 yuan, compared with 1,434,650,000 yuan for the private enterprises; in 1993 the private sector surged to employ a total workforce of 112,814, of which private business stood for 73,630, an increase of 153 per cent in just one year.

TABLE 4 Numbers of Employed in Individual and Private Enterprises in Haikou City, 1991–1993

	Total	Individual	Private
1991	46,640	26,282	20,358
1992	57,531	28,450	20,358
1993	112,814	39,184	73,630

Sources: Hainan Tongji Nianjian 1992, 70; *Hainan Nianjian 1993*, 59; *Hainan Tongji Nianjian 1994*, 44.

Turning to the countryside, the private sector is not particularly strong in agricultural production, which is still heavily dominated by the state farms. However, Hainan's township industries are to a large extent in private hands. In 1991 private enterprises constituted 92 per cent of the total number of Hainan's township industries. The number of people employed were 160,306, or 62.7 per cent of the total number of employed in this sector, and the income of private enterprises came to 58.4 per cent of total income of the township industry sector. If joint or cooperative enterprises are included in the number of private enterprises, the respective figures are 97.5, 73.3, and 75.5 per cent (see Table 5).

The state sector's role in Hainan's countryside peaked in 1991. New statistics show that from 1991 to 1993 the number of state farms dropped

TABLE 5   Township Industries in Hainan: Number of
Enterprises and Employees, 1991

Ownership	Number of enterprises	Number of employees
Total	90,540	255,780
Township and village	2,292	68,239
Joint/cooperative	4,772	27,235
Private/individual	88,476	160,306

Source: *Hainan Nianjian 1992*, 106.

from 97 to 92 and their total workforce was reduced from 454,500 to 418,600.[43] This trend is in line with official policies and will further improve the conditions for the development of the private sector in Hainan's countryside.

In short, there has been a rapid expansion of the private economy in Hainan in recent years. The process towards private economic activity and marketization gained momentum in 1993 and central control now plays a minor role in the economy. This has created a sphere of economic activity independent of the state and has stimulated the emergence of new social groups such as private entrepreneurs and businessmen. Thus, the economic part of 'small government, big society' appears to have been realized in practice.

Social Associations (Shetuan)

As mentioned above, an important and inventive part of the programme of 'small government, big society' is the proposal to set up various institutions and organizations for the assistance of individual persons, such as law and accounting offices and labour employment bureaus. These are supposed to represent the interests of their members and to function as a bridge between the state organs and the citizens. Self-governing associations in the villages, townships, and at the local level in major cities are also to be formed. Moreover, 'small government, big society' involves the establishment of various business associations and consumer associations.

There are currently 253 social associations (*shetuan*) in Hainan. Of these, 189 cover the whole province, 30 are specific to Haikou, and the rest (44) are located in cities like Tongsha and Sanya and counties such as Lingao, Wenchang, Qiongshan, Qionghai, Chengmai, Dingan, Tunchang, Dongfang, Changjians, Ledong, and Dan.[44]

We will divide these social organizations into eight categories (see Table 6).[45]

TABLE 6 The Formation of Social Organizations (*shetuan*) in Hainan, 1956–1992

Type of organization	1956	1982	1983	1984	1985	1986	1987	1988	1989	1990	1991	1992
Academic and cultural		1	2	2	1		1	8	13	19	18	3
Economic							1		5	6	8	
Science and technology	1			2		1			9	11	12	5
Political									5	4	1	1
Branch		1							3	12	5	7
Health									5	3	1	1
Sports		1	1				1	1	2	3	5	
Friendly							1	2	3	4	6	
Total	1	3	3	4	1	1	4	11	45	62	66	17

1. *Academic and cultural*   This category is the most numerous and comprises sixty-eight different organizations and associations. Examples range from academic study associations such as the Hainan Pacific Rim Study Association and the Hainan Physiology Association to cultural associations and groups such as the Hainan World Languages Association and the Hainan Philatelist, Calligraphy, and Photography Association of the Staff and Workers of the Non-Ferrous Metal Industry.

2. *Scientific and technological*   There are forty-one associations under this category. They are based primarily on particular professions or specialized skills and include organizations and groups like the Hainan Irrigations Works Study Association and the Hainan Accounting Associations.

3. *Economic*   There are twenty of these organizations in Hainan including associations engaged in land reclamation, basic economic construction, grain economy, aquatic products, tropical fruit, and tax affairs. Like the scientific and technological associations, these are engaged in training, research, exchange of information, arranging conferences, gathering and publishing of materials, etc.

4. *Political*   These eleven associations are directly organized by the party and state organizations and units and function as 'transmission belts' linking the party with specific groups, policies, or initiatives. Examples of this category of associations include the Hainan Association of the Study of Scientific Socialism, the Associations for the Study of Dialectics of Nature, the Hainan Minorities Study Association, and the Hainan Family Planning Association.

5. *Health*   This category of ten organizations, including the Hainan Association for the Study of the Economics of Public Health, the Hainan Association of Cancer Prevention, and the Association for the Prevention of AIDS, is clearly formed in the hope that citizens will take part in government-sponsored initiatives in the health sector. There are also some based on specific skills, e.g. the Hainan Acupuncture Association and the Combination of Western and Chinese Medicine Study Association of Hainan.

6. *Sports*   There are fourteen such organizations in Hainan, ranging from the Hainan Weight Lifting Association and the Hainan Badminton Association, to associations concerned with specific hobbies such as the Hainan Bridge Association and the Hainan Old People's Fishing Association.

7. *Friendly associations*   The sixteen friendly associations include associations of overseas Chinese in Hainan (e.g. Association of Overseas Chinese from Singapore and Malaysia) and of mainlanders living and working in Hainan (e.g. Association of Hunans living in Hainan). This category also

includes associations of mainland enterprises operating in Hainan (e.g. Association of Shanghai Enterprises and Undertakings in Hainan).

8. *Trade associations* There are twenty-eight of these, which organize the staff and workers within a special branch or trade. They include the Hainan General Chamber of Commerce, the Hainan Individual Labourers' Association, the Haikou Private Enterprises Association, the Hainan Real Estate Association, and the Hainan General Merchandise Association. The most numerous are those that organize people within a special profession, such as the Hainan Registered Accountants Association, the Hainan Translators Association, and the Hainan Association of Dancers. Although the independence and influence of these associations should not be overrated, they often function as interest groups representing the interests of their members *vis-à-vis* the provincial government.

As can be seen from Table 6, most of the social organizations were formed after the establishment of Hainan as a province in 1988. Only one—the Hainan Building Construction Study Association—was formed in the 1950s, i.e. in 1956. There was then a sixteen-year period before the next three associations were formed in 1982; 1983 also saw the formation of three associations, while in 1984 the number of new associations increased to four, although only one was formed in 1985 and again in 1986. From 1987, and especially from 1988, the establishment of new associations accelerated, with sixty-six new associations formed in 1991.

The new social organizations vary considerably in size. Almost half of them (46 per cent) have fewer than 100 members. There is also a relatively high percentage of associations with a membership of between 100 and 200 (28 per cent). Only 6 per cent of the associations have more than 1,000 members, but they hold 87 per cent of the total membership. The largest is the Hainan Individual Labourers' Association with a membership of 140,000; next comes the Haikou Individual Labourers' Association with 24,453 members; then the Hainan Red Cross and the Hainan General Merchandise Association.

All in all, these organizations have a membership of 218,762. There is no reliable information on the size of the forty-four local associations that are based in different counties and cities outside Haikou; it is estimated that they may increase the total membership to about 300,000.

The formation of all these associations indicates that, in addition to the old official organizations like the General Trade Union Federation and the Communist Youth League, a broad group of new social organizations is emerging. In sum, it appears that this part of Liao Xun's programme of 'small government, big society' is being realized.

To be sure, it could be argued that the new social organizations do not really represent a new phenomenon, since they all must register at a department in charge (*zhuguan bumen*) which normally is part of the state apparatus. However, this procedure does not necessarily entail their being run by the state (*guanban*). Some do have their leaders and staff appointed by a state agency as part of their official establishment and are allocated office in government buildings.[46] But others are spontaneously formed and are *minban* in the sense that they run their own affairs without interference from the state bureaucracy.[47] Such organizations clearly have a high degree of independence from the state.

Concluding Remarks

Civil society and public sphere have become popular concepts in the China field. Although it might be too early to use the term 'paradigmatic change', it is clear that a major change of our understanding of modern Chinese history is taking place. Instead of focusing on individuals, the development of different policy positions, bureaucratic infighting between different bureaucracies, etc., the new understanding emphasizes state–society relations in a broad sense. Not only that: it shows that state–society relations in China are not static, but positioned in a process of multidimensional change.

In the literature on civil society in China, the Chinese discourse has too often been neglected. Although Liao Xun seldom uses the concept of civil society, his ideas do in fact represent a Chinese contribution to the debate. His concept of 'small government, big society' involves a substantial cutback of government functions; instead, an autonomous sphere consisting of the independent activities of the citizens and their own associations and organizations is to be established. A full implementation of these plans will lay the foundation of a civil society introduced from above.

'Small government, big society' is applicable not only to Hainan. In fact, it is the general idea that the new political and social system introduced on Hainan will serve as a testing point for a long-term reform of the political system in China overall. Thus, the concept has national implications and an importance that reaches beyond the confinement of Hainan. In fact, Liao Xun's concept establishes a bridge or perhaps a beachhead for the Chinese political discourse to become integrated with Western political thought, *in casu* the civil society debate.

After the *gengsheng* reforms of 1980 were pushed aside, there was for many years a lull in the Chinese political reform debate. To be sure, separate ideas were advanced by Chinese intellectuals, but no comprehensive

programme involving substantial shifts in state–society relations was formulated or discussed in any detail. Liao Xun's ideas on 'small government,
big society' represents an attempt to remedy this situation. At the same
time, the concept re-establishes the link with the *gengsheng* reforms. Since
Liao Xun is the son of Liao Gailong, this is true in more than one sense.
History has turned full circle.

NOTES

1. In August 1980, at an enlarged meeting of the Politbureau, Deng Xiaoping gave a talk
   on thorough reform of the leadership systems of party and state. In the wake of the
   speech a debate on the issues raised by Deng unfolded in the party and in the media.
   The policy proposals that were formulated as a consequence of this debate came to be
   known as the '*gengshen* reforms'. The most elaborate of the reform proposals was the
   one put forward by Liao Gailong, a prominent member of the policy study office
   under the Central Committee. See Kjeld Erik Brødsgaard, 'Economic and Political
   Reform in Post-Mao China', *Copenhagen Papers in East and Southeast Asian Studies*,
   1 (1987), 31–56.
2. Liao Xun, *Makesi Engesi 'xiao zhengfu' sixiang yu dangdai jingji gaige* (Marx and
   Engels's Thoughts on 'Small Government' and Current Economic Reform) (Haikou:
   Hainan renmin chubanshe, 1988).
3. Liao Xun, *Xiao zhengfu da shehui: Hainan xin tizhi de lilun yu shijian* (Small
   Government, Big Society: The Theory and Practice of Hainan's New System) (Hunan:
   San huan chubanshe, 1991).
4. Liao Xun, *Kaifang de chengben* (The Results of Openness) (Haikou: Hainan chuban-
   she gongsi, 1993).
5. Other discussions on the concept of civil society in relation to China include Kjeld Erik
   Brødsgaard, 'Civil Society and Democratization in China', in Margaret L. Nugent,
   From Leninism to Freedom: The Challenges of Democratization (Boulder, Colo.:
   Westview Press, 1992), 181–93; David Kelley and He Baogang, 'Emergent Civil
   Society and the Intellectuals in China', in Robert Miller (ed.), *The Development of Civil
   Society in Communist Systems* (North Sydney: Allen & Unwin, 1992), 24–39; William
   T. Rowe, 'The Public Sphere in Modern China', *Modern China*, 16:3 (July 1990),
   309–29; David Strand, 'Protest in Beijing: Civil Society and Public Sphere in China',
   Problems of Communism, 39:3 (May–June 1990), 1–19; Mayfair Mei-hui Yang,
   'Between State and Society: The Construction of Corporateness in a Chinese Socialist
   Factory', *Australian Journal of Chinese Affairs*, No. 22 (July 1989), 31–60; and Tom
   Gold, Ch. 7 above. There is also a special issue of *Modern China* devoted to the issue
   of civil society in China, with articles by e.g. Heath Chamberlain, Philip Huang,
   Richard Madsen, William Rowe, and Frederick Wakeman: see *Modern China*, 19:2
   (April 1993).
6. The report appears as ch. 8 in Liao Xun, *Xiao zhengfu da shehui*.
7. ibid. 226.
8. ibid. 233.
9. ibid. 244.
10. ibid. 245.

11. ibid. 246.
12. ibid. 247.
13. ibid. 249.
14. ibid. 250.
15. ibid. 251.
16. ibid. 253.
17. ibid. 255.
18. ibid. 259.
19. ibid. 260.
20. ibid. 261.
21. Elsewhere I have argued that it is possible to locate six different discourses on civil society: (1) the traditional; (2) the classical–liberal; (3) the Hegelian; (4) the Marxian; (5) the Gramscian; and (6) a newer, Havelian, which transcends Marx and Gramsci and takes its inspiration in the East European and Soviet transition to post-communism: see Brødsgaard, 'Civil Society and Democratization'. Liao Xun's ideas relate to three of these discourses. Important works on the general concept of civil society include Perry Anderson, 'The Antimonies of Antonio Gramsci', New Left Review, 100 (1976–7), 5–78; Janina Frentzel-Zagorska, 'Civil Society in Poland and Hungary', Soviet Studies, 42:4 (1990), 759–77; Salvador Giner, 'The Withering Away of Civil Society?', Praxis International, 5:3 (1985), 247–67; Edward Shils, 'The Virtue of Civil Society', Government and Opposition, 26:1 (Winter 1991), 3–20; Charles Taylor, 'Modes of Civil Society', Public Culture, 3:1 (Fall 1990), 95–132; John Keane (ed.), Civil Society and the State (London: Verso, 1988); Jean Cohen and Andrew Arato, Civil Society and Political Theory (Cambridge, Mass.: MIT Press, 1992). See also the papers on the emerging democracies in Eastern Europe by, among others, Eugene Kamenka and Andrew Arato in Nugent, From Leninism to Freedom.
22. John Locke, The Second Treatise of Civil Government (New York: Prometheus Books, 1986).
23. ibid. 50.
24. ibid. 54.
25. ibid. 56.
26. See the interview with Liao Xun in Hong Xiaobo, 'Da gouxiang, da jiyu, da chaotou: "xiao zhengfu da shehui" de tiqi' (A Good Idea, a Good Opportunity, and a Widespread Tendency: The Talk about 'Small Government, Big Society'), Hainan Kaifa Bao, 8 April 1988.
27. See also the article on Thomas Jefferson in Hainan Tequ Bao (Hainan Special Zone News), 31 August 1993.
28. ibid.
29. John Stuart Mill, Utilitarianism, On Liberty, and Considerations on Representative Government, ed. H. B. Acton (London: J. M. Dent & Sons, 1988), 78.
30. ibid. 180–1.
31. See also Adam Ferguson, An Essay on the History of Civil Society, ed. Duncan Forbes (Edinburgh: Edinburgh University Press, 1966).
32. See G. W. F. Hegel, Elements of the Philosophy of Rights, ed. Allen W. Wood (Cambridge: Cambridge University Press, 1991), 220–74.
33. Karl Marx, 'The Eighteenth Brumaire of Louis Bonaparte', in Karl Marx, Surveys from Exile, ii, edited and introduced by David Fernbach (London: Allan Lane, 1973), 186.
34. See Andrew Arato, 'Civil Society against the State: Poland 1980–81', Telos, 47 (1981), 23–47.

35. See Robert F. Miller (ed.), *The Development of Civil Society in Communist Systems* (Sydney: Allen & Unwin, 1992), 5.

36. See Jürgen Habermas, *The Structural Transformation of the Public Sphere: An Inquiry into a Category of Bourgeois Society* (Cambridge, Mass.: MIT Press, 1991).

37. ibid. 50.

38. The 1994 commentaries are published in Liao Xun's most recent book, *Tianya shiping* (Comments on Current Affairs in Hainan) (Haikou: Hainan chuban gongsi, 1995).

39. Liao Xun, 'Tongye gonghui: "xiao zhengfu" yu "da shehui" bu ke queshao de zhongjie' (Trade Association: an Intermediary Organization 'Small Government' and 'Big Society' Cannot Lack), *Hainan Tequ Bao*, 1 March 1994.

40. ibid.

41. This problem is also discussed by Xu Shijie, former party secretary of Hainan province, in an interview carried in *Qiushi*: see Liu Wei, 'Hainan sheng: "xiao zhengfu, da shehui" de gouxiang he shishe' (Hainan Province: The Concept of 'Small Government, Big Society' and its Implementation), *Qiushi*, 6 (1989), 9–12.

42. *Hainan Tongji Nianjian 1994* (Beijing: Zhongguo tongji chubanshe, 1994), 153.

43. *Hainan Tongji Nianjian 1994*, 153.

44. Hainan sheng minzheng ting shetuan dengji guanlichu bian, *Hainan sheng shehui tuanti* (Social Organizations in Hainan Province) (Haikou, n.d.). The establishment of one association, the Haikou Private Enterprises Association, is dated April 1900. This must be a mistake. Since we do not have information on the correct date, the association is not included in the following table.

45. For a discussion of the new Chinese social associations, see Gordon White's study, 'Prospects for Civil Society in China: A Case Study of Xiaoshan City', *Australian Journal of Chinese Affairs*, 29 (January 1993), 63–87. For a more detailed study on the formation, typology, and nature of social organizations in Xiaoshan City, see Wang Ying, Zhe Xiaoye, and Sun Bingyao, *Shehui zhongjian ceng: gaige yu Zhongguo de shetuan zuzhi* (Social Intermediate Strata: Reform and the Formation of Social Organizations in China) (Beijing: Zhongguo fazhan chubanshe, 1993).

46. A good example is the Hainan Consumer Association (Hainan sheng xiaofeizhe ziehui), which was established in December 1993. The membership consists of 94 persons most of whom are heads or deputy heads of official organizations. See Hainan sheng xiaofeizhe xihui, *Hainan sheng xiaofeizhe xiehui chengli dahui* (The Founding Congress of the Consumer Association of Hainan Province) (Hainan sheng xiaofeizhe xiehui bangongshi bianyin, December 1993).

47. An example is the Hainan Individual and Private Economy Research Association (Hainan sheng geti siying jingji yanjiuhui). This association, which was formed spontaneously, elects its own chairman and sets its membership dues without government interference (private communication).

9

Is a Participant Culture Emerging in China?

Torstein Hjellum

There is an ongoing discussion among scholars about whether a civil society is developing in China, especially against the background of the mass protests of 1989.[1] The civil society concept refers to institutions, formal or informal, that exist and act independently of the state and are capable of developing their own views on local or national issues. They do not necessarily oppose the state, but they enjoy a great deal of autonomy.

Are the changes in the economic realm in China which began in 1978 somehow reflected in changed orientations by the populace towards the political sphere? Are the Chinese coming to participate more in official and political matters as a consequence of economic pluralism? Are they moving from being mere passive objects of party policy to becoming agents of historical change, organizing on their own and articulating their grievances in public? Is a participant political culture emerging in China?

Until now, evidence concerning the nature of Chinese political culture has been drawn from interpretive studies, based on documentary sources, interviews, and field observation.[2] In this paper I will present some results from nationwide surveys combined with in-depth interviews in urban areas in China. To my knowledge, there is only one other example among the political–scientific literature of a study of political culture in China by means of random sampling.[3]

What is Meant by a 'Participant Culture'?

According to Almond and Verba, a participant political culture is one in which the members of a society tend to be explicitly oriented to the system as a whole and to both political and administrative structures and processes. They also tend to be prepared to take an 'activist' role in the polity, although their feelings and evaluations of such a role may vary from acceptance to rejection.

What are the characteristics of a participant political culture? The citizens are expected to be active in politics and to be involved. They are supposed to be rational in their approach to politics, guided by reason, not by emotion. They are supposed to be well informed and to make decisions. A participant political culture model can be labelled 'rational–activist'.

How are these characteristics to be operationalized? To be active presupposes a *wish* to be active, a wish for circumstances that make activity possible. The citizens want the right to speak freely, to have access to mass media, to have formal and informal settings in which discussions and decisions may be undertaken, to have access to information about decision-making processes, especially those relevant to their own interests, and to intervene in such processes if they see fit. Participants should also be knowledgeable about politics, about political systems and their functioning, political leaders, the outcome of state politics, and so on.

When we wish to study changes or developments, a point of reference is needed. I am in possession of survey data from three dates: 1988, 1991, and 1993. Unfortunately, these surveys are too close together in time to be useful for a study of such developments; also, this kind of instrument is not really sensitive enough for the measurement of political cultures. The point of reference in analysing the data therefore will have to be primarily general and theoretical. The data will be related to an ideal model of a participant culture, developed within a Western democratic tradition, and to an understanding of some crucial elements of traditional Chinese political culture.

Civil Society and Political Culture

After the Tiananmen Square upheaval in 1989, the question arose to whether the modernization period in the 1980s had accelerated the move towards a 'civil' society in China. Brødsgaard discusses this, referring to a concept of civil society as developed by Moshe Lewin:

By 'civil society' we refer to the aggregate of networks and institutions that either exist and act independently of the state or are official organizations capable of developing their own, spontaneous views on national or local issues and then impressing these views on their members, on small groups and, finally, on the authorities. These social groups do not necessarily oppose the state, but exist in contrast to outright state organisms and enjoy a certain degree of autonomy.[4]

This definition focuses on movements that have explicitly voiced their opposition to an existing political system and also have tried to build up a leadership of their own, independent of state and party. Tony Saich has described the structural changes in the economy during the reform period and has outlined the social strains those changes have produced.[5] He also argues for the emergence of a civil society in China as a consequence of these strains. However, he is not able to present empirical evidence for his proposition apart from describing the spontaneous mushrooming of action groups during the dramatic events in May–June 1989. These numerous groups were immediately suppressed by the government, and no evidence has been given that they represented a growing participant political culture in China. The same may be concluded on the basis of Brødsgaard's analysis of the subject.[6] All the groups listed by Brødsgaard supposedly represented nothing more than a spontaneous protest against actual policies, and not a more deep-seated opposition representing an alternative political culture.

Another approach to the study of an eventual emergence of civil society is to focus on individual attitudes and orientations towards politics among the Chinese according to the political culture prescribed by Almond and Verba in 1966:

Political culture is the pattern of individual attitudes and orientation toward politics among the members of a political system. It is the subjective realm which underlies and gives meaning to political actions. Such individual orientations involve several components, including (a) *cognitive orientations*, knowledge, accurate or otherwise, of political object and beliefs; (b) *affective orientations*, feelings of attachment, involvement, rejection, and the like, about political objects; and (c) *evaluative orientations*, judgements and opinions about political objects, which usually involve applying value standards to political objects and events.[7]

The concept 'civil' refers to societal processes in the Western world associated with the Industrial Revolution, processes that resulted in a political culture that may be identified by concepts such as liberalism, civil rights, democracy, etc.[8] A civil society has its 'civic culture'. This was a concept developed by Almond and Verba in their 1963 book. They distinguished between three 'ideal' types of political culture—'parochial', 'subject', and 'participant'—differing from one another according to individual orientations towards the polity (Table 1).[9]

According to Almond and Verba, the political orientation of individuals can be tapped systematically if we explore the following questions:

1. What knowledge do people have of their nation and of their political system in general terms, its history, size, location, power, 'constitutional' characteristics, etc.? What are their feelings towards these systemic characteristics?
2. What knowledge do people have of the structures and roles, the various political élites, and the policy proposals that are involved in the

TABLE 1   Three types of Political Culture

Types of political culture	System as general object	Input objects	Output objects	Self as active participant
Parochial	0	0	0	0
Subject	1	0	1	0
Participant	1	1	1	1

upward flow of policy-making? What are their feelings and opinions about structures, leaders, and policy proposals?
3. What knowledge do people have of the downward flow of policy enforcement, the structures, individuals, and decisions involved in these processes? What are their feelings and opinions of them?
4. How do people perceive of themselves as members of their political system? What knowledge do they have of their rights, powers, obligations, and strategies of access to influence? How do they feel about their capabilities? What norms of participation or performance do they acknowledge and employ in formulating political judgements, or in arriving at opinions?

In a 'parochial political culture' there are no specialized political roles: headmanship, chieftainship, and 'shamanship' are diffuse political–economic–religious roles, and for the members of these societies the political orientations to these roles are not separate from their religious and social orientations. There is a comparative absence of expectations of change initiated by the political system, and the parochial individual expects nothing from the political system.

In a 'subject political culture' there is a high frequency of orientation towards a differentiated political system and towards the output aspects of the system, but orientations towards specifically input actions, and towards the self as an active participant, are very low. The subjects are aware of specialized governmental authority; they are affectively oriented to it, perhaps taking pride in it, perhaps disliking it, and evaluate it as either legitimate or not. There exists no differentiated input structure. The subject orientation is likely to be affective and normative rather than cognitive.

The 'participant political culture' is one in which the members of the society tend to be explicitly oriented to the system as a whole and to both the political and administrative structures and processes. Members tend to be oriented towards an 'activist' role of the self in the polity, though their feelings and evaluations of such a role may vary from acceptance to rejection.

These three cultures are pure types. In reality there is a cultural hetero-geneity, or cultural mix, in any society. The 'citizen' is a particular mix of participant, subject, and parochial orientations, and the civic culture is a particular mix of citizens, as both subjects and parochials.

How is political development and cultural change handled by the model? Political cultures may or may not be congruent with the structures of the political system. In general, a parochial, subject, or participant cul-ture would be most congruent with, respectively, a traditional political structure, a centralized authoritarian structure, and a democratic political structure. Political systems change, and culture and structure are often incongruent with each other. Schematically, these relations of congru-ence/incongruence between political structure and culture are represented in Table 2.

TABLE 2   Relationships between Political Structure and Culture

	Allegiance	Apathy	Alienation
Cognitive orientation	+	+	+
Affective orientation	+	0	–
Evaluative	+	0	–

[a] A plus-sign means a high frequency of awareness, or of positive feeling, or of evaluation toward political objects. A minus sign means a high frequency of neg-ative evaluations or feelings. A 0 means a high frequency of indifference.

Incongruence between political culture and structure begins when indif-ference is overcome and negative effect and evaluation grow in frequency. As we move from left to right in the table we move from a situation of alle-giance, in which attitudes and institutions match, to a situation of alien-ation, where attitudes tend to reject political institutions or structures. Almond and Verba use the term 'systematically mixed' for political cul-tures in which there are significant proportions of both the simpler and more complex patterns of orientations.

A criticism of this theory is that it does not sufficiently take into account the fact that variation in political attitudes and values within countries is often greater than that between countries.[10] The following questions may be asked: Are 'civil society' and 'civic culture'—and the theoretical con-text wherein these concepts are developed—of relevance in describing developments in political life and culture in China during the moderniza-tion period since 1978? Are the processes in China in the latest modern-ization period similar to the processes in the West during the period of industrialization, or would it be more proper to regard them as qualita-tively different processes that need qualitatively new concepts to describe them? Are concepts such as 'civil society' and 'civic culture' valid or fruitful when describing new tendencies in Chinese political culture? If they are, how strong are these tendencies? Is the leadership losing the confidence of the people? Is the modernization of China causing an attack on the traditional and predominant bases of legitimacy?

I suggest that, in order to achieve the goals of the economic reform, a loosening of the grip of the Communist Party has been inevitable. The development of private markets has also required the institutionalization of new links between the state and emerging groups of businessmen and other new social and economic strata of the population. Have developments in this direction given birth to new and autonomous interest organizations in China? I suggest that a possible development in China during the late modernization period may be a tendency towards a more participant political culture, away from a traditional mixture of parochial and subject cultures. However, I do not think that the tendencies towards a participating culture are yet very strong; instead, I think we will find that traditional political culture has been remarkably resistant to changes, and that the problem facing China today is rather to establish patterns of coexistence between a traditional authoritarian culture and the needs of different groups stemming from changes in the economic structure.

Political Cultures in China

The Tradition of Confucianism and Maoism

The word 'emerging' in the title of this chapter would suggest that traditionally, and before the latest reform policies, China did not have a participant political culture. I suggest that the dominating cultures historically were Confucianism and Maoism. Neither of these was a participant culture according to Western concepts. Some general traits of these historical legacies may be sketched.

In a first attempt to establish a Chinese sociology, Fei Xiaotong takes differences in fundamental organizational principles as a basis for understanding Chinese political culture compared with Western political culture.[11] In the West, he argues, individuals create their society by applying an 'organizational mode of association'. They form groups that have clear boundaries. Membership in these groups is unambiguous; everyone knows who is and who is not a member. The rights and duties of members are clearly delineated. Such organizations are everywhere and serve as devices for framing individualism in modern Western societies.

By contrast, people in China create their society by applying another logic, the logic of *chaxugeju*, the 'differential mode of association', whereby society is composed not of discrete organizations but of overlapping networks of people linked together through differentially categorized social relationships. These networks have four features. First, they are discontinuous. They do not link people together in a single, systematic way; rather, they centre on the individual and have a different composition for each person. Therefore Chinese society is 'egocentric' in contrast to the Western individualistic society. The Western mode of association presupposes the autonomy of individuals, whereas the Chinese mode of association presupposes multiple linkages of self with others. The differences may be traced back to Christian versus Confucian ethics.

Second, each link in a Chinese person's network is defined in terms of a dyadic social tie. These are *guanxi*, conventionally understood to connote strictly personal connections. Third, these networks have no explicit boundaries; they can link people who are separated by considerable social and geographical distance. Fourth, the moral content of behaviour in a network society is situation-specific. In sum, the differential mode of association is an egocentric system of social networks. This network-based Chinese society is also group-oriented and based on considerations of order, not laws.[12]

According to these different modes of association, power, i.e. how people control and are controlled by others, is configured very differently in China than in the West. In the West, individuals are presumed to be autonomous and hence necessarily able to exercise their will; authority is based on a rule of law. Chinese society is ruled through rituals; people pay obedience to their principal social obligations.

According to Fei, the state, as the constitutional embodiment of its people, is the highest level of organization in Western society. In China, the state does not even exist as an organization. The fundamental nexus of control is not a jurisdictional top-down system that controls the actions of every individual through the imposition of rules. The means of control is traditionally not located in the imposition of rules. State officials are responsible for managing the whole, but they do not intervene in the parts. When disorder occurs, all within that immediate network are at fault, and each successive circle has a duty to intervene and re-establish order. If everybody supervises and upholds the morality of his or her close relations, then the entire world is at peace and people can prosper. The ideal government should *wuwei*, do nothing. According to Fei, the Chinese have become merchants to the world largely because they have been able to create highly efficient, flexible commercial networks. On the other hand, social change is difficult because the Chinese cannot simply change networks in the same way that Westerners join or leave organizations. In conclusion, Fei argues that China should be considered not a class-based but a network-based society.

Writing some twenty years before Almond and Verba, Fei Xiaotong compares crucial aspects of the civic culture with Chinese counterparts. The main difference is that the Chinese are not oriented towards the state by associations representing their rights and interests. There is no system of representation institutionalized within the state; the citizens have no right to be taken into account when state decisions are taken. They can only hope that their *guanxi* may be of help if they are confronted with state authority. Each citizen is a subject of the state, and the authority of the state in the Chinese mind is parochial, based traditionally on the Mandate of Heaven.

On the other hand, Chinese culture and tradition do have strong elements of participation. In commerce the Chinese have been very active, participating far beyond the boundaries of China as a state. And in politics, history contains numerous examples of widely supported actions opposing state authority. These have been spontaneous, but also well organized—peasant revolts, the Taiping Rebellion, the formation of the Guomindang, and the Communist Party are examples. The legitimation of such activities may be traced back in part to Confucianism and Maoism. However, there is a fundamental difference between the civic culture participation and this Chinese tradition of participation. While the Chinese scope of action has been to attack one parochial authority, seeking to replace it with another parochial authority, the Western civic scope of action takes the form of competition for positions based on a respect of individuals' rights and the rule of law.

Although he does not refer to Fei Xiaotong in his two major books on Chinese political culture, Lucian Pye may be interpreted in the tradition of Fei Xiaotong.[13] China is a polity, he argues in *The Mandarin and the Cadre*, with politics but without organized interests. Therefore it is easy to rule:

people rule themselves. China has always been a nation of participants—participants, however, not in a coherent system of national politics, but in parochial groupings. At one time such groupings included the family, clan, *bao-chia*, village, guild, and secret society, all of which looked inward to the disciplining of its members and to ideals of self-sufficiency. Today the family is strong in spite of its battering, and there are the powerful disciplining realities of the neighborhood communities, small groups, or *danwei* . . . The private institutions never evolved into assertive pressure groups, organized to mobilize support to publicly change national politics . . . State and society were keeping their members out of trouble with the authorities . . . The odds favored success by corruption over public manifestos.[14]

This of course does not mean that different interests are lacking in political life. As in the past, there is constant politicking among officials, and local officials today follow their predecessors' example of challenging their superiors at the centre. Such practice takes place, however, within the context of the established policies, as part of the realm of the state, not of society. The politicking does not take place on the basis of organized civil societies, but rather on the basis of networks.

According to Pye, the two strongest ways of life in China have been hierarchy and egalitarianism:

the fundamental polarity of China's traditional cultures was between . . . an elitist high Confucian culture that glorified the established authority of the better educated and rationalized their claims of superiority on the basis of possessing specialized wisdom, and a passionate, populist heterodox culture that glorified the rebel and trusted magical formulas to transform economic and social reality.[15]

It should be added, however, that the heterodox culture itself functioned on the basis of hierarchy.

If we use the concepts of the cultural theory of Mary Douglas, based on dimensions of grid and group,[16] China's strongest ways of life have been hierarchy and egalitarianism. The first may be associated with the élitist high Confucian culture, the other with the passionate, populist heterodox culture that glorified the rebel and trusted magical formulas to transform economic and social reality, traditionally rooted in Taoism. But fatalism too is a Chinese way of life. And fatalism, egalitarianism, and hierarchy are all in different ways organized so as to restrict individual autonomy. While fatalism pacifies the individual, egalitarianism and hierarchy stress the importance of the group over the individual.

Pye argues that cultural factors dominate public life in China more than in just about any other country, for three reasons. The first is that in China there has developed a strangely potent mixture of Confucianism and Leninism, a marriage of Confucian habits and Leninist imperatives. More than with almost any other people, the Chinese believe that children must be taught to do right and should not just be allowed to grow up. All the communists needed to add was a new vision of how the product of unrelenting socialization pressures should look.

The second reason for the exceptionally dominant role of cultural factors in Chinese political life is, according to Pye, that Confucian Leninism places supreme value not just on ideology, but on highly moralistic versions of ideology. And few cultures can compare with the Chinese in suppressing the id and extolling the superego. Displays of deference by subordinates and grace in asserting command by superiors are the hallmarks of Chinese political culture. There is a marked instinct for hierarchy. These are not command structures but rather prestige alignments. The powerful urge for orderliness is driven by the intense Chinese fear of *luan*, disorder and confusion.

Finally, and supposedly most important, Pye claims, is the unique relationship between the primary institutions that are so important in socializing the Chinese and the public institutions of national politics. Confucianism fitted the ideals and needs of both the rulers in their political realms and the common people in their family and clan settings. These two still reinforce each other through Confucian Leninism. The family, work groups, and the *danwei*, basic structures in today's China, provide cultural continuity with the past (clan, *baojia*). The rule of men is superior to the rule of law.

The one aspect of Mao's personality that stands in sharpest contrast to China's traditional cultural pattern is his strong element of self-assertiveness, in a society which for millennia stressed social interdependence and personal dependence.[17] Mao was a man who had known the harsh reality of filial subordination, and in his political life he tried to pass on to the Chinese people a system of political participation in which subordinate opinion becomes a powerful element in checking the abuses of authority. Where Confucianism lauded the virtues of tranquillity and interpersonal harmony, Mao made activism the key to the behaviour of the ideal party cadre. Where fear and avoidance of conflict characterized the 'cultivated' response to social tension in the traditional society. Mao stressed the importance of criticism and controlled struggle in resolving those issues that blocked China's social advance. Perhaps Mao's most innovative reaction against tradition was his effort to liberate, in a disciplined, politicized fashion, the aggressive emotions which were denied legitimate expression in the political culture of dependency. Where the Confucian order stresses emotional restraint as the basis of personal discipline, and 'eating bitterness' as the only appropriate response of the subordinate, Mao developed 'speak bitterness' meetings. Through the mobilization of such aggression, the peasants dared to attack those who carried the authority of tradition, and acquired new perceptions of their altered political status and of possibilities for social change.

While Confucianism rejected open social conflict, Mao sought to 'liberate' aggressive emotions in the service of political ends by subjecting them to disciplined release. Political education was a way of making people conscious and disciplining aggression into purposeful action. Mao and his supporters sought to restructure China's political life so as to sustain popular participation and prevent a return to bureaucratic rule by an élite administrative class. However, many of the institutions of the People's Republic continued to bear the stamp of the social traditions from which the revolution grew. On the one hand, Mao introduced the 'big character poster', to diffuse political authority to the people and as a symbol of greater popular political participation, and Mao's writings were popularized through the *Little Red Book* of quotations from his writings. At the same time, however, these efforts to activate the masses of the people propelled Mao into the limelight as a new divine authority and built up a personal cult around the Communist leader.

One political value that merged with tradition was an uncompromising stress on the collective good above the interests of the individual. A slogan of the Cultural Revolution was 'Destroy the Self and Establish the Collective'. It was the difficulty of changing mature personalities, and the endurance of traditional Chinese social values and behavioural patterns, that ultimately led Mao to resort to the upheaval of the Cultural Revolution. By mobilizing the masses to criticize their leaders, he sought to give them a participant role in the political process.

The other tendency that Mao strongly encouraged was a strengthening of the old social practices in the Communist Party and in Chinese society at large. In this, he was affirming Max Weber's observation that revolutionary leadership eventually becomes routinized into bureaucratic administration. A political party that sought to exercise total social control by penetrating all areas of a society, even down to the basic social unit of the family, sowed in its striving for total influence the seeds of its own psychological self-destruction.

A distinctive feature of Maoism was mass mobilization. Peoples in their millions were mobilized into political actions in the revolutionary war, in rectification campaigns, and during the Cultural Revolution: 'for the last thirty-five years [the Chinese] have lived in one of the most participatory societies in history'.[18] Almost all aspects of social life became politicized during the Cultural Revolution. But did this mean that a participant political culture developed under Mao? Was Mao himself thinking in terms of a participant democracy?

There was a democratic tradition in China that can be dated back to the end of the nineteenth century. The extent to which this tradition became internalized in Mao's thinking is not easy to deduce. His policy of 'trusting the masses, relying on the masses, and respecting the creativity of the masses' was intended to be implemented into democratic institutions, in the tradition of the Paris Commune, during the Cultural Revolution.[19] On the question of Mao as a promoter of the democratic tradition, Andrew J. Nathan replies in the negative:

Under Mao [the weak tradition of criticism] seemed to come to an end. Although Mao still spoke about democracy, it was one in which the masses kept watch over the bureaucracy under the monocratic guidance of the national leader. Power was tightly concentrated in the leader's circle, while all aspects of life were controlled by vast bureaucracies of economic management, police surveillance, political supervision, and propaganda.[20]

Mao had realized that the feudal practice of arbitrary dictation was deeply rooted in the minds of the people and also the party members. However, democracy could at least serve as a measure of politics:

Democratic centralism can be widely and effectively practised in mass organizations only when its efficacy is demonstrated in revolutionary struggle and the masses understand that it is the best means of mobilizing their forces and is of the utmost help in their struggle.[21]

The legacy of Maoism with respect to participatory democracy can probably be summed up as follows. The Maoist mass line politics did not represent a principal step towards a civil society. The policy was not to build institutions to protect the interests of the people, in order to secure the representation of the collective will. Rather, the goal was to win the revolutionary war, and in that war the revolutionary party was dependent on the support of the masses. The support of the masses could be achieved by serving the masses. This was not a pure utilitarian approach from the party's side. The Communists could borrow a traditional principle, a Confucian heritage of moral obligation to serve the community. The test of regime legitimacy was the welfare of the people. And this coincided with the Communist ethos of solidarity with the working people.[22] Thus, a culture of participatory democracy does not seem to have made any progress during Maoism and the Cultural Revolution.

Perhaps the most significant change in China *after* Mao has been a depoliticization of social life.

As epitomized by the slogan *dagong wusi*—literally, 'all public and no private'— the Cultural Revolution was the culmination of a fifty-year trend toward the politicization of increasingly greater areas of life. By depoliticizing large areas of social life, the Dengist reforms moved to rectify that imbalance, creating a 'zone of indifference' in which 'private' activities were permitted far greater scope. In doing so, the Dengist reforms seemed much more in harmony with China's tradition of 'totalistic' but noninvasive political power.[23]

Regarding the reform era under Deng, what is striking is not the resistance or opposition of the people to sudden and fundamental shifts in politics—shifts with huge effects on their living conditions—but the extraordinary, inexplicable flexibility and pragmatism of the people. This flexibility may explain a hypothesis which postulates that no dramatic shift in political culture or political structure has taken place in China since 1978, in spite of great changes in the economy during the reform period—and that none will. Spontaneous and furious riots and rebellions may occur, as earlier in Chinese history, but not a political revolution.

According to this hypothesis, it seems that, whatever attitudes Chinese profess, their practical responses are to be channelled through larger cultural and social fields. That is, an activist sentiment which might mean letter-writing or joining an interest group in the West might in China well mean waiting for a 'parochial' catalyst, such as discontent among classmates, or the appearance of a friend from home or a cue from a patron, for the act itself to occur.

Pye presents a list of arguments for a pragmatism of feigned compliance. The passive spirit of the public reflects a combination of realism and fatalism, a fatalism that tells the public that it can do little to affect politics. The power of the Chinese leaders verges on the omnipotent because the masses have so little sense of political efficacy. A conventional explanation of this capacity for adaptability is that Chinese cultural norms tend to be highly particularistic, and therefore people learn early that, with different relationships and with changing contexts, behaviour too ought to change. Therefore the Chinese culture is spared the tensions common in those cultures that have more universalistic norms and that require behaviour in different situations to be made to appear consistent with absolute principles. The system of *guanxi* seems to be based on particularism and to represent a reality seemingly unaffected by changing circumstances in public policies. Furthermore, Pye argues that the Chinese can easily live with cognitive dissonance and contradictive emotions. To give action priority over thought, to be optimistic about the future disregarding former problematic experiences, to seek monocausal explanations instead of critically seeking complex causes of events—these traditional features of Chinese culture may be boundaries of critical reflections that could be seeds for the development of new political institutions. Moreover, to be critical has been regarded as unpatriotic by Chinese intellectuals, a tradition that can be traced back to the May Fourth Movement. Patriotic pride may also be a barrier to adopting models of politics from abroad. As legitimacy is based on a claim to moral superiority, the political leaders under pragmatism will be constantly vulnerable to ideological constraints. To argue for changes in political culture or political structures is therefore an uncertain strategy, as the leaders are quite inclined to regard such tendencies as anti-systemic.

The lack of thinking in competitive and conflicting interests has its counterpart in the people's understanding of the role of the supreme leader or leaders. A Chinese tradition seeks models and positive examples rather than critical analysis. The leaders should have the proper answers; they should be the teachers of the people, not representatives of their interests.

How is the Chinese concept of leadership a premiss for a possible development of a participant political culture? First of all, it is a reality in China, as in other countries in the Third World, that the general level of political institutionalization is low. Much depends upon the idiosyncratic wishes of the leader of the moment. The Confucian tradition of rule by men and not by law, combined with the Marxist–Leninist doctrine of the preciousness of the Party, have produced a heightened glorification of the concept of the infallible leader, the indispensable figure. There is in China a tradition of mystification of the leader as a great man, a tradition that may be traced back to the role of the emperor as Son of Heaven. This combination of transcendental and worldly authority makes it a tricky matter, fraught with dangers, to question such a leader. It borders on treason.[24] Giving authority to the man and not to the office allows China's supreme leader extraordinary flexibility, and absolves him from accountability. The ideal of the omnipotence of authority has been passed from generation to generation by the imperative of filial piety. Filial piety appears to be at the base of the explosive anger the Chinese seem to manifest when they feel that authority has not lived up to their belief in its omnipotence.

We now have a theoretical background for an analysis of the survey data. To sum up, an individual in a participant political culture should be affective, evaluative, and oriented towards the system as a whole, should be well informed about the political system and how it works, should want to be involved, and should possess an activist attitude.

An Empirical Approach: Structured Mass Surveys combined with In-Depth Interviews

As mentioned earlier, I was given access to data from three surveys carried out in forty cities in China in 1988, 1991, and 1993. Although the surveys were not originally designed to throw light upon issues concerning political culture, many of the questions asked are relevant for the present purpose. In addition to the surveys, we conducted in-depth interviews in Beijing in 1993, mainly to check the validity of the mass survey method. At these interviews the interviewees were asked to answer some of the questions in the survey questionnaire, and thereafter to explain and comment on their answers.

The method of random sampling was used in the mass surveys. However, the representativeness of the sample population is not outstanding. The forty cities would seem to represent an average of the *urban* population (in bigger cities). The distribution of men and women in the

230   *Is a Participant Culture Emerging in China?*

sample is acceptable. The answers to the question, 'What is your main job?' in the survey population are summarized in Table 3. The cadres categories are very rough, and in particular the category 'governmental cadres' is over-represented in the survey; 'workers' seem to be under-represented. The distribution of the interviewees according to education confirms this impression. The more highly educated people are considerably over-represented: in 1993 one out of four interviewees reported education at university level. This should not be forgotten in the interpretation of the data.

TABLE 3   Occupations of Survey Respondents

Occupation	1988		1991		1991	
	No.	%	No.	%	No.	%
Workers	808	35	630	26	567	27
Government cadres	325	14	496	21	455	22
Enterprise cadres	459	20	361	15	281	13
Professionals and technicians	371	16	576	24	502	23
Others	325	14	239	10	288	14
No value	22	1	93	4	24	1
Total	2,310	100	2,395	100	2,117	100

Interviews of people in China on sensitive political questions have to be carefully conducted. Secrecy is a must. The procedures undertaken in carrying out the surveys seem to have been satisfactory in this respect.

Most of the questions are formulated with multiple choice answers. On many questions the interviewees have frequently resorted to the 'middle' category;[25] for most of the questions this category has been chosen by 30–50 per cent of the respondents, for some up to 60 per cent. This high score may be interpreted in different ways. It may be a 'middle' position between substantial extremes, or an expression of indifference or unwillingness to answer; it may have been chosen because the interviewee had no special opinion; or it may simply express a lack of understanding of the question. The problem of interpretation of the middle category will be dealt with separately below.

The 1989 mass protests and the increase in control and restrictions on political activity that followed it came in between the survey of 1988 and those of 1991 and 1993. We would expect that respondents to a questionnaire with sensitive questions on politics would be more cautious in expressing their opinions in 1991 (and 1993) than in 1988. However, while there might have been a slight tendency for interviewees to be more careful in reporting critical opinions in 1991, two years later the in-depth interviews do not indicate a growing fear of expressing an opinion. Indeed, people were very free and open in the interview situation in 1993. It was an easy task to solicit persons to interview on the streets. This may indicate that the party's grip on the individual has been dissolving during the reform period. A weakening of the party's social control would mean freedom from the minute and daily supervision of individuals.

Concerning validity, there is a possibility that we are too ready to draw conclusions. Some of the expressions used in the questionnaire have an explicit meaning in a Western political tradition, but may not have similar connotations for the Chinese respondents. Particularly for less educated groups, the meaning of some of the questions could be difficult to grasp. This may be one reason for the generally high rates of middle-category answers to many of the questions. In-depth interviews on the basis of the standardized questionnaire may be a fruitful method for going deeper into the problem.

The Data and the Interpretation of Them

Our question is whether a participant culture is emerging in China. Are Chinese more oriented as activists towards the political system than before? Are they more informed, do they have more knowledge about what is going on in politics, do they want to be informed, do they want to be involved? To what degree do they have affective, evaluative, and cognitive orientations towards politics?

The Chinese urban population was concerned about *how their society is governed*. Of those interviewed, 69 per cent said they cared about the government (Table 4). They wanted to have an active state and a government that invites them to participate in decision-making. A majority did not want to be mere subjects (63 per cent) and had an idea of what an 'ideal government' should be like. Almost everyone was concerned about social and economic development (Table 5). They reported that they felt a duty and a responsibility to the state, and that they had a right to be informed and to participate. Some felt that they did not have the right to participate, but that they should have it.

The interviewees were asked to evaluate *the government's performance* on the basis of their own experiences (Table 6). On average, one third of the respondents were indifferent about it or without any clear opinion. Among those who had an opinion, a majority was very critical: in 1993, 60 per cent felt that the government was corrupt. There seems to have been

TABLE 4   Answers to the question: *What is the ideal government? Some statements about this question follow: do you agree with them?*

	Agree %	Disagree %
I never care about the government.	13	69
The government should take care of everything, while the ordinary people should just follow the decisions of government.	22	63
The government should be involved only if there are problems.	25	61
The government should be like a friend, with whom the ordinary people could discuss matters. And the government should invite people to participate in the decision-making.	74	14
I do not know what an ideal government should be.	27	57

a significant growth in negative evaluation from 1988 to 1993. The in-depth interviews revealed that people were well informed—through their personal experiences, from newspapers, and from rumours about growing corruption during the reform period. This belief seemed to exist at all levels. Everything was possible to get if you could pay—education, production licences, personal favours in daily life, etc. People seem to resent this development. As a comparison and a positive model, some of the interviewees referred to the situation in China under Mao. Corruption was most strongly felt as a problem among intellectuals, while 'upper-class people'[26] comprised the least critical social group (Table 7). However, among every group the problems have been perceived to be increasing. Even among party members, the dissatisfaction with corruption was very high (62 per cent).

TABLE 5   Answers to the question: *What is your attitude towards the country's economic and social development?*

	Yes %	No %
I am concerned about it.	93	7
I have the right to get information about it.	86	14
I have a duty and a responsibility towards it.	86	14
I have the right to participate in it.	74	26
I should have the right to participate in it.	82	18

TABLE 6 Answers to the question: *Please assess the following aspects of the social situation in the light of your own personal experience (from 1 to 5)* (percentages)

	The government is Corrupt		Acceptable/don't know	Honest and clean	
	1	2	3	4	5
1988	16	22	39	13	9
1993	27	33	29	6	3
	Government efficiency is Low		Acceptable/don't know	High	
	1	2	3	4	5
1988	35	22	31	8	5
1993	33	29	28	6	3
	Transparency (*toumingdu*) of government is Low		Acceptable/don't know	High	
	1	2	3	4	5
1988	25	23	35	10	6
1993	63		29	9	

TABLE 7 Answers to the question: *Please assess the following aspects of the government's performance* (percentages)

Category of respondent	The government is Corrupt		Honest and clean	
	1988	1993	1988	1993
Intellectuals	54	68	14	6
White-collar workers	47	62	17	8
Workers	29	56	29	12
Upper-class people	35	45	18	16
Party members		62		8
Total	39	60	22	10

	Government efficiency is Low		Acceptable/don't know		High	
	1988	1993	1988	1993	1988	1993
Intellectuals	74	69	19	25	7	5
White-collar workers	63	65	29	28	8	7
Workers	45	58	36	30	18	11
Upper-class people	62	61	26	26	12	12
Party members		64		29		6
Total	57	62	31	28	13	9

More than 60 per cent of respondents had the opinion that the government was inefficient. Again, the 'intellectuals' were the most negative in evaluating the regime's efficiency. But also, nearly two thirds of party members had the same opinion about 'their party's' government (Table 7): 63 per cent felt that the transparency of the government (*glasnost*) was low. We learned from the in-depth interviews that the question on transparency was fairly well understood. A party member for nearly forty years commented on the question of transparency as follows: 'After the 14th Party Congress I did not understand what was going on. But it does not matter because it cannot be of any relevance for me anyway.' On the other hand, a 19-year-old student marked '4/5' (high transparency) on the survey question and explained her answer: 'When something important happens, we can read about it in the newspapers or watch it on TV. Secrecy is necessary sometimes. I read *People's Daily* and the newspaper of the Youth League almost every day.' The critical evaluations seem to have been more common in the years following 1988.

One third of the respondents felt that the general public order was turbulent, while more than half of them felt that social morality was degenerate. The respondents in the surveys gave highest priority to public order among thirteen alternatives (32 per cent in 1988, 26 per cent in 1991, and 30 per cent in 1993). Very few (about 1 per cent) mentioned transparency of government as the most important; few rated the item even as second or third in importance. This may be interpreted as in accordance with a weak participant orientation. If one wants to have influence through participation, we should suggest that a high degree of *glasnost* should be required. The second highest preference among the respondents was honesty of government (15 per cent), higher than social morality, which was rated third (12 per cent).

According to these surveys, the Chinese feel that the quality of government is of great importance for their daily life. Their awareness of the government and what it provides is high.

Six out of ten urban people participating in the 1993 survey did not believe that the leaders' main motive is to serve the people (Table 8). A clear majority believed that leaders are most concerned about their own interests, and are representatives primarily of their own interests, not the interests of the common masses. If this is a roughly correct picture, Chinese politics seems to be a long way from a democratic culture, even if we understand this in terms of the Maoist 'mass-line democracy'. These findings may also be interpreted in terms of Fei Xiaotong's 'differential mode of association' as a culturally based weakness in positive orientations towards the state.

In the surveys respondents reported a big change in 'people's mentality'

TABLE 8   Answers to the question: *What is your opinion on the following statements about the cadres of the central and local government?* (1993 survey)

	Agree %	Disagree %
Leaders will always use their influence to help and serve the people in the best possible way.	29	58
Leaders of our country and localities will use their influence to serve the people, but they also use their positions to serve their own and their friends' interests.	82	11
Leaders of our country and localities only pretend to serve the people, while in reality they are most concerned about how to create benefits and gains for themselves.	68	22

as a result of the reforms (Table 9). How did the respondents understand this question? Judging by the in-depth interviews, the associations were uniform and categorical: the privatization of people's lives has increased during the reform period. People have become much more inclined to fight for an improvement in their personal material conditions. This is reflected in a change in their attitude towards others: how can personal relationships be exploited for personal gain? There was however no indication of a new collective mentality resulting in people grouping together to articulate their interests and fight for them.

The *guanxi* culture seems to have been strengthened during the reform period. When respondents were asked about their relations to others, a great majority reported views corresponding to *guanxi* relations: human relations are relationships of exchange, a kind of mutual exploitation, and 'debts of gratitude' are endless (Table 10). Combined with what we know about the lack of functioning of formal organizations as measures of promotion of the interests of individuals in China (a lack of industrialization), these data strongly underline the importance of interpersonal ties of

TABLE 9   Answers to the question: *After ten/fifteen years of reforms, what do you think of the situation in the country regarding changes in people's mentality (*guan nian*)?*

	No change %	Little change %	Big change %
1988	20	8	71
1993	23	10	67

TABLE 10   Answers to the question: *What do you think of the following statements?* (percentages)

Essentially, human relations are one of exchange.			
	Very true/true	Indifferent	False/not so true
1988	53	10	37
1993	51	13	35
Nowadays, human relations is just a kind of mutual exploitation.			
	Correct	Yes and no	Wrong
1988	65	22	13
1993	59	30	10
To do anything, one needs humbly to ask favours of others.			
1988	71	17	12
1993	61	23	15
Debts of gratitude are endless.			
1988	64	18	18
1993	65	23	12

dependence. This aspect of human relationships does not seem to have weakened among younger generations compared with older. And the tendencies do not seem to have weakened over time from 1988 to 1993.

How do the Chinese evaluate entitlement to political participation? More than one third of the respondents in the surveys reported that this was most or very important (Table 11). The suggestion is that the distribution of answers would be nearly the same if the question were put to people in Western Europe.

TABLE 11   Answers to the question: *Everyone has their own hopes in life. For instance, a peasant's desire throughout his life may be to build a new house, but a professor's wish may be to have a big collection of books. Following are some aspects that affect your life. Please offer your answers in the light of your actual conditions.* (percentages)

	Entitlement to political participation is				
	Most important	Very important	Not so important	Important	Not important at all
1988	19	27	33	8	12
1991	12	25	38	12	11
1993	11	23	37	13	12

When the interviewees in 1993 were asked to choose among eighteen items of life content, however, entitlement to political participation scored very low: 44 per cent gave first, second, or third priority to a nice flat; 41 per cent to a happy marriage; 29 per cent to a satisfactory government; and 28 per cent to a harmonious family life; only 4 per cent ranked entitlement to political participation among their first three priorities.

Only 29 per cent of the respondents in 1993 believed that 'Who rules is a question that ordinary citizens should care about' (Table 12); 40 per cent agreed with a statement that the main task of the ordinary citizen is to follow the decisions of the government in the best possible manner. The Chinese tradition is to obey authorities (filial piety), and the influence of this tradition seems still to be fairly strong. On the other hand, bad leaders should be opposed (agreed by 76 per cent of the interviewees). This, however, is also in accordance with tradition. Confucius taught that emperors who had lost their Mandate of Heaven could be overruled by the people. The answers to these questions illustrate a continuing strong subject orientation among the urban people in China.

TABLE 12   Answers to the question: *Somebody has to be the leader/s of our country and make decisions on behalf of the rest of us; what is your opinion on the following statements?* (1993 survey)

	Agree %	Disagree %
Who rules is not a question that the ordinary citizen should care about.	29	52
The main task of ordinary people is to follow the decisions of the government in the best possible manner.	40	43
Citizens should openly express their disapproval of bad leaders.	76	8

In which area of interest would urban Chinese want to involve themselves if they had a chance? An overwhelming majority were willing to join non-political associations. As many as one in three respondents said they would be willing to join a political party. (That should be regarded as a rather high figure.) However, there is a big gap between being willing to involve oneself in a political party and being ready to take the practical consequences of such involvement. In any case, the answers should be interpreted as a participant-political attitude (Table 13).

Traditionally, individual rights are not ascribed to people in China as in Western countries. There is no equivalent word to 'right' in the Chinese

TABLE 13   Answers to the question: *If there are the following kinds of social groups or organizations, which are you most willing to join in?*

	Yes %	No %
Leisure-time organizations such as clubs	88	12
Organizations for protecting your own interest such as consumers' associations	84	16
Political organizations such as parties	34	66

language. According to the Constitution of the PRC, the power belongs to the people. During Maoism citizens' entitlements in society depended on whether they belonged to 'the people' or were defined as among 'the people's enemies'. In the latter case, they were considered beneath the law and could be treated arbitrarily.

Under Deng there was a struggle for the rule of law. Was this reflected in the people's minds? If people demand an extension of rights, or express dissatisfaction with the lack of rights, this may be interpreted as a desire for more influence in the decision-making processes, that people want to be participants or to extend their roles as participants. Are such wishes and demands of extension of rights an increasing tendency among the Chinese?

In the surveys, people were asked to express their views on their rights as citizens. Several questions were related to their political rights: the extent to which they were satisfied with their right to express personal views openly and freely; the freedom of press and publication; their right to make criticisms of their leaders; the right to join different kinds of mass organizations; and the right to vote and to freely assemble and take part in processions (Table 14). On average, slightly more than half of the respondents reported either a negative or a positive evaluation; 48 per cent in 1988, 46 per cent in 1991, and 52 per cent in 1993 had no specific opinion or refused to express an opinion. These high frequencies of middle-category answers demand a closer look.

There is a remarkable variation in opinions from question to question. On two questions the respondents were less ready to express positive or negative views, namely concerning the right to join different kinds of mass organization and the right to assemble and to take part in processions. One possible interpretation of this may be that these two topics are especially sensitive. To form autonomous organizations and to rally in the streets are activities that traditionally have been regarded by the government as very critical; to report a negative satisfaction with the extent of

TABLE 14   Answers to the question: *Are you satisfied with your personal rights in the following aspects?*

	Dissatisfied %	Satisfied %
The right to express your personal views openly and freely		
1988	11	52
1991	16	40
1993	35	14
The freedom of the press		
1993	30	14
The right to express your own views to leaders of your unit (*danwei*)		
1988	33	21
1991	34	22
1993	44	11
The right to vote		
1988	23	47
1991	22	39
1993	43	11
The right to participate in all kinds of social organizations and groups		
1988	15	24
1991	19	23
1993	21	19
The right to assemble and demonstrate		
1988	26	27
1991	27	27
1993	25	15

these rights, especially after 1989, could be perceived to be a dangerous thing to do, even if the procedures of secrecy in the interview situation appeared to be reliable. However, this hypothesis got no support in the in-depth interviews: people were not afraid to respond and perceived this lack of fear as a freedom given to them over the last decade.

A more plausible explanation of this high frequency of middle-category answers is that the right to form and join mass organizations independent of state and party institutions represents a form of political activity that is very unfamiliar within a traditional Chinese political culture. There is a tendency in China for people to develop formal organizations on the basis of their own felt interests, as opposed to the interests of other people. This kind of argument may explain the significant difference between the answers to questions on individuals' rights compared with answers to questions asking for evaluations of the functioning of the government: two thirds of the interviewees gave either a positive or a negative evaluation of the performance of the political system and the government in general, compared with slightly more than one half on the questions about political rights.

While there is little tradition of thinking along the lines of individual rights, the tradition of criticizing the rulers is much stronger. In the in-depth interviews most of the interviewees reported that they did not understand the meaning of the concepts of mass organization and freedom of assembly. They reported that they were obliged to be members of mass organizations (work units/*danwei*); that they had no idea of organizations outside state or party control, or that they simply had no idea of whether such organizations were needed. If they did wish to have such organizations, they regarded the possibility as unrealistic.

Generally speaking, there was a strong tendency to be more dissatisfied and less satisfied over the years. This tendency was most significant regarding the right to express personal views openly and freely and the right to vote. The respondents reported highest degree of dissatisfaction on the right to make criticisms of leaders. To criticize leaders if their behaviour is judged to have been bad by the outcome of their policies is a right embedded in traditional Confucianism, whereas the other rights are more associated with Western liberalism. The high figures of dissatisfaction with the right to criticize leaders, therefore, may be interpreted as a dissatisfaction with a right to which the Chinese people have traditionally been entitled.

Asked whether they were satisfied or not with the right to vote, about 20 per cent were dissatisfied in 1988 and 1991 and between 40 and 50 per cent were satisfied. In the 1993 survey this had changed dramatically: only 11 per cent of the respondents said they were satisfied, and more than 40 per cent expressed dissatisfaction. In 1988 it had been nine years since the introduction of election reforms that permitted more than one candidate to stand for a post.[27] In practice, the reforms did not seem to have resulted in much real political competition in the 1980s. This situation may have changed to some degree in the 1990s.[28] The high degree of satisfaction with the right to vote in 1988 and 1991 may be interpreted as a lack of concern about free elections. The in-depth interviews support such an interpretation. The respondents who were satisfied with their lives did not pay very much interest to the question of voting. They didn't seem to be able to perceive of voting as a means of registering personal views; some had never voted and said they did not know much about the candidates. One respondent reported that she had voted once, for the candidate who had the same family name as herself, but without knowing anything about the candidate. Among the dissatisfied, the lack of importance given elections and a lack of information about the candidates were mentioned as objections. Another group had ideas about alternative systems with competing political parties as in the West, which they would have preferred. But no one seemed to be thinking about voting in terms of civil rights or as a means of registering personal views. In the 1993 survey, the interviewees were asked to comment on the following question: 'By voting, how much influence do you think you have on the decisions made by the national government?' In reply, 5 per cent reported 'much', 20 per cent 'very little', and 65 per cent 'no influence at all'. The same distribution of answers arose from the question: 'How much influence do you think you have on decisions made by your local government?' Here, 3 per cent reported 'some influence', 72 per cent 'no influence at all'.

Half of the respondents in the 1988 survey reported satisfaction with the right to express personal views openly and freely. This situation seems to have changed dramatically, according to the surveys: in 1993 only 14 per cent reported satisfaction with the right to speak while one third reported dissatisfaction. The in-depth interviews tell us that the group of satisfied respondents knew that there were very real restrictions even with respect to this freedom. One person said that it was impossible to complain about corruption for fear of reprisal. However, he reported satisfaction with the situation! Arguments for such seemingly contradictory positions were that no one can always say exactly what they want; 'it will produce too many words'; 'there have to be restrictions to avoid disorder'; 'it is understandable that politicians will monopolize decisions'; etc. More important than demonstrating behind the symbol of the US Goddess of Freedom on Tiananmen Square was to have real power, one interviewee stated. On the other hand, we interviewed several people who were very critical of the general lack of freedom of speech in China. The situation seems to be a bit confusing, with a growing wish for change.

What is the relative importance of political, or politically relevant, rights compared with other needs or rights? The politically relevant rights listed in Table 14 scored very low when mass survey respondents were asked to express their priorities. Without exception, 'the right as a consumer' and 'the right to choose your own way of life' scored highest and were given first, second, or third priority by nearly 60 per cent of respondents in 1993. Then followed 'the right to free marriage' and 'the right to change jobs'. Very few gave top priority to a politically relevant right. The highest score among these was given to the right to express personal views openly and freely, 24 per cent altogether (first priority 4 per cent, second 9 per cent, and third 11 per cent). In the beginning of the 1990s, the Chinese seemed to be giving highest priority to a widening of personal freedom and space.[29]

In these surveys people were asked to give their opinions about the results of the reforms. The respondents were asked to evaluate the consequences they may have experienced personally, and to report on their general impressions. Judging by their own personal experience, the Chinese feel that the reform policy has been successful, and two out of three urban Chinese dwellers were optimistic on behalf of the reform policy in the future (Table 15).

TABLE 15   Answers to the question: *In view of your personal experience, has the reform over the past ten years, generally speaking, been:*

	1988 %	1991 %	1993 %
A great success	30	11	24
Some success	59	71	61
No result—better without	4	7	5
I do not know	6	10	9

The nation's *economic conditions* were perceived to have improved (Table 16). People have experienced an improved supply of commodities on the markets, a higher personal living standard, and a richer cultural life. There can be no doubt about an absolute real growth in market supply in urban areas during these years. 'A richer cultural life' was related to a possibility of a generally more relaxed and varied daily life. The most negative evaluation concerned the social order; the negative reports were related to a perceived growth in lawlessness and corruption at all levels in society.

Only 10–15 per cent of the respondents were of the opinion that the conditions of democracy had worsened. There was, however, a decreasing satisfaction with the way it was developing. But how did the interviewees understand this question? From the in-depth interviews, we learned that many Chinese did not have anything comparable to our understanding of the concept of 'political democratization'. Whether they reported a positive or a negative view, they did not associate the concept with extensions of democratic rights: what they were really evaluating seemed to be more a relaxation of the totalitarian control imposed upon them in job relations, market operations, and in other daily circumstances. The data thus

TABLE 16   Answers to the question: *After ten/fifteen years of reform, what do you think of the situation in the country regarding the aspects listed below?*

	Worse %	Better %
National economic condition		
1988	20	42
1993	14	46
Market supply		
1998	24	52
1993	8	69
Your own living standard		
1988	14	71
1993	5	80
Social order		
1988	40	27
1993	54	15
The extent of democratization		
1988	13	50
1993	14	39
International position		
1988	5	67
1993	5	61
	More uninteresting	Richer
Cultural life		
1988	11	55
1993	12	55

do not allow us to conclude that there is an increasing consciousness of Western democratic values in China.

Two out of three respondents reported that the international position of the country had been raised. An in-depth interviewee explained her positive evaluation on this question in the following way: 'China has historically been at the centre of the world. This position was lost because of the humiliation of China by the colonial powers. China should again be a superpower and is now set to regain such a position.' She felt embarrassed when challenged to argue in favour of this national ambition. We may possibly understand her position as a reflection of a national ambition propagated by national political leaders.

Evaluating six different aspects of reform, respondents emphasized rural reform as the most successful (61 per cent in 1988, 52 per cent in

1991, 38 per cent in 1993); reform of the political system scored lowest and was mentioned by only 4 per cent of the respondents in 1993 as the most successful reform.

A general conclusion seems to be supported by these data. The Chinese are highly aware of the reform policy and have opinions not only on aspects of the policy which they can experience personally. At least in principle, the Chinese seem to be strongly oriented towards the opening out of the political system.

Is there a *generational gap* in the Chinese population? Are young people more critical of the existing political regime, for example, and do they have stronger interests in political participation than older generations? Table 17 reveals that young people are clearly much more negative in their evaluations of the rights they have than older people. The differences are so marked that we may indeed talk about a generational gap. Although younger and older people alike have become far more dissatisfied with

TABLE 17   Answers to the question: *Are you satisfied with your personal rights?* (percentages)

	Dissatisfied		Satisfied	
	1988	1993	1988	1993
The right to express your personal views openly and freely				
Young	14	32	43	26
Mid-aged	9	30	48	8
Old	5	16	66	18
The right to express own views to leaders of your unit (*danwei*)				
Young	39	36	18	13
Mid-aged	33	46	20	13
Old	18	49	29	23
Personal basic rights and freedom				
Young	34		20	
Mid-aged	22		29	
Old	11		41	
Freedom of political beliefs				
Young	10	17	40	26
Mid-aged	7	15	47	30
Old	3	10	51	41
The right to vote				
Young	28	44	40	11
Mid-aged	19	44	48	8
Old	11	33	66	18

their rights as participants in social and political life, the differences between the generations has remained almost the same from 1988 to 1993. However, the general picture of a high degree of indifference is valid also for the younger generations, although answers to the general question on basic personal rights and freedom may illustrate a tendency for individualism to be growing among younger people in China.

There is a marked difference between young and old people and their formal relationship to the Communist Party (Table 18). Will younger generations be more involved in the party as they grow older, or will they seek other channels of influence and power? Their growing dissatisfaction with their rights may be incompatible with membership in a political party with a clear hierarchical structure of power.

TABLE 18   Membership in CCP according to age, 1993

	Member of CCP %	Not a member of CCP %
Young	13	87
Mid-aged	37	63
Old	55	45

Do CCP party members represent a greater participant orientation than non-members? Are party members more inclined to defend the government, and do they therefore tend to be less critical of the government than non-members? Do party members feel that they have more influence or power than non-members? Respondents' answers in 1993 (Table 19) demonstrate no significant differences between party members and non-members, generally speaking. Party members may feel less powerlessness, but the difference is really marginal. The party membership does not seem to represent involvement in a more participant political culture for the rank-and-file member.

According to *occupation*, the overall picture is that workers are more satisfied with the government and its policies, less critical, and also more satisfied with their rights, compared with cadres. However, workers also tend to fit the general pattern described.

For the variables analysed above, there are small differences between men and women. There is a rather weak tendency for men to express more dissatisfaction with their rights and the political situation in general and for men to be slightly more negative in their evaluations of government. Also, women express extreme views, either negative or positive, to a lesser degree than men. However, these differences do not change an overall picture of similarity in men's and women's opinions.

TABLE 19   Evaluations of government, rights and influence: members and non-members of the Communist Party, 1993

	Member %	Not a member of CCP %
The government is		
Corrupt	62	59
Honest and clean	8	10
The government's effectiveness is		
Low	64	62
High	6	10
Reported influence on decisions by local government		
Much	3	3
Little	19	12
No influence at all	65	74
The right to vote		
Satisfied	12	10
Dissatisfied	39	44
The right to express personal views openly and freely		
Satisfied	26	25
Dissatisfied	29	31

The survey data make it quite clear that the most highly educated people, those with degrees from college and university, are more critical of the government, its policies, and the political situation in the country than people with less education. And better educated people are more dissatisfied with their rights.

Geography is another variable that reveals some significant differences in response patterns. The general trend is that the respondents living in cities in inland provinces report more dissatisfaction with political rights and the political system than those living in cities in coastal provinces. If we compare the three major cities—Beijing, Shanghai, and Guangzhou—with the rest of the urban population, the difference between 'periphery' and 'centre' is illustrated. Outside the three big cities, people are more critical of the corruption in government and are clearly more dissatisfied with government efficiency; they are also clearly more dissatisfied with their political rights.

Much of the writing on the relationship between economic reforms, opening to the outside world, and a developing cultural pluralism assumes a positive relation between these processes on the one hand, and pressures on the political system in the form of popular participation on the other. Knowing that these processes are most advanced in the coastal areas, these findings of greater dissatisfaction in the inland provinces, concerning both political rights and the political system, contradict such a hypothesis. They also question the basis for the development of a civil society, indicating that attitudes favourable for the development of such an independent sphere are stronger in areas that have a less developed economy and have been less exposed to cultural exchange with the outside world. On the other hand, the data may indicate a growing tension along territorial divides. This may be a result of both historical traditions and different extents of involvement in the reform processes.

Some Concluding Remarks

Is a participant political culture emerging in China as a result of the reform policies?

The data do not allow conclusions on development trends. What I can do is to interpret the survey data against the background of a theoretical frame of reference relating to traditions of Chinese political culture.

Judging by the experiences of the Chinese people, it seems that a traditional mode of association—the differential mode of association characterized as an egocentric system of social networks—still is of great importance. Hypothetically, we can express this even more strongly: the *guanxi* system seems to have been reinforced by the needs produced by reform policies.

People are very aware of the functioning of the government and express strong critical views on what are perceived as its defects. However, this orientation towards politics seems relatively unrelated to their coming to regard themselves as agents of history. From a common-sense point of view, the Chinese may be far more critical of their government than people in Western democracies. On the other hand, the possibility of changing the political system seems most unrealistic to them, and the idea of political rights as measures of interest representation and political change, very remote.

The satisfaction with the material results of the reform policies is overwhelming. This may compensate for the negative evaluation of other aspects of government. The improvement in people's material living conditions probably constitutes the overwhelming basis of legitimacy of the Chinese political regime. However, people are uneasy about a tendency towards social disorder as a consequence of the reforms.

Does Chinese society harbour the potential for a participant culture? Chinese express growing dissatisfaction with their rights. This is the dominating trend according to our surveys. Young and well-educated people in particular are critical, but not on behalf of general or universalistic principles of democracy: they do not advocate alternative political systems, and do not see themselves as agents of oppositional political alternatives. This growing tendency to criticize the system may lead to activism if the reform processes constrain people too much in their daily fight for survival. But this activism should be assumed to be of traditional kind, based on a Confucian and Maoist justification of the right of the people to oppose 'bad emperors' and 'enemies of the people'.

Western-based optimism on behalf of civil society and a growing democratic pluralism in China seem to be considerably exaggerated. It is more realistic to expect political mass activism in the tradition of the Tiananmen Square incidents of 1976 and 1989.

A premiss of this discussion has been that the emergence of a civil society should be rooted in changes in the people's minds, in their orientations towards the polity. On such a basis, new and autonomous institutions could grow. Compared with an image of the totalitarian state, controlling the people's minds and behaviour in every aspect of their daily lives, the survey data may be summarized as follows. Surprisingly many Chinese were willing to make evaluations on public policy in their country and on aspects of their political system. They dared to express critical opinions in a survey guaranteeing them secrecy.

The fact that there is a relatively high evaluative orientation towards the system should represent a potential for a participant political culture. However, it is not easy to conclude that people want a change of political system. To be satisfied with the level of democracy, as many Chinese are, or indifferent on the question, which half of them are (as expressed in survey attitudes on people's rights), in a system that clearly suppresses oppositional tendencies indicates a low level of readiness to participate in public affairs. It is a great paradox that Chinese seem so satisfied with their voting rights in an electoral system where the real opportunity to act independently of the state and the monopolizing party is so limited and controlled. It might be supposed that we should find the strongest interests in reforming the political situation among the more educated social strata in the urban population. However, even among this part of the population, the likelihood of a participant political culture arising seems to be very weak.

There are, however, nuances in this general picture. There is a marked difference between generations, with regard to both the perceived satisfaction with the output from the political system and the right to influence decisions. There is also a marked difference according to educational level: the higher one's education, the more inclined one is to be negative and critical to both output and rights.

Summing up, the data can be interpreted as demonstrating some *potential* of participatory attitudes among the Chinese population. This is particularly true for the highest educated group, and for the youngest part of the population. This may suggest a potential for a strengthening participant civic culture. However, there is a long way to go before a change in the political system can begin to be based on movements among the people.

NOTES

1. Cf. the optimistic hypothesis by Thomas B. Gold in Ch. 7 above: 'The demonstrations . . . made clear to the world, and to the Chinese people themselves, that the people were not . . . passive objects of party policy, but were capable of acting as subjects, as agents of historical change, organizing on their own . . . and articulating their grievances in public' (p. 165).
2. An overview of the field of study is given by Søren Clausen, 'Chinese Political Culture: A Discussion of an Approach', *Stockholm Journal of East Asian Studies*, 3 (1991), 39–78.
3. Andrew J. Nathan and Tianjian Shi, 'Cultural Requisites for Democracy in China: Findings from a Survey', *Dædalus*, 122:2 (1993).
4. Kjeld Erik Brødsgaard, 'Civil Society and Democratization in China', in Margaret L. Nugent, *From Leninism to Freedom: The Challenges of Democratization* (Boulder, Colo.: Westview Press, 1992), 231–57.
5. Tony Saich, 'The Reform Decade in China: The Limits to Revolution from Above', in Marta Dassu and Tony Saich (eds.), *The Reform Decade in China* (London: Kegan Paul International, 1992).
6. Brødsgaard, 'Civil Society'.
7. Gabriel A. Almond and G. Bingham Powell, Jr, *Comparative Politics: A Developmental Approach* (Boston: Little, Brown, 1966), 50.
8. How the concept 'civil' is to be understood in a Chinese context, is discussed by W. Theodore de Bary, 'China, Confucianism and Civil Society', *Newsletter of the State and Society in East Asia Network*, 2 (1993), 2–17.
9. Gabriel A. Almond and Sidney Verba, *The Civic Culture, Political Attitudes and Democracy in Five Nations* (Boston: Little, Brown, 1963/1965), 16.
10. Michael Thomson, Richard Ellis, and Aaron Wildavsky, *Cultural Theory* (Boulder, Colo.: Westview Press, 1990), 219.
11. Fei Xiaotong, *From the Soil: The Foundations of Chinese Society*, transl. and with an introduction by Gary G. Hamilton and Wang Zheng (Berkeley: University of California Press, 1992).
12. There has been a certain development, however weak, towards rule of law in China during the reform period since 1978: see Ronald C. Keith, *China's Struggle for the Rule of Law* (London: St Martin's Press, 1994).
13. See Lucian Pye, *Asian Power and Politics* (Cambridge, Mass.: Harvard University Press, 1985); and Lucian Pye, *The Mandarin and the Cadre: China's Political Cultures* (Ann Arbor: University of Michigan, 1988).
14. Pye, *Mandarin*, 14.

15. ibid.
16. See Thompson *et al.*, *Cultural Theory*, which also has an interpretation of Pye's discussions in *Mandarin*.
17. Richard H. Solomon, *Mao's Revolution and the Chinese Political Culture* (Berkeley: University of California Press, 1971).
18. Andrew J. Nathan, *Chinese Democracy* (New York: Alfred A. Knopf, 1985), x.
19. Cf. Ryosei Kokubun's contribution (Ch. 3 above).
20. Nathan, *Chinese Democracy*, xii.
21. Solomon, *Mao's Revolution*, 208.
22. Brantly Womack, 'In Search of Democracy', in Brantly Womack (ed.), *Contemporary Chinese Politics in Historical Perspective* (Cambridge: Cambridge University Press, 1991), 71, 59.
23. Joseph Fewsmith, 'Dengist Reforms in Historical Perspective', in Womack, *Contemporary Chinese Politics*, 25.
24. Samuel Eisenstadt elaborates this argument in *European Civilization in Comparative Perspective* (Oslo: Norwegian University Press, 1987).
25. There are no 'Don't know' alternatives, but 4 types of expression are used, which gives the respondent an opportunity to express different modes of indifference or reluctance to give a clear answer. The first is '*yi ban*', designated as category 3 with 'very satisfied' and 'very unsatisfied' being 5 and 1 (or 'most important' and 'not important at all/indifferent'). Another is '*wu suo wei*', indicating indifference, or that the topic does not matter to the respondent. In this connection category 1 is 'I very much agree' (*tong yi*), and 5 is 'I very much disagree'. A middle category is also available when respondents are asked for their opinion on a matter, e.g. ethnic relations, and are given a scale from 5 to 1, with 5 being 'harmonious', and 1 being 'conflicting'. Another example of this is 'man–woman relations', where 5 represents equality and 1 is inequality. The last type of middle category occurs when one is asked to indicate whether a statement is correct or incorrect, on a scale where 1 is very correct, 5 is very incorrect, and 3 is '*ye dui, ye bu dui*', meaning that the statement is partly correct, partly incorrect.
26. Top cadres in state administration and in private and state-owned companies.
27. Bruce J. Jacobs, 'Elections in China', *Australian Journal of Chinese Affairs*, 25 (1991), 171–99.
28. This development is argued by Merle Goldman, 'Is Democracy Possible?' *Current History* (September 1995), and by the Chinese government: 'Elections Alter Face of Local Politics', *China Daily*, 15 November 1995.
29. 'When the Communist Party took power, it destroyed the personal space of the people, and this destroyed civil society . . . But now the personal space is coming back. The worst thing in the old days was that there was no pluralism whatsoever. You depended absolutely on your niche in the vertical hierarchy. If you stepped out, you had nothing.' From an interview in Nicholas D. Kristof and Sheryl Wudunn, *China Wakes* (New York: Vintage Books, 1995), 300.

III
NATIONAL IDENTITY

10

Party Policy and 'National Culture': Towards a State-Directed Cultural Nationalism in China?

Søren Clausen[1]

> China's national culture is long-standing, well-established, rich, pro-
> found and influential . . . Our ancestors have bequeathed us extremely
> rich and extremely precious cultural legacy, which we should cherish,
> protect and explore.
>
> Li Ruihuan[2]

High on the list of mankind's current ills since the late 1980s is the rekin-
dling of ethnic and nationalist fervour from the Balkans to the Indian sub-
continent; and apparently the fever is spreading to East Asia too.
'Ignorance is torn apart, / The dragon can now scream into the heavens,'
goes a song by the Chinese rock band with the heavily symbolic name
'Tang Dynasty', and the Chinese government quietly approves of the
imagery. The Chinese bid in 1993 to host the year 2000 Olympic Games
turned into a massive display of nationalist emotions. Towards the end of
1993 *Newsweek* captured much of the ongoing concern with a special issue
on reawakened nationalism in East Asia; the cover illustration shows a
Japanese samurai warrior battling a Chinese dragon.[3] Are we going to see
a global replay of Europe's tragic mistakes?

In close conjunction with the rise of nationalist feelings, a rejuvenated
Chinese cultural self-confidence has manifested itself in recent years,
inside and outside China, from the treatises of Chinese–American academics (i.e. Professor Tu Wei-ming's concept of 'Cultural China', denoting
Chinese culture as an inalienable treasure constituting the true 'homeland'
of all Chinese) to the wave of popular interest surrounding the esoteric
breathing techniques of *qigong* and the geomantic lore of *fengshui*. In fact,
China would appear to fit into an emerging pattern of global cultural
nationalism, which continues to escalate despite a growing sense of des-
peration in the old heartlands of cultural nationalism.

Cultural nationalism has been defined in various ways. In Kosaku Yoshino's terms, 'cultural nationalism is concerned with the distinctiveness of the cultural community as the essence of a nation', in contrast to political nationalists, who seek to 'achieve a representative state for their community and to secure citizenship rights for its members, thereby giving their collective experience a political reality'.[4] Historically, cultural nationalism has been particularly manifest in the process of shaping political nation-states or in connection with the continued separatism within or break up of such nation-states. In most parts of western Europe, the red-hot passions associated with nationalistic cultural symbols in the 100 years from the mid-nineteenth century to the middle of the twentieth century have largely petered out. But one need only look at the aggressive 'cultural engineering' presently at play in the former Yugoslav republics or in India to be reminded of the potential virulence of cultural nationalism. When Western intellectuals are confronted with these phenomena in the global arena, they approach them with a measure of resignation and disillusionment, like old people looking at youthful—and dangerous— passion. With experience, however, follows also a responsibility to study such occurrences and to breathe cool sense into the hot passions. That involves identifying the rules of the game and the key players.

With the post-1978 economic reforms, the Chinese Communist leadership discarded the revolutionary legitimacy provided by Maoism; then, with the Tiananmen Square disaster of 1989, the Chinese Communist Party (CCP) forfeited much of what had been gained during the 1980s in terms of restoring the legitimacy of party rule by means of economic growth. There is universal agreement among China specialists that the *crisis of legitimacy* today is the pre-eminent expression of China's predicament. Furthermore, there is broad consensus that the CCP leadership is striving to invoke the energies of nationalist feeling in its effort to establish a new foundation of legitimacy, including a 'rehabilitation' of China's past glory and traditions. In post-1989 China one can indeed find many manifestations of a new state-directed cultural nationalist drive, focusing on the historic splendour and cultural identity of China: party and state leaders pay homage to the Confucius Temple; the mythical Yellow Emperor is likewise officially honoured; and the positive values of Chinese tradition are mentioned in central party documents.

After seven decades of May Fourth cultural iconoclasm and three decades of heavy-handed Maoist attacks on traditional culture, has the CCP élite finally settled down and joined the rising tide of Chinese cultural self-esteem? In a number of recent studies of Chinese culture, nationalism, and identity, it has been suggested that this is in fact the case. For example, Lowell Dittmer and Samuel S. Kim claim that '[t]he lack of international enemies and reference groups seems to leave China no choice but to resort to tradition to ground its national identity'.[5]

The purpose of this essay is to argue that the present concern in the West with state-sponsored cultural nationalism in China is exaggerated. Official cultural–nationalist rhetoric does indeed exist, but it is a thin smokescreen for a party ideology which has not in any way abandoned its primary focus on economic modernization.

Official cultural nationalism and the partial rehabilitation of 'tradition' may be understood within four different contexts. First, the regime wants to tap the potential for patriotism and use it for its own purposes. Second, there is a growing concern over social anomie and moral decay in connection with the unfolding of economic reforms, and traditional values are perceived as a remedy that may serve purposes of social control.[6] The use of cultural–nationalist notions by official China must be seen as instrumental in relation to this primary goal. Third, the regime wants to maintain control over the authoritative discourse on culture and tradition with the aim of preventing the emergence of ideological rivals basing themselves on a cultural–nationalist foundation.[7] Fourth, the promotion of symbols related to the Chinese tradition provides a convenient bridge to reach the hearts of Chinese 'compatriots' (*tongbao*) in Hong Kong, Taiwan, Singapore, and elsewhere.

There are a number of powerful reasons, however, why the CCP regime does not endorse an all-out programme of cultural nationalism. Even if it wanted to do so, there are strong historic counterforces, and the room for manoeuvre in the field of cultural-nationalist rhetoric has narrowed during the 1980s rather than widened. The aim, then, is to examine the current conditions of state-sponsored cultural nationalism and to discuss the constraints and future prospects.

Looking at Chinese nationalism in this perspective, the general picture of China in the 1980s and early 1990s is one of false starts and ambiguity. 'National culture' has in fact moved on to the stage since the early 1980s, without, however, assuming a central position in official ideology. As the 1980s progressed divisive implications of 'national culture' became visible, peaking in 1988 and 1989. The crackdown on the Democracy Movement in 1989 brought expectations of a more vigorous political effort at controlling the public discourse on 'national culture'. Such efforts appear to have fizzled out, however, after an initial burst of energy in 1989–91. It is ironic that in China, a country with a rich tradition of political control over cultural symbols and the interpretation of the past, the present regime has very little to say about 'national culture'—except to prevent others from expressing themselves on the matter.

Cultural Nationalism: The Concept

The contemporary Western scepticism towards cultural nationalism has produced a vocabulary of 'deconstruction' which is neatly encapsulated in the titles of two influential books that appeared in 1981: Benedict Anderson's *Imagined Communities*[8] and E. J. Hobsbawm and T. Ranger's *The Invention of Tradition*.[9] The general trend of cultural studies since the 1960s, to see culture as a creative activity rather than just the passive imprint of the past on the present, has been given full momentum in these and other contemporary studies of culture at the national level. The ongoing review of the concept of culture has been summarized by R. G. Fox:

> Culture, we are coming to think, is not a heavy weight of tradition, a set of configurations, a basic personality constellation that coerces and compels individuals. Culture is a set of understandings and a consciousness under active construction by which individuals interpret the world around them . . . Similarly we have drained off much of the necessity and teleology of the nation-building literature. National culture is not an inevitable output of infrastructural investment. It is a contingent product, of history, of struggle.[10]

There are, of course, considerable differences of opinion in this body of literature. Ernest Gellner tends to emphasize the elements of masquerade and fabrication inherent in cultural nationalism, which he sees as directly and functionally related to capitalism and modern nation-building.[11] Anthony Smith, in contrast, points at ethnic foundations of modern nations and a measure of continuity between pre-modern concepts and modern nationalism.[12] Anderson, Hobsbawm, and Ranger occupy a middle position between these two views.

Differences aside, the basic point in all of this is that 'tradition' and 'national culture' assume reality only when perceived as such by a contemporary mind. Not *all* past history is 'tradition', and not *all* culture is 'national culture'. The 'editing of tradition' is a universal condition, and, with the emergence of modern nation-building and rapid social transformation, this process has assumed a prominent and highly visible role under the heading of 'national culture'. In the more fortunate cases, 'national culture' faithfully serves the purpose of unity and harmony (e.g. the Japanese cultural industry related to the concept of *nihonjinron*— 'Japanese uniqueness'), but every so often it is a spearhead of social or political conflicts (e.g. contemporary Hindu revivalism in India).

Where does China fit into this picture? New approaches to understanding the relationship between culture and nationalism in China are currently being suggested. In an article published in 1992, James Townsend has presented a valuable survey of Western perceptions regarding Chinese nationalism.[13] The dominant paradigm in most of the existing scholarship on Chinese nationalism is described by Townsend as the 'culturalism-to-nationalism thesis', i.e. China's shift from 'cultural entity to political entity'. The implications of this paradigm are summarized in three points:

First, it [the culturalism-to-nationalism thesis] tries to explain why the Chinese empire was so much more durable than the other pre-modern systems, finding the answer in China's kind of cultural identity. Second, it argues that China's entry into a world of sovereign nation-states was unusually prolonged and traumatic because it forced the Chinese to reject their age-old cultural identity and adopt a new politicized one. Third, it suggests that this long, wrenching 'identity crisis' makes contemporary Chinese nationalism unusually intense, becoming in the resolution of the crisis something like the religion of modern China.[14]

The main thrust of Townsend's argument is the refutation of certain aspects of this culturalism-to-nationalism thesis. Without negating the thesis entirely, Townsend points out that:

[t]he thesis's main weakness is that it exaggerates the totality and clarity of the change in question. It overstates both the dominance of culturalism and the weakness of pre-modern nationalism in imperial times, as well as overstating the eclipse of culturalism and triumph of nationalism in modern times. Contrary to the thrust of the thesis, culturalism could co-exist with other ideas about state and nation, could lend support in modern times to both state and ethnic nationalism, and hence could retain some influence on Chinese nationalism down to the present. Culturalism and state nationalism have been dominant elite doctrines in their respective eras, but neither has monopolized the field of ideas and sentiments about the Chinese nation.[15]

Taking this line of argument up to the contemporary age, Townsend finds that 'Chinese nationalism remains an elusive and unpredictable phenomenon'[16] and that '[n]ationalism continues to divide the Chinese as often as it unites them'.[17] State nationalism is the official doctrine, but it coexists with the ethnic notion of Chinese 'compatriots' outside Mainland China as well as with unofficial ethnic nationalism on the popular level within China. And 'culturalism' remains a powerful influence alongside official state nationalism.

The Townsend article offers a broad view of the various current ideas on Chinese nationalism. In a historical perspective, China has experienced a whole range of 'nationalisms' in this century, including varieties of ethnic nationalism (particularly in the first decades of the twentieth century) and the universalistic 'modernizing nationalism' of the May Fourth generation. And in periods of Maoist radicalism, particularly the Cultural Revolution, 'class struggle' tended to overshadow any form of nationalism, unless one chooses to see 'class struggle' as precisely the expression of

nationalism during the Maoist era. In the overall picture, state nationalism has been the mainstay from the Guomindang Chinese Republic of the
1930s to the People's Republic of China, and in a sense one can find
antecedents of this in late Qing official policy. But 'culturalism' has never
been completely off the stage, and certainly *history* has always occupied a
central position, even during the high peaks of Maoist attacks on the 'four
olds'. In the words of Ann Anagnost:

> In the culture of Chinese socialism, history was not destroyed but reinvented
> (again and again) throughout the socialist era. Much of Chinese socialist culture
> was based precisely on the power of narrative to recall the past, albeit an invented
> one (as are all national pasts). The 'speaking bitterness' narratives that fueled the
> land reform, the graphic depictions of the 'rent collection courtyard', the repre-
> sentations of class and market in local histories, the historiography of peasant
> uprisings that helped to construct the historic inevitability of the Liberation in the
> creation of a mythic history, the historical metaphorization of political debate
> (e.g. Mao as Qinshihuang) are just a few examples of how the exercise of histori-
> cal memory was deployed.[18]

The contemporary Chinese wranglings with culture and nationalism
are in fact only the last chapter in a history of a hundred years, and we
must accept the reality of a 'fuzziness' in the vocabulary of nationalism,
ethnicity, and identity which 'comes not from scholarship but from social
life'.[19]

An up-to-date sophisticated theoretical analysis of Chinese national
identity has been produced by Lowell Dittmer and Samuel S. Kim.[20] The
introductory chapter on the theories of national identity makes the step
from standard *analytical definitions* of national identity (i.e. definitions
revolving around questions of boundaries) to *synthetic definitions* aimed
at the questions of 'why' and 'what'. At the core of their argument is the
focus on 'a relationship of identification between nation and state'.[21] The
identity of the state is a 'symbol system known as the national essence,
which consists of the myths, rituals, ceremonies, and folklore that relate
how the nation came to be and what it stands for',[22] and this symbol system is subjected to a historical evolution influenced by '(1) the projected
aspirations and demands of the citizenry (both masses and élites); (2)
domestic political history, particularly those epoch-making events (like
Tiananmen) whose reverberations are felt by the population at large; and
(3) foreign policy experience, as the ship of state navigates unpredictable
international waters'.[23]

The theoretical definitions of Dittmer and Kim provide an opportunity
to establish some of the important dimensions—with implicit constraints—that constitute the 'field of operation' regarding current official
Chinese attempts to employ the symbolic resources of 'national culture'.

1. Globalization and 'national culture' are intertwined, and in more than one way. First, there is the complex process of replication mixed with metamorphosis, and of diachronic and synchronic aspects, involved in the global spread of nationalism. The negation of classical imperialist nationalism in the form of Third World anti-imperialism is only the first and simplest level of complexity; to use the words of Arjun Appadurai, global cultural flows move in a number of 'non-isomorphic paths',[24] creating an increasingly complex interplay between global cultural homogenization and disjunction. Second, the significance of international 'reference groups' must be recognized; in the case of China, the global demise of state socialism and Third Worldism alongside the rise of the East Asian 'little dragons' is of prime importance in setting the agenda of Chinese cultural nationalism. Third, significant cultural symbols always involve a degree of international exchange. For example, Arthur Waldron has produced an interesting study of the interplay between China and the West in the establishment of the Great Wall as a key Chinese cultural symbol in this century.[25]

2. Cultural nationalism, while aiming at an imaginary and mythical point of unity, in fact always involves a 'package' of symbols, drawing on different sources. The contradiction between the proclaimed unitary core and the heterogeneity of the symbol sources renders cultural nationalism particularly vulnerable to the eroding influence of 'deconstructionism', not just as a discourse undertaken by Western scholars but in fact as everyday expressions by all individuals and groups in a given society. All approaches to cultural nationalism and 'Chineseness' during the last decade, whether produced by the political élite or by any other group, have been immediately challenged or even ridiculed by other Chinese. In this process, the ideal of an apparently 'natural' and indisputable symbolic core becomes increasingly remote.

3. The propositions and counter-propositions regarding cultural nationalism since the mid-1980s form a significant part of the political arena in China. Various social groups, segments, élite strata, etc., manifest themselves in the ongoing efforts to come to terms with cultural nationalism and identity. To borrow the words of Helen F. Siu, 'Instead of upholding the prevailing image of a reified China enshrouded with primordial sentiments, one may see how advocates on different ends of the spectrum have negotiated their respective positions to generate a complex, open cultural process.'[26] To take the point a bit further, the contestation over national culture is in itself a breeding ground for élite conflict and general social differentiation, for widening cultural differences between city and village, between the political leadership and the new business élite, etc.

'Culture Fever': The 1980s Discourse on Culture and Nation

Views from the Top

In describing the different levels of discourse regarding cultural nationalism in China in the 1980s, the metaphor of a *mountain* might be helpful.
At the very top, we have official party declarations and ideological guidelines. A bit below the top there is a level of 'authoritative discourse' conducted in the main national media, directly or indirectly under official
control, with establishment intellectuals playing the leading role. This level
of discourse is challenged from below by less established intellectual
rebels, and here one also finds inputs from a much broader culture debate
involving art, literature, and so on. At the bottom we have the level of popular culture, involving the cultural aspects of lifestyles and popular opinion.

Seen in this perspective, the Chinese culture debates of the 1980s reflect
the climatic conditions of a mountain: at the top there is coolness, coupled
with occasional mists and high winds; further down it gets warmer, and
there is a greater profusion of life forms. The 'culture fever' (*wenhua re*) of
the mid-1980s started at the lower and middle levels of the mountain, and
from there it gradually spread to levels below and above. The central
organs of party and state were for a long time very slow and passive in
responding.

Since 1978 the 'ideology machine' has been preoccupied with two concerns. One is the reinterpretation of Mao, i.e. neutralizing the Maoist concept of class struggle under socialist conditions without abandoning Mao
altogether. The second concern is the ideological justification of economic
reforms. Since 1989 the global collapse of state socialism has added a third
concern to these original tasks. The key concept that emerged during the
1980s to deal with these problems is that of 'China's special characteristics' (*Zhongguo tese*). This formula, canonized at the 13th Congress of the
CCP in 1987 and reaffirmed at the 14th Congress in 1992, addresses all
three problems: it establishes a continuity of sorts with Maoist pronouncements regarding 'combining the universal truth of Marxism with
China's concrete conditions', it legitimizes economic reforms by pointing
to China's low level of economic development, and it serves to explain why
socialism should be able to survive in China despite its collapse in Eastern
Europe and the Soviet Union.

Quite strikingly, however, one finds no references—certainly not in a
positive sense—to *cultural* aspects of 'China's special characteristics' in

the official statements on the concept. To take Zhao Ziyang's report to the 13th Congress of the CCP, 'Advance Along the Road of Socialism With Chinese Characteristics', as an example, the 'special characteristics' are uniformly described as 'backwardness', first and foremost in terms of the productive forces, but not only there:

In the realm of the superstructure, a number of economic and cultural conditions that are necessary if we are to promote a high degree of socialist democracy are far from ripe, and decadent feudal and capitalist ideologies and the small-producers' force of habit still have widespread influence in society and often corrupt party cadres and public servants.[27]

Zhao Ziyang's 1987 report echoes similar statements in Hu Yaobang's 1982 report to the 12th CCP Congress, and essentially it reflects the spirit of the September 1986 Resolution on 'Guiding Principles for Building a Socialist Society with an Advanced Culture and Ideology', adopted at the Sixth Plenary Session of the 12th Central Committee of the CCP. This Resolution stands out as the single most comprehensive and authoritative party statement of the 1980s regarding issues related to cultural nationalism, and in principle it has remained in force ever since despite its links with the reformist leadership of Hu Yaobang. The 1986 Resolution for the first time provides glimpses of an official reevaluation of traditional culture in advocating a new culture 'that incorporates the best from historical tradition', and in its ambition to 'inspire a sense of national pride, self-respect and self-confidence'.[28] However, the main thrust of the Resolution is towards a *scientific* world view and culture:

We should work actively to change those undesirable customs that still prevail in cities and the countryside, to advocate cultured, healthful ways of living that are in keeping with scientific principles and to eliminate ignorance and backwardness. Bad wedding and funeral customs have to be changed, and superstitious, feudal beliefs and practices must be eradicated. On condition that sound folkways are respected, these reforms should be carried out voluntarily by the masses themselves . . . As a higher stage in human moral progress, socialist ethics naturally incorporate all the best elements in the various ethical systems and traditions developed throughout history and reject all decadent ideology and ethics. Feudal ideology is deep-rooted in our country . . . It is therefore a formidable, long-term task to eradicate all these pernicious influences.[29]

In this perspective, Zhao's 1987 report and similar official pronouncements on 'Chinese characteristics' during the 1980s, with their insistence on a universalistic and unilinear pattern of development, have a core message that is in fact the exact opposite of the proclaimed regard for China's 'special characteristics'. The only concession to unscientific popular culture is the vague term 'sound folkways', and the values of traditional Chinese culture are described as not essentially superior to traditional cultures worldwide.

Establishment Intellectual Discourse

There is considerably more substance to the discourse on tradition and 'national culture' when the focus is widened to include what might be called 'the level of authoritative discourse'. This concept is meant to cover primarily the main national media such as the *People's Daily* and *Guangming Daily*, as well as a number of national-level academic journals, which serve not just as organs of the political élite but also as a 'testing ground' for variations in the official line. A very large number of articles on the topic of tradition and 'national culture' have appeared in these newspapers and journals since 1984; according to one estimate, more than 1,500 articles were published during the great academic debate on culture in China in 1984–9; several new journals were founded, and over twenty centres for cultural study were established.[30] There are innumerable variations in this highly complex debate, yet it is possible to distinguish between a few major schools of thought.

An *'orthodox Marxist'* position was quite apparent in the first few years of the debate, but its influence gradually waned as the 1980s progressed. This position basically rejects traditional values as a core element of 'national culture', since they belong to a mode of production that has now been superseded. Instead, 'national culture' must be based on contemporary values congruent with socialist modernization: patriotism and socialist values.

'*Syncretism*' could serve as the common denominator for the large number of debaters who propose a happy marriage between 'the best features of tradition' and contemporary scientific and socialist values. This school of thought is well in line with the mainstream of 'cultural engineering' in the countries surrounding China; towards the more pro-traditionalist end of the spectrum in this large body of literature one finds views akin to the '*Confucian ethic*' hypothesis popular in Taiwan and among some Western scholars. This hypothesis suggests that Confucian culture is not only compatible with modernization but in fact is a valuable asset contributing to economic growth. Prominent exponents of this line of thought are Zhang Dainian, Pang Pu, Xiao Jiefu, and Tang Yijie. The 'Confucian ethic' discourse is in itself an example of a highly successful case of 'cultural engineering': originating in Japan in the 1970s, the idea was taken over by US academics around 1980 (Herman Kahn was probably the first to embrace the concept[31]) and transplanted to Taiwan and Singapore from there. For the People's Republic of China, the 'Confucian ethic' concept is politically unacceptable because it is so closely associated with a rival—and highly successful—political regime. But at the same time, it is a tempting line of thought in a period when economic growth is the top priority in China, and although the hypothesis is rarely voiced without reservation by PRC scholars, adherents of the 'Confucian ethic' theory are frequently invited to express their ideas at academic conferences in China.

The many different views lumped together here under the heading of 'syncretism' all share the common premiss—and problem—of 'combining the best of two worlds'. Sometimes the problem is addressed in a straightforward manner that carries an air of naïvety: various concepts associated with the classical Chinese philosophers are brought forward as 'valuable elements of traditional culture' that qualify to be combined with the most valuable elements—having gone through a similar screening—of contemporary Western civilization, without much apparent thought to the question of *who* should conduct this experiment in cultural chemistry, and *how* the results are to be communicated to society.

'*Critical acceptance*' is meant to cover those debaters who basically deplore the influence of tradition on contemporary China while at the same time arguing that all-out rejection amounts to closing one's eyes to reality. The power of tradition, including the negative features of it, must be accepted as a reality and starting point of the debate. Some of the most sophisticated debaters of the 1980s can be identified with this line of thought, with Liu Zaifu, the former director of the Institute of Literature under the Chinese Academy of Social Sciences (CASS), and former minister of culture Wang Meng as prominent examples. In this trend of thought we find establishment intellectuals with a reputation of independent thinking, and the events of 1989 brought them close to the dividing line between acceptable independent thought and dissent: Liu Zaifu chose exile, although he was not a prominent supporter of the Democracy Movement, and Wang Meng stepped down as minister of culture after the events of 1989.

The 1987 book by Liu Zaifu and Lin Gang, *Tradition and the Chinese* (*Chuantong yu Zhongguo ren*) is a prime example of the 'critical acceptance' school of the 1980s. The basic orientation of the book is a defence of the iconoclastic May Fourth movement, with Lu Xun as the main hero. The main weaknesses of May Fourth—avantgardism, utopianism, etc.—are fully recognized, but the writers see these phenomena as dictated by historical circumstances and quite understandable. In contrast, the pro-traditionalist current—in this book exemplified by Tu Wei-ming—is criticized in great detail.[32] The argument against Tu Wei-ming is that the contemporary Chinese cannot even begin to consider the potential value of traditional culture until they have basically liberated themselves from the shackles of that same tradition.

On the other hand, Liu and Lin distance themselves from what is seen as superficial contemporary iconoclasm. No matter what contemporary Chinese think of traditional Chinese culture, it is still the logical starting point of any cultural strategy. No matter how much tradition is rejected, it still plays a role. Therefore the book suggests as its central argument that attention is focused on those 'mechanisms' (*jizhi*) within traditional culture that in themselves 'invite' modernization or at least are not hostile to modern transformation.[33] In this way certain traditional elements may actually aid the necessary breakup of 'tradition as a *system*'. When it comes to identifying such 'mechanisms', however, Liu and Lin remain abstract. The closest they get to a positive identification is the suggestion that such 'mechanisms' must be of value to the 'mainstay of the nation' (*minzu zhuti*), in line with earlier pronouncements by Lu Xun on this subject.[34]

Wang Meng has contributed significantly to the line of thought described here as 'critical acceptance'. In early 1989 he wrote a short article challenging the whole approach of the culture debate of the 1980s in a refreshing and provocative manner, 'The Cultural Tradition and the Tradition of Non-culture'.[35] Starting out with a string of examples of stupidity, greed, and vandalism taken from contemporary Chinese social life, he asks ironically, which aspects of traditional culture are manifested here? Confucianism, or perhaps Taoism? Of course not. What is really the problem in contemporary China, according to Wang Meng, is not traditional culture but the *tradition of non-culture* (*wu wenhua*) or even *anti-culture* (*fan wenhua*). Wang Meng refuses to subscribe to the pro-traditionalist notions of the 'syncretist' approach, but his basic position is that 'building a new culture' is not facilitated by an all-out attack on the vestiges of traditional culture.

The work of philosopher Li Zehou from the CASS Institute of Philosophy also falls within this scope.[36] Among his many significant contributions to the 1980s culture debate, probably the best known is the concept of 'Western substance—Chinese application' (*Xiti Zhongyong*), originally put forward by the historian Li Shu and adopted and elaborated on by Li Zehou from 1986 onwards. The formula turns the famous late Qing formula 'Chinese substance—Western application' (*Zhongti Xiyong*), combining cultural conservatism with technological modernization, upside down. At the same time, it keeps a distance from the 'total Westernization' (*quanpan zihua*) approach. Li defines '*Western substance*' in a very broad sense which includes all aspects of modern reality: material production, science and technology, and the pattern of everyday life. 'Chinese application' in this context means that certain features and institutions of Chinese traditional culture must be brought to serve as a vehicle for modernization, that is, an approach similar to the 'mechanisms' of Liu Zaifu and Lin Gang.

The 'Western substance' formula was immediately provocative and refreshing in the context of the Chinese culture debate of the 1980s, and it has been the target of official criticism after 1989. In another perspective, however, the 'issue of how to sinicize "Western substance" '[37] runs parallel to the official CCP rhetoric on 'socialism with Chinese characteristics'. Like the other establishment intellectuals in the 'critical acceptance' school, Li Zehou is struggling to preserve a dialogue between ruling CCP ideology and independent currents of thought; despite official condemnation, he managed to keep a foothold in China after 1989. (More recently Li Zehou, along with a number of other Chinese establishment intellectuals, have voiced their explicit criticism of the radicalism and iconoclasm that formed part of the background to the 1989 Democracy Movement and, by implication, have moved closer to the current ideological mainstream. The most striking example of this move is the 1995 book by Li Zehou and Liu Zaifu, *Farewell to Revolution* (*Gaobie Geming*).

Anti-Establishment Discourse

A very prominent role was played in the late 1980s by the 'iconoclasts' representing a young generation of critical scholars.

During the last few years of the 1980s a revived anti-traditionalism in the spirit of the May Fourth movement had swelled to become a major tributary of the growing wave of protest and dissent, culminating in the television epic *Heshang* (River Elegy), which sparked a nationwide debate in the second half of 1988. *Heshang* is a devastating critique of traditional Chinese culture, cast in the image of the Yellow River—inward-looking, despotic, and unpredictable—and contrasted with the openminded and explorative 'azure blue' civilization of the West, thus defying the party leadership's fear of 'spiritual pollution' from abroad. An estimated 70 million Chinese saw *Heshang*, and the ensuing debates turned into a kind of popular referendum on the merits and demerits of Chinese tradition. A large body of literature discussing the *Heshang* phenomenon has been produced since 1989; most agree that it displays a rather totalistic and sometimes naïve approach to traditional culture. In the words of one critic '*Heshang* is less than satisfactory to anyone who has studied Chinese history. It is an overwrought and inchoate mélange . . . '[38] In fact, one important weakness of the iconoclast approach has been very clearly pointed out by none other than the *Heshang* director Su Xiaokang himself in a November 1989 interview:

We, as authors, did not dare to confront the CCP system, and therefore we attacked our ancestors instead . . . the reason for China's backwardness [is] not the traditional culture, but on the contrary the fact that by 1840 traditional culture had been destroyed by many factors, one of which was the impact of the West. The new culture which arose after the destruction of the old was a disastrous combination of Oriental despotism and Stalinism. What we now have in China is Communist culture, not traditional Chinese culture . . . [39]

Perhaps the significance of *Heshang* does not rest with its historical accuracy or lack of it. In Anagnost's words, the TV series was a 'calculated effort to displace the discursive field' and a reinvention of 'Chinese tradition as a counterdiscourse to the state's own inventions'.[40] The politically crucial feature of *Heshang* iconoclasm was the attempt to conquer the mantle of May Fourth modernizing nationalism from the gerontocracy within the CCP leadership.

Until his arrest in 1989, Liu Xiaobo was the most outspoken and eloquent proponent of this line of thought, and he has produced a whole range of provocative statements concerning the necessity of total demolition of traditional culture, including a refutation of the views of the 'critical acceptance' line of thought. The iconoclasts have been universally persecuted or driven into exile in the wake of the June 1989 events.

Non-establishment Inputs and Popular Culture

The third level of the debate on tradition and 'national culture' is the wider, non-establishment level of intellectual discourse, including literature, art, and cinema. It is here that the main body of the 'culture fever' of the 1980s is located. There is an authentic air of enthusiasm and intellectual curiosity in much of this discourse which sometimes makes the debaters of the two first-mentioned levels look like tired schoolteachers in comparison.

Generalization is impossible when looking at the 'culture fever', because *diversity* is precisely the point. In the enthusiastic search for cultural roots, 'tradition' has been relativized and transformed into the *many* traditions. A case in point is the 'rediscovery of Chu culture', which attracted much attention in the 1980s. The southern state of Chu flourished in the middle of the Zhou period (*c.* 1000–221 BC), and recent archaeological discoveries indicate that Chu contained many cultural traits in aesthetics, art, and religious symbolism that were later erased by the victorious northern Chinese Confucian culture and have since come to be seen as 'un-Chinese'. Many contemporary Chinese now project their dreams of a more individualistic, free, and sensuous lifestyle on to the idealized image of Chu. Others dig for valuable experience in the Chinese

Taoist or Buddhist traditions. All of these efforts are true expressions of modern cultural inventiveness, but the leitmotif of *unity* is lost in the process. Like nationalism, culture also has turned into a force that divides the Chinese as much as it unites them.

In literature and art, the 'culture fever' of this level of discourse is clearly expressed in the 'roots' *xungen* literature and cinema of the mid-1980s, with writers such as A Cheng, Han Shaogong, and Gao Xingjian as prominent examples. But the 'roots' sought after are far from the ortho-dox Confucian culture; instead, attention is directed towards the symbols, magic, and narrative tradition of popular culture. And from this there is only a small step to fascination also with non-Han popular culture. But looking for 'roots' invites new paradoxes and challenges. In the words of Leo Ou-fan Lee:

> If we bear in mind the somewhat ironic fact that most *xungen* writers come from urban centers, it is not surprising that they too are strangers to these peripheral regions which they wish to uncover as authentic 'centers' of Chinese civilization; the Other as the primordial source of their culture thus seems unfamiliar and even exotically 'foreign'. Herein lies their paradox: like exiles returning home after a long absence, they find the homeland of their own culture foreign, and the jour-ney to their roots becomes one of increasing 'defamiliarization'.[41]

The last level of discourse to be mentioned here is that of popular cul-ture itself. It is the general impression that the economic reforms and ide-ological relaxation of the 1980s have produced a growing bifurcation of Chinese society, with urban China becoming increasingly cosmopolitan while rural China experiences a re-emergence of many traditional cultural features. The return of traditional forms of life-cycle rituals and religious worship has been documented in a rapidly expanding literature. It is often observed, however, that this apparent re-traditionalization is not simply the mechanical reproduction of past patterns, and that contemporary rit-uals are in fact a creative expression of and adaptation to current condi-tions.[42] Once again, the political authorities are not in a position to harness this creative energy into a 'national culture' project because of the obvious challenges to central policies and indeed party authority itself implicit in rural China's embrace of 'traditional' rituals.

The Official Counter-Offensive, 1989–1991

The events of 1988–9 forced official China to take a stand. *Heshang* was made the target of condemnation during the second half of 1989, and the principal writer of the series, Su Xiaokang, was put on a list of intellectu-als wanted by the state for 'counter-revolutionary crimes'.

The celebration of the 2,540th anniversary of Confucius in October 1989 offered an opportunity for the CCP leadership to make a public demonstration of its new-found pride in the glory of Chinese tradition. The celebration was cast as a major event with several high-ranking leaders attending. Gu Mu, then vice-chairman of the State Council, gave a speech on the correct attitude towards traditional culture, concentrated in the formula 'discarding the dross and retaining the essence' (*qi qi zaopo, qu qi jinghua*).[43] A few weeks after this propaganda, boss Wang Renzhi delivered a key hardline speech where, among other things, the Democracy Movement was accused of 'negating the 5,000 years' history of Chinese civilization and of the whole Chinese nation . . . [they] finally walked down a road of preaching national nihilism and national betrayal'.[44] Similar pronouncements were intermittently aired during 1990. As for 'discarding the dross and retaining the essence', it is actually a quotation from Mao Zedong, and the meaning is vague. *What* is the 'essence', and *how* is it 'separated from the dross'? The weakness of this often-repeated formula has been aptly brought out by Liu Xiaobo in the sarcastic comment: 'The essence is always in the dross'!

Finally, in 1991 it appeared that the CCP leadership was ready to put substance into its proclaimed commitment to respect traditional culture. In March 1991 CCP General Secretary Jiang Zemin instructed Li Tieying, chairman of the State Education Commission, and former minister of education He Dongchang to initiate a nationwide programme of improved education in 'modern and contemporary history as well as national conditions [*guoqing*]'. A 'General Programme—preliminary draft' was published in the October 1991 issue of *Renmin Jiaoyu* (Popular Education).[45] In actual fact, the Programme covers the entire range of history, and it offers a comprehensive view of how the CCP leadership defined national identity at the time. It should be remembered that in 1991 the Chinese economy was still in low gear and the collapse of the Soviet Communist Party loomed very menacingly on the horizon. The post-1989 defensive mood and general gloom within the CCP was in full force, and it was against this background that the political élite produced the 1991 Programme, which provides Chinese educators with a detailed list of requirements regarding the teaching of national culture and Chinese identity.

The Programme does not establish itself as a new, separate subject for the schools to teach; rather, the core content of 'socialist patriotism' is to be integrated with the already existing curriculum, particularly with subjects such as history, geography, morality, and politics. Chinese language classes must 'organically' integrate the spirit of the Programme in the classroom activities. The main target group of the Programme is primary and middle school students; in principle, it should also extend to the pre-school activities of kindergartens and to university classes. It should be noted that the Programme is by no means the first example of central guidelines on the teaching of history and nationalism. The value of the 1991 Programme for the purposes of this essay is that it offers a concentrated statement of the official position regarding 'tradition' and 'national culture' in the early 1990s.

The Programme is divided into six main chapters. The first chapter, 'Five Thousand Years of Splendid Chinese Civilization', covers premodern history. The second chapter covers the 1840–1949 period under the heading 'The Humiliation of More than a Century of Invasions, and the Struggle to Save the Country from Destruction'. As the title suggests, the emphasis is on the evils of imperialism rather than 'feudalism', i.e. on external rather than internal causes of China's decline in the nineteenth and early twentieth centuries. Similarly, the rise of the CCP is described as the culmination of a century of anti-imperialist popular resistance. Chapter 3 is on the post-1949 period: 'The People's Republic Opens Up for Progress: Gigantic Changes in the Holy Fatherland for More than Four Decades'. This chapter mainly covers the period up to 1978, leaving the reform decade for separate treatment. Comment on the Maoist period is strongly affirmative with no trace of self-criticism regarding Party policies; for example, the only comment on the Cultural Revolution is that it saw 'the struggle of some eminent old comrades to resist "the Great Cultural Revolution"—the so-called "February Countercurrent" ';[46] there is no mention, however, of *what* the 'old comrades' were struggling against, and thus the material contains nothing that could help illuminate the young generations in China about the causes or the nature of the Cultural Revolution.

Chapter 4 deals with the issues of 'Population, Resources, Environment and Nationalities'. The general tone of this chapter is remarkably different from the rest of the text, and it appears to have been written by worried technocrats rather than the party ideologues in charge of the other chapters. A rather dark picture of demographic, resource, and environment problems, loaded with many grim facts, is presented. Chapter 5 addresses the current political line under the heading 'Building Socialism with Chinese Characteristics'. The focus once again is on *struggle*— against 'bourgeois liberalization', 'peaceful evolution', 'counter-revolutionary rebellion', etc., and on upholding the 'socialist orientation' in the implementation of economic reforms. Finally, Chapter 6 deals with the current international situation: 'Keep a clear orientation regarding the fundamental nature of capitalist exploitation and aggression, maintain vigilance against the imperialist plot to achieve peaceful evolution—a correct understanding of the international environment that we face.' An unbroken line of imperialist aggression is drawn up, from the slave trade to the contemporary Western human rights concern as a thin disguise for the plot to achieve 'peaceful evolution' in China. In the economic sphere the imperialists 'use "exchange", "help" and "technology transfer" to lure the socialist countries into privatization and marketization . . . '[47] Comments such as these appear to be actually directed towards an internal party policy debate in early 1991.

The overall gist of the 1991 Programme is to conjure up an inherently good Chinese essence challenged by evil outside forces. Resistance to those forces constitutes the crucial feature of Chinese identity in the modern and contemporary age. *Socialism* is the embodiment of anti-imperialist patriotism, and the serious problems presented in the chapter on population, resources, etc., are seen as entirely external to the socialist system. The feeling of encirclement experienced by the CCP leadership in the wake of Tiananmen is reflected in the treatment of the global situation. Not much is said about international socialist or Third World solidarity; China must fend for itself and build self-confidence on its independent power status: 'Socialist China stands firm as a rock in the world, and it increasingly has a decisive influence on international affairs.'[48] In sum, according to the Programme Chinese identity must rest on a trinity of *ancient civilization*, *anti-imperialist resistance*, and *great power status*.

What, then, constitutes the cultural core as defined under the heading of 'ancient civilization'? In Chapter 1 the following points are highlighted:

- the very long history of China, its splendid culture, and its contributions to global civilization;
- 'outstanding wisdom' in practical as well as spiritual matters;
- fruitful collaboration among the different nationalities of China: 'learning from each other, conducting exchange, amalgamation';
- a tradition of absorbing the valuable elements of foreign cultures.[49]

In the section dealing with the specific teaching plan, the first and third points in particular are elaborated in great detail. It is hardly surprising to find a long list of Chinese 'firsts' in the field of technological invention. However, turning to the field of cultural accomplishments, it is a bit more surprising to find a similar 'we were first' approach. The oracle book Yijing is acclaimed for its 'dialectics', and similarly the Taoist masters Laozi and Zhuangzi are credited with developing 'simple dialectics'. The Confucian philosopher Xunzi is seen as having attained a 'tendency towards materialism', which was later fully developed by the Han scholar Wang Chong. Kongzi (Confucius) himself is praised as an 'outstanding historian and chronicler'. These accomplishments were achieved 'centuries before the ancient Greeks and Indians', and in this way traditional culture is seen as providing yet another list of 'Chinese firsts' set to the tune of contemporary official ideology.

The approach of the 1991 Programme to China's historic cultural achievements in fact has a striking precedent in the *Guocui* (National Essence) movement associated with the journal *Guocui Xuebao* (Journal of National Essence), 1905–11. The *Guocui* movement, which included scholars such as Zhang Binglin, Liu Shipei, and Huang Jie, was an intermediate stage in the intellectual transition from the 1898 Reform generation to the 1919 May Fourth cultural iconoclasts; its purpose was to establish and promote an authentic Chinese identity in the face of growing Western influence. But as Ying-shih Yü argues, 'what they identified as 'China's "national essence" turned out to be, more often than not, basic cultural values of the West such as democracy, equality, liberty and human rights . . . [T]hey took these Western values as universal and insisted on their genesis in an early China completely independent of the West.'[50] The 1991 Programme has replicated this intellectual somersault, substituting Marxism–Leninism for democracy and human rights, and insisting on an independent origin of historical and dialectical materialism deep in the womb of Chinese cultural history.

The 1991 Programme was worked out at a time that also saw the appearance of 'new conservatism' on the ideological stage. There is a close connection between these two currents, and they may in fact be seen as branches of a single ideological project. According to Gu Xin and David Kelly, the term 'new conservatism' was aired for the first time at a December 1990 conference on 'China's Traditional Culture and Socialist Modernization' by the Shanghai scholar Xiao Gongqin. Xiao's views were summed up at the conference in the following words:

Make use of a transitional authority with a modernizing orientation; make use of mediating traditional values to bring about the internal social change; when the success of this internal social change is assured, gradually introduce Western democratic institutions, and thus bring about a steady impetus towards modernization in Chinese society.[51]

'New conservatism', a reworking of the late 1980s 'new authoritarianism', is closely associated with the so-called Princelings' Party, i.e. the sons and daughters of party gerontocrats, who share a common concern regarding how to maintain power and party legitimacy after the passing away of the old revolutionaries. In August 1991, just after the attempted coup in the former Soviet Union, an internal document was produced by the Ideological and Theoretical Board of *China Youth Daily*.[52] The document, entitled 'Realistic Responses and Strategic Options for China after the Soviet Coup', was reportedly commissioned by Chen Yuan (son of Chen Yun) and Deng Yingtao. The document, following Gu Xin and Kelly, suggests that 'emphasizing China's size, poverty, overpopulation, relative lack of resources, its history of division and foreign humiliation in the last century is "the most effective means of persuading the people at present" '.[53] The parallels between the 1991 Programme and the 'new conservative' position are striking, and one might see Jiang Zemin's embrace in 1991 of cultural nationalism as an attempt to co-opt the 'new conservatives'.

The political and ideological climate in China changed in 1992, however, starting with Deng Xiaoping's southern inspection tour in early 1992, and the renewed 'reform and opening' drive. Furthermore, the Princelings' Party suffered a major political defeat in connection with the 14th National Congress of the CCP in October 1992. This also changed the tone of the official 'national culture' discourse. A faint echo of the efforts of 1989–91 to enlist traditional culture in the struggle to regain legitimacy can be found in Jiang Zemin's report to the 14th Congress, in the remark that 'w[e] should maintain and enrich the fine traditions of the Chinese nation'.[54] Occasional quotations from the Confucian classics in recent public speeches by Jiang Zemin have also been noted.[55] But generally speaking, references to traditional culture in official statements have become less conspicuous since 1991. Recent articles in the party theoretical organ *Qiushi* (Seeking Truth) have essentially returned to the 1980s position on the primacy of science and modernization and the concomitant need to maintain a critical attitude towards traditional culture.[56] A 1994 article in *Qiushi* dealing with the relationship between tradition and modernization warns:

While we oppose national nihilism, we also oppose the tendency indiscriminately to accept ancient culture without asking about the needs of the socialist era—for example, to exaggerate irresponsibly and indiscriminately the historical position and contemporary significance of Confucianism, or even to the extent of proposing 'the resurrection of new Confucianism', attempting to place Confucianism once again in a leading position in contemporary Chinese culture. In the theatres, some plays that propagate feudalistic ideology are performed unmodified. In cultural activities, a 'fever for imitating the old' is currently on the rise; some tourist spots and public places display objects that possess an aura of feudal superstition, parading them as splendid cultural objects. All these things are unacceptable.[57]

Judging from a superficial glance at the academic debate in other journals since 1991, it would similarly appear that the general profile of the 1980s culture debate has been restored, albeit without the enthusiasm and fervour of that time.

In the short period of 1989–91, official attempts to enlist the support of 'national culture' never moved beyond the very formalistic approach of the 1991 Programme. 'Traditional culture' is directly translated into 'national pride' and is never allowed a voice of its own. The significance of this flirtation with traditional culture is the fact that the CCP leadership, despite obvious pressures to develop themes related to traditional culture more fully, actually resisted the temptation. Even under the present economic circumstances of 'anything goes', the ideological machine of the CCP maintains a kind of discipline that is dictated by deep-rooted historical blockages.

A Century of Frustrations

The many problems and obstacles involved in the contemporary Chinese search for an identity and a 'national culture' are in fact only the most recent expression of a century-old endeavour riddled with frustrations. The late nineteenth-century slogan, 'Chinese substance—Western application' (*Zhongti Xiyong*) associated with the late Qing modernization-oriented General-Governor Zhang Zhidong is a clear programmatic expression of the need for a 'national culture' project; but the bureaucratic Yangwu modernization movement of the late Qing dynasty had little to offer in terms of a creative adaptation of the 'substance'. Considerably more creativity was at work in Kang Youwei's reinterpretation of Confucianism in the 1890, particularly his 'Confucius as a reformer' (*Kongzi gai zhi kao*) from 1897. But the political defeat of the 1898 Reform Movement and the subsequent rise of new social forces as well as the emergence of radical nationalism in the early twentieth century showed that the task of reformulating 'national culture' had already left the hands of the classical scholar élite. An intermediate position between the classical scholastic approach to national culture and modern nationalism was manifest in the early twentieth-century *Guocui* movement, as mentioned above.

Chiang Kai-shek's 'New Life Movement' in the mid-1930s, with its curious mixture of Confucian and Christian values as well as elements of fascist ideology, is another example of a short-lived 'national culture' project. The movement had a measure of academic support in the *benwei* (Chinese uniqueness) school of thought. In 1934 a number of pro-traditionalist scholars organized the 'Association for Chinese Cultural Construction', and their main manifesto was published in January 1935. The ensuing academic debate lasted into 1936, but the efforts of the *benwei* group to 'roll back' the effects of the May Fourth movement and restore faith in traditional Chinese culture never achieved a breakthrough in intellectual circles.[58] The educational work of Liang Shuming in the 1930s could be seen as the embodiment of a sincere and practical attempt to construct 'national culture' from below, but all such efforts were frustrated by the difficulties of implementation.

Mao Zedong's 'sinification of Marxism' in the Yan'an era touched on the issue of national culture, albeit in a fairly general way:

Foreign stereotypes must be abolished; there must be less singing of empty, abstract tunes, and dogmatism must be laid to rest; they must be replaced by the fresh, lively Chinese style and spirit which the common people of China love.[59]

Throughout Mao's political life he saw the culture of the masses as the genuine level of cultural creativity, which had been infiltrated and polluted, however, by the reactionary features of gentry-class Confucian culture. In this perspective, 'revolution' in the cultural sphere meant digging deep for the true mass culture and liberating it from its feudal fetters. To quote Mao's 1942 speech at the Yan'an Forum on Literature and Art:

The life of the people is always a mine of the raw materials for literature and art, materials in their natural form, materials that are crude, but most vital, rich and fundamental; they make all literature and art seem pallid by comparison; they provide literature and art with an inexhaustible source, their only source.[60]

Maoist notions of mass culture influenced CCP policy in varying degrees. They were particularly influential in the Yan'an period and in the movement for promoting the 'art of the masses' in the late 1950s. The farcical degeneration of this approach during the Cultural Revolution once again demonstrated the difficulty of 'separating the dross from the essence', and the ultimate failure of Maoist cultural policies has in itself contributed to the obstacles surrounding the 'national culture' project in contemporary China.

To summarize these obstacles, the problem of 'the people' is obvious. *Which* people? In Chinese political jargon, the word *renmin* (the people) has political connotations as a concept covering loyal and 'true' citizens in contrast to 'counter-revolutionaries'. The concept *Zhonghua minzu* (the nationalities of China) is often used to invoke a sense of unity among the national groups and to counter *Dahanzhuyi* ('Great Han-ism' or Han chauvinism) as well as 'separatism' among national minorities. Contemporary Western scholarship has argued that ethnicity is itself a cultural construct,[61] but ethnic conflict is nevertheless also a reality in China. For political reasons ethnic nationalism must necessarily be restricted, although solidarity with the *tongbao* and the overseas ('ethnic') Chinese confuses the picture. The CCP must try to maintain a delicate balance in this matter.

'Language', like 'the people', is another classical ingredient in the repertoire of 'national culture'. Once again China is a complicated case. Even within the dominant Han Chinese language the official language of *putonghua* (the common language) is not an obvious equivalent to the 'mother tongue' of romantic European cultural nationalism. Only written Chinese is the shared language, whereas oral Chinese is divided between several major regionalects and dozens of local dialects.

The official ideology of China, i.e. Marxism–Leninism–'Mao Zedong Thought', constitutes yet another obstacle to a 'national culture' approach. A key concept of Marxist–Maoist theorizing during the last fifty years is that of *correspondence*. Do production relations correspond to the level of the productive forces, and how does the superstructure correspond to the economic base? In the terminology of correspondence, traditional culture is nothing but a burden left over from the past, and creative 'cultural engineering' thus contradicts the very core of the official ideology.

In a wider perspective, the 'battle against traditional culture' has been the common unifying platform of progressive Chinese intellectuals since the May Fourth movement of 1919. After 1949 no major intellectual current has successfully challenged this platform, and, as the events of the 1980s have demonstrated, the CCP finds itself far more vulnerable to charges of 'abandoning the May Fourth ideals' than of the opposite. In this sense, the May Fourth spirit still plays a decisive role, even within the CCP élite. The temptation to drum up a state-sponsored 'national culture' is obvious, but the counterforces have the upper hand, at least in the foreseeable future.

Concluding Remarks

It has been argued in this essay that contemporary Chinese regime rhetoric concerning the value of traditional culture is only superficial and instrumental. The official promotion of traditional culture in no way amounts to an attempt at 're-Confucianization' but serves, in Børge Bakken's words, 'as a direct instrument of reform and modernization'.[62] In this perspective there is a strong affinity between the official Chinese position regarding traditional values and the new Confucian rhetoric of Singapore's Lee Kuan-yew and other Southeast Asian political leaders. In a thought-provoking essay, Jonathan Friedman has argued that

In those areas of the East characterized by rapid economic growth there are new forms of modernism. These have to be seen in relation to the declining dominance of the West in order to understand the difference between their particularistic cultural character and the universalistic evolutionism they embody. On the one hand they have emphasized the moral core of the Confucian order, expressed in neo-Confucianism ['new Confucianism' might be a better term to avoid confusion with the Neo-Confucianism of Song China—SC], an order that stresses the ethics of the bureaucratic public sphere, an abstract morality, but one extracted from the ideals of the family and elevated to a set of generalized social principles . . . In this sense, it might be said that neo-Confucianism appears as a cultural movement, and is a cultural movement from the point of view of the declining hegemony, but in the same sense that Renaissance Europe was a cultural movement with respect to the declining centres of the East, and in the sense that Englishness arose as a particular cult of modernity in opposition to the rest of the world, not least the rest of Europe. But in such terms, it belongs to the family of modernist cosmologies.[63]

The crucial difference between PRC official views regarding traditional values and those of for example Lee Kuan-yew is to be found in the many constraints surrounding PRC ideological discourse. As argued above, there are a number of significant obstacles to a more resounding endorsement of 'tradition', some of which are related to the structure of Chinese society, others to the political history of China in the twentieth century. These obstacles have dictated official China's reluctant approach to traditional culture during the 1980s and early 1990s. It is highly ironic that the initial introduction of 'new Confucianism' into Chinese academic circles in the 1980s to a large extent appears to have been the result of a *defensive* move intended to blunt the perceived danger of China being flooded by 'new Confucian' ideas from abroad. In a recent article by Lin Tongqi, Henry Rosemont Jr, and Roger T. Ames, it is argued that '[p]aradoxically enough, this spread of *xinrujia* [new Confucianism] has been fostered less by its own "landing" on the mainland than by a government-sponsored research project set up to meet the challenge of the "landing". This large-scale project was established in late 1986 with the expressed purpose of conducting a "critical study" of *xinrujia* as an intellectual force alien to Marxism.'[64] The end result has been a fluctuating semi-endorsement of traditional culture, and only in a high abstract sense, which sees pride in China's long cultural tradition as the main message.

The abstract nature of cultural-nationalist discourse in China today is an indication of yet another frustration in the century-old struggle to come to terms with 'tradition'. Just as the iconoclasts, from the Taipings to the May Fourth movement, from Mao's Red Guards to Liu Xiaobo, have shared the common problem of how to identify and attack the vital nerves of 'tradition', so the proponents of 'dialogue with tradition' have all shared the problem of identifying 'the essence', 'the positive factors', or 'the elements compatible with modernization', as the desired but elusive object is variously termed. In this broad perspective, most Chinese debaters of 'national culture' actually have a lot in common. The idea of re-interpreting the Chinese classics with the aim of making them compatible with democracy and science was shared by Kang Youwei and the *Guocui* movement. In Mao Zedong's Yan'an discourse, popular peasant culture was described as the healthy marrow of a Chinese tradition waiting to be liberated from the dead wood of gentry culture. For Liu Zaifu as well as Li Zehou, the issue is how to identify those elements (or 'mechanisms') of tradition that are compatible with or may even promote modernization. Contemporary official discourse never forgets to emphasize a selective and critical approach to 'tradition'. But throughout, all debaters share a fuzziness regarding the specific content of the 'positive elements'. Perhaps the conclusion is simple: the discourse is the message!

NOTES

1. I should like to express my thanks to Graham Young, University of New England, Australia, for his comments on the draft of this essay.
2. Li Ruihuan, 'National Culture Important for Literature to Flourish', *Beijing Review*, 33:9 (1990), 20.
3. 'Japan vs. China: Asia's Power Struggle', *Newsweek* (15 November 1993), 10–23. For a more recent example of this concern, see Nayan Chanda and Karl Huus, 'China: The New Nationalism', *Far Eastern Economic Review* (9 November 1995), 20–6.
4. Kosaku Yoshino, *Cultural Nationalism in Contemporary Japan* (London: Routledge, 1992), 1.
5. Lowell Dittmer and Samuel S. Kim (eds.), *China's Quest for National Identity* (Ithaca, NY: Cornell University Press, 1993), 228.
6. A superb treatment of this dimension can be found in Børge Bakken, 'The Exemplary Society: Human Improvement, Social Control and the Dangers of Modernity in China' (Ph.D. dissertation University of Oslo, 1994), esp. 5–14.
7. e.g. James L. Watson's concluding remarks in his 1992 essay on 'The Regeneration of Chinese Cultural Identity in the Post-Mao Era': 'Henceforth, the Communist Party intended to control the redefinition of Chinese cultural identity. This was too important a matter to be left to "unreliable" intellectuals and ordinary people. Thus . . . the party propaganda apparatus appeared to be gearing up for yet another attempt to dominate the ongoing debate regarding the future of "Chineseness".' See James L. Watson, 'The Renegotiation of Chinese Cultural Identity in the Post-Mao Era', in Jeffrey Wasserstrom and Elizabeth Perry (eds.), *Popular Protest and Political Culture in Modern China* (Boulder, Colo.: Westview Press, 1992), 80–1.
8. Benedict Anderson, *Imagined Communities: Reflections on the Origin and Spread of Nationalism* (London: Verso, 1983).
9. E. J. Hobsbawm and T. Ranger (eds.), *The Invention of Tradition* (Cambridge: Cambridge University, 1983).
10. R. G. Fox, 'Introduction', in R. G. Fox (ed.), *Nationalist Ideologies and the Production of National Culture* (Washington: American Anthropological Association, 1990), 10.

11. Ernest Gellner, *Culture, Identity and Politics* (Cambridge: Cambridge University, 1987).

12. Anthony Smith, *The Ethnic Origins of Nations* (Oxford: Blackwell, 1986).

13. James Townsend, 'Chinese Nationalism', *Australian Journal of Chinese Affairs*, 27 (1992), 97–130.

14. ibid. 102.

15. ibid. 123–4.

16. ibid. 128.

17. ibid. 130.

18. Ann Anagnost, 'Cultural Nationalism and Chinese Modernity', in Harumi Befu (ed.), *Cultural Nationalism in East Asia: Representation and Identity* (Berkeley: Institute of East Asian Studies, University of Berkeley, 1993), 67–8.

19. Fox, 'Introduction', 3.

20. Dittmer and Kim, *China's Quest*.

21. ibid. 30

22. ibid.

23. ibid.

24. Arjun Appadurai, 'Disjuncture and Difference in the Global Cultural Economy', in Mike Featherstone (ed.), *Global Culture: Nationalism, Globalization and Modernity* (London: Sage, 1990), 301.

25. Arthur Waldron, 'Representing China: The Great Wall and Cultural Nationalism in the Twentieth Century', in Befu, *Cultural Nationalism*, 36–60.

26. Helen F. Siu, 'Cultural Identity and the Politics of Difference', *Dædalus* (Spring 1993), 27.

27. Zhao Ziyang, 'Advance along the Road of Socialism with Chinese Characteristics', *Beijing Review*, 30 (9–15 November 1987), iv.

28. 'Resolution of the Central Committee of the Communist Party of China on the Guiding Principles for Building a Socialist Society with an Advanced Culture and Ideology', *Beijing Review*, 29 (6 October 1986), iii.

29. ibid. iv–v.

30. See Tongqi Lin, 'A Search for China's Soul', *Dædalus* (Spring 1993), 183.

31. Herman Kahn, *World Economic Development: 1979 and Beyond* (London: Croom Helm, 1979).

32. Liu Zaifu and Lin Gang, *Chuantong yu Zhongguo ren* (Tradition and the Chinese) (Beijing, 1987).

33. ibid. 385–8.

34. ibid. 388

35. Wang Meng, 'Wenhua chuantong yu wuwenhua de chuantong' (The Cultural Tradition and the Tradition of Non-Culture), *Dushu* (The Reader), 4 (1989), 58–81.

36. It should be noted in this context that Li Zehou was in fact the first PRC scholar to open the debate in the post-Mao era on the re-evaluation of Confucianism. His seminal article, 'The Re-evaluation of Confucius', written in 1978 and published in 1980, suggests a substratum of 'primitive democracy' in early *rujia* philosophy which was later eradicated by official state Confucianism. See Li Zehou, 'Kongzi zai pingjia' (A Re-evaluation of Confucius), *Shongguo Shehui Kexue* (Social Sciences in China), 2 (1980).

37. Lin Min, 'The Search for Modernity: Chinese Intellectual Discourse and Society, 1978–88: The Case of Li Zehou', *China Quarterly*, 132 (December 1992), 987.

38. Waldron, 'Representing China', 52.

39. W. L. Cong (interview), 'Su Xiaokang on his Film "River Elegy"', *China Information*, 4:3 (1989–90), 46–7.

40. Anagnost, ' Cultural Nationalism'.
41. Leo Ou-fan Lee, 'On the Margins of the Chinese Discourse: Some Personal Thoughts on the Cultural Meaning of the Periphery', *Dædalus* (Spring 1991), 210–11.
42. e.g. James L. Watson, 'The Renegotiation of Chinese Cultural Identity in the Post-Mao Era', in Wasserstrom and Perry, *Popular Protest*, 67–84; Helen F. Siu, 'Reconstituting Dowry and Brideprice in South China', in Deborah Davis and Stevan Harrell (eds.), *Chinese Families in the Post-Mao Era* (Berkeley: University of California Press, 1993), 165–88.
43. *Guangming ribao*, 8 October 1989.
44. Wang Renzhi, 'Opposition to Bourgeois Liberalization', *Beijing Review*, 33 (23–9 April 1990), 15.
45. 'Zhong-xiaoxue jiaqiang Zhongguo jinxiandaishi ji guoqing jiaoyu de zongti gangyao' (General Programme for Strengthening Education in Modern and Contemporary History and National Conditions), *Renmin Jiaoyu* (People's Education), 10 (1991), 2–24.
46. ibid. 15.
47. ibid. 22.
48. ibid. 15.
49. ibid. 8–9. The last two points would appear to contradict the notion of 'essence'.
50. Ying-shih Yü, 'The Radicalization of China in the Twentieth Century', *Dædalus* (Spring 1993), 130.
51. Quoted from Gu Xin and David Kelly, 'New Conservatism: Intermediate Ideology of a "New Elite" ', in David Goodman and Beverley Hooper (eds.), *China's Quiet Revolution: New Interactions between State and Society* (Melbourne: Longman, 1994), 223.
52. ibid. 219.
53. ibid. 225.
54. Jiang Zemin, 'Accelerating Reform and Opening-Up', *Beijing Review*, 35 (26 October–1 November 1992), 25.
55. *Far Eastern Economic Review* (22 May 1995), 36; (9 November 1995), 21.
56. e.g. a statement in the January 1993 issue of the authoritative journal *Qiushi*: 'To resist national nihilism in no way implies a wholesale affirmation of tradition': Zhou Zhiliang, 'Patriotism and Opening Up', *Qiushi*, 1 (1993), 31.
57. Xun Chunrong, 'Jianshe you Zhongguo tese de shehuizhuyi' (The Building of a Socialist Culture with Chinese Characteristics), *Qiushi* (Seeking Truth), 3 (1994), 26–32.
58. Chen Song, '30 niandai guanyu wenhua de zhenglun' (The Debate on the Issue of Culture in the 1930s), *Lishi Yanjiu*, 1 (1991), 65–77.
59. Mao Zedong, 'The Role of the Chinese Communist Party in the National War', in *Selected Works*, ii (Peking, 1965), 209–10.
60. Mao Zedong, 'Talks at the Yan'an Forum on Literature and Art', in *Selected Works*, iii.81.
61. e.g. Pamela Kyle Crossley, 'Thinking about Ethnicity in Early Modern China', *Late Imperial China*, 11:1 (1990), 1-35.
62. Bakken, 'The Exemplary Society', 9.
63. Jonathan Friedman, 'Narcissism, Roots and Postmodernity: The Construction of Selfhood in the Global Crisis', in Scott Lash and Jonathan Friedman (eds.), *Modernity and Identity* (Oxford: Blackwell, 1992), 356–7.
64. Lin Tongqi, Henry Rosemont, Jr, and Roger T. Ames, 'Chinese Philosophy: A Philosophical Essay on the "State of the Art" ', *Journal of Asian Studies*, 54:3 (1995), 735.

11

Fostering 'Love of Learning': Naxi Responses to Ethnic Images in Chinese State Education

Mette Halskov Hansen[1]

This paper, based on a local study, describes and analyses some of the ethnic images that national minorities are presented with in Chinese state education today. It goes on to discuss how Chinese minority education, as part of a modernizing and homogenizing process, has unintentionally caused members of the Naxi minority in Yunnan to strengthen their ethnic consciousness while enabling them to utilize this to their own potential political and economic advantage. Without running counter to the government's ideology of 'national unity', the Naxi in Lijiang have started to make use of their high level of education by providing alternative and supplementary education in Lijiang Naxi Autonomous County.[2]

In different periods of China's history, élites have attempted to promote Chinese education among the peoples who lived in the periphery of the Chinese state—peoples who were regarded as having less culture (*wenhua*) and being less civilized than the élites and even less than the peasants in central China. These former 'barbarians' and present national minorities have to different degrees been subjected to, and have often freely participated in, various forms of education that were intended to foster cultural homogeneity based upon the moral values of Confucianism, and (later) to implant in the students the ideological values of nationalism and communism. They have taken part in what Stevan Harrell has called China's 'civilizing projects', of which education certainly constitutes one of the most essential and powerful components.[3]

It is in the Communist era, especially, that specific measures have been taken to involve the various non-Han peoples in the building of the state via a strengthened emphasis on specific 'minority education' (*minzu jiaoyu*) as opposed to the 'regular education' (*zhenggui jiaoyu*) received by the Han and the more acculturated minorities. Ideally, minority education is expected to facilitate ethnic amalgamation (*ronghe*) and the unity of the nationalities (*minzu tuanjie*), mainly by allowing and encouraging bilingual education, and by setting up special boarding schools for minorities from poor, rural, underdeveloped areas.

The limited research that has so far been conducted into the implementation of the policy of minority education in different regions of China suggests marked local variations. A general trend has been to promote the establishment of bilingual education in regions where the Chinese language is used only to a very limited degree, or where the authorities have met local resistance to the standardized Chinese education. While bilingual education has been applied at different levels (and at different times) in for example Inner Mongolia, Tibet, Xinjiang, and Yanbian (among the Koreans), most of the smaller minorities living in the province of Yunnan have received no, or only few hours of, instruction in their own language, and examples of teaching materials incorporating local minority history and culture are few. Often it is local financial limitations and the local cadres' own attitudes towards bilingual education that determine whether or not some sort of special content of education in the minority regions is established.

Minority Education and the Drive towards Modernization and Integration in China since 1980

Education of minorities in the People's Republic is directed towards the fifty-five groups of people who have been officially categorized as 'national minorities' (*shaoshu minzu*). Based upon intensive fieldwork in the early 1950s and Stalin's criteria of a nation (common language, territory, economic life, and a common psychological makeup manifested in a common culture), the Chinese government decided that, although more than 400 different ethnic groups of people in the whole of China, and 260 groups in the province of Yunnan alone, wished to be acknowledged as distinctive national groups, only fifty-six groups in China are recognized today. Of these, the Han nationality (Hanzu) encompasses the vast majority of the Chinese people, i.e. 92 per cent.[5] Consequently, the official classification of people in the People's Republic often does not correspond to their subjective feelings of ethnicity. Groups of people may, and some in fact do, apply to be reclassified, but this is very difficult to achieve. For example, the Mosuo 'branch' of the Naxi minority (the Na or Nare) wish to be identified independently from their Naxi classification, although other Naxi generally insist that for historic reasons they all belong to one ethnic group. The official classification of each Chinese citizen probably supports the Naxi's (as well as many other national minorities') feelings of belonging to a distinctive group, of being different from the majority Han. Identities have been mapped and counted, and the relation between minorities and the majority has been firmly consolidated.[6]

On the basis of a very pessimistic conclusion about the general state of minority education in China, the Chinese Ministry of Education and the State Nationalities Affairs Commission suggested in October 1980 a renewal of political emphasis on the education of minority nationalities.[7] By this time, Chinese politicians and educators had realized that the People's Republic of China (PRC) had not accomplished the ambitious goals and expectations of the early 1950s concerning the education of national minorities. With some exceptions (mainly the Hui, Manchu, Koreans, and Russians), the level of school education among minorities was significantly lower than the national level, and their numbers of illiterate and semi-literate adults significantly higher; according to the Third Census of 1982, 59.4 per cent of the non-Han population in Yunnan were illiterate or semi-literate.[8]

The above mentioned document marked the start of new political efforts to strengthen and improve minority education through measures such as the re-establishment of a Department of Minority Education under the State Ministry of Education,[9] the reinstatement of political organs specifically concerned with minority education at all levels of the autonomous governments, and the increasing of finance earmarked to improve minority education. Since then, new goals and aims for minority education have been formulated at local levels. The government of Yunnan, for instance, decided in 1993 to strive to establish six years of compulsory education in *all* the minority areas in the province by the year 2000, and nine years in *70 per cent* of the minority areas. (The national goal is nine years by the year 2000.) In areas with a very low percentage of educated people (for instance Ninglang County) the aim is to establish four years of compulsory education by the end of 1995. In Lijiang Autonomous County, where six years of compulsory education has been achieved in most villages, the goal is to establish nine years of compulsory education by the end of 1997.[10]

Following the crack-down of the students' movement in 1989, more concern has been raised about the education of minorities in China's 136 border counties (twenty-six of which are in Yunnan province). Patriotic education is considered to be especially important in these areas where non-Han peoples have ethnic relations across the borders and often have a relatively short history of integration into the Chinese state. Furthermore, the border areas are still considered to be among the most backward (*luohou*) and underdeveloped in China. As early as 1931, the first decrees were made public in Yunnan accentuating the need to build up modern style Chinese education in the border and mountain areas inhabited by non-Han peoples, with the purpose of securing loyalty to the Chinese nation.[11]

Since the 1980s there has been widespread agreement in the government and the party on the overall principles behind the investment of money and human resources in minority education: (1) education is essential for modernizing the economy in the minority regions, which are among the poorest in China; (2) especially in border regions, the so-called 'patriotic education' (including a greater knowledge of Chinese language and history) is regarded as necessary to improve integration and stability; (3) more highly educated minority members are needed in the minority regions to work for the modernization and to function as mediators between the central government and the local people; and (4) education is regarded as an indispensable tool for eradicating presumed backward customs which are seen as obstructors of economic development. However in the local areas, cadres, teachers and educators continue to discuss the organization, form, and content of minority education, which is still often criticized for not adapting to local conditions and for reflecting discriminatory views of the Han as the 'older brother'. The most urgent problem for local governments is still the lack of steady and sufficient central financial support for the development of the education of the national minorities.

The curriculum, the length of study, and the choice of languages in school may to a certain degree be decided by the autonomous governments. However, whether or not a certain school teaches a minority language as a subject, uses it as the means of instruction, or incorporates local history into the curriculum is often arbitrarily determined by local demands, individual teachers' capacity and interests, financial possibilities, and, not least, local cadres' judgements on the need or desirability for specific considerations of minorities in education. Since the aim of Chinese education is to promote ethnic and national unity based upon a common Chinese language, common history, atheism, and nationalism, many Han Chinese cadres and teachers regard the extended use of minority languages in school as a potential threat to this goal of homogenization. Classes are conducted in minority languages mostly in schools where it is considered to be necessary in a transitional period until the members of the minority in question have learned sufficient Chinese.

Han Chinese cadres and teachers in minority areas often express their belief in the developing, civilizing effects of Chinese education based upon the Chinese language, history, and culture. As one government leader in Sipsong Panna Tai Autonomous Prefecture explained during an interview:

Experiences from some of the advanced nationalities in this province, such as the Baizu, and the situation among the Jinuozu and Hanizu in this prefecture, prove that if you let minority children study Chinese rather than their own language from the beginning it has great advantages for developing minority education and raises the quality of the *minzu* [*minzu suzhi*].

There is a myriad of local variants of government-sponsored minority education, but all share the common goal of spreading the knowledge of standard Chinese (*putonghua*), turning national identities towards an identity with the People's Republic, reducing religious influence, and educating loyal citizens. Thus, minority languages, history, culture, etc., are incorporated into education not for their own sake but rather to the degree to which they are: (1) considered necessary to prevent strong local dissatisfaction with education, and/or (2) considered necessary to facilitate the transition to a purely Chinese-based education. This also explains why Han children, though living in regions of Yunnan where members of minorities constitute the majority, are not expected to learn any minority language in school. In the words of one of the cadres at the Minority Education Department in Sipsong Panna, 'The Han children are certainly allowed to participate in the Tai lessons [one non-compulsory hour per week in the particular primary school we were talking about] . . . but they never do!' and, we could add, 'why should they?' when all minorities are expected to learn Chinese, the use of minority languages in administrations is mostly a pure formality, and the general status of the minority languages, customs, and religions of the Chinese society is low and most tend to be valued only for their exotic attractiveness, or for their role in constructing a contrasting image of a developed, modern, and 'normal,' Han majority.[12]

Minority Education for the Naxi

Primary and Secondary School Levels

The officially classified Naxi nationality (Naxi*zu*) consists of 277,750 people including the Nare (mostly called 'Mosuo' in Chinese), who live near Lake Lugu in Ninglang and prefer to distinguish themselves from the Naxi.[13] Except for approximately 4,000 Naxi residing in the provincial capital of Kunming, most Naxi live in Lijiang Naxi Autonomous County (established in 1961) in the north-western part of Yunnan.[14] The county capital is Lijiang Town (Dayanzhen), inhabited by more than 60,000 people of which more than half are Naxi.

The Naxi live in close contact with several other ethnic groups, including the Bai (Baizu), Nuosu (Yizu), Tuo'en (Yizu), Premi (Pumizu), Lisu

(Lisuzu), Tibetans (Zangzu), and of course the Han Chinese (Hanzu). Throughout history, the Naxi living on the Lijiang plain in particular have been strongly influenced by Tibetan and Chinese culture and social organization. The town of Lijiang was situated on the important trade route between South China and Tibet, and the ruling Naxi Mu lineage was very open towards incoming Han craftsmen, artisans, and scholars. When the Qing Empire in 1723 took over direct control in Lijiang (*gaitu guiliu*) and deposed the local hereditary Naxi chief (the *tusi*), contacts with the Han Chinese accelerated and a number of new Confucian schools (academies, charity, and private schools) were started up in what was then Lijiang Prefecture (Lijiang Fu).

Although Confucian education among the Naxi in Lijiang was received mainly by the male relatives of the Mu family and other well-off families in Lijiang Town, literacy and school attendance was probably similar to that of many rural areas in central China. The teachers in the local Confucian private schools were themselves Naxi, and they enjoyed a high status in the local community. When the first modern schools were introduced in Lijiang in the early twentieth century, the Naxi population in Lijiang Town was already accustomed to Chinese Confucian education which they had adapted as their own. Many Naxi participated in the transformation of the traditional Confucian education into an education based upon the study of modern subjects and the propagation of nationalism, and the proportion of Naxi teachers and educational leaders in Lijiang has steadily increased ever since.

The Naxi have their own language and three written scripts. The most famous one is the dongba[15] script, a pictographic script developed and used by the Naxi ritual specialists, also called the dongba, for recording rituals and legends. The dongba script has more than 6,000 characters, most of which are pictographic symbols. There exist approximately 20,000 dongba scriptures, of which almost half are found in foreign collections and museums. The Naxi ritual specialists or dongba performed various rituals in connection with such occurrences as death and illness, assisting people in exorcising evil spirits. The second Naxi script, usually called the *geba* script, is a syllabic phonetic script which was never widely known. Both scripts were used exclusively among dongba and neither was standardized.

The third script is a romanized Naxi script which Chinese linguists in cooperation with intellectual Naxi developed in the 1950s. In 1951 a national committee was set up to suggest guidelines for the development of written languages for the national minorities. Thirty-two minority languages were considered, and after years of extensive research a plan was put forward in 1958 to create eighteen scripts for twelve different *minzu*.

Because the ordinary Naxi had never used the dongba script, the Naxi nationality was chosen as one of the ten groups to be given a new script.[16] However, this script has never gained widespread influence among the Naxi and has mainly been taught in adult literacy campaigns, and in a few schools in rural areas where the Naxi have little knowledge of Chinese.

The Naxi in Lijiang have a relatively high number of intellectuals, cadres, teachers, and graduates beyond the level of junior secondary school, and quite a few possess influential posts in the county, prefecture, and provincial governments. Moreover, some of the Naxi urbanized intellectuals in Kunming in 1986 established a Society of Naxi Culture (Naxi Wenhua Xuehui) in order to promote Naxi culture, increase Naxi research, and improve chances for extending their own political and economic influence in the Naxi areas. In spite of their small number, the Naxi constitute a very visible minority in the political and cultural life of Yunnan.

In Lijiang County national minorities make up 82 per cent, and the Naxi 58 per cent, of the whole population. Therefore many educators say that in Lijiang 'All education is minority education.' Lijiang Nationalities Secondary School (Lijiang Xian Minzu Zhongxue) is not reserved for non-Han *minzu*, but is for all *minzu* from the poorest, remotest areas with the fewest secondary school graduates. Since 1987 it has enrolled students for three years of junior secondary education, and like all nationalities' secondary schools it is a boarding school.

It is much more difficult to get into the Lijiang Nationalities Secondary School than into a regular junior secondary school, though special consideration is given to about twenty-five students each year from townships in which only very few primary school graduates are able to continue into junior secondary school. (Naxizu, Hanzu, and Baizu do not receive extra points.) Generally students need about 142 points to get into the school, compared with 90 points for the regular junior secondary schools. The school is very popular because students get 23 yuan in support every month from the government; also it has strict regulations concerning the students' spare-time activities, and students do not have to cook for themselves. Most importantly, it has a relatively high proportion of graduates continuing into senior secondary school or specialized secondary school (*zhongzhuan xuexiao*); therefore each year a number of parents attempt (and many manage) to enrol their children through the 'back door'.

For the poorest parents it is a heavy economic burden to have a child in the Lijiang Nationalities Secondary School because a student needs a minimum of 100 yuan per month for living expenses and, as in other schools, has to pay for books. Each class in the school has a small piece of land that it may cultivate to support poorer students. The Naxi constitute the largest group of students at the school with almost 60 per cent, and twenty out of twenty-three teachers are Naxi. Boys make up the vast majority of students with as much as 74.5 per cent between 1985 and 1991. This probably reflects the fact that most villagers of all ethnic groups in Lijiang prefer a son to get an education, not least when they can afford to support only one student in the family.

Two other secondary schools in Lijiang arrange special nationalities classes (*minzu ban*). One of these, the Lijiang First Secondary School, is exceptional because its nationalities classes are reserved for the students with the *highest* scores in the junior and senior secondary school examinations rather than for students from poor areas with few graduates, which is otherwise common practice in nationalities schools and classes. Students (including Hanzu) need 160 points to enrol in its junior *minzu ban* (compared with 90 points in a regular junior secondary school) and 470 points for its senior *minzu ban* (compared with 430 in a regular senior secondary school). In fact, students who get into the *minzu ban* at the Lijiang First Secondary School have scored higher than what is required to get into a specialized secondary school (*zhongzhuan xuexiao*), even though the latter are generally the most prestigious and popular secondary schools because graduates are guaranteed a job. Some students can get up to 30 extra points towards the entrance requirement for the *minzu ban* if they come from areas without a senior secondary school, and again, some manage to enrol through the 'back door'.

The purpose of the *minzu ban* is 'to educate specially clever minority students', and the students in these classes get the best teachers and the most extra-curricular support. According to the administration of the Lijiang First Secondary School, approximately 80 per cent of students continue into tertiary education. Therefore, it is considered very prestigious to get into the *minzu ban*, and students from the regular secondary school classes have given it the nickname of '*guizu ban*', 'aristocracy class'. The majority of students in the *minzu ban* are Naxi, especially from Lijiang Town or Shigu, where the influence of Chinese language is strongest and students have some of the best possibilities for school education.

The *minzu ban* at Lijiang First Secondary School are even more prestigious than the regular classes at the provincial keypoint school, the Lijiang Prefecture Secondary School, although the latter school has the best facilities, and financial support from the provincial government and private sponsors. Like the other major secondary schools, the Lijiang Prefecture Secondary School is situated in the capital of Lijiang County. It too arranges special *minzu ban*, but these recruit minority students from the poorest and least developed townships of the four counties in Lijiang

Prefecture.[17] The Lisuzu, Mosuo,[18] and Yizu get extra points to get into this senior secondary school class, from which most graduates return as cadres to their own townships, because only 15–20 per cent of them pass the university entrance examination.

Tertiary-Level Education in Institutes of Nationalities

The only institution at the tertiary level in Yunnan specifically designed and reserved for education of national minorities is the Yunnan Institute of the Nationalities (YIN) in Kunming, one of thirteen nationalities institutes in China.[19]

When this institute was founded in 1951, its main purpose was to train political cadres from among the people living in the periphery of the People's Republic who would then be able to implement the policy of the Chinese Communist Party (CCP) in the newly created autonomous regions in Yunnan. Thus, the content of education was centred on teaching 'socialism', 'patriotism', 'unity of the nationalities', 'CCP minority policy', and the Chinese language.[20] Students were recruited among local religious leaders, local aristocracy, and minority students from secondary schools. Later, in the 1950s and early 1960s, 'culture classes' (*wenhua ban*) started to train 'cultural workers', who were supposed to improve the level of the presumed backward cultures of the minorities and to function as minority teachers and translators. Classes to teach selected minority languages were also started.

After a period of severe criticism, periodical disruptions of education, and one-sided emphasis on political training during the Cultural Revolution, all classes and departments were restarted at the YIN in 1976, and since 1977 enrolment has been determined basically by examination results. In 1979 the enrolment of students was integrated into the national common examination, and education became oriented towards the demands of the new modernization policy. This meant that common university subjects became relatively more important than the short cadre-training courses.

At present, the Institute organizes short-term training courses for locally employed cadres, preparation courses for the university exam, senior secondary school courses, and specialized courses in common university subjects. In addition, the Department of Minority Languages (Minzu Yuwen Xi) educates teachers and translators in the 'Xishuangbanna-Dai', 'Dehong-Dai', Jingpo, Lisu, Lahu, Yi, and Wa languages. Some Naxi, Tibetans, and Hani are currently urging the authorities to set up courses in their languages, but as yet there are no concrete plains to do so. The History and Anthropology Departments at the institute include the history of minority regions in their curriculum, and there is a special Minority Research Department. In a recent development, students who pay for themselves are permitted to take short university courses without the right to be assigned a job (*fenpei*) after graduation. In 1996 a new Department for 'Minority Art', specializing in minority dances and painting (*minzu yishu xi*), began enrolling students.

Students, and many teachers as well, tend to regard the Institute's technical departments as the 'strong' ones, with the minority language courses in particular being not highly rated. One teacher of 'minority psychology' (*minzu xinlixue*) explained that 'The students with the lowest level of education [*wenhua shuiping dī*] are the Wa, Jingpo, Lahu, Lisu, and Nu, and therefore most of them study minority languages.' Many students in the Language Department have not been accepted for a university course on the basis of their examination results, but instead have been chosen and sponsored (*baosong*) by a senior secondary school or a special or technical school (*zhongzhuan*), to which they are expected to return after graduation. Most of the students in this department are painfully aware that their specialization is regarded as an inferior study in an inferior university, and it is extremely difficult for them to find jobs upon leaving the university, other than those they are allocated.

Since the Institute began to enrol students in accordance with their examination results, special measures have been taken to ensure that all minority groups are represented. At present the rules are confusing, and often individual judgement determines whether or not a student is accepted. The maximum score that can be achieved in the unified university entrance examination is 600 points; in 1994 a student needed 430 points to get access to the YIN as opposed to 480 points to enter a key-point university such as Yunnan University. Generally speaking, minority students get 10 to 30 extra points depending on their household registration (*hukou*). Baizu, Naxizu, Yizu, and Huizu do not get extra points if they are from a city, e.g. Lijiang Town, but they normally get 10 extra points if they are from a border region or have a peasant household registration. Minority people residing in the provincial capital of Kunming get extra points only if they belong to minorities that have very few educated members. Normally the Nationalities Affairs Commission (Minzu Shiwu Weiyuanhui) accepts a maximum of 5 per cent of Han students from poor border areas. For the 'preparation class' (*yuke bu*), where students study for one or two years before they try once again to pass the normal entrance examination, students may be allocated between 30 and 100 extra points. In all higher education applications, a member of a national minority is given preference if he or she has scored equal marks to a Han. Today approximately 95 per cent of the students and 33 per cent of the staff at

YIN belong to national minorities. Compared with their total number in Yunnan, the Huizu, Baizu, and Naxizu are best represented at the Institute and many Naxi study in the 'hard' high-status departments.

There is a very unequal distribution of the different minorities in higher education in general in Yunnan (and indeed in the rest of the country). According to one source, 11 per cent of all 3,519 minority students who passed the entrance examination for tertiary education in Yunnan in 1985 (including the special minority preparation class in Yunnan University) were Naxi.[21] This is a rather high number considering that the Naxi constitute only about 2 per cent of the minority population in Yunnan. In 1990, 20 per cent of all students in higher education in Yunnan belonged to minorities.[22] The relatively high proportion over the years of Baizu, Huizu, and Naxizu students in higher education is explained by Chinese researchers mainly as a reflection of their long history of contacts with central China, and by the early establishment of Confucian and later modern Chinese schools in their areas. Most certainly, the widespread or exclusive use of the Chinese language among the Bai and the Hui respectively have helped them to be relatively successful within the Chinese school system. Unsurprisingly, the majority of Naxi students come from the capital of Lijiang County, which is most influenced by Han Chinese and has the best secondary school in the area in terms of preparation for further studies.

The system of job assignment (*fenpei zhidu*) for the graduates is an important tool in realizing the political purpose of the institute. The idea behind the special education for minority people is that graduates should return to their local areas as transmitters of official government policy, as competent Communist cadres capable of playing the role as the indispensable link between the central government and the local minority population. Therefore the guiding principle is still that 'where they come from they should return to' (*na lai na qu*), and the majority of graduates are still sent back to their native places, with or without their own approval. This has generated a growing dissatisfaction among students, and last year the Yunnan government decided to release graduates from the obligation to be sent back if they paid 4,000 yuan for a regular course (*benke*) or 3,000 yuan for a short-term course (*zhuanke*).[23]

Pu Linlin estimates that as many as 92 per cent of students at the Central Institute of the Nationalities in Beijing in 1991 wished to stay in the capital after graduation, and about one third of the students at YIN wanted to stay in Kunming.[24] This tendency is obviously of concern to many teachers and political authorities in Yunnan, who need the minority graduates as a link between the local minority population and the central government, and to assist in the modernization programmes in these areas. Consequently, students are often criticized for being more concerned about their own individual aspirations than about the common good. Clearly, the problem for the political authorities and many educators alike is how to solve the dilemma of teaching minority students to dissociate themselves from their parents' and grandparents' world view, religion, customs, etc., while at the same time convincing them of the need to return as civilizers of these same 'backward' customs.

The students of YIN may expect other problems after graduation. Their education is very often regarded as second-rate and quite often units are not interested in employing them. They are turned down on grounds that they are less qualified than other university graduates or have inadequate knowledge of the Chinese language. According to Pu, the proportions of graduates who had to be reassigned jobs a second time were 85.2 per cent in 1989 and 71.5 per cent in 1990.[25] Students themselves are aware of this, and many criticize the teaching at YIN for being of a lower standard than at the Yunnan University. Some teachers at YIN expressed concern that the minorities were not sufficiently motivated for studying; they were too 'wild' and were not respectful enough towards the authorities. 'Especially until a few years ago, there was a lot of fighting and drinking, and uncivilized students who were not accustomed to life here in the city were not motivated for studying.'

Teaching Ethnic Categories and Social Evolution

Closely related to the classification of all people of China into different *minzu* in the 1950s was the political aim of determining the stage of development of each group. This was required in order for the party to decide how and when to implement land reform in the minority areas—how to 'salvage the backward', as the slogan of the party went.[26] Engels's and Morgan's theories of a social evolution were applied to identify living non-Han peoples with what was described as ancient forms of society; and conversely, the different stages of evolution that were determined for the minorities served to prove the very correctness of their theories.[27]

Through their education, minorities in China are confronted with the state-defined ethnic categories and the objectified theories of social evolution. Students learn, for instance, that they are members of a definite *minzu*, that by definition they are distinct and different from the Han and the other nationalities, and that all *minzu* are first and foremost Chinese citizens in a 'unitary multi-ethnic country' (*tongyi de duo minzu guojia*) and members of the 'Chinese nationality', the *Zhonghua minzu*. They also often come to realize that the very reason why they are enrolled in higher education is because of their belonging to a national minority.

Students in regular secondary schools tend to believe that, although they themselves do not learn anything specifically about the history of their own area and their own nationality, or even study their own language, the students in the nationalities schools (*minzu xuexiao*) do learn about these things. However, this is rarely the case. The idea behind the nationalities schools from primary to tertiary level is to recruit minority students, from rural areas in particular, and to provide them with boarding facilities in order to improve their educational opportunities and prevent them from wasting time working at home and practising their religions. Among educators and cadres, I have often heard the boarding school system being praised for its ability to 'change students' traditional way of thinking' (*chuangtong sixiang*) by changing their surroundings. In Yunnan Province only a few classes in some of the teacher training schools offer bilingual education at a secondary level; all the regular and nationalities secondary schools follow the common standardized Chinese teaching material.

In primary and secondary schools all over Yunnan, a short course of Yunnan history might be included as a supplementary part of the curriculum. The two brief volumes of *Yunnan History* (*Yunnan lishi* for the regular secondary schools and *Yunnan difang shi* for the teacher training schools) were edited by the Provincial Education Department in 1990 after the 1989 massacre in Beijing, which led the central government to issue demands for strengthened focus on nationalism in education. The government's basic idea behind the support of more local teaching material is that 'love of one's local native area' should be explicitly put into a close relationship with broader nationalist feelings. To promote 'love of the country and the party', students today have to learn to 'love their native place' as an inseparable part of the Chinese state represented by the Communist Party.

To this end, the Lijiang government is currently preparing a collection of articles about Lijiang history, cultural relics, nature, the Red Army in Lijiang, famous local people, etc. Within the next few years this volume will probably become teaching material in primary and secondary schools in Lijiang County. The present draft of this material consists of a compilation of brief papers about a variety of subjects, and the only *minzu* that is described in more detail is the Naxi: there are small sections about dongba, Naxi music, and famous Naxi scholars, authors etc., while the other *minzu* in Lijiang are mentioned a few times only briefly.[28] Many Naxi teachers today complain that they would like to teach students about Naxi history even though it is not included in the curriculum, but, since they themselves have never learned anything about it in school, they find it impossible. The intellectual Naxi élite in Lijiang are very influential, and the teaching materials they succeed in eventually putting together are likely to be widely accepted among teachers at all levels.

One of the important purposes of teaching Yunnan history is to transmit the message that Yunnan, with all its inhabitants, has been an inseparable part of the Chinese empire for two thousand years. In this way, the government hopes to create among minority students a strong sense of belonging to the modern Chinese communist state and of being an historical part of the Chinese nation. The introduction to one of the history books, here quoted in full, clearly illustrates the importance of this purpose:

Yunnan is an inseparable part of China. Yunnan local history is an organic part of China's history. Yunnan is a place of the origin of mankind. On this piece of land man has lived and laboured since ancient times, opened up land, created civilization and made history with his own hands.

Since Qin established a fully unified centralized state power more than two thousand years ago, Yunnan has been an administrative unit in China. First it was called a county, then a prefecture, and then the Yuan Dynasty established Yunnan Province. The political connections between Yunnan and China in dynastic history have varied, in that sometimes Yunnan was directly ruled by the Empire, while at other times rule was indirect. However, in spite of different kinds of rule, Yunnan has always been an inseparable part of China.

The great People's Republic is a unified multi-ethnic country. Today all minority nationalities within the borders of China are members of the Chinese nation (*Zhonghua minzu*). Yunnan is the province in our country which is inhabited by the largest number of nationalities. It is a miniature of our multi-ethnic fatherland. Almost all forefathers of each nationality can be traced back to the times before Qin. They all have a very long history.

The purpose of studying Yunnan history is to deepen the knowledge of Yunnan, to receive patriotic teaching, education in revolutionary tradition, to develop feelings of love of one's local area, a love of its people, a love of the fatherland and a love of China's Communist Party. Furthermore, the purpose is to protect the unity of the fatherland, strengthen the unity of the nationalities, and actively participate in building socialism in Yunnan.[29]

The history of Yunnan is studied in most secondary schools and teacher training schools throughout the province and is part of the 'patriotic education' that the government emphasizes as essential for ensuring the integration of the minorities. The books present a general survey of events in Yunnan's history profoundly influenced by Morgan's and Engels's theories of social evolution which still dominate much of China's social sciences. Apart from the focus on Yunnan's historical incorporation into the Chinese Empire, a dominant theme is the close relationship between Han and non-Han in Yunnan. Ethnic conflicts in history are generally interpreted as being essentially class conflicts, sometimes initiated by previous unjust governments' oppression of the ethnic minorities. The books discuss relations between two groups: the 'Han', and the 'minorities' (covering all the officially recognized national minorities in Yunnan). Only in connection with major ethnic clashes with, for instance, the Hui in the late nineteenth century are specific non-Han groups mentioned. Cultural influence and exchange are generally presented as a one-way process in which the developed Han people influence and develop an unspecified group of grateful 'minorities'. Thus, two sorts of culture are constructed and presented to the student: advanced Han culture, and less advanced non-Han culture. This becomes explicit in the teaching of social evolution of mankind, which is established as a scientifically proven, and therefore indisputable, theory to the students:

All nationalities [in Yunnan] live in different areas and their economies are not equally developed. Therefore, on the eve of Liberation different developmental stages still existed: primitive society (*yuanshi shehui*), slave society (*nuli shehui*), serf society (*nongnu shehui*) and feudal society (*fengjian shehui*). And therefore, Yunnan has long been called 'a living history of social development'.[30]

Students learn that some minorities possess a world outlook and system of values which still belong to 'primitive society', and that for instance the 'high cultural level of the Bai' was achieved thanks to strong Han Chinese influence during the time of the Dali Kingdom'.[31] They learn that large-scale immigrations of Han into Yunnan during the Ming Dynasty brought advanced agricultural tools and techniques to Yunnan, and that the dismissal of the local hereditary chiefs during the Qing Dynasty was greatly beneficial to the minorities because the previous system of granting power to local chiefs blocked the development of production, made society unstable, and prevented progress.[32] When non-Han groups are mentioned specifically, it is not for their technical advancement but for their 'prosperous minority cultures'; for instance, minority dances and music are used as examples of 'mankind's earliest forms of singing'. In this way, the books reinforce a picture of the technically and politically advanced Han contrasted with the primitive but sensitive minorities whose main contribution to society is to be living examples of 'traditional and colourful ancient culture'. Students also learn about the establishment of education in Yunnan, but this concerns exclusively the Confucian education and the early Chinese modern education, both of which 'disseminated advanced Han culture'. Nothing is mentioned about other groups' various forms of education.[33]

The Naxizu is a rare example of a small minority in Yunnan that is actually mentioned a few times in the two booklets about Yunnan history referred to above. Lijiang is used as an example of an area where the transference of direct power in 1723 to bureaucrats of the Qing Empire resulted in economic development.[34] In the Yunnan history book for students at Yunnan's teacher training schools, the Naxi are mentioned for their 'dongba religion'. This book explains that, in accordance with the different stages of development among the *minzu*, different 'primitive religious beliefs' prevailed and some *minzu*, among these the Naxi, had their own specific type of religion.[35]

Apart from the 'Yunnan history', the common national teaching material, especially in the subjects of politics and history in secondary schools, also gives strong priority to patriotic education and social evolution. The primary school course in 'ideology and morals' (*sixiang pinde*) focuses on proper moral behaviour including love of the country, the flag, the Communist Party, the national anthem, etc. In Yunnan the Education Department has edited a small book intended for supplementary reading in 'ideology and morals' which also includes stories of heroic people (for instance the famous revolutionary hero Lei Feng) and the Communists' achievements in Yunnan. In addition, it contains a one-page chapter specifically about Yunnan, entitled 'Yunnan—The Home of National Harmony'. Here children learn the names of the twenty-six different *minzu* living in Yunnan who before the liberation 'did not trust each other' and fought against each other in this area where 'production and economy was utterly backwards'.[36] Then came Liberation:

After Liberation all nationalities in our country became equal. Socialist ethnic relations based upon equality, unity, and mutual aid were established. The country also granted special consideration to minorities. The formerly oppressed minorities became masters of the country. . . . The party and the country were deeply concerned about the minorities in the border regions. They sent minority work teams [*minzu gongzuo dui*] to the minority regions to help them develop trade, education, science, culture and hygiene. . . . The party's minority policy promoted unison among nationalities, so that former 'enemies' [*yuanjia*] become 'relatives' [*qinjia*]. All the nationalities in Yunnan lived in harmony, united to help each other, and to develop and protect the borders of the fatherland.[37]

In an exercise that follows, pupils have to remember the names of the twenty-six nationalities in Yunnan and they have to fill in two key words from the text: namely, that all nationalities in China are 'equal' and that they have to 'unite'. The Han are not directly mentioned since the text only speaks about the party helping the minority nationalities (*shaoshu minzu*), which are pictured as backward and helpless groups of peoples receiving the help they need from the Communist Party. Indirectly, the Han appear as the majority which is representing the party, is not specifically backward, and does not need the same kind of help as the non-Han peoples.

In secondary school the teaching of evolution and ethnic categories is intensified, and students learn, for instance, that 'if we look at the whole country the Han nationality constitutes the vast majority and generally speaking their level of development is also the highest, so, with regard to equality and the unity of the nationalities, the Han people carries the gravest responsibility'.[38] In the second year of junior secondary school the students study in detail Morgan's and Engels's different stages of social evolution, and beneath a picture of the 'Beijing man' from the Stone Age they see a picture of men from the Jinuo nationality (Jinuozu) who are dividing meat into equal portions for their villagers—a so-called 'trace from primitive society'. The book's rather dull descriptions of the different stages of mankind's social evolution are sometimes given life through examples of minorities whose productive methods and social organization fit into some of the evolutionary stages. For instance, the Yi in Liangshan are put forward as examples of how the extremely backward developmental stage of 'slave society' still existed at the time of Liberation, and Tibet is used as one example of a 'feudal serf society' that existed until 1949.

In political classes in the third year of senior secondary education many more examples are given to illustrate the point that all of China's *minzu* belonged historically to the same Chinese nation (Zhonghua minzu) since the time of Qin, and that most of them fitted into different (low) stages of development before 1949. It is also repeatedly concluded that the minority areas are still backward where economy and culture are concerned, although they are rich in natural resources. With their higher level of development, the Han are obliged to help the minorities to develop, and this will also help the Han themselves, because of the wealth that the exploitation of natural resources in minority areas will bring to the whole country.[39]

'Love of Learning' as an Ethnic Marker

During their school education, minority students are confronted with the powerful depiction of the minorities as groups of backward people. In many cases this has created among students feelings of cultural inferiority. However, by focusing on 'love of learning' (*ai xuexi*) and 'love of culture' (*ai wenhua*) as specific ethnic markers, e.g. as being 'typical Naxi', Naxi intellectuals have reinterpreted the official descriptions of them as an ethnic minority.

Today the Naxi have a relatively high proportion of graduate and undergraduate students compared with most other *minzu* in China.[40]

Owing to the early establishment of Confucian education in Lijiang and the relatively successful spreading of modern education in Lijiang, the Naxi*zu* is often described in Chinese media and publications as a *minzu* with a 'high level of education', a *minzu* that has proved 'willing to learn from more advanced cultures'. This way of characterizing the Naxi has come to occupy a significant position in Naxi identity—even, to an extent, in the countryside where education is not so developed. It has become an ethnic marker in the consciousness of many Naxi who consider it a typical Naxi feature, a sort of inherited inclination towards 'love of learning' or 'love of culture'. In rural Naxi villages many people explained to me that, unlike many other *minzu* (notably those higher up in the mountains), the Naxi are very interested in learning and in acquiring an education, and that it is only their economic limitations that prevent more Naxi from getting an education.

Most Naxi are very proud of the Naxi researchers, teachers, government members, etc., who have positions in Kunming or other places in China. In spite of the fact that they are intellectuals whose way of living, customs, and occupations are profoundly different from the majority of Naxi, they have nevertheless come to symbolize (even among many rural Naxi) the Naxi as a numerically small ethnic group still capable of developing and manifesting itself in the Chinese state. Many Naxi peasants and teachers in rural areas criticize the government in Lijiang Town for not paying enough attention to the rural situation in Lijiang, for focusing on development in the town of Lijiang. This, however, does not prevent many of them from talking about the intellectual Naxi as a specific group of Naxi (rather than as representatives of the government), proving that the Naxi constitute an ethnic group partly characterized by intellectual capacity and openness towards 'advanced culture'. The intellectuals, on the other hand, are very concerned with the development in Lijiang—even those who live in Kunming and plan to stay there.

Most parents in the town of Lijiang hope that at least one of their children can continue in specialized senior secondary school or go on to tertiary education. This is the most obvious reason why so many younger Naxi parents in Lijiang Town have decided to speak only Chinese at home. Since the only possible way to a higher education is through the Chinese language, many parents hope to facilitate their child's upward social mobility by teaching it Chinese from birth. The general attitude in the town of Lijiang is that 'the children learn Naxi anyway on the street among their friends, so we had better prepare them for school as early as possible'. This also explains why many Naxi intellectuals who are themselves occupied with Naxi history and culture, or who have strong opinions about the need for protecting and developing Naxi culture (see next section), find it necessary to teach their children Chinese only. It is beyond doubt that only those who are very fluent in reading and writing Chinese will eventually manage to continue into senior secondary school, not to mention tertiary education. Therefore, the major reason for teaching children Chinese in Lijiang, where most parents speak Naxi at home and with each other, is based upon pragmatic considerations that are very realistic considering the form and content of Chinese school education. However, many interviewees emphasized 'love of learning' as a major explanation of why they wanted to educate their children in Chinese. They would argue that their wish to have their child receive a higher education was extremely strong because of the 'love of learning' which they considered to be a common Naxi characteristic. Since the Naxi 'loved learning', and since learning in schools happened to be Chinese learning, they were more motivated to bring up their children in Chinese than were most other minorities.

The Naxi's focus on 'love of learning' as a specific ethnic characteristic is in my view closely related to the teaching of social evolution discussed in the previous section and to the pervasive conceptualization in China of the minorities as backward. In one particular aspect the Naxi escape the label of being backward, namely when it comes to the adaptation of and to Chinese education throughout history. Thus, the focus on 'love of learning' establishes the Naxi as a *minzu* fairly close to the Hanzu in some aspects of level of civilization while distinguishing them from the minorities in the mountains (and to a certain degree from the Mosuo part of the Naxi*zu*, who are not included as sharing this Naxi characteristic).

Clearly, the perception of 'love of learning' as a typical Naxi feature is most widespread among Naxi with a higher education. It is mainly through education that the concept of the 'backward minorities' is impregnated in the minds of the students, often instilling feelings of cultural inferiority. When I interviewed Naxi students at YIN, several of them told me about how they had tried to avoid being recognized as belonging to a presumably backward non-Han group, and how students from other universities tended to look down on them as minority students. When I asked Naxi students or graduates in Lijiang and Kunming what they had learned about their own *minzu* during their time in secondary school, most would immediately answer a plain 'nothing' (*mei you xue*). When asked more specifically if teachers sometimes taught about the Naxi even though it was not in the textbooks, many of those who had had Naxi teachers recalled that they sometimes told Naxi stories or told a bit about Naxi history, for instance why most Naxi are called either Mu or He.[41] Many had also heard that the Naxi were always 'good at studying' and 'at learning from Han Chinese culture'. When asked what they had learned generally about the different *minzu* in China, they virtually all pointed to the descriptions of social evolution. All students without exception were well aware that the minorities were found on the most backward stages, and for the most part they believed this to be an indisputable fact, since it was never discussed in class but was simply presented as the truth.

The concept of social evolution and the construction of the minorities as backward had a very strong impact on most students' self-perception. Though all students were very well acquainted with the official policy of promoting political and economic equality between the *minzu*, their confrontation with the objectivized hierarchic understanding of cultural development clearly influenced them emotionally, and coloured their perceptions at least as much as the positive propaganda. However, owing to the idea of the Naxi as a *minzu* characterized by 'love of learning', and to the 'dongba culture', which I return to in the following section, many of the Naxi students managed to compare themselves favourably with the other *minzu* in Lijiang. As one of them remarked: 'of course the Lisu and the Yi in our class do not feel comfortable hearing about their own history, but for us it is quite interesting because we have our own literary tradition [*you ziji de wenhua*].

The concept of the backward minorities is one that is extremely difficult to escape in the Chinese context because it saturates so many levels of society, but perhaps mainly because it is reproduced in schools in the form of scientific objective truth. Students are not encouraged to develop a critical approach to the content of school education and its textbooks, and therefore they rarely express any doubts about the truth of what is written. In this way, the official categorization of the minorities as basically backward is reproduced in the minds of the educated minorities. They internalize this external interpretation of the content of their ethnic identity, so that the categorizers' definition becomes 'true' and comes to constitute a part of their identity as a national minority.

A more positive side of the Chinese categorization of the Naxi has been the conception of them as a minority 'willing to learn'. This perception has existed at least since the time of Qing, when the royal Mu family was praised by Chinese bureaucrats for its openness towards Confucian education and culture. It has been repeated in publications of all kinds about the Naxi. It has also become a strategy in the Naxi's attempt to establish an alternative picture of the Naxi as a group that might have been backward at the time of the Communist take-over, but nevertheless was so inclined towards learning that it always had the potential for development. In this regard, the more positive aspect of the Chinese categorization of the Naxi has also come to play a significant role in the remaking of Naxi identity. The external definition of Naxi identity has influenced the identity itself and helped to refute the negative aspect of the external categorization.

Naxi teachers in institutions of earlier learning, such as Lijiang Prefecture Teacher Training School and Yunnan Institute of the Nationalities, have turned out to be particularly influential in spreading the concept of the Naxi as an ethnic group that loves learning. Many Naxi students at YIN mentioned that, through the influence of their Naxi teachers, they had come to change their perceptions of themselves as Naxi and of the Naxi as a group. Their teachers had not opposed the general theory of social evolution for all ethnic groups, but had presented alternative understandings of the presumed backward elements of Naxi culture. One of the positive features was the 'love of learning'; another was the 'dongba culture', which was reformulated as a strength of the Naxi rather than as proof of backwardness. Thus, especially in recent years, the process of transforming and strengthening Naxi identity by presenting alternative interpretations of cultural features previously considered backward has intensified.

The Dongba: From Superstition to Culture

Anyone who travels to Lijiang (and many Chinese, Asiatic, and Western tourists now do so) inevitably encounters a wide range of local expressions of Naxi identity. Apart from the typical Naxi architecture, the old Naxi women's blue costumes, and the musical performances, the visitor is certain to notice the abundant representations of the dongba script in the town of Lijiang. In the 1990s especially, many shopkeepers started to paint dongba characters on their signs; several Naxi now paint and sell calligraphies with dongba characters; well-known Naxi painters incorporate dongba pictures in modern paintings; the local bookshop has a whole shelf reserved for publications about the Naxi and the dongba; and two dongba museums are open for visitors. In the ongoing process of formulating a modern Naxi identity, the various aspects of dongba—the script, rituals, recorded stories, and myths—have been put together into the concept of a 'dongba culture'. The 'dongba culture' has acquired a significant place in the ethnic identity of the educated Naxi in particular. Both inside and outside China, an unprecedented interest in the dongba script and rituals has developed in recent years, starting from the mid-1980s when Lijiang opened up to foreigners. Many Naxi in the town of Lijiang agree that the tourists and researchers from outside Lijiang and China have stimulated and encouraged the Naxi's own interest in the dongba script; it has certainly also initiated several local shops selling and producing handicrafts. There is, however, much more at stake than direct economic advantages in the Naxi's process of formulating a modern ethnic identity that has 'dongba culture' as perhaps the most prominent feature.

By 1949 there were dongba practising only in the rural areas of Lijiang. We have no figure on the exact number, but according to interviews many Naxi villages had a dongba at that time, or would invite one from a neighbouring village. After the Communist take-over the dongba's activities were prohibited as expressions of feudal superstition (*mixin*), and partly for this reason there are extremely few dongba today. The Institute of Dongba Cultural Research[42] (Dongba Wenhua Yanjiusuo) in Lijiang was started in 1981 as a branch of Yunnan Academy of Social Sciences with the purpose of promoting dongba research and translating dongba texts. The Institute has employed a few dongba to assist in, for instance, translation work and the reconstruction of rituals. One of them, a dongba from the area of Tai'an, was born in 1921, and started to learn the dongba rituals and the script from his father when he was 14 years old. At that time there were two dongba families in his village. He recalled:

From 1949, when I was 28, it was forbidden to practise the dongba rituals. So I stopped. Nobody asked me to come any more. Then from the 1980s people again started to invite me as a dongba, and later I was invited by a unit [the Institute of Dongba Cultural Research] to work there. My wife and children were very much against my starting practising again. Now they are not against it any more; they accept it because so many people are interested in it . . . *previously dongba rituals were called 'superstition' [mixin], now it is 'culture' [wenhua].* [my italics]

The fact that 'dongba superstition' has turned into 'dongba culture' is manifested, for instance, in the way more and more Naxi intellectuals describe the dongba: they are no longer representatives of feudal culture or peasants' superstitious beliefs, but are 'the Naxi's own intellectuals' (*Naxizu de zhishifenzi*). The same point was clearly illustrated in a speech held by a former head of a local propaganda bureau in connection with a local Naxi celebration in a village in 1995:

Earlier the dongba activities were labelled 'feudal superstition'. This was not right [loud expressions of agreement among the audience, who were mostly old Naxi]. It is important that we Naxi not only learn from the Han culture, but also try to disseminate [*xuanchuan*] our own culture.

'Dongba culture' has become central in Naxi identity as it is expressed publicly in China today. Dongba rituals are still performed in several Naxi villages, but that does not necessarily imply that the concept of a 'dongba culture' as such plays a significant role in local Naxi peasants' ethnic identity. In the early 1980s, after the end of the Cultural Revolution and with the renewed acceptance of ethnic identities and expressions, it was mainly a relatively small group of Naxi intellectuals in Kunming who started to promote research into dongba activities and to focus on 'dongba culture' as a specific feature of the Naxi as an ethnic group and a national minority in China. In the last ten to fifteen years this has gradually spread to other strata of the Naxi community in Lijiang, and it is a process that has been developing very rapidly in these years. Dongba rituals are no longer merely objects of research; very recently, some intellectual Naxi with high official positions have even started to invite dongba to perform rituals in their homes in connection with family events. They have also initiated other projects where the modern use of 'dongba culture' is directly combined with education in an attempt to spread the knowledge of the dongba, to develop the Naxi's ethnic pride based on 'dongba culture', and to reject the construction of the Naxi as backward.

One of these projects is the 'Minority Culture and Ecology Village' (Minzu Wenhua Shengtai Cun), which has been set up on a local initiative in a small Naxi village in the proximity of Lijiang Town. During the Qing Dynasty this village had a private Confucian school, but when the Republic was established a local public primary school took over all school-based education. Before the 1950s there were two dongba families in the village, but the last dongba died about twenty years ago. In 1934 the local teachers started a 'common people's school' (*minzhong xuexiao*) where adults participated in Chinese literacy courses in the evening. More than fifty years later, in March 1994, the village was the centre for a celebration of the Naxi's guardian spirit, Sanduo, where a dongba was invited by a few prominent Naxi to perform a traditional dongba ritual for the villagers and for some Japanese dongba researchers. The event was an interesting mixture of photographing and filming and making serious offerings to, and honouring, the Naxi protecting spirit of Sanduo. It was also part of a larger local project initiated by a native, retired Naxi intellectual, Mr He.

The guiding idea behind Mr He's Minority Culture and Ecology Village is to promote 'traditional Naxi culture', which he finds is threatened by the mainstream of modernization. He's vision is to create a synthesis of old values and modern techniques, to combine 'The Confucian analects + dongba + propagation about the Communist part + computers'.[43] One of his major ideas has already been realized, namely the restarting of a locally based 'common people's school', the Peasants' Evening School, which is a completely private initiative fully independent of government financial support. A small library has been opened in connection with the evening school. The local peasants may freely attend the school, which arranges courses almost every evening in agricultural techniques, the breeding of animals, etc., but also offers classes in Naxi Romanized script and dongba characters. The Naxi Romanized script is taught because it is very easy for the Naxi to learn, and is useful in collecting and recording local stories, myths, songs, etc. The initiators of the school expect a revival of dongba rituals, since a few younger dongba are now being trained in neighbouring villages, and more and more families plan to restart the tradition of inviting a dongba to perform rituals in events of death, marriage, illness, etc.

The village project is a serious intellectual attempt to utilize education for the dual purpose of promoting local agricultural modernization and ethnic consciousness among local Naxi. Another recent major local project is also directed towards strengthening the role of 'dongba culture' in the common Naxi identity, while at the same time promoting the utilization of its economic potentials. The Naxi Dongba Cultural School of Lijiang[44] (Naxi Dongba Wenhua Xuexiao) was started in Lijiang Town in the beginning of 1995. The idea behind the establishment of this school was to offer a short-term education for all people in Lijiang county who had at least graduated from junior secondary school. The first class was started in February 1995, when forty students (all Naxi from the neighbourhood of Lijiang town) enrolled, paying 200 yuan for the course during which they would learn to read and write 1,000 dongba characters, learn about dongba history, rituals, art, etc., and study basic English for the purpose of future employment in the tourist business. Some of the students were unemployed youths, some were primary schoolteachers, and some worked at local museums or travel agencies. Some were motivated by a wish to find work in the tourist industry, others were simply interested in learning more about dongba. Approximately half of the students completed the course.

The head of the school and its teachers are very enthusiastic about the project and have plans for a further development of the school. Within the next year they hope to raise money for a class of about fifty students of 14 and 15 years of age from the poorest mountain areas, for instance students who have not continued their regular studies because their parents could not afford it. The plan is to build dormitories for these students who will then study for two years. In a small leaflet produced to raise money for the project, its purpose is described in this way:

Our purpose is to save the dongba culture via living people, expand our nationality culture [*minzu wenhua*], stimulate our nationality spirit [*minzu jingshen*], and promote local economic development. After a period of practising teaching, we want gradually to enrol more students, so that the school will turn into a cradle for qualified people who study and carry on dongba culture [*dongba wenhua*]. It will also become an international study institution for dongba culture and a centre for dongba art. We are trying our best to achieve this great goal.[45]

Furthermore, the initiators behind the school hope to be able in the future to start a dongba university, or at least a research and study institution under one of the established universities. As one of them said, 'The Tibetans, Koreans and the Mongols have their own universities, so why not we Naxi? Previously most Naxi thought that only Han culture was interesting and developed. Now many realize that we have a culture and a tradition with its own value.'

Both of the schools described here are interesting because they how how intellectual Naxi engage in local economic development in Lijiang through the establishment of alternative education that incorporates (or is even built upon) the teaching of local Naxi culture and history lacking in regular state education. Initially directed by a relatively small group of Naxi intellectuals, the concept of dongba as feudal superstition has now been turned into that of a 'culture' (*wenhua*) carrying implications of script, art, history, and civilization. Whereas 'superstition' is a burden of a backward people, 'culture' is a force, a proof of civilization, and a justifier for demands of local influence and control of economic and cultural development.

The concept of dongba culture as a typical, unique Naxi ethnic marker helps to refute the powerful construction of the Naxi as a backward minority. It establishes the Naxi as a *minzu* with a *wenhua*. It also solves the dilemma of how a *minzu* that has been characterized by its 'love of learning' and positive attitudes towards 'advanced cultures' nevertheless remained backward and resisted assimilation with the Han: dongba was not a 'superstition' but a 'culture', and therefore it was valuable as a rather refined expression of local Naxi culture different from the culture of the Han and the other groups in the area and in the rest of China. The Naxi 'loved learning from the advanced Han', but they also had their own characteristics. They had their own 'culture' and even their own 'dongba intellectuals'.

Dongba ritual practice was only one of several religious practices among rural Naxi and one that for a long time did not exist even in the town of Lijiang. Never the less, the Naxi have been very successful in turning the various aspects of the dongba into a modern symbol of the Naxi in China. When asked, most Naxi today mention 'dongba' 'or dongba culture' as a major 'typical Naxi feature'. This is not because dongba culture as such plays an important practical role in most Naxi villages, but because the educated Naxi élite's formulation and strong voicing of Naxi identity is spreading into the countryside where the same élite is regarded with respect and approval, just as the Confucian educated Naxi élite before them.

Conclusion

The reason why the Naxi have been so successful in turning public perceptions of dongba into those of a culture and a strength, rather than a form of superstition, is I believe closely related to the relatively high educational level of the Naxi and their own belief in 'love of learning' as a typical Naxi characteristic. The educated Naxi élite consists of a comparatively large number of people, many of whom hold prestigious and influential positions in Kunming or Lijiang. There are Naxi at all levels of government in Yunnan province and Lijiang County, and considering their overall numbers they have many influential teachers and researchers. Many come from families where the fathers and grandfathers were students in Confucian private schools and they value education very highly. They have a well developed network, for instance through the Society of Naxi Culture, and they are therefore also capable of articulating their feelings and expressing their demands within the politically acceptable framework in China.

As a result of the level of Chinese state education they have attained, the Naxi have been able to establish an alternative education which will most likely have more far-reaching consequences at the local level than the more exclusive Society of Naxi Culture. Thanks to their own education, the Naxi who initiated these projects know how to play by the rules so that this education is not regarded as a threat to regular state education, but is even supported by the local autonomous government and most heads of state schools in Lijiang (mostly Naxi themselves). Even so, the creation of the new alternative schools in Lijiang is a way of reacting against a state education that almost completely ignored non-Han culture, language, and history and fails to show that minorities in China have more to offer than picturesque costumes, dancing, and singing. In fact, state education involuntarily supports, perhaps even creates, a focus on ethnic identity. Minority members can never escape their label as minorities, because they are officially classified as such and learn in school that the classification relies on objective, scientific proof. Neither can they escape the label of being backward, because this too, they learn, is a scientifically proven fact. Finally, through an education that ignores local history, language, stories, religions, etc., they indirectly learn that much of what they have experienced and learned at home is without value in the broad context of the Chinese state. While this creates feelings of stigmatization for some educated minority people, for the Naxi education has been instrumental in the development of a stronger and forcefully expressed Naxi identity. This has been made possible by the fact that they possess relatively many educated members, believe that 'love of learning' is a typical Naxi characteristic, and have found a potential in their dongba script.

Many of the intellectual Naxi have themselves participated in the Communist project of defining *minzu* and disseminating the theories of social evolution, but they have never the less started to react against the perception of themselves as members of a group that is backward by definition. In this sense they are reacting against an external definition, an ethnic categorization, of what it implies to be Naxi. In other words, they do not (unlike the 'Mosuo branch' of the Naxizu) reject what Jenkins has called the nominal aspect of ethnicity, that is the name or the boundary of the group, but they do reject the context of this name and seek to reinterpret it.[46] Since the nominal ethnic categorization was based on an already existing social category with which most Naxi (excluding the Mosuo) already identified—they did not doubt that they were Naxi—this identity has been further strengthened. At the same time, it has become vitally important for the Naxi intellectuals to redefine the content of the external ethnic categorization which was the public and official version of their experiences as an ethnic group.

Education plays several roles in the remaking of Naxi identity. First of all, it is one of the most significant means through which the officially sanctified categorization of the 'backward minorities' and the definite ethnic boundaries of *minzu* are communicated. Therefore, it is also the educated Naxi who most strongly 'feel backward' and who experience a strong contradiction between this and their perception of themselves as a group with potential for learning and developing. Most likely the individual motive plays a significant role as well, because the Naxi are successful in terms of education and therefore experience a personal conflict between this and the inescapable fact of being classified as members of a backward minority. Success in education, partly resulting from a high degree of integration into the Chinese state and the adoption of the Chinese language and cultural values through lengthy contact with the Han Chinese, is in itself a factor that provides the Naxi with the abilities to reinterpret the content of the constructed ethnic categorization in a way that is acceptable in the present political climate in China. In this way, ethnicity is remade through the reinterpretation of the original content of an external categorization.

Of course, education alone does not explain why the recent strong expressions of ethnicity among the Naxi have met no political sanctions or have not been regarded as a threat to the government. The Naxi are a very small ethnic group in China; they have no ethnic relations across borders and absolutely no aspirations to political independence. Their expressions of ethnicity, to the degree that they are directed by instrumentalist motives, seek to define a room for the Naxi as a group that has adopted a lot from Han Chinese (Confucian) culture and language, but at the same time has maintained its own culture (*wenhua*). This also justifies further control over local resources and political decision-making, all clearly within the context of the Chinese state.

NOTES

1. I am indebted to Stevan Harrell, Stig Thøgersen, and Koen Wellens for invaluable comments on earlier drafts of this paper. I thank the authorities at the Yunnan Institute of the Nationalities for their cooperation, and all the Naxi who agreed to participate in my interviews. The research presented is part of a larger fieldwork-based Ph.D. project concerning the relationship between education and ethnic identity among the Naxi in Lijiang and the Tai in Sipsong Panna, Yunnan Province. I am grateful for the funding of this project provided by the Danish Council for Development Research (RUF).
2. The article is based on different periods of fieldwork between 1991 and 1996. The main part of the fieldwork was carried out between September 1994 and June 1995 and consisted of formally arranged interviews with Naxi intellectuals, teachers, heads of schools, peasants, students, and workers; participation in various local events, informal interviews, and sitting in on classes.
3. Stevan Harrell, 'Introduction: Civilizing Projects and the Reaction to Them', in Stevan Harrell (ed.), *Cultural Encounters on China's Ethnic Frontiers* (Seattle and London: University of Washington Press, 1995).
4. See e.g. Chae-jin Lee, *China's Korean Minority: The Politics of Ethnic Education* (Boulder, Colo.: Westview Press, 1986); Wurlig Borchiged, 'The Impact of Urban Ethnic Education on Modern Mongolian Ethnicity, 1949–1966', in Harrell, *Cultural Encounters*; Wang Xihong *et al.* (eds.), *Zhongguo bianjing minzu jiaoyu* (Minority Education in China's Border Areas) (Beijing: Zhongyang minzuxueyuan chubanshe, 1990); Sun Ruoqiong *et al.* (eds.), *Zhongguo shaoshu minzu jiaoyuzue gailun* (An Introduction to the Education of China's National Minorities) (Beijing: Zhongguo laodong chubanshe, 1990).
5. See e.g. Fei Xiaotong, 'Ethnic Identification in China', in Fei Xiaotong (ed.), *Toward a People's Anthropology* (Beijing: New World Press, 1981); and Lin Yaohua, 'Zhongguo xinan diqu de minzu shibie' (Ethnic Identification in the Southwest Region of China), in *Yunnan shaoshu minzu shehui lishi diaocha ziliao huibian* (Kunming: Minzu chubanshe, 1987) about classification.
6. See e.g. Koen Wellens, 'What Is in a Name: The Premi in Southwest China and the Consequences of Defining Ethnic Identity', *Nations and Nationalism*, (forthcoming).
7. *Minzu gongzuo wenxuan* (Selected Documents on Nationalities Work) (Nanning, 1986), 274–81.
8. Chen Hongtao *et al.* (eds.), *Yunnan minzu jiaoyu yanjiu* (Research on Minority Education in Yunnan) (Beijing: Zhongyang minzu xueyuan chubanshe, 1989).
9. Since 1985, the State Education Commission.

10. Especially among the Lisu, Miao, Tuo'en, Nuoso, and in the poorest Naxi villages, it is still the norm for most children to attend school for less than six years.

11. See Mette Halskov Hansen, 'Lessons in Patriotism: State Education and Ethnic Identity among Tai and Naxi in Southwest China' (Ph.D. thesis, Aarhus University, 1996) concerning the history of Chinese Confucian, Nationalist, and Communist education in the non-Han areas of Yunnan. See also Cai Shoufu *et al.* (eds.), *Yunnan minzu jiaoyu fazhan gaikuang* (A Brief Introduction to the Development of Minority Education in Yunnan) (Kunming: Yunnan daxue chubanshe, 1992).

12. See Dru Gladney, 'Representing Nationality in China: Refiguring Majority/Minority Identities', *Journal of Asian Studies*, 53:1 (1994), 92–123, for a discussion of the functioning and purpose of the exotic representation of minorities in China.

13. The figure is from *Zhongguo minzu tongji* (Statistics on China's Nationalities) (Beijing: Zhongguo tongji chubanshe, 1992). The Nare, mostly called 'Mosuo' in Chinese, are now locally recognized as a branch of the Naxizu called Mosuoren. When students are recruited for the 'minority class' in the prefecture secondary school, the Nare are admitted on terms different from the other Naxi students.

14. The Austro-American botanist, Joseph Rock, who lived for almost 20 years in Lijiang and conducted one of the most famous and comprehensive studies on the Naxi, transcribes Naxi as 'Na-Khi'. In the Romanized Naxi script it is transcribed as 'Naqxi'. I prefer to use the most commonly used form of Naxi, which is very close to the pronunciation of the Naxi themselves.

15. The transcription dongba is closer to the pronunciation in Naxi language, but in China and among the Naxi élite the form 'dongba' is commonly used when talking about different aspects of the so-called 'dongba culture' *dongba wenhua*).

16. These ten were: Zhuangzu, Buyizu, Miaozu, Dongzu, Yizu, Hanizu, Lisuzu, Wazu, Lizu and Naxizu. Other nationalities, such as the Daizu, had their script simplified: Shi Jun, *Minzu falü fagui gaishu* (A Summary of the Laws and Regulations Concerning the Nationalities) (Minzu chubanshe, 1988), 247–52.

17. Lijiang, Huaping, Ninglang, and Yongsheng counties.

18. With regard to admission of students, the Mosuo (or Nare) are not considered to be Naxi, but get special consideration.

19. One of them, the Central Nationalities Institute in Beijing, has recently been rearranged into a Minority University (Minzu Daxue).

20. See e.g. *Minzu gongzuo shouce* (A Handbook to Nationalities Work) (Kunming: Yunnan renmin chubanshe, 1985) and Li Li *et al.* (eds.), *Yunnan minzu xueyuan sishi nian, 1951–1991* (Forty Years of Yunnan Nationalities Institute, 1951–1991) (Kunming: Yunnan daxue chubanshe, 1991).

21. Yunnan Province Education Commission Office for Educational Gazetteers, *Yunnan minzu jiaoyu fazhan gaikuang* (A Brief Introduction to the Development of Minority Education in Hunnan) (Kunming: Yunnan daxue chubanshe, 1991), 177.

22. ibid. 179.

23. The policy of payment to be released from the duty to accept an assigned job is very unclear at the moment (1995) and there are considerable individual differences in how much graduates have to pay. Furthermore, even when some graduates manage to pay the money, it is sometimes impossible for them to get a household registration in the city so that they have to return to their home county anyway. Only a very small number of graduates from YIN have so far managed to find a job themselves.

24. Pu Linlin, 'Minzu yuanxiao biyesheng fenpei gongzuo gaige chuyi' (My Opinion on the Distribution of the Graduates from the Minority Schools), *Minzu jiaoyu yanjiu*, 1 (1994), 64.

25. ibid. 65.
26. Guo Xialin, 'Review of Chinese Research on the Yongning Naxi Matriliny', *Stockholm Journal of East Asian Studies*, 2 (1990), 77.
27. See Charles McKhann, 'The Naxi and the Nationalities Question', in Harrell, *Cultural Encounters*.
28. Lijiang County Educational Commission *et al.*, *Lijiang Naxizu Zizhixian zhong xiao xuexiao deyu difang xiangtu jiaocai* (Local Moral Teaching Material for Middle and Primary Schools in Lijiang Naxi Autonomous County) (Lijiang: unpublished draft, 1995).
29. *Yunnan difang shi* (Yunnan Local History) (Teacher Training Department of Yunnan Province Education Commission, 1993), 'Introduction'.
30. ibid. 64.
31. ibid. 43.
32. ibid. 59.
33. ibid. 47, and *Yunnan lishi* (The History of Yunnan) (Commission for Examining and Revising Teaching Materials for Primary and Secondary Schools in Yunnan Province, 1990), 47.
34. ibid. 40.
35. *Yunnan difang shi*, 68.
36. *Sixiang pinde* (Ideology and Moral) (Supplementary teaching material for third year of primary education in Yunnan) (Kunming: Chenguang chubanshe, 1991), 19.
37. ibid. 19–20.
38. *Sixiang zhengzhi* (Ideology and Politics) (Compulsory teaching materials for three years of junior and three years of senior secondary education) (Guangdong gaodeng jiaoyu chubanshe, 1993), i.57.
39. ibid. 131–3.
40. Only the Huizu, Manzu (Manchu), Mengguzu (Mongols), and Chaoxianzu (Koreans) have more university graduates per 1,000 members than the Naxi. Owing to the policy of providing the smallest minorities with university graduates in spite of low examination results from the entrance examination, some very small *minzu* also exceed the Naxi in percentage of university graduates: see e.g. *Zhongguo tongji nianjian* (Statistical Yearbook of China) (Beijing; Toingji chubanshe, 1993), 91.
41. Mu was the Chinese name given to the royal family during the Ming Dynasty, which then decided that the commoners should adopt the name He. Today many Naxi still have these family names.
42. The institution's own translation.
43. Quoted from a small leaflet written by He Wanbao about the Dalai Minority Culture and Ecology Village.
44. The school's own English translation of its name.
45. Quoted from a leaflet to raise money for the Naxi Dongba Cultural School of Lijiang.
46. See Richard Jenkins, 'Rethinking Ethnicity: Identity, Categorization and Power', *Ethnic and Racial Studies*, 17:2 (1994), 197–223.

12

China Deconstructs? The Future of the Chinese Empire-State in a Historical Perspective
Harald Bøckman

Introduction

The bottom line of any assessment of the future development of China—
be it economic, cultural, social, or political—is its survival in its present or
some modified form. Only a dozen years ago, such a problematique would
swiftly be relegated to the files of the oddities of futuristic research. Today,
it is a theme that is being discussed as an important issue not only outside
China, but also seriously—albeit reluctantly—within China as well.

This abrupt change is a useful reminder of the increasing curtailment of
our collective historical memory: in spite of recurrent social and political
upheavals since 1949, the present geopolitical configuration of China has
been more or less taken for granted.[1] It is therefore easily forgotten that
China had been neither united nor fully sovereign for more than one hundred years preceding the Communist victory in 1949.

It we want to assess the prospects for a 'deconstruction' of China,[2] it is
my assertion that a parallel to the breakup of the Romanov/Soviet Empire
is of only limited relevance. Those who extended their analysis to the
Chinese scene after the breakup of the Soviet Union did so primarily from
a 'communist systems' approach. They tended to forget that the Chinese
Communists also inherited—as a deliberate policy—the geographical
configuration of the former empire,[3] and along with that a fair portion of
its implied thinking. However, the Chinese imperial tradition is infinitely
more entrenched and durable than the—comparatively speaking—brief
Romanov empire. Because of the dominance of the systemic approach to
our understanding of China, it is frequently overlooked that China is the
only major imperial geopolitical structure that is still intact today.[4]

Still, the prospects for a breakup of China are real enough, and have
been envisaged in two ways: the major ethnic regions (Tibet, Xinjiang, and

Inner Mongolia) would attempt to secede, and the major cultural–
economic regions within China proper would constitute themselves as
semi-independent autonomous regions. In worst-case scenarios, at least as
seen from Beijing, some of these regions may even attempt a total break
with Beijing's dominance and establish new, independent, and sovereign
states.[5]

None of these scenarios are so far in the process of being realized. If one
agrees that an imperial geopolitical structure is an aberration in this *fin de
millenaire*, one should be equally curious about the evident resilience and
durability of such a structure. In considering the reasons why China once
again seems to be following its own course, it is insufficient to analyse the
successful manoeuvrings of the present Beijing regime during the last two
decades only. We need to go to the root of the matter, and try to account
for a tradition that Angus Graham half jokingly called 'the Chinese secret
of social immortality'.[6]

The reason for deliberately avoiding a comparative systemic approach
to the Chinese political scene is to make room for an undeniable but frequently slighted fact: that the traditional Chinese political system was a
highly sophisticated and unique political *system* in its own right. At the
same time, modern China has developed to such an extent that it is possible to 'compare China with China', that is, to sort out links and transfor-
mations, ruptures and substitutions with the past.

From this, it should be needless to say that I am of the opinion that the
modernization and transformational processes in modern Chinese society
have been overstated at the expense of serious inquiries into how traditional notions about politics and society have survived and been transformed in this process.[7] I feel that these notions are not merely vestiges,
but are very much alive. Evidence for that can be observed in different
fields, including resurging Confucian-derived ethics among the intellectuals, renascent nationalist attitudes, and of course the reappearance of the
domestic unit as an economic unit. The past, the present, and the future
are very close in time and also are more intertwined in their Chinese context than in most other polities. I do not want to imply that history is
merely repeating itself, but rather that it is used in a transactional manner
in order to make sense of the strains of modernization. It is in many
ways—in the wording of the popular French adage—a process in which
plus que ça change, plus ça reste le même.

The issue of the transformation of tradition (rather than the 'tradition
and transformation' scheme) is huge indeed. In this paper there will only
be room to bring up some historical features that I regard as important for
furthering our understanding of contemporary Chinese political syntax.
To illustrate the depth and scope of the issues involved, we may say that

adopting a macro-perspective in its Chinese context makes *la longue durée* approach of French structuralism look like a single chapter in a long historical novel. Of course, a macro-perspective can easily become so generalized that it loses much of its explanatory power.[8] But equally we also find that micro-perspectives—especially in the case of China—become so particularistic that their messages become anecdotic.

China as 'a Great Systemic Whole'

It is no coincidence that China is the only major imperial structure left: it is beyond comparison in terms of durability. Whereas the Western imperial constructions reckon their history in terms of the rise and fall of one or two dynasties, China's history may be seen as *recurrent* dynasties that have diverged considerably, but have retained a basic common notion of their political and cultural order.

While the nation-states of Europe evolved (and are still evolving) on the basis—real or imagined—of a common Judaeo-Greek foundation, the perceived common cultural framework itself became the basis of the Chinese empire-state. Within this conceptual framework, there has been no room for a notion of developing different nation-states within the Chinese cultural realm. The aim of all local pretenders was always to restore the imperial order. This is not only abundantly documented in Chinese historical records, but is also in popular sayings like 'Strive to gain the political power of the Central realm' (*zhulu zhongyuan*).[9] Looking outward, the aim was to seek congruence between the imperial order and the cultural realm, even if that was rarely feasible.[10]

The authors of the Chinese television series 'River Elegy' (*Heshang*),[11] ask themselves what kind of powerful force it is that has been able to unify such a large state for more than two thousand years. They point to the riddle of 'the Great Systemic Whole' (*Da yitong*), which, according to the authors, has caused Chinese and Western scholars alike to rack their brains.[12] The term occurs throughout the television series as a central concept for understanding the peculiar nature of China in the imperial epoch.[13]

The term *Da yitong* is not easily translatable,[14] and its origin can hardly be said to be impressive. It occurs the first time in the Gongyang commentary to 'The Spring and Autumn Annals', or Chunqiu, where—in the fashion of the New Texts scholars of Han times—a brief and simple passage may be elaborated upon *ad absurdum*. It was then taken up by Dong Zhongshu, the most influential Confucian syncretist during the Western Han dynasty.[15] While Dong may not be said to be an outstanding philosopher, his political thinking had a decisive impact both on his contemporaries and on posterity. With Dong Zhongshu, *Da yitong* became a catchword for expressing the syncretization and unification of politics and thought that took place in his own time.[16] It was Dong himself who, in a memorial to the Emperor, proposed that Confucianism be given preference over the other schools of thought (*duzun rushu*). Thus, in the words of Fung Yulan, 'the Period of the Philosophers came to an end, and . . . the Study of the Classics commenced'.[17]

While the origin of the term *Da yitong* may be obscure, it conveys a strong notion of unitarianism, which was a basic notion in early Chinese philosophy and political thought. This ranges from the notions of cosmological unity between Heaven and man, that is, unity between the natural and the mental realms (*tian ren heyi*),[18] to various terms expressing the unitary origin of things. This is illustrated by the prevalence of the concept *yi*, which in this context means 'oneness' or 'totality', and by terms like 'The Great Oneness' (*tai yi*). The philosopher Meng Zi, when asked by King Hui of Liang how *Tianxia*, or 'the world below Heaven', can be settled, answers that it can be settled through unification (*yi*).[19] In the mid-third-century BC eclectic work *Lü shi chunqiu* we find the following passage: 'If there is unity, then one can govern; if there are divergences, then there will be disorder. If there is unity, then there will be peace; if there are divergences, then there will be crises.'[20] Unitarianism is a basic premiss in Taoism, as it is expressed in this passage from the *Dao de jing*: 'Lords and princes possessed the One and became thereby leaders of the empire.'[21] The *dao* itself has a supreme quality of oneness. Oneness becomes a principle of Heaven, and the ruler who emulates Heaven is expected to conform to it. Constructs of traditional rudimentary dialectics such as *yin* and *yang* dualism are merely constituent and fluctuating parts within a single whole.

Thus, the unifying process by the Qin may be seen as the enactment of a unitarian strain that had been crystallizing throughout the later Zhou period. The succession by the Han may be seen as the modification of this strain into an enduring, unified, and centralized state. The establishment of syncretic Confucianism as the state ideology during the Han period constituted an ideological framework that would show both great inclusiveness and great adaptability. By 'Confucianism' I mean Han Confucianism, which adapted many features from Legalist, Taoist, Mohist, and Yin-Yang strains of political thought.[22]

Determining the ultimate reasons why this system proved to be of unequalled durability may be the most tricky issue in our understanding of Chinese history. Clearly, it cannot be ascribed to a singular cause, but to multiple factors and their interrelationship. Here, I list only what I consider the most important of these factors:

- Confucianism continued its adaption to changing and at times other (dominant) currents of thought, primarily Buddhism and Taoism, without losing its basic identity and tenets.
- Confucianism rarely had to vie with proponents of political power that sought divine legitimation. The Chinese thus have not been victims of our Western schizophrenic split between the secular and the sacred. The state in China therefore was not conceived of as 'secular', because there never was an alternative model.
- The continued tradition of ancestor worship created a pull towards the past that promoted a sense of common origin and destiny that has no equivalent in Western civilization. This created a horizontal orientation towards the past instead of a vertical orientation towards a personal God.
- The vertically layered structure of social status, rank and classes had the Emperor, the Son of Heaven, at its apex. This vertical structure and the horizontal structure of ancestor worship were complementary and rooted in the same ideological system.
- Dualism as expressed in the *yin–yang* scheme was basically a model for the harmonization of opposites (but also was a ruling technique that gave prominence to the patriarchal *yang*). The ideal was to merge conflicting elements into a unified harmony by promoting interdependence, complementarity, and the Golden mean, or *zhong yong*. The ideal however was not a free and harmonious union, but a *controlled* model of harmony.
- This system was maintained by a meritocracy of civil servants who shared a common code of ruling techniques and norms and a common interest in upholding this code. The ideological basis for this meritocracy became routinized and increasingly ossified through an elaborate system of examinations based on the Confucian classics.
- An administrative system of commanderies and prefectures, or *junxian*, which had already been introduced in pre-Qin times, remained dominant over the sometimes recurring 'feudal' (*fengjian*) structure. The *junxian* system was a regional administrative network that secured central control which was not equalled in Europe until the nineteenth century.[23]
- The Chinese morphosyllabic script was the most important of several 'tools' of governance that became subject to standardization.[24] The script and its language was not, however, sacred in the same sense as the script of the other universalist high cultures of antiquity. It shared the same status as a truth-language with Church Latin and Qur'anic Arabic,[25] but it was first and foremost a *statist* language, in the sense

that it was first and foremost applied in connection with the upkeep of the 'secular' state.

- A concept of cosmic centrality structured this system spatially as well as symbolically. In traditional China, there were five cardinal directions, the centre constituting the fifth 'direction'. The other directions were meaningless without the centre.[26]

The notion of unitarianism has been pervasive in traditional Chinese thought, and may be seen as the underlying principle of a tradition that probably has been more holistically oriented than any other major political culture in the traditional world.[27] It is my assertion that it is still very much alive in the minds of the average Chinese today, the only exception being the emerging new Taiwanese identity. This obsession with 'unity' (*tongyi*),[28] and the corresponding abhorrence of 'splittism' (*fenlie*), still constitute a potent political lever in present-day Chinese politics; moreover, it can be explained from the fact that China has experienced several periods of disunity, which will be discussed below.

The Traditional Chinese World Order

What is usually termed as 'the Chinese World Order' may be regarded as the notion of unitarianism applied to the various Others. For a Chinese of the Great Confucian tradition, the world was a coherent whole. The Empire constituted the entire civilized world, which was surrounded by layers of barbarians of the various directions, the most troublesome of which were the northern and north-western barbarians. In traditional Chinese historical and ethnographic sources, there are hundreds, if not thousands, of appellations and descriptions of various peoples beyond the imperial pale. Thus, we must not confuse the traditional Chinese notion of superiority with a lack of interest in the world around them. However, as we will see below, this interest was based primarily on strategic considerations.

The salient features of the traditional Chinese world order may for our purpose be briefly stated as follows.

The fundamental strategy was to control the surrounding barbarian world, instead of striving to conquer as much as possible in a Napoleonic manner. The only way barbarians could be *included* into the empire was 'to come and be transformed' (*lai hua*) through a process of acculturation, by initiating a Lévi Straussian process of going from a state of being 'raw' (*sheng*) to becoming 'cooked' (*shu*), i.e. becoming civilized in the Confucian sense. The Chinese and the Others were distinguished on the basis of a set of cultural markers, the most important of which was the prescribed system of Confucian rites. A popular traditional appellation of China is 'The Land of Rites and Righteousness' (*Li yi zhi bang*).

The various strategies for achieving control ranged from the purely conciliatory ones, i.e. by promoting the positive example of the Confucian 'virtue' (*de*), to the purely practical Legalist punitive (*zhengfa*) strategies. The strategy adopted tended to be synchronized with the status of the various peoples involved. Those who resided nearer and were already accultured to some extent were regarded as 'inner' (*nei*) barbarians, while those further away were termed 'outer' (*wai*), and for them different 'medicines' were prescribed.

The comprehensive strategies for regulating the relation between the Empire and its neighbours has in Western usage been termed the 'tribute' system. It originated in early Zhou times, and became fully developed during the Ming.[29] There is, significantly, no single term in Chinese for this regulatory system, but rather a number of different terms, such as 'to keep loose reins' (*ji mi*), encompassing different political measures and strategies towards the barbarians' polities. The reason for the absence of a general term is that the system as such did not involve the conceptualization of one dominating country versus the other lesser countries.

The claims of universal kingship were however frequently intercepted by starkly different realities in times of dynastic decline and disorder. The policies could be accommodating, if forced by circumstances, to the extent of accepting adversaries on an equal footing. This was the case with the militarily weak Northern Song Emperor who conceded to the Qidan ruler the title of Emperor (*Huangdi*),[30] and the Qing court's acceptance of Russia as an equal partner in the Treaty of Kiakhta in 1727.[31]

In spite of bowing to the practical realities at times, one cannot infer that the traditional order contained rudiments of an 'international system'.[32] It was a system in which the Emperor was the apex of the whole civilized world and whose orders were expected to be obeyed even in the most remote parts of the World below Heaven. 'Foreign relations' in the Westphalian and Vienna traditions thus may hardly be said to have existed: rather, relations with neighbouring and more remote polities were conceived of as extensions of the social hierarchy that existed within China. In this sense, they were of utmost importance for diagnosing the state of affairs inside the Empire, as illustrated by expressions like 'internal problems or trouble abroad' (*nei you wai huan*).[33] Frequent tributary missions calling on the borders were a sign of great imperial authority, and less frequent missions a sign of the opposite.[34] As Mark Mancall has expressed it, 'for the Chinese, the emergence of problems [in the border regions] was a sign of failure, not their solution a sign of success'.[35]

In spite of imperialist encroachments in the nineteenth century, China succeeded in retaining sovereignty over most of the regions that had been incorporated into the Empire during the heyday of the Qing. But the world of the tribute system received a lethal blow with the treaty of Tianjin in 1858. The age of 'soft' frontiers was withering, and was having to be replaced by 'hard' frontiers. That meant that former barbarian buffers like Mongolia, Xinjiang, and Tibet had to be either excluded or included. Faced with different imperialist designs, late Imperial, early Nationalist, and Communist leaders went for the second option: the vast ethnic regions of the former Empire were transformed into inalienable parts of the motherland.[36]

Even during the heyday of Chinese ethnic nationalism around 1911, when the revolution brought the imperial order down, the calls for an ethnically based Chinese nation were quickly replaced by a modified version of traditional Confucian cosmopolitanism.[37] During the decennia of the Republic, the ethnic regions were either left to tend to themselves, or ruled by Chinese warlords. It was only with the advent of the socialist order that the various ethnic minorities were elevated to the status of nationalities. On the whole, this was a remarkable change both in an international context and especially in its Chinese context. But in some cases it involved lumping several distinct ethnic groups together, and in other cases it created nationalities where before there had been no sense of ethnic identity. This process may thus be seen both as an effort to dismantle the former imperial geopolitics by creating 'nations by design',[38] and as an attempt to apply the former imperial strategy of retaining the loyalty of local chiefs (*tusi*), by establishing new autonomous regions where the local upper strata were invited to take part in political affairs. Thus, while the Chinese Communists recognized the legal status of the ethnic minorities, they retained the old unitarian notion of China. The first Constitution of the People's Republic proclaimed China to be 'a united, multi-national state' (*tongyide, duo minzude guojia*).

The notion of the Great Systemic Whole in traditional Chinese world order is of utmost importance in assessing the future of China. This field may easily become both sensitive and emotional, because it involves notions of cosmic centrality that remained dominant in Chinese thought until the end of the last century. I do not want to imply that this tradition still constitutes the main conceptual framework of the Chinese policy-makers and people, but there is no denying that it is a unique and rich tradition that forms a common heritage for both the political élites and the people. It is a tradition that in no way is limited to dealing with the outside world, but extends to the political and social realms as well. In essence, it is a tradition that deals with the arts of governance.

One could choose a number of phenomena to illustrate this. One telling example is the Chinese tradition of strategic thinking as it is expressed in the formulation of stratagems, *mouliie*, or *jimou*, which draws heavily on popular classical works like the Intrigues of the Warring States (*Zhanguo ce*), and The Romance of the Three Kingdoms (*San guo yanyi*). A recent selection of around five hundred commonly used Chinese stratagems, published in 1990, contains, besides sections on stratagems for politics, military, economics, arguments, and fraudulence, lengthy sections on foreign policy and on ways of exercising universal authority (*tongyu mouliie*).[39]

When characterizing China as an empire-state, I may misleadingly allude to modern Western imperial images. The imperial heritage of China is in most respects quite different, with a rationale of its own. One significant difference is that it was Napoleonic in its drive for conquests to a much lesser degree than Western imperialism. Rather, the world was to be ordered through the tribute system. Admittedly, during the great dynasties such as the Han, Tang, and Qing, large-scale military expeditions did occur; but on the whole, the main strategy was to keep the empire intact through *controlling* its environments, not conquering as much land as possible. In this respect, the present-day empire-state is not at all dissimilar with its predecessors, except for the fact that the former border areas have become strictly delineated either as a part of China or as independent polities. It is very unlikely that China will take on an expansionist policy in Asia, but the present territorial make-up of China will be defended at all costs. In this respect, there is unlikely to be any substantial difference between the Communists and the Guomindang.

One incident that certainly contributed to the restoration of imperial geopolitics was Outer Mongolia's proclamation of independence from China as a kingdom under the Jebtsundamba Khutuktu in 1911.[40] Mongolia's independence was not recognized by China until 1952, as a result of Soviet pressure that originated with Mao's visit to Moscow in 1950. The Guomindang government in Taiwan has never recognized Mongolia's independence, and Mongolia has accordingly been safely delineated within the borders of China on the official maps published in Taiwan. However, both national and local borders should be seen more as a blank denial of any treaties and administrative changes carried out by the CCP government in Beijing than as an actual political claim.

Another aspect of the traditional Chinese world order is that external politics and domestic politics were seen as being different expressions of the same state of moral–political order of a regime. Of late, it has become quite the vogue to claim that the old guard of Chinese Communist leaders in general, and Mao Zedong in particular, developed their domestic and foreign policies primarily from studying traditional Chinese works of history. This is taken as evidence for the limited mind-set of the old guard of revolutionaries. While this is certainly true at least in part, such preoccupations are meant to illustrate how hopelessly out of touch with the present-day realities the Chinese leaders have been. But what do those who pass such judgements know of the works in question?

This issue may be illustrated by referring to Harrison Salisbury's repeated reference to the general history of China called *Zizhi tongjian* (Comprehensive Mirror as an Aid to Government). Salisbury characterizes this work as 'designed as a practical handbook for the emperor, telling him how his predecessors had handled difficult questions',[41] or as a 'dynastic commentary'.[42] In actual fact, the *Zizhi tongjian* is a general history of China written in the annalistic style, and covering the period from 403 BC to AD 960. It was compiled by Sima Guang, a leading scholar and politician of his day, and took nineteen years to complete. The 294-chapter work was presented to the throne in 1085. It is true that Sima Guang was conservative as a politician, and it is likewise true, as the title indicates, that the work had a didactic purpose, but that was a central concern of all Chinese historiography. However, it surpassed by far any historical work up to the advent of modern historiography in the West.

Methodologically, *Zizhi tongjian* featured two innovations: it made use of extensive source-material, including literary and inscriptive materials; and it contained thirty chapters of *kaoyi*, or 'inquiries into the divergences of the source material', where problems of source critique were discussed in a manner that is surprisingly scientific. Above all, the work is much more than a mere 'practical handbook'. It is an original work written in an extremely clear and readable style, and it gives invaluable insight into the traditions of the politics of the Great Systemic Whole and the Chinese world order. We are free to close our eyes to a sophisticated tradition that probably has been more systemic than any other autochthonous political order in the history of mankind; but in so doing we would thereby make ourselves less able to understand the significance that this great tradition has for the Chinese of today and in the future.

From a Cultural to a National Identity?

In the proliferation of studies on nationalism since the early 1980s, the experience of China is treated in a most perfunctory and conventional way, if mentioned at all. Indeed, this is frequently also the case with works that pretend to present the topic in its Asian context.[43] If we compare China's history with the central themes about the origins of nations and various forms of nationalisms, one feature stands out: most of the theoretical issues related both to the origins of Western nationalism and to colonial nationalism are in one way or another relevant to China, but mostly as a *contrast* to the evolution of classical Western nationalism and forms of colonial nationalism. This is because one can—from the earliest times—talk about a continuous and contiguous cultural–political entity called 'China', even if there has been a multitude of different stage settings and actors down through history. If there is one single country that convincingly aspires to have been a 'nation before nationalism', it must be China. But China is conspicuously absent in the most influential works on nationalism that discuss this issue.[44]

An influential trend in American sinology has maintained that the Chinese traditionally have had a cultural identity, rather than an identity based on race or ethnicity. In this scheme, a perception of a Chinese state or nation apart from its cultural heritage was simply unthinkable. The discussion about unitarianism and the traditional Chinese world order above may be taken as a basic acceptance of the validity of such a claim. However, there remains the problem of how to delineate the cultural artefacts that constituted this identity. Such a venture would probably prove to be futile, because one will quickly be carried out from the realm of culture into the realm of politics. This illustrates the insufficiency of the term 'cultural identity', because it misses the specific relation between culture and politics in its Chinese context: *the one was embedded in the other, and it would thus be extremely difficult, if not impossible, to ascertain where 'culture' stops and 'politics' starts, or vice versa.*[45]

The Harvard sinologue Tu Wei-ming has coined the term 'Cultural China' (*Wenhua Zhongguo*) to express the preponderance of the cultural identity of the Chinese. Such a term tends to underscore the conceptual problem rather than solving it, because there is no term in traditional Chinese for the modern Western concept of 'culture'. The term that comes closest is probably the comprehensive term *li*, or 'rites'. The term *wenhua* is a modern invention by the Japanese, who borrowed this little used traditional term to coin the Western word 'culture', or *bunka* in Japanese.[46] This conceptual framework was never seriously challenged until modern Western ideas about alternative world orders began to make themselves felt in China. It is only with the disintegration of the traditional imperial order in the last half of the nineteenth century that the concept of 'culture' becomes a distinct realm in Chinese perceptions. It is therefore no exaggeration to say that, if the current popular term 'political culture' has ever had a manifest and unequivocal meaning, it must be in the description of the relationship between governance and culture in traditional China.[47]

The peculiar configuration of Chinese nationalism has been explained as tensions between the disintegration of culturalism in the late nineteenth century and the budding of nationalist ideas that developed from the last decennium of that century until the May Fourth Era under the influence of various Western trends of thought. In the same period, China underwent several earthshaking incidents, including the Sino-Japanese war in 1895, the quelling of the Reform movement of 1898, the Boxer Rebellion in 1900, the downfall of the Empire in 1911, the ensuing Warlord period, and finally the growth of radical nationalism around the New Culture Movement and the May Fourth Movement in 1915–19. During this epoch, the argument goes, the Chinese underwent a transformation from having a (traditional) cultural identity to a (modern) national identity.[48] A more precise way of phrasing it would probably be to say that the Chinese for the first time became aware of a distinction between culture and politics as separate fields.

The basis for nationalist thinking in China is rather distinct from most types of colonial nationalism, where traditional societies were fragmented and reassembled in a way that mirrored the colonial experience more than their former societies. In spite of colonial encroachments, the Chinese were not welded into new post-colonial entities and identities. In this respect, the Chinese feel more 'at home'—maybe too much so—in their modern nation than do most other Third World peoples. For the Chinese, it has not been the case of 'inventing' or 'imagining' their past to the same degree as for many other peoples, but rather a case of continuing their unbroken dialogues with their own past.

Nationalism in one form or another has been of central concern to all political leaders in twentieth-century China. After the foundation of the People's Republic, state nationalism became an integral part of the nation-building process. In the 1920s and 1930s, the Chinese Communist Party subscribed to Comintern ideas of a federal structure for a future liberated China, but these were quietly dropped during the Yan'an period.[49] As mentioned earlier, the People's Republic was from the outset 'a unitarian, multi-ethnic state'. Nationalist sentiments and propaganda peaked during the Korean War, at the height of the Sino-Soviet split, and during the Vietnam War. However, they were overshadowed by socio-revolutionary strategies during the Maoist period, when the issue of class took preference over the concern of the nation. Also, traditional Han Chinese sentiments *vis-à-vis* the minority peoples of China—dubbed 'Great Han Chauvinism'—were at times curbed in order to facilitate the nation-building process.

The reason why the transition from the traditional Chinese world order to China's becoming a member of 'the family of nations' was such a painful process that it necessitated a fundamental break with Confucian universalism. The traditional imperial order and its social ethics were merely different expressions of a holistic system. The historical significance of the various groups of reformists around the turn of the century was that they accepted a disjunction between the political order and its cultural foundations. By distinguishing between the two, political reforms were conceivable without Heaven coming tumbling down. The idea of The World below Heaven as a centre of the civilized world had to be relinquished, but the idea of The World below Heaven as a *moral* universe— that is, the notion of the superiority of Chinese culture—could be retained.

The ideological groundwork for this was elaborated both by constitutional reformists such as Liang Qichao and by a group that rallied around the concept of *guo cui* (national essence). This latter was an anti-Manchu movement at the beginning of the century which promoted cultural conservatism.[50] Its supporters accepted the fact that the traditional imperial order might disappear physically, provided that the national essence could be externalized, so to speak, in cultural forms.[51] This attitude clashed with reformers like Liang Qichao (1873–1929), who saw a modernized, Western-inspired nation as the basis for a new constitutional system,[52] and above all with the New Culture Movement from 1915 onwards, which advocated political *as well as* cultural modernization.

Modern Chinese conservatism has thus primarily taken the form of *cultural* conservatism, with no clear programme of *political* conservatism. Certainly, there were attempt to save the imperial institution in some modified form or other, such as Kang Youwei's short-lived 'Party for the Protection of the Emperor' (Bao huang dang), but the odds against the imperial institution were great. Events like the humiliating defeat for Japan in 1895, the *coup d'état* by the Empress Dowager Ci Xi in 1898 against the young and reform-minded Emperor, the inertia against foreign encroachments on China, and above all the fact that the royal house was of Manchu stock and not ethnically Chinese, were factors that effectively sealed the fate of the Chinese imperial order. Because of this historical constellation, one will not find in China any basis for restoring the former imperial house, unlike in Russia. If there are any likely candidates for future nativist heroes, it will be early Republican martyrs like Tan Sitong, Ming loyalists like Wang Fuzhi and Gu Yanwu, who refused to cooperate with the new Manchu dynasty, and Yue Fei, the Southern Song general who fought bravely against invasion from the north.[53]

There is another aspect that complicates our understanding of the nature of Chinese nationalism. That is the relation between nationalism and modernization. The uniform and widespread focus on the present Chinese efforts of modernization frequently blurs the fact that China has been trying to modernize in some way or other for the last 140 years. Not only that, the basic issues have remained more or less the same, and are as valid and contested today as they were a hundred years ago, when they were succinctly formulated by the conservative reformer Zhang Zhidong. He coined the slogan 'Take Chinese learning as the basics and Western learning for application' (*Zhong xue wei ti, xi xue wei yong*). Since then, the Chinese have been hotly debating what constitutes 'the basics' and what 'application'.[54]

Why has this been such a touchy topic? Because it goes to the core of how the Chinese react to the consequences of modernization. As always, modernization involves both embracing and rejecting. Since Chinese modernization from the outset was a fruit of its forced encounter with imperialism, it made the proponents of modernization vulnerable to hostile populist sentiments. The culturalist basis could be mobilized for fanning anti-modernization sentiments, thus making Chinese nationalism rather unpredictable. It seems—in the parlance of the theoreticians of nationalism—that the universalization of the particular features (*yong*) of nationalism is especially difficult to carry through in China, because it runs up against refractory and potent remnants of traditional Confucian universalism (*ti*). Another way of describing this phenomenon is to say that the pervasive tradition of Confucian universalism has perhaps rendered Chinese ethnic identity more primordial and less situational than is the case for most other peoples. It seems that the more bravely they fight tradition, the more they are likely to get trapped in it.[55]

During the drastic changes of ideological orientation that have taken place in the Chinese political leadership as well as among the Chinese populace during the 1980s and 1990s, the socialist rhetoric has been retained, but the real issues tend more and more to be addressed in a language that is rather a contradictory combination of traditional symbolism and the symbols of modernity. What we have witnessed during the past decade or so is that ethnic Chinese nationalism has not only been given freer rein, but has been used more actively by the political leadership as a lever for implementing the politics of economic reform, as a lever in the efforts to regain Hong Kong and Taiwan, and finally as a source of legitimation for the ailing regime. This fits well with Hobsbawm's assertion that Marxist movements and states tend to become not only national in form, but also nationalist in substance.[56] Mao Zedong has already become a part of the modern nationalists' mythology, and it may seem that the Chinese Communist Party also aims at reserving a 'natural' place for itself in the organic evolution of modern Chinese history. At any rate, the year 1949 in no way looms as high as it used to. The symbols of national liberation seem to be more associated with their national aspects than with their liberating aspects.

One striking example of this reorientation is the revival of the term *Zhonghua minzu*, usually rendered 'the Chinese nation', a term that dates from the formative period of Chinese nationalism around the turn of the century. The term has been used all along in Taiwan, but in the People's Republic it has been used mostly for ceremonial purposes. Of late, however, it has been revived in China and has quickly caught on not only in political parlance, but also in scholarly circles.[57] Chinese history is interpreted as a continuous and organic growth of 'the Chinese nation' from its mythological origin, with the present regime as the natural and legitimate heir to this vast historical legacy. But this concept, which seems to establish 'the Chinese nation' as a supranational concept, implies that the ethnic and national minorities are relegated to various forms of appendices of history, even if their 'contributions' (*gongxian*) to the great unitarian enterprise are duly recognized.[58]

The mobilization of traditional symbols for popular consumption has developed so far and so quickly during recent years that one can talk about a formidable revival of culturalist symbols. This is also taking place in the upper political echelons, as the following report from *Renmin ribao* (the *People's Daily*) illustrates. On 5 April 1993, around 10,000 Chinese, all 'descendants' from the legendary Yellow Emperor, Huang Di, assembled in front of his alleged grave in Qiaoshan, Huangling County in Shaanxi province, to cherish the memory of their first ancestor. In an exceptionally solemn and respectful atmosphere, the graveside rituals commenced. The governor of Shaanxi province was master of ceremonies, and political representatives, overseas Chinese, and people of Chinese descent from Singapore presented wreaths. An advisor to the Chinese Study Society of the Yan-Huang culture performed the ritual sweeping of the grave on behalf of comrades like Bo Yibo and the historian Zhou Sucheng. Then Zhang Liangzhou, a scientist with the rocket division in the American Rockwell aerospace company, read out the ceremonial text on behalf of those who had come from overseas. The day before, persons and organizations from home and abroad had donated around $350,000 for an overall remodelling of the site.[59] Three days later, the same paper reported on its first page that the nation's president, Jiang Zemin, had presented an inscription entitled 'The Chinese Civilization has Distant Origins and has Run a Long Course'[60] for the ongoing remodelling of the site. In one move, 1,500 years of China's history was pushed back. It is as if the work of modern scepticist historians such as Gu Jiegang and his colleagues has been all in vain.[61]

It is however noteworthy that this re-imagination takes place mostly along culturalist lines, and not political ones. If purely political movements along nationalist lines were to be launched, it is more likely that they would seek legitimation from traditional catchwords such as 'national strength' or 'national renewal' rather than from more woolly terms like 'democracy'.[62] Even if the ageing Communist Party seeks legitimation in culturalist symbols, as the example above illustrates vividly, the dominant tendency seems to be more in the spirit of a *guo cui* in reverse, that is, an acceptance of a disjunction between politics and culture if the *political* order can be retained. In this sense, the party may to some extent be able to capitalize on the 'habits of the heart' of former Confucian universalism. After all, the Communist doctrines—at least until recently— have also had clear universalistic and holistic pretensions.

As conservative reformers, Deng and his colleagues on several occasions raised the scenario that the party is the only guarantee of continued reforms and thus the only guarantee for saving the nation (*jiuguo*). If, on the other hand, the party goes down the drain, the state will follow suit (*wangdang, wangguo*)—or so the argument runs. The precedents for the party are gloomy indeed: when the Qing government initiated conservative reforms when the *guo cui* movement was active, it took only a few years before the whole imperial order collapsed in 1911.[63]

If one is to assess the future of Chinese nationalism, one must start from the premise that the presumed tradition from a traditional culturalist identity to a modern political identity was much too neat and not nearly as complete as was formerly thought. Above all, it missed the fundamental point that culture and politics have been much more intertwined in China than elsewhere—and still are. This is the cause of both its depth and its peculiar contours. At any rate, nationalism is bound to remain an important and perhaps determining factor in the political development of China as the socialist slogans are gradually being shelved. It may take on a number of forms and cloaks. It tends to return in force in times of political change and social insecurity. It may develop into an explosive situation where, literally, 'the Empire strikes back'; but it may also be used in the service of further dialogue between China and the world, since—as James Townsend reminds us—many Chinese favour a continued *kaifang*, or opening towards the world, precisely on nationalistic grounds.[64]

Regionalism and Separatism

What was described earlier as the Chinese obsession with unitarianism is easily explained from at least one perspective. China has often been politically and geographically fragmented. This goes even for the periods of dynastic rule, which frequently saw regional attempts at breaking away from imperial control. Periods of disunion are unequivocally viewed as negative, because they are inevitably associated with the forces of disunion (*fenlie*) and/or chaos (*luan*).[65] Those who tried to carve out their own independent lesser polities (*geju*),[66] be they challengers of the dynastic order, regional military satraps, or barbarian chieftains, were doomed to have their deeds chronicled in the most inauspicious parts of the official histories.

The irony of history is that the periods of political disunion turned out to be periods of great cultural and institutional innovation. This is generally recognized for the Spring and Autumn and the Warring States periods (eighth to third centuries before Christ), less so for the period between the Han and the Sui dynasties (third to sixth centuries after Christ), and hardly at all for the other shorter periods of disunity.

Thus, the centrifugal forces in Chinese history have been strong, and also have prepared the ground for periods of cultural and institutional creativity, even if the inclination towards the centripetal has been pointed out as one of the basic-virtues characteristic of Chinese history. Viewed in *la longue durée*, the last thousand years of Chinese history, relatively speaking, have shown more imperial cohesiveness than the first millennium of our era: the last time China was fragmented into several lesser states was in the period AD 960–970, the so-called Five Eras (*Wu dai*) between the Tang and Song dynasties.

The Spring and Autumn period saw the gradual growth of cooperation between the centrally located states, or *Zhong guo* (written as two words!), as defensive measures against the outlying and less civilized states, notably the southern state of Chu. The central states were located more or less in the regions that had been controlled by the former dynasties of Shang and Zhou. It is however misleading to regard the Zhou and its predecessor as territorial dynastic entities in the same sense as the later Qin and Han. They were more the political and ritual apex of a complex array of vassals, allies, and enemies.

When the great age of Chinese thought (sixth to third centuries before Christ) sought inspiration in the Early Zhou in order to remedy the deplorable inter-state relationships, it was primarily as an ideological epitome rather than as a factual great and unified dynasty. The evolution of the political cultures in the various states blended the various strains of political thought with the local indigenous cultures. This resulted in regional cultural diversification, but not to such an extent that it would have laid the foundation for alternative cultural identities or political orders that were inherently non-Chinese. Quite the contrary: the ruling strata in the various states and regions literally wrote and spoke the same language, and the pull was rather towards the central regions as a symbol of commonality.

Shortly after the downfall of the Han dynasty at the beginning of the third century after Christ, a qualitatively new situation arose on the Chinese political scene: northern China, the heartland of the ancient Chinese culture and polities, was conquered by non-Chinese northern barbarians. This had its precedents in the Xiongnu encroachments on northern China during the Han, and was to become a basic pattern in the relationship between Chinese and non-Chinese: almost without exception, the military threat against China has come from peoples inhabiting the vast regions north of the Chinese core areas.

The new barbarian dynasties were to last for nearly three hundred years. To the weaker dynasties in the south, who saw themselves as the legitimate successors to the Qin and Han empires, the situation looked bleak indeed.[67] However, in spite of being the carriers of many 'alien' features that were introduced into the affairs of state (this was the heyday of what we may call statist Buddhism but also of statist Taoism, the latter of which of course was of Chinese origin), these lesser dynasties gradually became sinicized. Not only that, they also promoted institutional innovations that became part of a reinvigorated Chinese political order.

The reasons why this process of sinicization—which was to become a pattern in later ages—took place are rather evident. Here, I can highlight only some of the aspects. In the first place, there was no alternative universal order (like Islam) that could replace the disgraced Confucian order after the downfall of the Han. Buddhism did not offer a sufficiently complete 'programme' for matters both temporal and spiritual. In the second place, even if the Chinese imperial order was the adversary of the alien conquerors, its secrets of the art of statecraft were very tempting to emulate; at least, these skills, be they administrative or military, were more suited to run such a huge, sophisticated agrarian society than any other institutional import. Furthermore, the new conquerors had to solicit the assistance of the former local ruling strata in order to achieve this aim. Finally, the sheer size of the Chinese population (it is estimated that both the Han and the Tang dynasties had populations of about 50 million) hardly gave the new rulers any choice. The net results of these processes were that the moment the new rulers descended from their horses, they started the transformation of their own identities.

In periods of general disintegration in China, the various regions—even those striving to retain their independence *vis-à-vis* the others—invariably strove to emulate the former imperial order. If sufficiently strong, they would also be pretenders to the restoration of 'the Great Systemic Whole'. This is reflected clearly in the appellations of their lesser orders: they would invariable choose names that related to some former meritorious dynasty. Thus, the states in the Five Eras between the Tang and the Song called themselves Later Liang, Later Tang, Later Jin, Later Han, and Later Zhou respectively.

On the other hand, and this is important for our argument, each major historical region of China has traditionally applied the historical names of the various regions—which in most cases go back to the most ancient appellations—as some kind of basic but secondary identity. For example, even today, any phenomenon relating specifically to Yunnan or Sichuan would in many contexts by Dian or Shu, respectively,[68] rather than bearing the formal names of the provinces. A person from Guangdong Province in the south does not speak 'Guangdong-ese' (i.e. Cantonese), but the Yue regionalect.[69] The inherited regional cultural identity has been applied to features such as language, arts, cuisine, etc., and also used in an informal, political sense. But such appellations may be said to be cultural rather than culturalist. These regions might constitute independent states, like Shu during the romanticized Three Kingdoms period in the third century after Christ, but would not have imperial pretensions.[70] However, these regional names would have been conceived of as meaningless unless there were some larger and more basic culturalist tradition which they could relate to in one way or other.

Thus, these regions and their appellations have left their definite imprint on the Chinese political landscape, but the status of such regions was of a nature that we, in perhaps a somewhat contradictory term, could call basic but secondary. This order of things could be mobilized (and in fact, still is!) when the larger imperial order waned, and would recede to its place in the hierarchy when the imperial order waxed. Even if this was frequently exploited to its full extent (and it still is!), it would rarely go beyond semi-independence and local satrapy. There was never any 'breakthrough' in the European sense: there was simply no conceptual space in which to create an alternative world order or particularistic nations beyond the 'Great Systemic Whole'.[71]

The relation between the centripetal and centrifugal forces in Chinese history is extremely complicated. The centripetal tendency has been regarded almost as a virtue.[72] On the other hand, there has also been sufficient conceptual room for a state of disunions, even if that has been regarded as uniquely undesirable. The oscillation between unity and disunity becomes a basic feature of historical time, which in its traditional Chinese context is more cyclical than linear. As Arthur Wright says: 'While political disintegration was thought of—in terms of various life-cycle analogies—as periodically inevitable, reunification, by the same analogies, was regarded as inevitable.'[73] The opening passage of the famous historical novel Romance of the Three Kingdoms (*Sanguo yanyi*) sums up this train of thought. As a backdrop to an account of the waxing and waning of the various dynasties of antiquity, it says, with an air of populist authority, that, 'after a long separation, there is bound to be unity; after a long unity, there is bound to be separation [*fen jiu bi he, he jiu bi fen*]'.[74] This adage is also brought up in the *Heshang*,[75] which is understandable, since Jin Guantao was one of the advisors to the series. According to Jin, the hyperstability (*chao wending*) of the Chinese feudal structure can be explained by the shift between the recurrent breakdowns and reinvigorations of the dynastic order that in the long run came out as a hyperstable structure.[76] It may seem that the price of unity has been the acceptance of periods of disunity.

While it is true that Chinese history seems hyperstable at the first glance, it is not a simple matter to assign primacy to specific features such as structural features, ideological features, geopolitical features, contingencies,[77] etc. Above all, the notion of the cyclic and stagnant nature of Chinese history is nothing but a dated sinological notion, and the nineteenth-century Western origin of such a notion can hardly be taken as sufficient proof of its modernity.[78]

Warlordism and Federalism

The big uprisings against the Qing dynasty in the middle of the nineteenth century, including the Taiping and Nian rebellions, were the last traditional peasant uprisings in China's history. However, before and after the downfall of the imperial order, China experienced three types of regional movement arising from the chaotic political landscape that followed the emperor's abdication in 1912: these were the plans for local self-government, the warlord regimes, and the federalist movement. During the eight years from 1916 to 1923, these three movements were concurrently played out.

The provincial level of China had been the scene of various modest reforms during the last part of the nineteenth century. This was initiated by provincial governors who were mostly ethnically Chinese. In their terminal years, the Qing had promulgated political reforms that would have resulted in a considerable degree of local self-government (*difang zizhi*). The developments of such politics were particularly noteworthy in the provinces of Guangdong, Guangzi, Hunan, and Shanxi. Philip Kuhn says that this movement may be seen as an effort to solve the problems of the internal conditions which were not solved during the Qing and which in some respects still remain to be solved today. He continues: 'Though local self-government can be considered something of a blind alley in China's political evolution, the techniques and assumptions that underlie it form vital components of the larger process whereby the relations between China's local society and government have been modernized.'[79] He concludes by saying that it was invariably connected with political programmes that promised more than they delivered: 'in practice, [it] was associated with all the evils of the age: the arbitrary exercise of power by rapacious local élites and petty functionaries; the ambitions of provincial warlords; and the preachments of a political party that promised democracy but delivered dictatorship'.[80]

When the dynasty fell and the attempts to create a national republic ended with Yuan Shikai's attempt at monarchical restoration in 1915, the provinces and regions became the principal stages for further political stratagems. In several places, military governors took the reins. This situation lasted until 1928, and in some regions even longer. These military figures are popularly called warlords,[81] and their heyday is called the Warlord Period. Fairbank describes them as 'essentially men in between. They were not in a dynastic interregnum, where "change within tradition" would bring forth a new dynasty. Yet they were not modernizers with a new order in mind.'[82] There is probably a fair degree of agreement about such a description, even if other views have been presented.[83] However, the new access to modern military technology made the relationship between civilian politics and military power look like an 'unbalanced modernization' in favour of the latter.

The political discussions of the day about the nature of warlordism merged with the discussions on the status of the provinces and their role in the problem of China's unity. The central issue in this respect was the discussion on federalism and the federalist movement from 1920 to 1923. When the whole nation succumbed to warlordism, the reformers of the day extended the perspective to an inter-provincial federal self-government (*liansheng zizhi*).[83] Jean Chesneaux, in an early study, concludes that the federalist movement in the early 1920s can best be interpreted as the provincial level in the Chinese political hierarchy asserting the provinces as clearly delineated political, economic, and social entities, without aspiring to create a separate state order.[85] But he also stresses that it was more a movement by conservative forces in Chinese society than a radical and occidentalist movement.

Recently, occasioned by the fact that the debate on federalism has been brought back in the political discourse about China's future, Arthur Waldron has summarized the debate on warlordism versus federalism that took place in the 1920s, with actors such as Liang Shuming, Hu Shi, and Chen Duxiu.[86] The main question concerned whether the development of provincial- and regional-based federalist politics was advantageous to warlordism or was a good way of coming to grips with the phenomenon.

The debate also took up the looming issue of the day, namely China's disunity, and how federalism would influence that. Hu Shi was of the opinion that a development of a more civil and democratic society at the provincial level would be the best guarantee of a future strong and democratic China, since the country's fundamental problem and main source of weakness, as he saw it, was the traditional forced unification from above.[87] The pioneer reformers Kang Youwei and Liang Qichao, for their part, argued that it was only by remaining united that China would be able to constitute itself as a modern nation. According to them, China's main problem at the time of transition was that parochial localism impeded the formation of a modern nation.[88]

The radical Nationalists and Communists had initially supported the federalist ideas,[89] but from 1922 on they relinquished the idea altogether, primarily because of the split between Sun Yatsen and the warlord Chen Jiongming in Guangdong. The chairman of the CCP, Chen Duxiu, argued that 'Those advocating federalism did not understand that the historical basis of disunity in China lay in the efforts of militaristic hegemons (*ba*) [to] control a particular area and its resources'.[90] When the radical Nationalists and the Communists withdrew their support, the whole movement folded within a year.[91]

The Future of the Chinese Empire-State

There are a number of important factors that will decide the future of China. Deliverance from Communist Party domination is bound to be a long and complex process, and will constitute a major leap in the mentality history of the Chinese. Regional politics, with the issues of Hong Kong and Taiwan as the pivot, may cause major dislocations. The social costs of a transformed economy provide a rather grim outlook. The widening gap between the urban and rural populace in terms of both life-style and cultural values will create new social conflicts. On one level, China seems to be heading for a state where 'all that is solid melts into air',[92] where traditional identities are being mobilized but at the same time being recast in a quicker and quicker pace. The vastly increased physical and occupational mobility, and above all the rising general expectations among the populace, have created a restlessness that is very unlikely to recede and which will be very difficult for any political leadership to handle.

On another level, even if China is almost bursting in its social seams, it is still very much a *functioning* country. China has been eminently governable, both as a Confucian and as a socialist empire, but will this huge country be governable in a state of relative modernity as well? This essay has stressed the necessity of understanding certain aspects of traditional Chinese thought as a key to understanding likely scenarios in China's development. The rapid developments in China since the early 1980s may seem more novel to us than they are to the actors themselves. When we marvel over the emergence of ethnic or sub-ethnic identities we had not heard of before, perhaps we overrate their significance because *we* have not been aware of them. When we point at strikingly new features of personal or social values, we easily forget that in no way means that *entire* personalities or social values are being recast. What is most spectacular to us may turn out to be the least significant.

With these precautionary words in mind, I will end this essay with a brief return to the main theme. I have termed the Chinese state—perhaps provocatively to some—an empire-state. This neologism is an attempt to characterize the special nature of the topic of our investigation. It points to the enormous format of the imperial order, and also to the fact that in many ways it has continued to this day. Lucian Pye in a much quoted passage has said: 'The struggle for modern Chinese nationalism has been a Herculean effort to squeeze a civilization into the framework of a nation-state.'[93] In line with this, Tu Wei-ming discusses the Chinese state as a 'civilization-state'.[94]

When characterizing China as an empire-state, I imply that the country is not a nation-state in the regular sense of the term, and that it probably never will be. I find it unlikely that 'the Age of the Nation-States' will ever reach China, effecting the creation of independent states from the major Chinese regions. One serious obstacle for such a development is the dual integrative effects of the international economic order and of the nascent Chinese bureaucrat–capitalist order. But the decisive factor is that the political unity of China has always been regarded as being of fundamental value in itself, and probably will continue to be so regarded in the foreseeable future.

An outstanding feature of nationalism is that it is supposedly universally copyable, but the dissemination of such ideas in China did not lead to attempt to create lasting independent entities from the former Chinese Empire (with the exception of Mongolia). Rather, the solution for China became a new type of Western ideology that in many ways had universalist pretensions. With the waning of this socialist ideology, it is a modified universalist notion of *Da yitong* that seems to be returning, rather than ideal-type nationalism. In this scheme, the notions of *fenlie* or *geju* will remain as patently negative concepts as ever. The efforts of China to become a nation among others seem—ironically—to have secured prolonged life to the notion of the *Da yitong*. An increased Chinese nationalism will definitely take the whole of present-day China as its basic point of attention.

But does not the increasing disobedience from the provinces and regions point towards a development that works counter to the perpetuation of the empire-state? This is certainly true, but we are still a far way from serious contemplations about forming separate nation-states. Again, we may be misled by the notion of China as a uniformly unified state during our own time. The centrifugal forces have been there all along, even during the People's Republic.[95] They have only become more vocal during the last decennium. Even if the various coastal provinces like to compare themselves with the various small economic dragons or tigers beyond their shores, no intellectual or political force of any conviction has attempted to formulate an actual programme for full independence. It is only in a situation with a general breakdown of the political centre (*zhongyang*)[96] that different regions will proclaim their independence. This happened in 1915, for example, when the warlords of Yunnan, Guizhou, and Guangxi declared their independence in protest against Yuan Shikai's attempt to restore the imperial order. But it is highly doubtful that regional sentiments will grow so strong that the regional identity will become a primary identity and the Chinese identity secondary. The pronouncements and symbolic actions of the regional leaders of today express first and foremost a discontent with the state of affairs in Beijing, but only as a means of getting the best of two—not worlds—but situations.

Several writers, the most vocal of whom is Edward Friedman, have lately raised the prospect of China being divided into a northern and a southern part as a result of the modernization processes.[97] While it is true that there are both important and interesting historical contradictions on many levels between the North and the South that may be exploited by both 'parties' today, and which may be aggravated in the future, Friedman reveals a surprisingly shallow understanding of basic historical facts and argues in a reductionist manner to make his point: the North is uniformly regarded as 'Leninist' and is subject to procrastination, while the 'southern project' is regarded as 'dynamic' and is presented in a romanticized manner.[98] Friedman seems, among others, to believe that the theory of the Yellow River region as the cradle of Chinese civilization is a Communist invention, and that the ancient near-coastal cultures of Wu and Yue belonged to the ancient inland Chu culture,[99] a view that would not sell well even if presented to business-minded people in today's Wu and Yue regions. Friedman is right in pointing to the increased importance of the South in the construction of a modern Chinese identity, but his claim that this will be the main constituent part in a new Chinese *national* identity rests more on wishful thinking than on historical insight.[100]

The Taiwan experience shows that it is indeed possible to develop a notion of a primary affiliation that is independent of the great unitarian order of the Mainland. But the case of Taiwan, strategic considerations aside, illustrates only too well how difficult it will be to implement something similar under the infinitely more complex relations on the Mainland. It should rather, I think, be regarded as a case of *xiao guo gua min*—a small state with few people.

Still, the former debate on federalism has recently been raised again, the most vocal voice being the prominent dissident Yan Jiaqi.[101] The debate is likely to become more intense in the years ahead, because such a solution can possibly encompass the questions of the major ethnic regions, the questions of Hong Kong and Macao, the question of Taiwan, *and* the provincial voices. In seeking appropriate precedents, the United States and Switzerland have been presented as possible models.[102] But one can hardly imagine two countries more dissimilar than China and the United States, and Switzerland has been a neat and orderly small confederation almost from its very inception. A federal solution for China would clearly first and foremost have to be a 'Chinese-style' federation, because of the constraints of the heavy baggage of traditional thought. In this context, the formal features of a federation in conventional Western thinking, which presupposes that federations are democracies, are of limited relevance to China in the foreseeable future.[103]

Contemporary federalist arguments echo the view of Hu Shi, referred to earlier, that the basic evil in Chinese society is the autocratic power structure in Beijing. More regional power would thus be an efficient way of encouraging a democratic development. Fang Lizhi, who is not an outspoken federalist, nevertheless voices similar ideas: 'As soon as Deng Xiaoping dies, central control will weaken and local forces will rise, Guangdong, Fujian and Shanghai will ask for more democracy . . . The strong autonomous tendency among local authorities is not entirely a bad thing. Maybe it can put an end to the oligarchy in China.'[104]

While few would deny that Beijing is autocratic and has wielded excessive power, it does not necessarily follow that a transfer of authority to the regional level would result in less authoritarianism and more democracy. Nobody has yet seriously proposed that the Chinese democrats all reside in the provinces. The result may just as well be the opposite, namely that the traditional autocratic modes of governance are reproduced in degenerated forms on a lower level, such as was witnessed during the Warlord Period. I remain convinced that any major transformation of the Chinese state cannot take place in a reasonably orderly manner unless such changes are sanctioned by Beijing. The questions of reform from above or reform from below in the context of centralized and regionalized power seem surprisingly to have been rather peripheral to the recent Chinese debates over neo-authoritarianism. The discussion has been centred primarily around regime types.[105]

While the 'strong state' argument may not sound very attractive when linked to the present Chinese regime, we easily forget that this has been the prerequisite for the spectacular economic development of all the authoritarian Confucian-inspired East Asian states and Singapore. The Communist-led authoritarian Chinese state has shown that it is able to initiate and lead equally spectacular economic and social changes. The prospects of a unified China, however, is 'tainted' by the prospect of continued CCP rule, which to many seems like a worst-case scenario.

Common wisdom in the West sees a close link between the development of the nation-state and the evolution of democratic institutions, but recent experiences in Europe itself have proved that such an equation is too facile. Similarly, the demands on China for a set course of development will most likely turn out to be mere wishful thinking. One phenomenon in the reform process in China is that former state companies are more than happy to be responsible for their profits, but they turn to the state when confronted with losses. There is a similar tendency in Western thinking: Western liberals are happy to give advice on which medicine is best for China, but they have shown less interest in calculating the social costs of their prescription.

A continued unified China will in my opinion almost certainly retain many of the authoritarian features of the present regime. To a large extent, I believe that such features will be independent of the name of the party in power. Proponents of the worst-case scenario of continued party rule are unlikely to be willing to consider the possibility that a future non-CCP-led China may become both more authoritarian and more chauvinistic than the present regime.

If China is to remain united, we must expect that a fair part of the 'feeling' of *Da yitong*, or the Great Systemic Whole, in some way or other will remain as an identifying element. If the notion of *Da yitong* is removed, the Chinese will certainly experience a national deprivation; if, on the other hand, the notion of *Da yitong* is retained, they will certainly continue to feel burdened by their history. The Chinese remain victims of their own historical success, and the transformation of tradition is therefore bound to be a very long-drawn-out process.

If, on the other hand, China were to divide (*fen*), never again to reunite (*he*), this would constitute a fundamental shift in the basic cultural orientations of the Chinese. The politics of economic reform have had an *uprooting* effect, but have also had an *integrating* effect on society. In these days of entrepreneurial bonanza and rampant corruption, it may be difficult to discern the Chinese genius of social immortality, which is really a sophisticated sense of the primacy of politics. My guess is that this will prevent China from collapsing in the process of modernization. The country will certainly be battered, but not necessarily shattered.

NOTES

1. With the obvious exception of Tibet.
2. Used as a pun on the former Chinese magazine, *China Reconstructs*, rather than a methodological approach. The 'reconstruction' of China continued on the pages of this magazine well into the 1980s, when its name was changed to *China Today*.
3. With the exception of Outer Mongolia, the regions east of the Ussuri/Wusuli River, and the easternmost drainage area of the Heilongjiang/Amur River.
4. In this context, I disregard modern colonialist constructs like India and Indonesia.
5. The future fate of the major ethnic regions of China will clearly have great domestic and international repercussions. It is however impossible to fit a meaningful discussion of this issue into the framework of this paper. The primary focus here therefore will be to present and analyse central aspects of how the Chinese state has been perceived by the Han Chinese.
6. Angus C. Graham, *Disputers of the Tao: Philosophical Argument in Ancient China* (LaSalle, Ill.: Open Court, 1989), 4–6; 372–3.
7. Notable exceptions to this are Paul Cohen, 'The Post-Mao Reforms in Historical Perspective', *Journal of Asian Studies*, 47 (1988), 518–40; and some contributions in Brantly Womack (ed.), *Contemporary Chinese Politics in Historical Perspective* (Cambridge: Cambridge University Press, 1991).
8. This is for example, in my opinion the case with the lionized article by Samuel Huntington, 'The Clash of Civilizations?' *Foreign Affairs*, 3 (1993), 22–49.
9. This concept has its origin in a passage from the Shi Ji or 'Records of the Historian': see *Zhongguo chengyu da cidian* (Shanghai: Cishu chubanshe, 1988), 1774.
10. See John K. Fairbank, 'A Preliminary Framework', in John K. Fairbank (ed.), *The Chinese World Order: Traditional China's Foreign Policy* (Cambridge, Mass.: Harvard University Press, 1968), 3. Cf. Gellner's definition of nationalism as a political principle, 'which holds that the political and the national unit should be congruent': Ernest Gellner, *Nations and Nationalism* (Oxford: Blackwell, 1983), 1.
11. This was a six-part television series which set out to analyse the roots of the ills of the traditional landlocked and inward-looking Chinese society and the reasons for its 'yellow' backwardness, as contrasted with the dynamic and modern Western civilization that was based on communication across the 'blue' seas. The word *yang* in Chinese means 'ocean', but also has the derived meaning of 'foreign', i.e. 'that which came from across the seas'. *Yang* is also used in the sense of 'modern' in some contexts, as an antonym to the word *tu*, or 'homespun' (literally, 'earth'). The series was an instant success when it was run on Chinese television in the summer of 1988, but met with swift condemnation by the cultural orthodoxy. The script has been assessed as politically explosive but historically feeble by Western and Chinese critics alike. See e.g. the penetrating critique by Wang Jing, '*He Shang* and the Paradoxes of Chinese Enlightenment', *Bulletin of Concerned Asian Scholars*, 3 (1991), 23–32. One of the scriptwriters, Su Xiaokang—who lives in exile in the West—later modified his views considerably.
12. Su Xiaokang and Wang Luxiang, *Heshang* (Yellow River Elegy) (Henan, 1988), 107.

13. This is understandable as far as the basic message of the series is clearly inspired by the theories of Jin Guantao and Liu Qingfeng, who say that the *Da yitong* is 'a starting point for our dissection of the structure of the feudal Chinese society': see Jin Guantao and Liu Qingfeng, *Xingsheng yu weiji: lun Zhongguo shehui chaowending jiegou* (The Cycle of Growth and Decline: On the Hyperstable Structure of Chinese Society) (Hong Kong, 1992), 20. Jin and Liu are also interviewed about their analysis in the television series.

14. Stephen Field proposes the 'Paramount unified order' ('He Shang and the Plateau of Ultrastability', *Bulletin of Concerned Asian Scholars*, no. 3 (1991), 4–13). 'The Grand coordinating unity' is proposed by Michael Loewe, 'Imperial Sovereignty: Dong Zhongshu's Contribution and His Predecessors', in Stuart Schram (ed.), *Foundations and Limits of State Power in China* (Hong Kong: Chinese University Press, 1987), 50, and 'the Principle of unification' by Derek Bodde in Fung Yulan, *A History of Chinese Philosophy* (Princeton, 1952), i.16. My own translation as 'the Great Systemic Whole' is tentative and provisional. I am discussing this concept in depth in a forthcoming paper. The term *da yitong* is frequently confused with the quite different term *Da tong*, or a utopian 'Great Community': see e.g. Prasenjit Duara, 'Provincial Narratives of the Nation: Centralism and Federalism in Republican China', in Harumi Befu (ed.), *Cultural Nationalism in East Asia* (Berkeley: Institute of East Asian Studies, 1993), 15. The *Da tong* appears for the first time in the Taoist-inspired chapter 'Evolution of the Rites' (*Li yun*) in the Book of Rites (*Li ji*). For the original use of this term, see Hsiao Kung-chuan, *A History of Chinese Political Thought: From the Beginnings to the Sixth Century AD* (Princeton: Princeton University Press, 1979), 124 ff.

15. For a recent attempt to link the concept of *Da yitong* ideologically to the Jixia Academy of the pre-Qin state of Qi, see Sun Kaitai, 'Shilun "gongyang zhuan" de da yitong sixiang' (Probing the Thought on 'the Great Systemic Whole' in the Gongyang Chronicle), *Zhongguo shi yanjiu* (Studies in China's History), 2 (1993), 32–41.

16. The passage in the Chunqiu simply reads: 'It was in the spring of the first year, the first month of the royal [i.e. Zhou] calendar.' On the basis of this, the Gongyang commentary construes catechismically: 'It was in the spring of the first year of Duke Yin, the first month of the royal calendar. What is meant by "the first month of the royal calendar"? It is the great systemic whole.'

The relevant exposée by Dong Zhongshu is rendered as follows by Bodde: 'The principle of unification [*da yitong*] in the Ch'un Ch'iu is a permanent warp passing through the universe, and an expression of what is proper extending from the past to the present. But the teachers of today have diverse standards [*tao*], men have diverse doctrines, and each of the philosophic schools has its own particular position, and differs in the ideas it teaches. Hence it is that the rulers possess nothing whereby they may effect general unification, the government statutes having often been changed; while the ruled know not what to cling to. I, your ignorant servitor, hold that all not within the field of the Six Disciplines or the arts of Confucius should be cut short and not allowed to progress further. Evil and licentious talk should be put a stop to. Only after this can there be a general unification, and can the laws be made distinct, so that the people may know what they are to follow.' Fung, *History of Chinese Philosophy*, i.16–17; *Han Shu* (The History of the Han Dynasty), The Zhonghua (ed.), lvi.2523.

While the term *Da yitong* is in the process of becoming a popular catchword among present-day Chinese historians (cf. Yang Xiangkui, *Da yitong yu rujia sixiang* (The Great Systemic Whole and Confucianist Thought) (Beijing, 1989); Zhou

Qingzhi, 'Shixi xian qin "da yitong" minzuguan' (Attempt at Analysis of 'Great Systemic Whole'-outlook concerning the Nationalities during the Pre-Qin Period). *Yunnan shehui kexue* (Yunnan Social Sciences), 5 (1992), 63–70; and Qiu Jiurong, 'Wei, Jin, Nan-Bei Chao shiqi de "da yitong" sixiang' (Thought on 'the Great Systemic Whole' during the Period of Wei-Jin and the Southern and Northern Dynasties), *Zhongyang minzu xueyuan xuebao*, 4 (1993), 45–51); it is surprisingly absent in standard works on Chinese political thought such as Hsiao, *History of Chinese Political Thought*.

17. Fung, *History of Chinese Philosophy*, i.17.
18. Also here, we owe the terminological summarization to Dong Zhongshu, *Tian ren zhi ji, he er wei yi*. The concept was further elaborated by the Song Neo-Confucians.
19. 'Abruptly, he [the king] asked me: "Through what can the Empire be settled?" "Through unity", I said. The king inquires further: "Who can unify it?' Meng Zi answers: "Those who are not fond of killing can unify it."' See D. C. Lau, *Mencius*, 2 vols. (Hong Kong: Chinese University Press, 1984), 10–11.
20. *Lü shi chunqiu jiaoshi* (The Annals of Sir Lü), collated and explained by Wang Qiyou (Shanghai: Xuelin chubanshe, 1984), 1124.
21. D. C. Lau, *Tao Te Ching* (Hong Kong: Chinese University Press, 1982), 190–1.
22. In spite of the reference to the passage in the *Mencius* above, pre-Qin Confucian political philosophy was only indirectly occupied with the issue of 'national' political unity. The idealized references to western Zhou society did not easily lend themselves to such a notion. This was developed first and foremost by the statecraft-oriented Legalism of the Qin state, which was much less preoccupied with the ideal forms of the past. But also in early Legalist writings, there is little theoretical substantiation of the practical aim they pursued. To the extent that classical Taoism was preoccupied by this issue at all, it was more in the sense of formulating alternatives. The ideal society in the *Dao de jing* was envisaged as 'the state should be small and its people few' (*xiao guo gua min*) (modified from Lau, *Mencius*, 115). This notion is not at all prominent in the minds of the Chinese today, even if the size of the land and its population is a popular topic of common complaints. When I tell Chinese people that my native country Norway has only a little more than 4 million inhabitants, they find it ridiculously silly. However, Sun Longji sees the traditional localism, small peasant consciousness and compartmentalism as expressions of the tradition of *xiao guo gua min*: see Sun Longji, *Zhongguo wenhua de shenceng jiegou* (The Deep Structure of Chinese Culture) (Hong Kong: Jixian chubanshe, 1983), 329 ff.
23. Some Chinese thinkers have voiced the opinion that a modified *fengjian*, or 'feudal', system would have been more efficient and also would have contributed to curbing the autocratic imperial system: see Wm. Theodore de Bary *et al.*, *Sources of Chinese Tradition* (New York: Columbia University Press, 1964), i.553 ff.; Philip A. Kuhn, 'Local Self-Government under the Republic: Problems of Control, Autonomy, and Mobilization', in Frederick Wakeman and Carolyn Grant (eds.), *Conflict and Control in Late Imperial China* (Berkeley: University of California Press, 1975), 261 ff.; and Alexander Woodside, 'Emperors and the Chinese Political System', in Kenneth Lieberthal *et al.* (eds.), *Perceptions on Modern China: Four Anniversaries* (Armonk, NY: M. E. Sharpe, 1992), 8 ff.
24. The most important other ones being the calendar, weight, measures, and the wheel-axle.
25. Benedict Anderson, *Imagined Communities: Reflections on the Origin and Spread of Nationalism* (London: Verso, 1983), 22.
26. This may be observed in every spatial scheme, from the cosmological layout of the

classical capital to the position of the remains of Mao Zedong in the centre of Beijing today: see Rudolf Wagner, 'Reading Chairman Mao Memorial Hall in Beijing: The Tribulation of the Implied Pilgrim', in Susan Naquin and Yü Yingshi (eds.), *Pilgrims and Sacred Sites in China* (Berkeley: University of California Press, 1992), 378–423. Several of the great cultures of antiquity conceived of themselves as cosmically central, but since they have receded into history the continued Chinese notion of centrality seems rather unique.

27. Benjamin Schwartz, when discussing dominant Chinese cultural orientations in a recent article, refers to Jacques Derrida's claim that holistic structures must have a central, underlying principle that acts as an organizing core and governs the elements within the structure. While Schwartz discusses this in terms of cultural orientations, we may borrow this claim for our notion of unitarianism, where the notion of centrality is the symbolic representation of this underlying principle: Benjamin Schwartz, 'Culture, Modernity, and Nationalism: Further Reflections', *Dædalus*, 3 (1993), 208–9.

28. This term occurs already in the *Han Shu*. It has been carried over to the present, where it is applied for the notions of 'unity', 'unify', and 'united' in Communist parlance.

29. See Choon S. Lee, 'The Origin, Function, and Nature of the Tributary System in Chou Times', Ph.D. thesis, University of Kansas (1980); and Mark Mancall, *China at the Center: 300 Years of Foreign Policy* (New York: Free Press, 1984), chs. 2 and 3.

30. See Tao Jingshen, 'Barbarians or Northerners: Northern Sung Images of the Khitans', in Morris Rossabi (ed.), *China among Equals: The Middle Kingdom and its Neighbors, 10th–14th Centuries* (Berkeley: University of California Press, 1983), 66–86.

31. See Rossabi, *China among Equals*, 136–8. On the other hand, if the power relations were different, there would be no concessions. One example is the claim of the southwestern Nanzhao ruler that the relation between the Nanzhao and the Tang should be one of elder and younger brother, and not the prescribed relation of lord and vassal. The Tang never gave in to this claim, even when the Nanzhao for some period occupied Sichuan and Chengdu: see Charles R. Backus, *The Nan-Chao Kingdom and Tang China's Southwestern Frontier* (Cambridge: Cambridge University Press, 1982), 135; 149; 154–8.

32. During the later part of the Zhou period (the so-called Spring and Autumn Period of 8th–5th cent. BC and the so-called Period of the Warring States of 5th–3rd cent. BC), one may arguably discern a 'multi-state system' (see Richard L. Walker, *The Multi-State System of Ancient China* (Hamden, Conn.: Shoestring Press, 1953); and Hans Stumpfeldt, *Staatsverfassung und Territorium im antiken China* (Düsseldorf: Bertelsmann Universitäts Verlag, 1970)); but this in no way became a conceptual model which appealed to the proponents of the later imperial order. Quite the contrary, the period has been—in spite of its uncontested status as the golden period of classical political thought—associated with the antipode of the imperial order, i.e. political disunion and disorder.

33. The expression has its origin in the *Guanzi*: see Allyn W. Rickett, *Guanzi: Political, Economic and Philosophical Essays from Early China* (Princeton: Princeton University Press, 1985), 382.

34. In the period between 1662 and 1911, well over 500 tribute missions from 62 different states called at Beijing: see Mancall, *China at the Center*, 15.

35. ibid. xiii.

36. The present 'patriotic' appellation of China, *Zuguo*, is invariably translated into English as the 'Motherland'. This is also signalled in its Chinese pronominal form, which is the feminine form of the graph for *ta*. There have been various 'parents' allegories in modern Communist parlance, the most common being that of Mao as the father figure and the party as the mother figure. This again has an imperial precedent, cf. the following passage from the Mozi: 'Heaven and the Spirits rewarded them [i.e. the Sage kings], appointed them to be Sons of Heaven, and parents of the people'; see *The Ethical and Political Works of Motse*, trans. Mei Yi-pao (London: Probsthain, 1929), 44. A popular informal appellation of local officials was and still is *fumu guan*, or 'fatherly and motherly official'.

37. If Chinese ethno-nationalism had won out around the time of the revolution in 1911, China today would have been of about the size of Ming China. The present geographical extent of the country is matched only for about 400 years out of the last 1,000 years of Chinese history. This includes the Mongol period.

38. Anthony D. Smith, *National Identity* (London: Penguin, 1991), 110 ff.

39. See Chai Yuqiu (ed.), *Molüe ku* (A Repository of Stratagems) (Beijing: Lantian chubanshe, 1990). For examples of how a classical selection of stratagems—the so-called 'Thirty-Six Stratagems' (*Sanshiliu ji*)—is conceived of and applied today, see Harro von Senger, *Strategeme: Lebens- und Überlebenslisten der Chinesen: die berühmten 36 Strategeme aus drei Jahrtausenden* (Bern: Scherz Verlag, 1988).

40. See C. R. Bawden, *The Modern History of Mongolia*, rev. edn (London: Kegan Paul, 1989), 187 ff.

41. Harrison E. Salisbury, *The New Emperors, Mao and Deng: a Dual Biography* (London: HarperCollins, 1992), 9.

42. ibid. 94.

43. An exception is the recent volume on cultural nationalism in East Asia edited by Harumi Befu, *Cultural Nationalism in East Asia*. Moreover, the issue of Chinese nationalism in its wider context has been surprisingly absent in the discourse on the specificalities of Chinese contemporary politics. The study by James Harrison on modern Chinese nationalism from the late 1960s (James P. Harrison, *Modern Chinese Nationalism* (New York: Hunter College Research Institute of Modern Asia, 1969)) was the last systematic word on the topic until the article by James Townsend, 'Chinese Nationalism', *Australian Journal of Chinese Affairs*, 27 (1992), 97–130. However, the discourse seems to be gaining momentum in several ways. In the first place, it is being linked to the general theoretical discourses on nationalism, as illustrated by Prasenjit Duara's article entitled 'De-constructing the Chinese Nation', *Australian Journal of Chinese Affairs*, 30 (1993), 1–26. In the second place, related aspects of the problematique are being brought up, such as works examining various aspects of Chinese identity: see e.g. Sun Lung-kee, 'Contemporary Chinese Culture: Structure and Emotionality', *Australian Journal of Chinese Affairs*, 26 (1991), 1–41, which is based on his 1993 study in Chinese, *Zhongguo wenhua de shenceng jiegou* (Hong Kong: Jixian chubanshe, 1983); the Spring 1991 issue of *Dædalus* examining the changing meaning of being Chinese today; and the volume examining China's quest for national identity, Lowell Dittmer and Samuel S. Kim (eds.), *China's Quest for National Identity* (Ithaca, NY: Cornell University Press, 1993), where one finds e.g. a rare attempt to discuss the issue of national identity in pre-modern China; see also Michael Ng-Quinn, 'National Identity in Premodern China: Formation and Role Enactment', ibid. 32–61. Finally, Chinese scholars in the diaspora have started to examine various aspects of Chinese nationalism in earnest, as illustrated by the contributions to nos. 15 and 16 of the Hong

Kong journal, *Ershiyi shiji* (The Twenty-First Century), published by the Chinese University of Hong Kong.

44. Cf. John Armstrong, *Nations before Nationalism* (Chapel Hill, NC: University of North Carolina Press, 1982), 287; Anthony D. Smith, *The Ethnic Origin of Nations* (Oxford: Blackwell, 1986), 209 ff.; Smith, *National Identity*, 43 ff. Certain phenomena, e.g. the claim of universal kingship by the Chinese emperor and indeed the traditional Chinese world order itself, weaken the argument for the ancient origins of the Chinese nation. But there are many other phenomena that readily speak in favour of such an argument. Since this is a major topic in itself, which among others includes the question of the origin and nature of the Han people (which we in daily parlance call 'the Chinese'), it would go way beyond the confines of this brief essay.

45. There is a faulty use of terminology to express this tradition in Western sinology. The tradition is characterized by the term *zheng jiao heyi* (the fusion of the political and cultural order): see Schwartz, 'Culture, Modernity and Nationalism', 209; also Benjamin Schwartz, *The World of Thought in Ancient China* (Cambridge, Mass.: Harvard University Press, 1985), 36, 379, for a different wording; see also Oskar Weggel, 'Wo steht China heute? Die Rückkehr der Tradition und die Zukunft des Reformwerkes: Teil X', *China Aktuell* (August 1993), 803. The expression *zheng jiao heyi* in Chinese is a modern term that refers to theocratic ruling structures, as in medieval papal Europe and Tibet. It is true that one finds the term *zheng jiao* in several classical works, underlining the close relationship between governance and culture, but there also has other connotations.

46. The traditional Chinese term *wen* has many meanings, and may be said to partly cover the semantic field of the term 'culture' (considering the fact that there are probably several hundred different definitions of this term in its modern sense in the West). However, *wen* was not seen as a correlate to *zheng*, or 'politics', but rather to *wu*, or 'marital affairs'. *Wen* in this sense is thus better translated as 'civic'.

47. That this still holds good in certain contexts is illustrated by the rather strange term 'The Great Proletarian Cultural Revolution' (*Wuchan jieji wenhua da geming*). It was proclaimed a revolution in the political superstructure, but was termed a cultural concern.

48. The earliest and most eloquent proponent of this view is Joseph Levenson, *Liang Ch'i-ch'ao and the Mind of Modern China* (London: Thames and Hudson, 1959, 2nd rev. edn), 108 ff. The 'culturalism-to-nationalism thesis' still holds, but the field is clearly in need of both revision and refinement. Townsend's 'Chinese Nationalism' represents a commendable critique, as does Duara's 'De-constructing the Chinese Nation'; see also Søren Clausen's Ch. 7 above.

49. The veritable record of this fundamental transformation, beginning with Mao Zedong's comments in the interview by Edgar Snow in 1936 and consummated with the declarations at the 7th Party Congress in 1945, is still not available.

50. The *guo cui* movement sought inspiration in a Japanese movement after the Meiji restoration whose followers called themselves *kokusui* (written with the same characters), which in its turn was inspired by a Hegelian organic conceptualization of the nation. The *guo cui* movement was not a broad popular movement as such, but consisted of an extended circle of scholars who developed different political tendencies, especially before and after 1911, e.g. the erratic Liu Shibei (1884–1919) who turned into a royalist already in 1909. The *guo cui* lost its appeal after 1919, but its general ideas were incorporated into the Guomindang ideology in a social–Darwinist cloak. *Guo cui* was recast as *guo xing* (national character), which 'claimed to

establish, as both ideal and fact . . . the unitary nature of the Chinese people's historical experience and its fruit in their unique devotion to moral principle': Charlotte Furth, 'Culture and Politics in Modern Chinese Conservatism', in Charlotte Furth (ed.), *The Limits of Change: Essays on Conservative Alternatives in Republican China* (Cambridge, Mass.: Harvard University Press, 1976), 34.

51. In this respect, they found inspiration in the prominent Ming loyalist Gu Yanwu, who was the first one to express the idea that, whereas a change of dynasty (*wang guo*) implied only a change of names and eras, a change of the imperial order (*wang tianxia*) would imply a decline in the basic Confucian virtues to a state where men would be devouring each other. The ideas of the *guo cui* movement were carried on into the 1930s and 1940s by people like Qian Mu, who advocated that the universal moral values of the Chinese could be applied in more developed societal forms: see Furth, 'Culture and Politics', 35–6.

52. Levenson, *Liang Ch'i-ch'ao and the Mind of Modern China*, 114–15.

53. But in the age of veneration of things 'blue' and foreign, these candidates represent dynasties that were distinctly 'yellow' and introspective. In some circles the Tang and Yuan dynasties, with their cosmopolitan profile, are regarded as better suited ideals. It is no coincidence that one of China's most popular heavy-metal bands in the 1990s calls itself 'The Tang Dynasty'.

54. The slogan has been criticized since its conception. For example, it was maintained that it does not make sense to say that things Western have only an applicative aspect, as these must also embody Western 'basics'. The contemporary debate may be illustrated by the title of a paper by Li Zehou, 'Xiandaihua jiu shi "ti" de bianhua' (Modernization Means a Change of the 'Basics'), in *Zhongguo chuantong wenhua de zai guji* (A Reappraisal of Traditional Chinese Culture) (Shanghai: Shanghai renmin chubanshe, 1987). The present promise of 'building socialism with Chinese characteristics' may be seen as a variant of this problematique.

55. As Wang Jing writes: 'Even at those moments when Su Xiaokang preaches most eloquently for the elimination of such a nostalgia, his vision for the future is helplessly and unconsciously embedded in the same rhetorics of imperialistic nationalism. At its heart, *Heshang* often betrays the cause of enlightenment and lapses into the nationalist discourse it is struggling so hard to free itself from.' See Wang Jing, '*He Shang*', 24–5.

56. Quoted in Anderson, *Imagined Communities*, 12.

57. The most spectacular 're-launching' of this concept seems to have been the noted sociologist Fei Xiaotong's Tanner Lecture at the Chinese University of Hong Kong in 1988, entitled 'Zhonghua minzu de duoyuan yiti geju' (The Configuration of the Chinese People from Pluralism to an Organic Whole), printed in *Beijing dazue duebao*, 4 (1989), 1–19. I discuss the origin and the new uses of this term in the PRC in 'A Supra-national Identity? The Re-emergence of the Zhonghua Minzu in the PRC' (forthcoming).

58. This change in terminology becomes evident when browsing in any Chinese bookstore nowadays. Whereas most books dealing with aspects of China would have *Zhongguo* in its title only a few years ago, this field has almost totally been taken over by the term *Zhonghua*. One example is the latest survey of the nationalities in China, written by scholars from the Central Institute of Nationalities in Beijing, entitled *Zhonghua minzu* (Beijing, 1991) and blessed with Deng's calligraphy.

    Incidentally—and as a vivid illustration of how fast the symbols of the 'national' heritage are spreading—the name of the publishing company of *Zhonghua minzu* is Huaxia Publishing Company (*Huaxia chubanshe*). 'Huaxia' is allegedly the self-appellation of the Chinese before the Han dynasty, i.e. before they became the Han people, but in fact the term *Huaxia* is a post-Han dynasty invention which has been elevated to a national myth. The punch-line is, however, that the Huaxia publishers have not only (among others) published a Handbook on Education in National Conditions (*Guo qing jiaoyu shouce* (n.p.: Huaxia chubanshe, 1990)) (see Clausen, Ch. 7 above): they have also published the official Party Member's Handbook (*Dangyuan shouce*)—still a sure winner, at least in terms of printed copies. This made me curious about the organizational affiliation of the Huaxia Publishing Company. My inquiries revealed that it is run by the China Disabled Persons' Federation (CDPF) (Zhongguo canjiren lianhehui), which is a non-governmental organization financed by support from the Chinese state and donations from Japan and Europe. The Huaxia Publishing Company was said to be geared towards propaganda for humanitarianism (*rendao zhuyi*). As most readers will be aware, the leader of the CDPF is Deng Pufang, the son of Deng Xiaoping, who seems to be running the CDPF as his public property. Deng Pufang also figures as the advisor to the Handbook on Education in National Conditions cited above.

59. 'Haineiwai Yanhuan zisun gongcha Huang Di ling' (Domestic and Foreign Descendants of Yan and Huang Di Hold Public Ceremony at the Tomb of Huang Di). *Renmin ribao*, 4 April 1993.

60. *Zhonghua wenming, yuan yuan liu chang*. The last four characters have their origin in a grave inscription attributed to the Tang poet Bai Juyi.

61. See Laurence A. Schneider, *Ku Chieh-kang and China's New History: Nationalism and the Quest for Alternative Traditions* (Berkeley: University of California Press, 1971). The alleged grave sites of the cultural heroes Yan Di and Shun Di are also in the process of being restored. For some odd reason, they seem to be situated in the southern province of Hunan, far away from the traditional central regions of Chinese cultural mythology: see 'Yan Di lingmu chongjian gongcheng chuju guimo' (The Reconstruction of the Tomb of Yan Di is Beginning to Take Form), *Renmin ribao*, 9 March 1993; and 'Hunan chong xiu Shun Di ling' (Hunan Restores the Tomb of Emperor Shun), *Renmin ribao*, 8 April 1993. The traditional site of the birthplace of the Yellow Emperor in Shouqiu near Qufu, Shandong Province, is also being remodelled on a grand scale: see 'Huang Di yanshengdi guji zhengzai xiufu' (The Ancient Historical Birth Site of the Yellow Emperor in the Process of Renovation), *Renmin ribao*, 7 April 1993.

62. Unfortunately, the 'nationalist' image is already taken by the Guomindang even if its translation into English as 'The Nationalist Party' is quite forced.

63. See Paul Cohen, 'The Post-Mao Reforms in Historical Perspective', *Journal of Asian Studies*, 47 (1988), 518–40; and Yu Cong, 'Cong Man Qing zhi fuwang kan jintian de gaige' (A Look at the Present Reforms in the Light of the Fall of the Manchu Qing Dynasty), *Jiushi niandai* (The Nineties), 6 (1988), 46–9.

64. See Townsend, 'Chinese Nationalism', 407–8.

65. Those who may wonder what the Chinese associate with the term *luan* are advised to see Kurosawa's film *Ran*, which is the Japanese rendering of *luan*.

66. The expression *geju* occurs the first time in Pei Songzhi's commentary to the *San Guo Zhi* (History of The Three Kingdoms) (early fifth century).

67. As Wright notes, 'the effects of barbarian rule, the development of new institutions in the north, made the reconstitution of a Chinese ecumenical empire, the recreation of a homogeneous society, seem like the most improbable of dreams. And, as time went on, fewer and fewer Chinese, in the increasingly prosperous and comfortable south, dreamed or planned a new united empire or a new unified society.' See Arthur

F. Wright, 'The Formation of Sui Ideology', in John K. Fairbank (ed.), *Chinese Thought and Institutions* (Chicago: University of Chicago Press, 1957), 75.

68. *Dian* refers to the name of the ancient autochthonous kingdom of Central Yunnan, and the name *Shu* occurs already in the oracle bone records from Shang times.

69. The term 'regionalects' is a useful term introduced by John DeFrancis in order to place the status of the major Chinese 'dialects' in their proper context. See John DeFrancis, *The Chinese Language: Fact and Fantasy* (Hawaii: University of Hawaii Press, 1984), 52 ff.

70. e.g., the regional satrap of Sichuan during the Five Eras, Wang Jian, called his domain Da Shu (Greater Shu), but changed the name to Da Han (Greater Han) when he launched a northern military campaign with imperial pretensions: see Klaus-Peter Tietze, *Ssuch'uan, vom 7. bis 10, Jahrhundert* (Wiesbaden: Steiner Verlag, 1980), 83–4.

71. While the transformation of the lesser foreign dynasties that were established in the core regions of China was rather complete, the less accultured polities in the fringe areas of China offer some interesting contrasts: see Backus, *The Nan-Chao Kingdom* and Wu Tianchi, *Xixia shigao* (A Draft History of Xixia) (Chengdu: Sichuan renmin chubanshe, 1983); see also Herbert Franke, 'The Role of the State as a Structural Element in Polyethnic Societies', in Schram, *Foundations and Limits of State Power in China*, 87–112.

72. And still is—Clausen has a reference to the General Programme of 1991 (see Clausen, Ch. 7 above).

73. See Wright, 'The Formation of Sui Ideology', 74.

74. It is also applied by some authors today to describe the characteristic course of evolution of Chinese thought: see Zhou Guidian, *Zhongguo chuantong zhexue* (China's Traditional Philosophy) (Beijing: Beijing shifandaxue chubanshe, 1990), 334–6.

75. See Su and Wang, *He Shang*, 97.

76. See Jin and Liu, *Xinsheng yu weiji*, 196 ff.

77. For example, if the Southern Song dynasty had been allowed to continue, we might have seen a more permanent cleavage between a land-oriented, traditionalist and non-Chinese northern China, and a sea-oriented, 'early-modern' Han southern China. Instead, the Mongol conquest of the whole of China became an utterly traumatic experience to the Chinese. The mental makeup of the ensuing Ming upper strata was clearly conditioned by the trauma of the Mongol conquest.

78. Wang Jing provides an insightful discussion of the notion of ultra-stability. She ends rather caustically: 'The concept of ultra-stability thus not only speaks of but also speaks to the ethical and psychological inertia that conveniently blurs the distinction between the victim and the victimizer, and between conscious choice and choice by default. It is this same collective inertia of the Chinese people that finds expression in their unreflective condemnation of China's socialist past and in their worship of a vaguely conceived modernity as the new fetish.' See Wang, *'He Shang'*, 29.

79. See Kuhn, 'Local Self-Government', 258.

80. ibid. 257.

81. The traditional provincial military commander was called *dujun*, and is the term applied to the warlords in the beginning of their reigns. Another term, *junfa*, which today is generally used for the term 'warlord', was borrowed from Japanese to describe this specific historical phenomenon. It gradually replaced the former term in the 1920s.

82. John K. Fairbank, Edwin O. Reischauer, and Albert M. Craig, *East Asia: Tradition and Transformation* (London: Allen & Unwin, 1973), 757–8.

83. e.g. Lucian Pye, who says: 'I have sought to demonstrate that the modernization of China can be usefully viewed as a profound tension between tendencies toward the restoration in modern guise of an essentially monolithic structure and tendencies toward more open and competitive politics, of which the warlords were a principal but not always happy example.' See Lucian Pye, *Warlord Politics: Conflict and Coalition in the Modernization of Republican China* (New York: Praeger, 1971), 167.

84. Today one usually applies the term *lianbang* for things federal. *Lianbang* was actually the earliest rendering into Chinese of the term, but it was dropped by the early proponents of federalism because of the strong connotation of 'state' and 'sovereignty' of the word *bang*. See Duara, 'Provincial Narratives of the Nation', 16.

85. Jean Chesneaux, 'Le Mouvement fédéraliste en Chine (1920–1923)', *Revue Historique*, no. 236 (1966), 383.

86. Arthur Waldron, 'Warlordism versus Federalism: The Revival of a Debate', *The China Quarterly*, 121 (1990), 116–28.

87. Again, the early Qing scholar and thinker Gu Yanwu is the provider of ideological ammunition. In his essay 'On the Prefectural System' ('Junxian lun'), he says among other things that 'the fault of feudalism was its concentration of power on the local level, while the fault of the prefectural system is its concentration of power at the top': see De Bary *et al.*, *Sources of Chinese Tradition*, 557.

88. Levenson, *Liang Ch'i-ch'ao*, 114.

89. This was also the case with the young Mao Zedong around 1920. Hunan province was one of the early strongholds of federalist ideas. See his article 'Break Down the Foundationless Big China and Build Up Many Chinas Starting with Hunan', and several pieces on the issue of federalism in the entries for 1920 in Stuart Schram (ed.), *Mao's Road to Power: Revolutionary Writings 1912–1949* (Armonk, NY: M. E. Sharpe), i, *The Pre-Marxist Period, 1912–1920*.

90. Cited in Duara, 'Provincial Narratives', 29.

91. On the other hand, the Chinese Communists retained—from their second Congress in 1922 until the Yan'an period—the traditional Comintern policy of self-determination for subjugated peoples; e.g., a resolution on the national minorities on the first All-China Congress of Soviets in Ruijin, Jiangxi in 1931, stated that the CCP 'categorically and unconditionally recognizes the right of national minorities to self-determination. This means that in districts like Mongolia, Tibet, Xinjiang, Yunnan, Guizhou and others, where the majority of the population belongs to non-Han nationalities, the toiling masses of these nationalities shall have the right to determine for themselves whether they wish to leave the Chinese Soviet Republic and create their own state, or whether they wish to join the Union of Soviet Republics, or form an autonomous area inside the Chinese Soviet Republic': quoted in George Moseley, *The Party and the National Question in China* (Cambridge, Mass.: MIT Press, 1966), 164.

92. Cf. Marshall Berman, *All That is Solid Melts into Air* (Harmondsworth: Penguin, 1988).

93. Lucian Pye, *Asian Power and Politics: The Cultural Dimensions of Authority* (Cambridge, Mass.: Harvard University Press, 1985), 64.

94. Tu Wei-ming, 'Cultural China: The Periphery as the Center', *Dædalus*, 120 (1991), 14f.

95. See e.g. Stuart Schram, 'Decentralization in a Unitary State: Theory and Practice 1940–1984', in Stuart Schram (ed.), *The Scope of State Power in China* (Hong Kong: Chinese University Press, 1985), 81–125.

96. *Zhongyang* is a curiously Chinese concept. It conveys the idea of centrality on the political level, the locus of the autocratic power, the applied level of cosmic centrality. It is not at all a Communist invention, but has of course also been applied intensively by the CCP. There has been just as much *zhongyang*-talk in Guomindang circles in Taiwan. *Zhongyang* is also to some extent applied where we would use 'national'.

97. Edward Friedman, 'Reconstructing China's National Identity: A Southern Alternative to Mao-Era Anti-Imperialist Nationalism', *Journal of Asian Studies*, 53:1 (1994), 67–91.

98. A parallel mode of reductionist thinking is expressed, in my opinion, by Lucian Pye in a recent article on how Chinese nationalism was 'shanghaied', which implied that the true Chinese nationalists resided in Shanghai in their day: 'But the building blocks for a coherent nationalism are missing because the collective symbols and ideals of the culture have been so severely damaged. The rejection of the melding of Chinese nationalism and modernization, which was taking place in pre-war coastal China, in favour of the less authentic nationalism based on Leninism has left China without a satisfying sense of either modernization or national pride.' See Lucian Pye, 'How China's Nationalism was Shanghaied', *Australian Journal of Chinese Affairs*, 29 (1993), 130.

99. Friedman, 'Reconstructing China's National Identity', 85.

100. There is certainly a renewed interest today in China's ancient southern cultures, as exemplified by Wang Guanggao, *Chu wenhua yuan liu xin zheng* (New Evidence of the Origin and Development of Chu Culture) (Wuhan: Wuhan daxue chubanshe, 1988). But this is in no way limited to the southern regions; cf. Wang Zhimin (ed.), *Qi wenhua gailun* (Outline of Qi Culture) (Jinan: Shadong renmin chubanshe, 1993), which deals with the ancient Shandong culture of Qi. Such interests also extend to later regional dynasties; cf. Du Shifeng (ed.), *Bei Wei shi* (The History of Northern Wei) (Taiyuan: Shanxi gaoxiao lianhe chubanshe, 1992), which deals with the semi-barbarian dynasty of Northern Wei (368–534).

101. See Yan Jiaqi. *Lianbang Zhongguo gouxiang* (The Conception of a Federal China) (Hong Kong: Mingbao chubanshe, 1992).

102. See e.g. Chen Fangzheng, 'Minzu zhuyi de pouxi: qiyuan, jiegou yu gongneng' (Nationalism Analysed: Origin, Structure and Function), *Ershiyi shiji* (The Twenty-first Century), 16 (1993), 11–21.

103. Arend Lijphart, *Democracies, Patterns of Majoritarian and Consensus Government in Twenty-one Countries* (New Haven: Yale University Press, 1984), 170–9.

104. See *Free China Journal*, 2 August 1990, quoted in Friedman, 'Reconstructing China's National Identity', 84.

105. Barry Sautman, 'Sirens of the Strongman: Neo-authoritarianism in Recent Chinese Political Theory', *China Quarterly*, 129 (1992), 72–102.

Index

abortion practices 98, 100, 111(*n*29)
administrative management studies 69, 89(*n*1)
administrative reforms (Hainan province)
   203–8
   small government notion and 191–3
Asian Development Bank 18(*n*2)

badao (rule of force) 58
Balazs, Etienne 83
birth control 92–112
Buddhism 327
Bureau for the Administration of State Assets
   131
Bureau of Industry and Commerce (ICB)
   121, 125
bureaucracy in China 69–91
   big society notion and 193–5

Canton
   armed attack (1924) 58
   Sun Yat-sen's visit (1924) 57
Catholic Church 174
Cao Kun 48
CCP, *see* Chinese Communist Party
Chang Kuo-t'ao, *see* Zhang Guotao
Chen Duxiu 330, 331
Chen Jiongming 57, 65(*n*76)
Chen Qianfu 60
Chengdu Health Products 127–9, 132
Chiang Kai-shek 273
China Disabled Persons' Federation 343(*n*58)
China Reconstructs (magazine) 336(*n*2)
China Today (magazine) 336(*n*2)
Chinese Catholic Patriotic Association 174
Chinese Communist Party (CCP)
   1989 demonstrations 163, 172, 180
   administrative reform 77–9
   'China's special characteristics' 260–1
   corruption/bureaucracy 71–5, 83–4, 85–6
   cultural nationalism and 254–5, 272–3
   federalism and 331, 334, 345(*n*91)
   party membership survey 247
   post-1978 reforms 168–9
   on private enterprise 116
Chinese Democratic Alliance 177
The Chinese Intellectual (journal) 177
Chinese nationalism 19–24, 321–36, 340(*n*43)
Chinese People's Political Consultative
   Conference 169, 173
Chu culture 266
civil society concept 6–7, 9–19, 163–83,
   213(*n*5), 214(*n*21)

definition 217
historical perspective 198–200
Liao Xun's 191, 193–5, 198–203
political culture and 217–21
survey on 216, 229–49
class order/feudal society 83–4
'collective' enterprises 118–19, 121–4, 170–1
   shareholding 124–32, 194
contraception methods 98–102
corruption in CCP 71–5, 83–4, 85–6
criminal networks 175
'cultural identity' 320
cultural nationalism 253–79, 320–1
Cultural Revolution 71, 78, 180, 226
   current teaching of 269
culture (popular) 169

Da yitong (the Great Systemic Whole)
   312–13, 332, 335, 337(*n*14–16)
Dai Jitao 49
Dalai Lama 174
danwei (units) 171–2, 225
Daqiuzhuang village 185(*n*22)
Deng Pufang 343(*n*58)
Deng Xiaoping
   on bureaucratism 78–9, 84
   Dengist reform period 3, 71–5, 78–82,
   227–8
Deng Yingchao 49, 272
Denmark 143
Ding Shiqing 64(*n*37)
Dong Zhongshu 312–13, 337(*n*16)
dongba script/culture 285, 300–4

Eastern and Western Cultures (Liang
   Shuming, 1921) 140
education/schooling
   1991 Programme 268–71
   Liang Shuming's vision 140–3, 153–8
   minority education 280–309
   Zouping county pre-1931 145–9
electronic mail networks 177, 180
ethnic considerations 281–2, 317, 345(*n*91)
   chinese nationalism 19–24, 321–36,
   340(*n*43)
   minority education 280–309

family planning 92–112
Fang Lizhi 334
federalism 26(*n*16–17), 331, 334, 345(*n*91)
Fei Xiaotong 18, 223–5, 342(*n*57)
Feng Guozhang 48

feudal society 83–4
foreign investment 171
Friedman, Edward 333
The Friends of Nature 186(*n*40)
Front for a Democratic China 177
furniture production 122–3, 127

gengshen reforms 213(*n*1)
Gorbachev, Mikail 85, 183(*n*2)
Gu Mu 268
Gu Yanwu 322, 342(*n*51), 345(*n*87)
Guanyin Mountain 55–6
Guocui movement 271, 341–2(*n*50–51)
Guomindang (Nationalist) Party 38, 50, 59

Habermas, Jürgen 201–2
Hainan reform process 189–97, 203–13
Han Chinese language 275, 284
    bilingual education 280–1
Han nationality 281, 293–4
    'Great Han Chauvinism' 321
Havel, Vaclav 11, 27(*n*36)
He Yongji 51, 52
Heshang (TV series) 23, 265–6, 312, 329,
    336(*n*11)
Hong Kong 175
Hu Hanmin 49
Hu Shi 37, 55, 330, 331, 334
Hu Yaobang 74, 75
Huang Di tombside ceremony 324
Huaxia Publishing Company 342(*n*58)
human rights issues 92, 109(*n*3)
    population policies 92–3
Huntington, Samuel 80–1

ICB (State Bureau of Industry and
    Commerce) 121, 125
Imagined Communities (1981) 256
individuality in China 91(*n*36), 108
The Invention of Tradition (1981) 256

Jiang Zemin 272, 324
Jianshe (journal) 19, 55
jianshe (reconstruction) 1–2, 55, 56
Jin Guantao 84, 329, 337(*n*13)

Kang Baiqing 66(*n*93)
Kang Youwei 331
Kanghua Company 86
knife-making industry 116
Kornai, Janos 114

language issues 275
    bilingual education 280–1
    minority languages 281, 283–4, 285–6
lawyers 172
legal reforms 169, 172
Li Jialin 149

Li Ka-shing 186(*n*40)
Li Nai 148
Li Yizhe group 85
Li Yuanhong 47
Li Zehou 28(*n*54), 264–5, 277, 278(*n*36)
Liang Congjie 186(*n*40)
Liang Heng 177
Liang Qichao 6, 26(*n*15, 20), 322, 331
Liang Shuming 2, 5, 139–60, 274, 330
Liao Gailong 189, 202, 213
Liao Xun 189–215
Lijiang Autonomous County 280, 282, 284
    education issues 284–91
Lijiang (town) 285
Lin Biao 85
Liu Guoguang 189
Liu Junning 81
Liu Qingfeng 84, 337(*n*13)
Liu Qingyang 66(*n*93)
Liu Shibei 341(*n*50)
Liu Xiaobo 266, 268
Liu Zaifu 263, 265, 277
Locke, John 198–9
Lu Ji 41
Lu Xun 23–4, 52, 68(*n*142), 263, 264

Ma Liuwen 125–6
Mao Zedong (Mao Tse-Tung) 5, 23, 71,
    225–7, 268
    admires Wang Zhen 63(*n*25)
    on culture of the masses 274
    on federalism 345(*n*89)
    personal domination 78, 85, 226
market economy development 76, 113–14,
    168
Marx, Karl 200–1
May Fourth Movement (1919) 47, 65(*n*84),
    145, 263
May Thirtieth Movement (1925) 60–1
media management 176
Meng Zi 313, 338(*n*19)
Mill, John Stuart 199–200
Ministry of Civil Affairs 169
Mongolia 318
Muslim community 174

national identity 19–24, 321–36, 340(*n*43)
National People's Congress 173
nationalism (cultural) 253–79, 320–1
Nationalist (Guomindang) Party 38, 50, 59

Naxi people 22, 280, 281–2, 294–307
    education issues 284–91
New Culture Movement 322
New Life Movement 273
NGOs (non-governmental organizations)
    176
shetuan in Hainan 195–6, 208–12

1989 demonstrations 75, 163, 172, 180
North China Post (newspaper) 47

one-child family policy 17, 92–112
Operation Yellowbird 175

Pang Pu 262
Philippines 181
Poland 174, 184(*n*19)
  Solidarity 201
Political Order in Changing Societies
    (Huntington, 1988) 80–1
popular culture 169
population size
  current issues 92–112
  Han/Tang dynasties 327
  Sun Yat-sen's beliefs 49
privatization issues 12, 113–15, 171
  Hainan province 194–6, 205–8
  in Poland 135(*n*28)
  province comparisons 205
  rural private enterprise 115–21
  urban private and individual enterprise
    205–8

Qian Xuantong 36

railway building (1912 plan) 35
'reconstruction' (*jianshe*) 1–2, 56
  Jianshe (journal) 19, 55
  origin of term 1–2, 55
religion 174, 327
River Elegy (*Heshang* TV series) 23, 265–6,
    312, 329, 336(*n*11)
Romance of the Three Kingdoms (novel)
    328–9
rural enterprises 113–36
Rural Reconstruction Movement (RRM)
    139–62

Salisbury, Harrison 319
script 314
  dongba script/culture 285, 300–4
secret societies 175
Shangdong Rural Reconstruction Institute
    141
Shao Lizi 62(*n*11)
shareholding enterprises 124–32, 194
Shen Tong 175
social associations 208–12
social change programmes 95
  one-child policies 94–108
Solidarity trade union 201
Soros, George 177
South Korea 181
Soviet Union dissolution 13, 75
State Bureau of Industry and Commerce
    (ICB) 121, 125

student movements 175–6, 177
Su Xiaokang 265–6, 267, 336(*n*11),
    342(*n*55)
Subao (newspaper) 41
Sun Fo 35
Sun Yat-sen 5, 6, 26(*n*17), 33–68, 177

Taiwan 177, 181, 333–4
Tan Sitong 322
Tang Dynasty (rock band) 253, 342(*n*53)
Tang people 339(*n*31)
Tang Yijie 262
Tao Xingzhi 149
Taoism 327
Three Gorges Project 3, 56, 175
Three Principles of the People 34
  lectures by Sun Yat-sen (1924) 44,
    64(*n*56)
Three-Self Patriotic Movement 174
Tiananmen Square Incident (1989) 75
Tibet 174, 310, 317
trade unions 195
  Solidarity 201
Treaty of Kiakhta (1727) 316
Triads 175

USSR (dissolution of) 75

Wang Fuzhi 322
Wang Meng 263, 264
Wang Renzhi 268
Wang Yanan 82–3
Wang Zhen 63(*n*25)
wangdao (enlightened rule) 58
Warlord Period 330
Weber, Max 77
Whampoa Military Academy 40
writing/script 314
  dongba script/culture 285, 300–4
Wu Delu 48
Wu Jiaxiang 81

Xiao Gongqin 271
Xiao Jiefu 262
Xu Deheng 66(*n*93)
Xu Shichang 47
Xu Yongying 50, 51, 52, 53
xungen literature 267

Yan Jiaqi 334
Yang Xiaochun 147–8, 153
yin/yang dualism 313, 314
Yuan Shikai 5, 33, 39, 47, 62(*n*6), 65(*n*76)
Yue Fei 322
Yunnan Institute of the Nationalities
    288–91, 300
Yunnan province 282–3, 333
  education in 280–309

Zhang Bingjiu 80
Zhang Dainian 262
Zhang Guotao 66(*n*93)
Zhang Jianyuan 42
Zhang Jiayin 64(*n*37)
Zhang Park (Shanghai) 41, 64(*n*42)
Zhang Zhidong 6, 323
Zhang Zonglin 156–8
Zhao Ziyang 74, 79, 81, 85, 259
Zhengzhixue yanjiu (journal) 81

Zhili Provincial Education Society 48
Zhu Rongji 87
Zhu Xi 179
Zou Jiahua 90(*n*35)
Zou Lu 21, 49, 59, 64(*n*64)
Zouping county
    education pre-1931 143–7
    industrial organization 27(*n*26)
    Liang Shuming's RRM 143–60